EMBODIED NARRATIVES

Increasing quantities of information about our health, bodies, and biological relationships are being generated by health technologies, research, and surveillance. This escalation presents challenges to us all when it comes to deciding how to manage this information and what should be disclosed to the very people it describes. This book establishes the ethical imperative to take seriously the potential impacts on our identities of encountering bioinformation about ourselves. Emily Postan argues that identity interests in accessing personal bioinformation are currently under-protected in law and often linked to problematic bio-essentialist assumptions. Drawing on a picture of identity constructed through embodied self-narratives, and examples of people's encounters with diverse kinds of information, Postan addresses these gaps. This book provides a robust account of the source, scope, and ethical significance of our identity-related interests in accessing – and not accessing – bioinformation about ourselves and the need for disclosure practices to respond appropriately. This title is also available as Open Access on Cambridge Core.

EMILY POSTAN is a Chancellor's Fellow in Bioethics at the University of Edinburgh Law School and a deputy director of the J Kenyon Mason Institute for Medicine Life Sciences and the Law. Her principal research interests lie in the ethical and regulatory implications of the impacts of health technologies and health data on our identities, group memberships, and relationships with others. Her wider research includes work in neuroethics, reproductive ethics, and regulation of health research.

CAMBRIDGE BIOETHICS AND LAW

This series of books – formerly called Cambridge Law, Medicine and Ethics – was founded by Cambridge University Press with Alexander McCall Smith as its first editor in 2003. It focuses on the law's complex and troubled relationship with medicine across both the developed and the developing world. In the past twenty years, we have seen in many countries increasing resort to the courts by dissatisfied patients and a growing use of the courts to attempt to resolve intractable ethical dilemmas. At the same time, legislatures across the world have struggled to address the questions posed by both the successes and the failures of modern medicine, while international organisations such as the WHO and UNESCO now regularly address issues of medical law. It follows that we would expect ethical and policy questions to be integral to the analysis of the legal issues discussed in this series. The series responds to the high profile of medical law in universities, in legal and medical practice, as well as in public and political affairs. We seek to reflect the evidence that many major health-related policy and bioethics debates in the UK, Europe and the international community over the past two decades have involved a strong medical law dimension. With that in mind, we seek to address how legal analysis might have a trans-jurisdictional and international relevance. Organ retention, embryonic stem cell research, physician-assisted suicide and the allocation of resources to fund health care are but a few examples among many. The emphasis of this series is thus on matters of public concern and/or practical significance. We look for books that could make a difference to the development of medical law and enhance the role of medico-legal debate in policy circles. That is not to say that we lack interest in the important theoretical dimensions of the subject, but we aim to ensure that theoretical debate is grounded in the realities of how the law does and should interact with medicine and health care.

Series Editors

Professor Graeme Laurie, *University of Edinburgh*

Professor Richard Ashcroft, *City, University of London*

EMBODIED NARRATIVES

Protecting Identity Interests through Ethical Governance of Bioinformation

EMILY POSTAN

University of Edinburgh

Shaftesbury Road, Cambridge CB2 8EA, United Kingdom

One Liberty Plaza, 20th Floor, New York, NY 10006, USA

477 Williamstown Road, Port Melbourne, VIC 3207, Australia

314–321, 3rd Floor, Plot 3, Splendor Forum, Jasola District Centre, New Delhi – 110025, India

103 Penang Road, #05–06/07, Visioncrest Commercial, Singapore 238467

Cambridge University Press is part of Cambridge University Press & Assessment,
a department of the University of Cambridge.

We share the University's mission to contribute to society through the pursuit of
education, learning and research at the highest international levels of excellence.

www.cambridge.org
Information on this title: www.cambridge.org/9781108718196

DOI: 10.1017/9781108652599

First published 2022
First paperback edition 2023

A catalogue record for this publication is available from the British Library

Library of Congress Cataloging-in-Publication data
Names: Postan, Emily, 1973– author.
Title: Embodied narratives : protecting identity interests through ethical governance of
bioinformation / Emily Postan.
Description: Cambridge ; New York, NY : Cambridge University Press, 2021. |
Series: Cambridge bioethics and law | Includes bibliographical references and index.
Identifiers: LCCN 2021056539 (print) | LCCN 2021056540 (ebook) | ISBN 9781108483742
(hardback) | ISBN 9781108718196 (paperback) | ISBN 9781108652599 (ebook)
Subjects: LCSH: Medical records – Access control – Psychological aspects. | Personal information
management – Psychological aspects. | Patients – Psychology. | Identity (Psychology) | Data
privacy. | Medical records – Law and legislation. | BISAC: LAW / Medical Law & Legislation
Classification: LCC R864 .P57 2021 (print) | LCC R864 (ebook) | DDC 610–dc23/eng/20220107
LC record available at https://lccn.loc.gov/2021056539
LC ebook record available at https://lccn.loc.gov/2021056540

ISBN   978-1-108-48374-2   Hardback
ISBN   978-1-108-71819-6   Paperback

CONTENTS

Foreword   *page* ix
JACKIE LEACH SCULLY
Acknowledgements   xii
Table of Cases   xiv

1   Attending to Identity   1

1.1 Introduction   1

1.2 Terminology   12

1.3 Guide to the Following Chapters   28

2   Mapping the Landscape   31

2.1 Introduction   31

2.2 Legal Entitlements to Bioinformation   31

2.3 Seeking Conceptual and Normative
      Foundations   46

3   Narrative Self-Constitution   61

3.1 Introduction   61

3.2 Identity Narratives   62

3.3 Two Objections   70

3.4 Limits on Identity-Constituting Narratives   72

3.5 Practical and Evaluative Capacities   75

3.6 The Trouble with Coherence   79

3.7 Beyond Coherence   86

3.8 A Practical, Normative Conception of
     Identity   88

4 Bioinformation in Embodied Identity
  Narratives   89

4.1 Introduction   89

4.2 Embodied Lives, Embodied Selves   90

4.3 Bodies in Narrative Identity Theory   94

4.4 Personal Bioinformation as a Narrative
     Tool   98

4.5 The Suitability of Bioinformation: Responding
     to Concerns   110

4.6 Moving Beyond Theory   118

5 Encounters with Bioinformation: Three
  Examples   120

5.1 Introduction   120

5.2 Illustrative Example I: Encounters with Donor
     Origins   124

5.3 Illustrative Example II: Encounters with Genetic
     Risk   141

5.4 Illustrative Example III: Encounters with Psychiatric
     Neuroimaging   158

5.5 Narrativity across the Three Examples   172

6 Locating Identity Interests   181

6.1 Introduction   181

6.2 Our Identity Interests   181

6.3 Sources of Identity Significance   190

6.4 Filling a Conceptual and Normative Gap   197

6.5 Relationships between Structure and
     Contents   205

6.6 Distinguishing Identity from Other Interests 208

6.7 A Fresh Ethical Dimension 217

7 Responsibilities for Disclosure 218

7.1 Introduction 218

7.2 Responsibilities of Potential Disclosers 219

7.3 Ethical Foundations 221

7.4 Limiting Considerations 229

7.5 Ascertaining Where Interests Lie 232

7.6 Identity-Supporting Communication 238

7.7 Shared Social Responsibilities 244

8 Protecting Identity in Practice 247

8.1 Introduction 247

8.2 What Would Change? 248

8.3 Five Disclosure Contexts 252

8.4 Future Challenges 262

Bibliography 264
Index 287

Reading *Embodied Narratives: Protecting Identity Interests through Ethical Governance of Bioinformation* is a salutary reminder of how recently the circulation of mass data about our own and others' bodies has become a normal part of everyday life. Despite this relative novelty, bioethics has already generated an impressive body of literature on the ethical and legal issues connected with making human bioinformation easily available. Most of this existing work examines the actionable consequences of acquiring data about a person's genome, microbiomic profile, or neural architecture: how such knowledge might affect someone's cancer diagnosis, treatment choices, their chances of crossing a border, getting insurance, or being convicted in a court of law.

Much less attention has been given to the possibility that knowledge from and of one's body might have other important effects. There is curiously little discussion, for example, of why patients might find it important to know (or not to know) some aspect of personal bioinformation, even if that knowledge has seemingly no influence on their subsequent choices or actions. In this book and in clear and engaging style, Emily Postan demonstrates how the collection of information from and about the human body – and sometimes even just the expectation that such bioinformation will be gathered and used – affects our individual and collective identities in profound and often unexpected ways.

What does it mean to 'know who you are', and how is that affected by the historically unprecedented health and bio-related data now available to us? What we are concerned with here is identity as the set of characteristics that make each person a distinct and particular individual. Postan's view is that while information about our bodies has always played an important role in self-constitution, the massively expanded availability and variety of bioinformation, and the extent to which it is now generated and controlled by other people, fundamentally alters the landscape and tools of personal identity.

With this as her starting point, Postan draws on theories of identity as constituted through narrative, and the claim that a meaningful identity narrative is essential to making sense of our lives, to our capacity for self-determination, and to our exercise of agency. The argument then is that because of the role that knowledge and experience of the body play in our narratives about ourselves, personal bioinformation has profound consequences for our ability to 'occupy our own narrative accounts' of who we are. The abstraction that we call 'health data' is a confirmation of the embodied nature of identity: that the material actuality of body form and function provides a good part of who you feel you are. Personal bioinformation can provide a way to make sense of and articulate embodied experience and, in doing so, make it available to the composition of an inhabitable self-narrative.

This view differs in two important respects from more familiar claims in law, policy, and scholarship about the effect of knowledge about our bodies on identity. First, it directs attention away from concerns about how others' use of our information might affect us and towards our own reactions to and uses of such information. Second, in doing so, it directly confronts the easy assumption that if bioinformation has significance for building a sense of self, then that must mean personal identity in some way flows directly from, and is fixed by, bodily materiality. Postan's argument is that what people do with bioinformation is rather more sophisticated and complex than that, and to demonstrate this, *Embodied Narratives* tests out the emerging theory of bioinformation and identity against empirical evidence. This key part of the book uses three case studies of bioinformation, involving knowledge of donor origins, genetic predisposition to disease, and neuroimagery in psychiatric diagnosis, to examine how those involved talk about the effect of the personal information they receive on their self-conception and understanding of their past and future.

Recognising the importance of body knowledge to the construction of a working identity clearly has major ramifications for those public and private agencies that generate, hold, or control access to our personal bioinformation. Part of Emily Postan's argument is that people have real, justifiable, and ethically significant interests in their identity-relevant biodata, whether or not access to that information appears objectively 'useful' in terms of guiding healthcare or other decisions. This is an important conclusion not just for ethics and law but also for anyone trying to make sense of the bioinformation-saturated society in which we live. It sets a starting point for a detailed exploration of the governance and law that will be needed to protect these interests appropriately.

The appearance of Embodied Narratives is a milestone in the development of data ethics and in building a deep understanding of how technology can change individual and collective identities. More generally, it marks a significant evolution in empirically informed normative ethics. There will be bioethicists, bioinformatics specialists, and philosophers of identity who disagree with its arguments and conclusions, but what Emily Postan has provided them with is an account that is worth engaging with: serious, nuanced, and provocative.

Jackie Leach Scully

ACKNOWLEDGEMENTS

This book owes its existence to the many friends, colleagues, students, reviewers, and family members who have shared with me their wisdom and inspired and supported me. In addition to those named elsewhere on these pages, thank you to my friends and colleagues in the Liminal Spaces team, in the Mason Institute, and at Edinburgh School of Law – Ted Dove, Murray Earl, Anne-Maree Farrell, Isabel Fletcher, Steph Lewis, Katy MacMillan, Gerard Porter, Sam Taylor-Alexander, and Shauna Thompson – for their solidarity and humour. Particular thanks to Alexandra Braun, Niamh Nic Shuibhne, and Anna Souhami for pushing me to keep on keeping on. Thank you also to my friends and erstwhile colleagues at the Nuffield Council on Bioethics secretariat, including Rosie Beauchamp, Ran Svenning Berg, Kate Harvey, Cath Joynson, Pete Mills, Carol Perkins, Hugh Whittall, and Katharine Wright, from whom I learnt invaluable lessons about thinking, writing, and finishing.

This book began as a PhD thesis, and I owe more than I can say to my supervisors, now colleagues and friends, Sharon Cowan and Graeme Laurie, for their patient guidance, personal and intellectual generosity, and their uncanny abilities to understand which ideas I was reaching for, often before I realised so myself. The arguments presented in this book have evolved through discussions with many people, more than I can name individually. In particular, this book has benefitted immeasurably from the wisdom, insights, and challenges offered by Sarah Chan, Matthew Elton, Agomoni Ganguli-Mitra, Gail Harding, Emma Keir, Chloe Kennedy, Cicely Postan, Nayha Sethi, and Annie Sorbie, by my doctoral thesis examiners Richard Ashcroft and Martyn Pickersgill, and by the Cambridge University Press reviewers of my book proposal. I have been thinking about identity since my postgraduate philosophy days, and I am so lucky that my then-supervisors Antony Duff and Sandra Marshall have remained my friends and mentors for twenty-five years and that I continue to benefit from their kindness and razor-sharp questions. I owe enormous gratitude to Jackie Leach Scully for the inspiration her work always provides; for her generosity, encouragement, and advice; and for doing me the huge honour of contributing a foreword to this book.

I am grateful to the series editors at Cambridge University Press for giving me the opportunity to develop my ideas into this monograph and, in doing so, to join the Press's Bioethics and Law Series, which includes works of authors from whom I have learned so much. Thank you to Laura Blake, Marianne Nield, Finola O'Sullivan, Esakki Thangam, and all in the editorial and production teams at Cambridge University Press for their calm expertise. And particular thanks to Rebecca Richards for bringing her tireless, forensic eye to proofreading the manuscript, and to my father, Basil, for his additional readings and support. Much of the research contributing to this book was conducted with the support of an Arts and Humanities Reseach Council studentship award while the manuscript was written as part of the Wellcome-funded 'Confronting the Liminal Spaces of Health Research Regulation' project led by Graeme Laurie. I am grateful to these funders and, of course, to Graeme. Many thanks also to Wellcome for supporting open access publication of this book.

Lastly, incalculable thanks to my families, Postan and Peggie, for their love and support, for providing quiet spaces to write and happy places to escape, for knowing when to ask me how the book was going and when not to, and for countless hours of child wrangling. Most of all, thank you to my loves, Martyn and Eva, for bringing me so much joy, teaching me so much, and being at the heart of my own narrative and letting me be part of theirs.

TABLE OF CASES

ABC *v.* St Georges Healthcare and Others (2020) EWHC 455 (QB) 42, 88

Anayo *v.* Germany (no. 20578/07) (2012) 55 EHRR 5 37

Bensaid *v.* United Kingdom (no. 44599/98) (2001) ECHR 82 34

Gaskin *v.* United Kingdom (no. 10454/83) (1989) ECHR 13 34, 37

Haas *v.* the Netherlands (no. 36983/97) (2004) 1 FCR 147 36

Jaggi *v.* Switzerland (no. 58757/00) (2008) 47 EHRR 30 34–35

KH and Others *v.* Slovakia (no. 32881/04) (2009) ECHR 709 7, 37

Mikulic *v.* Croatia (no. 53176/99) (2002) 2 WLUK 216 34–36

Mizzi *v.* Malta (no. 26111/02) (2006) 1 FLR 1048 36–37

Montgomery *v.* Lanarkshire Health Board (2015) UKSC 11 41, 214, 256

Odièvre *v.* France (no. 42326/98) (2003) ECHR 3 34–36, 230

Rose *v.* Secretary of State for Health (2002) EWHC 1593 38

1

Attending to Identity

1.1 Introduction

Two Friends

Let us imagine two friends, who find themselves in situations that are at once similar and strikingly different. Ilana is a proud participant in a national research biobank project. Over several years, she has attended a clinic to provide blood and saliva samples, to undergo various observations, tests, and scans. She has filled in lifestyle questionnaires and agreed to grant access to her medical records. The biobank stores the data collected from her, and health and social researchers can apply to use them in their studies, in pseudonymised form and subject to conditions.[1] As she nears the age at which her late mother had a number of small strokes and started to experience problems with her memory and eyesight, Ilana wonders if she, and her daughters, might be similarly at risk. She would like to know if her brain scans show any abnormalities and whether she carries genetic variants associated with Alzheimer's disease or degenerative eye conditions. The biobank has not contacted her about any health concerns. But she knows that they will only do so if they find 'potentially serious abnormalities' in observations or scans, and she will not be contacted at all if subsequent research studies find, even serious, risk factors. Meanwhile, her friend Sam has been excited about receiving the results of her 'full health and ancestry' report from an online direct-to-consumer (DTC) genomic testing service. When Sam's results eventually arrive, she is fascinated to learn of unexpected southern Indian ancestry and amused to see she is disposed to fear public speaking. She is relieved she does not carry the cancer-related *BRCA* mutations but is not sure how to interpret her percentage risk of Alzheimer's disease – it seems

---

[1] Pseudonymisation replaces identifying details with, for example, a reference number so that personal data cannot be easily attributed to a specific data subject.

scarily high. Overshadowing all this, though, is Sam's acute distress to learn that the results indicate she is not related to her father.

There are undoubtedly many differences between these two examples. Ilana is a volunteer in an endeavour intended to deliver social benefits; Sam is a customer of a commercial business. Receiving results of genomic analyses is an explicit part of Sam's customer agreement, whereas Ilana assented to the biobank's limited feedback policy. The biobank, researchers using the banked data, and the DTC genomics service each have different aims and resources for analysing and reporting back findings. And, while we might want to take issue with any such differences, the legal duties and standards of care each of these parties owes to Sam and Ilana are also likely to differ. Yet the *kinds* of information Ilana is unable to access and Sam is simply sent and what this information *means* to them are not so dissimilar. Both involve insights relevant to the friends' health and well-being, some of which are significant. They include findings that both women might want to know despite being neither strongly predictive nor clinically actionable. Both include information that could affect how the friends feel about and describe themselves, their familiarity and confidence in their bodies and mental capacities, and their hopes and plans for their futures. Some findings could help explain recent experiences, and others might affect how the women see and conduct their relationships with those close to them. This is most starkly so in Sam's case, but Ilana too feels an urgent need to know if her experiences and anxieties are like her mother's and she feels guilty about failing in her parental responsibilities to protect her daughters from threats to their happiness and health.

The contextual differences listed above account for much, but not every aspect, of the friends' dramatically different access stories and the questions these raise. For example, why does the biobank only report back 'potentially serious' abnormalities, and what are the appropriate criteria for deciding seriousness? How does the genomic testing service justify providing results directly to customers without professional support, while the biobank sends serious findings via participants' doctors? Which, if either, arrangement is best protecting the friends' interests? Is it true to say that the DTC service provides insights into users' identities, as its advertising strapline 'Getting to know the real you!' shouts, while the biobank only collects and generates data about health?

This sketch is not simply about the so-called rights to know or not to know.[2] It is about the particular kinds of interests that are affected by

---

[2] See Chadwick et al. 2014.

'knowing' – or not – and also by the manner and context in which information subjects come to know.[3] It invites us to consider whether serious health threats are the only or most important consideration when presenting us with insights into our health and traits, or whether it also matters how these affect our understanding of 'who we are'. And what does that last question even mean? Are learning of serious disease risks and knowing who one is easily separable? Are matters of genetic related-ness and ancestral origins paradigm identity concerns? More so than a fear of public speaking or risk of Alzheimer's disease? Or are these all equally reductive, restrictive misconceptions about what actually makes us *us*? Ilana and Sam themselves do not quite agree on these questions. When confiding her shocking news to her friend, Sam says, 'I know your health is important, but this is different, it's about my *identity*. I am not sure I know who I am anymore.' Ilana comforts her but thinks to herself, 'This feels like it's about my identity too. At this point in my life, I feel oddly at sea. Knowing more about my body and what mum went through would help me feel close to her, to understand and plan some important things for me and my family, and to be more at home in myself.' Over the following chapters, I will explore the potentially valuable insights reflected in each of their perspectives.

The Bioinformation Explosion

Observations, accompanied by awe or trepidation, of the sheer quantity and variety of health and bio-related data being generated are now customary in bioethics and related fields of study.[4] The ubiquity of these observations should not, however, desensitise us to their truth or to the personal, social, ethical, and regulatory implications of the richness of this ever-expanding reservoir of data.[5] These data supply sources of information about our physical and mental health and well-being; our cognitive and physical traits; the states, functions, and capacities of our bodies and minds; the relationships between our bodies and those of other people; the ways we differ from others; and the traits we share. It is these kinds of information, our encounters with them, and, specifically,

---

[3] In what follows, I shall use the term 'information subject' to refer to an individual person to whom particular personal bioinformation pertains and to whom it is understood to pertain. This does not preclude the possibility that the same information may have more than one information subject and thus be 'personal' to each of them.

[4] See, for example, Raghupathi and Raghupathi 2014; Sharon and Lucivero 2019.

[5] Xafis et al. 2019.

how these encounters shape who we are that I am concerned with in this book.

To get some idea of the range of information in question, we can start by imagining those that are collected and recorded in the course of observations and tests conducted in healthcare. The quantity and variety of these are amplified by the uses of biotechnologies in delivering care. For example, genome sequencing, neuroimaging, biosensors, self-administered diagnostic tests, and implanted smart technologies are all increasingly part of screening, treatment, patient monitoring, public health surveillance, and targeting of interventions. Our health data are stored in electronic patient records, which in turn facilitates their subsequent use in health and social research. Vast amounts of data are also generated through health research itself, which includes clinical and observational studies, but also increasingly involves secondary uses of health records, data linkage, and biobanking projects. These methods offer the promise of new diagnostics and therapies, of delivering 'precision medicine' that targets subgroups of patient populations, and of informing public health interventions.[6]

The collection and analysis of information from and about our bodies are not, however, limited to healthcare or health research settings.[7] They extend to public health, administrative, justice, and surveillance applications, including biometric passports, forensic DNA databases, apps and databases designed to track the spread of pandemics, and uses of gait analysis or facial recognition technologies in law enforcement.[8] We are also active participants in the generation and dissemination of information about ourselves, for example, when we send off – as Sam did – saliva samples to commercial genomic testing services; use wearable devices and apps to track our own behaviours, fitness, or well-being; or share experiences and photographs on social media. The role of technology in all of this extends beyond methods of gathering fresh data. Data science, including uses of artificial intelligence (AI) and machine learning, plays an increasingly central role in generating new health-related, phenotypic,[9] or behavioural profiles from existing data collections that may be applied to people far beyond those who were the sources of the original data.

---

[6] Xafis et al. 2019.

[7] Sharon and Lucivero 2019.

[8] Henschke 2017.

[9] Phenotypic traits are observable, measurable characteristics of an organism such as eye colour or the symptoms of a genetic disease.

The proliferation of all these kinds of data and the insights they offer into our health, well-being, traits, behaviours, and relationships invite questions about how they should be used and how these uses should be governed. For example, who should be able to access and use them? How can their clinical, social, or economic value be realised? How can potential abuses and harms be averted? The network of laws, regulations, policies, guidelines, and professional and institutional norms governing how health and biological data may be collected, deployed, and disclosed include data protection regimes, laws governing human tissues and fertility treatment, property and personality rights, and laws protecting information subjects' confidentiality and privacy alongside others' interests in information access.[10] It is reasonable to expect that this network of laws, policies, and guidelines governing who can gather, use, and access information about our health, bodies, and biology and for what purposes will be informed by an appropriate, context-responsive, and well-grounded framework of relevant ethical considerations. This framework would account for all private and public interests that could be significantly affected by, amongst other things, disclosures of and access to these kinds of information.

The central concern of this book is to highlight one set of interests that, I will argue, belongs squarely in this framework but has not yet received sufficiently robust or clearly conceived attention in practical governance settings or academic debate. Specifically, my intentions over the following chapters are to characterise the impacts of our encounters with information about our own health, bodies, and biology – which I will collectively term 'personal bioinformation' – on our *identities*; to interrogate the nature and strength of our interests in whether and how we encounter this information; and to highlight when and why these interests are engaged. I will argue that our access, or lack of access, to bioinformation about ourselves can affect our capacities to develop, make sense of, and occupy our own narrative accounts of who we are. And because these capacities play a foundational role in many aspects of well-being and of a rich and engaged practical life, our encounters with this information can engage ethically significant interests. I will say more about what I mean by 'identity' and 'personal bioinformation' shortly.

---

[10] Those of particular relevance to the arguments in this book are discussed in detail in Chapters 2 and 5.

Retraining Our Focus

In focusing on the impacts of information subjects' own encounters with personal bioinformation, the arguments presented in this book look in a different direction from many of the most prominent debates about governance of health information and biodata. They look inwards rather than outwards. What I mean by this is that often, when proposals are mooted, for example, to make patient records available for research or to introduce a mobile app to track exposure or immunity during a pandemic, the value of such initiatives tend to be framed in terms of the benefits they will deliver for patient care, public health, or perhaps public administration and security. Meanwhile, the most commonly voiced ethical concerns tend to be whether such initiatives could threaten the privacy of those whose data are gathered and processed and whether uses of these data might be stigmatising or discriminatory, infringe upon participants' dignity and freedoms, or erode public trust.[11] In short, attention usually turns first to what *others* might do with bioinformation about us. Here, I am concerned instead with the less well-trodden territory of what *information subjects themselves* might do with this information and how this might have profound effects on who they are.

This is not to suggest that information subjects' interests in accessing bioinformation have been wholly neglected. For example, in recent decades, medical law and ethics have seen a shift in what patients can expect to be told about their health and care options, turning from what healthcare professionals think they need to know, towards what the patient themselves might want to know.[12] Health research ethics continues to wrestle with dilemmas about feeding back individually relevant research findings to participants, though increasingly, the focus is on what should be fed back, rather than whether it should happen at all.[13] There are contemporary debates about the extent and basis of information subjects' 'right to know' and 'right not to know', particularly in the context of disclosures of genetic information to close blood relatives.[14] And discussions about benefits and risks to users of DTC services or consumer technologies to find out about their genetic traits or to track their lives are vigorously pursued.[15]

---

[11] See, for example, Carter et al. 2015; Dubov and Shoptawb 2020.
[12] Chan et al. 2017.
[13] Eckstein et al. 2014.
[14] Chadwick et al. 2014.
[15] See, for example, Kreitmair 2019.

Nevertheless, despite growing attention to subjects' own interests in accessing, or being shielded from, bioinformation about themselves, closer examination reveals that a relatively small cluster of concerns and interests dominate the landscape.[16] For example, when it comes to legal obligations to disclose health-related findings and to weigh the value of disclosure against countervailing concerns; when policy decisions are made about whether to offer health screening or which individual findings from health research should be returned to participants; or when those undergoing genetic testing are encouraged to share their results with their relatives, it is – perhaps unsurprisingly – the clinical actionability of the findings and their utility for reproductive decision-making that tend to be the foremost considerations.[17] Meanwhile, reasons for *protecting* information subjects from, for example, uncertain indications of susceptibility to genetic disease in healthcare or DTC contexts tend also to focus on clinical actionability – or rather its absence – alongside the risks of harm to health and psychological well-being from misleading, vague, or hard-to-interpret results, false reassurances, or the absence of effective prevention or treatment options.[18] Appeals to information subjects' privacy and the protection of a metaphorical 'private space' from impositions of unwelcome information feature in academic proposals for a robust theoretical grounding for the right not to know.[19] And information subjects' autonomy – understood either as the bald exercise of choice (not) to know or as a capacity for self-determination enhanced by judicious information provision – also plays a prominent role in legal and academic reasoning. For example, European human rights law emphasises individual 'rights to know' and 'not to know' information gathered about them in healthcare.[20] And judgments of UK courts increasingly emphasise patients' entitlement to receive the information that a reasonable patient would deem relevant to their care and that would allow them to make choices reflecting their own values.[21]

---

[16] Here, I am referring specifically to the interests of information subjects as (prospective) recipients. The list of protections and recognised interests that follows would look somewhat different if the concern was how information subjects are affected by *others'* access.

[17] Wolf et al. 2008; UK National Screening Committee 2015.

[18] Bunnik et al. 2011.

[19] Laurie 2002, p. 67.

[20] See, for example, *K.H. and others* v. *Slovakia* (no. 32881/04) (2009) ECHR 2009/13; Council of Europe, 'Convention for the Protection of Human Rights and Dignity of the Human Being with Regard to the Application of Biology and Medicine' (4 April 1997), Article 1.

[21] Chan et al. 2017.

This brief sketch illustrates the prominence of clinical actionability, protection of psychological and physical health, autonomy, and, to some extent, privacy as the core considerations most commonly invoked when it comes to assessing information subjects' interests in accessing bioinformation about themselves. I am not seeking here to take a position on the extent to which these should be part of the ethical framework governing when information subjects can access information about their health or bodies. They are indeed likely to be relevant and important considerations. Rather, I want to highlight that by comparison there is a lack of consistent, serious, or well-developed attention to the ways that our own encounters with bioinformation may affect our *identities* – with a few notable exceptions, which will be discussed over the following chapters.[22]

At this stage, of course, I have yet to say what I mean by identity or identity-related interests, let alone explain why, if there is indeed an identity-shaped gap, anyone should care about it. Nevertheless, I would hazard that many of us have encountered the idea, in one form or another, that some kinds of insights into our biological selves can have a bearing on who we are or at least on how we view ourselves. The arts, media, commerce, and popular imagination are littered with insinuations and bald claims about the importance of particular kinds of bioinformation to our identities. These are perhaps most prevalent with respect to genetic information, including the discovery of genetic relationships. For example, in the UK, assumptions that knowledge of genetic 'origins' provides insights into the self are evidenced in the popularity of amateur genealogy and television shows documenting celebrities' search for their ancestry.[23] UK courts have erred towards protecting children's right to know their genetic parentage, even in absence of existing social bonds.[24] Searches for genetic parents populate the plots of literature and films.[25] And documentaries and memoirs bear witness to personal quests for genetic 'parentage' or ancestry in the context of adoption, donor-assisted conception, or where family histories have been shattered by legacies of

---

[22] I will return in Chapter 6 to map the relationships between our identity-related interests and the other more commonplace considerations I have listed here.

[23] For example, the BBC series *Who Do You Think You Are?* in which celebrities trace their family history is in its seventeen series at the time of writing.

[24] Fortin 2011.

[25] The feature film *The Kids are All Right*, in which adolescent siblings build relationships with their sperm donor, and the Scottish poet Jackie Kaye's memoir 'Red Dust Road' in which she recounts searching for her birth parents, Kay 2011, are just two such examples.

enslavement, colonialism, or conflict.[26] Meanwhile, DTC genomics services play upon ideas that our genes reveal or shape our identities in promoting their tests for genetic markers associated with disease and non-disease traits and ancestral heritage with marketing straplines such as 'getting to know you' and 'a story about you'.[27] Similar assumptions are evident in popular discussions of what images from brain scans or data gathered about neural activity might reveal. For example, reporting of neuroscience in the non-specialist media is notorious, and often criticised, for enthusiastic, credulous, and reductive treatments of the putative capacities of neuroscience to explain differences in behaviour, attitudes, or personality types or to read our minds.[28]

We might be justifiably sceptical that popular tropes and preconceptions such as those just described are reliable indicators of whether ethically significant identity-related interests are in fact engaged by encounters with personal bioinformation. Nevertheless, they join an accretion of bioethical and social science discussions that further signal that something worthy of investigation is afoot. In the early years of the twenty-first century, there was a considerable wave of bioethical and social science writing, both theoretical and empirical, exploring the relationship between genetic or genomic information – about disease risk, traits, or relatedness – and our identities, in which both this relationship and identity itself are construed in a wide variety of ways.[29] For example, Christine Hauskeller considers, with some concern, the ways genetics could be used to naturalise and reinforce social distinctions.[30] Meanwhile, in a different vein, Vardit Ravitsky argues that donor-conceived individuals are wronged when they are not told of their origins and denied the opportunity 'to choose what meaning they assign to the genetic components of their identity'.[31] Academic discussions of the

[26] Again, just a few examples are: Georgina Lawton's memoir 'Raceless' in which she explores her family history and sense of racial identity, Lawton 2021; the personal stories recounted in Alondra Nelson's discussion of the entanglements of genetic science and the history and politics of race in the USA, Nelson 2016; and the 2020 documentary *Enslaved with Samuel L Jackson*, in which actor Samuel L. Jackson and journalist Afua Hirsch trace connections to Jackson's African heritage.

[27] iSpot.TV websites '23andMe TV Commercials' www.ispot.tv/brands/Ias/23andme (accessed 18 July 2021).

[28] O'Connor et al. 2012; Racine et al. 2005.

[29] Unless, otherwise specified, in what follows I will use 'genetic' as an umbrella term to refer both to information about specific genes and about features of an individual's entire genome, even though the latter could more accurately be referred to as 'genomic information'.

[30] Hauskeller 2004.

[31] Ravitsky 2014, p. 36.

relationship between genetic information and identity have been joined more recently by those suggesting that insights into our brain states and functions may provide fresh ways of seeing ourselves. For example, Nikolas Rose and Joelle Abi-Rached observe how the adoption of concepts from neuroscience can offer fresh tools for self-characterisation, while Mary Walker sceptically explores propositions that brain data might be able to reveal our 'real' attitudes and motivations.[32] I will consider these and other views about the impacts of bioinformation on identity in the following chapters, where they will provide some of the illustrations, critical tools, and comparators for the conceptual and normative picture that I will develop.

Given both popular beliefs and scholarly discussions about the possible roles of genetic or neuro-information in understanding or developing our identities, it is perhaps striking that currently the only legal entitlements to access bioinformation about oneself on explicitly identity-related grounds in the UK are donor-conceived individuals' limited rights to knowledge of genetic parentage.[33] I will discuss these provisions in greater detail in Chapters 2 and 5. I raise them here because it was the ongoing debate about donor-conceived individuals' putative identity-based interests and legal entitlements to know about their conception and their donors that provided the original motivation for the enquiry at the heart of this book. This debate piqued my interest in finding out what such claims might mean and on what grounds they might be justified.[34] But my curiosity was matched by corresponding scepticism about the apparent exceptionalism of these claims. It seemed both arbitrary and implausible that, if we do indeed have significant identity interests in knowing about our genetic parentage, these interests uniquely attach to this one category of information. Furthermore, any claim to identity value must contend with the corresponding critique that proposing an important role for knowledge of genetic parentage depends on a troublingly deterministic and biologically essentialist view of the self that risks being exclusionary and oppressive.[35] Either way, this debate demanded closer scrutiny of the nature of any supposed identity value or detriment.

---

[32] Rose and Abi-Rached 2013; Walker 2012.

[33] Marshall 2014; Human Fertilisation and Embryology Act 1990, as amended. Hereafter, I will use the phrases genetic parentage, without inverted commas, and genetic origins to mean genetic progenitor while recognising that in many cases neither the legal nor the social relationship is one of a parent.

[34] I examine these reported experiences in detail in Chapter 5.

[35] For example, de Melo-Martín 2014.

As I will argue in the next chapter, the meaning of identity and its relationship to knowledge of genetic parentage – the very things existing legal provisions purport to be concerned with – remain ambiguous in existing legal and regulatory provisions. Some of the pictures of the relationships between identity and particular kinds of bioinformation proposed in academic debates are considerably more developed and nuanced. However, as I shall go on to explore, many still remain open to charges that the connections drawn are, in some cases, exceptionalist; while in others, they are ambiguous, contentious, or lacking in normative heft. This leaves us, and those responsible for governing access to personal bioinformation in particular, ill-equipped. We lack the necessary tools to conceptualise and formulate well-justified, consistent, and practical ethical approaches to providing access to personal bioinformation in ways that protect recipients' identity interests. In the course of the arguments to be presented, I will explain why I think this is a significant gap that warrants serious attention. I will suggest that it is not only a practical gap, inasmuch as existing laws and policies are inadequate to protect our bioinformation-related identity interests. More fundamentally, there is a lack of conceptual and normative clarity about the nature of the impacts of personal bioinformation on our identities, the strength and scope of the interests engaged, and, thus, how these interests might be appropriately recognised and met. Filling this more fundamental gap is essential to addressing the practical one, and it is my aim over the following chapters.

Aims of This Enquiry

My objective in this book is to offer a plausible, conceptually robust, normative account of the roles of personal bioinformation in our self-conceptions that is consistent with people's lived experiences. This will be an account that is capable of explaining why and how our encounters with this information can impact our identities in ways that engage ethically significant interests, without recourse to biologically essentialist claims.[36] The picture I will develop will be applicable across all 'personal bioinformation'

---

[36] By biologically essentialist claims, I will mean those that hold that our identities as individual persons are 'given', determined by particular biological characteristics such as our genetic inheritance, rather than created by other means and malleable.

conceived as a broad, inclusive category, rather than being limited to any one specific kind. However, it will also be capable of accounting for the diverse impacts of different kinds of bioinformation in different circumstances. Building from this conceptual and normative foundation, I will argue that our identity-related interests warrant serious attention when decisions are made about disclosures of personal bioinformation to those to whom it pertains. I will explain why these interests are engaged beyond the usual suspects – namely, information about genetic origins and genetic disease risk. I will further demonstrate that identity concerns are neither reducible to nor coextensive with those interests more commonly accounted for in decisions about disclosure – health protection, psychological well-being, autonomy, and privacy – and thus require attention in their own right.

My central claim will be that personal bioinformation, understood as a broad and inclusive category, plays critical roles in the development and maintenance of comfortably inhabitable and sustainable self-narratives – the narratives that constitute our identities. These roles, and their ethical significance, are accounted for by the practical functions of our self-narratives in our inescapably embodied and relational lives. I will argue that personal bioinformation can help us in the population and interpretive work of building narratives that are responsive to, and intelligible in light of, our embodied, relational experiences and that support us in making sense of and navigating these. I will also account for those instances in which bioinformation fails to fulfil these roles. In presenting and defending these claims, this book will contribute a vital plank in the ethical frameworks that guide laws, policies, and practices governing disclosures of personal bioinformation, equipping them to protect our identity interests. It will offer not only a picture of the nature of information subjects' interests in accessing this information but also a means of discerning when, why, and how these interests are engaged in different circumstances. It will also characterise the nature and extent of the corresponding obligations accruing to those who hold personal bioinformation about us.

1.2 Terminology

Before I can proceed with this argument, however, it is necessary to lay some groundwork by explaining what I will mean by 'personal bioinformation' and 'identity'. This will help to establish the conceptual and practical scope of the discussions to come.

Personal Bioinformation

This chapter opened with a brief sketch of the kinds of 'personal bioinformation' with which I am concerned. That provided some indication of the breadth and variety of information to which the arguments in this book are intended to apply. However, it will be useful to say a bit more about what I intend this phrase to include. My aim here is not to provide necessary and sufficient conditions for a precise definition, but rather a working understanding that will inevitably leave some fuzzy edges. I will also introduce the three categories of personal bioinformation that will serve as illustrative examples in the coming chapters. It is perhaps easiest first to say what 'personal bioinformation' is *not* intended to signal. I am not using it to introduce a novel or bespoke category distinction. Nor should the word 'personal' be understood as building in intrinsic identity-significance in a way that would be question-begging. The phrase is simply a contraction of 'personal biological information', adopted here for the purposes of brevity. It is intended to capture a broad and diverse set of information about our health, bodies, biological traits, and relationships to others – that is, the kinds of information about which the law, clinicians, policymakers, and bioethicists already ask questions regarding who may access it and for what purposes.

Information

In what I have said so far I have not been disciplined in distinguishing between data and information, slipping between the two as we often do in ordinary language. There is, however, a useful distinction to be made. The General Definition of Information (GDI) defines information as data plus interpretation.[37] Interpretation involves the processing, organisation, structuring, classification, and aggregation of data in a particular context and with a particular purpose such that it becomes about something.[38] The GDI further stipulates that information must comprise more than one datum and be 'well-formed' – that is, arranged so that it is 'meaningful'.[39] Data may be thought of as observed or recorded states of affairs that provide source material for information. The discussions in

---

[37] Taylor 2012. I am concerned here with semantic information communicated between people, not the information conveyed by genetic material for the construction of proteins, or transmitted by neural signals.

[38] Rowley 2007.

[39] Floridi 2019.

this book do not concern access to raw, unformed, and uninterpreted data but information that is comprehensible, at least in principle, to the person to whom it pertains – the information subject. All personal bioinformation will have meaning, which is not to say that it will always be useful or meaning*ful* – in the sense of significant – to the recipient. It may not even be true or reliable.[40]

Interpretation is not a one-off event. Different and successive interpretations can be applied to the same data or information, resulting in new information with new meanings. Consequently, information is not inert but dynamic and changeable as successive layers of interpretation supplant each other or accumulate palimpsest-like. In his discussion of genetic data, Mark Taylor observes that we can think of information as having an 'interpretive pedigree' – that is, the interpretation(s) that has or have already been applied to it – and 'interpretive potential' – referring to the ways that it could go on to be further interpreted.[41] I will follow Taylor in terming the context in and purpose for which interpretation takes place the 'interpretive framework'.[42] The nature and meaning of the information derived depends on the framework applied. Recognising the dynamic and cumulative nature of information will be useful when it comes to thinking in later chapters about the ways in which the impacts of personal bioinformation and its relevance to identity can vary in different contexts.

Due to the interpretive and dynamic nature of information, we cannot assume that the meaning invested by the party conveying it will be the same as that of the person receiving it. Each will bring different interpretive frameworks, including background knowledge, experiences, expectations, and interest perspectives. These are not limited to different capacities to make sense of complex, technical aspects of the information. For example, both discloser and recipient could be clinical geneticists. But, if one is a patient and the other their doctor, the same 'item' of genetic information conveyed – for example, that the patient has tested positive for the mutation responsible for the serious neurological disorder Huntington's disease – will have different meaning and significance for each.[43] And disclosures of the same kind of genetic test result to

---

[40] Some accounts hold that semantic information must, by definition, be true (see Floridi 2019). Here, I adopt an ordinary usage approach according to which information can be described as false, or indeed meaningless in the sense of being irrelevant or trivial.

[41] Taylor 2012, pp. 41–42.

[42] Taylor 2012, p. 53.

[43] For this reason, any suggestion that disclosing information entails handing over an inert information 'item' is misleading.

three different patients – for example, one with children, one aware of their family history of Huntington's, and one with emerging symptoms – are likely to convey three diverse meanings. As will be explored in later chapters, the context and manner of communication are themselves likely to further contribute to the interpretive framework.

Biological

'Bioinformation' is used here to capture more than information about health and disease. It is intended to extend to any information about ourselves as embodied, biological, and biologically connected human beings, our dispositions, states, functions, and capacities. Taylor's taxonomy of genetic data offers a valuable device here. Taylor proposes that 'genetic data' includes not only data derived from analysis of genetic material – those with a genetic source – but also those that have been, or could be, interpreted to be about genetic states of affairs – that is, with a genetic interpretive pedigree or interpretive potential.[44] The following discussion will adopt a parallel understanding of personal bioinformation, whereby this includes not only information derived from observation or monitoring of someone's body, tissues, or biomarkers but also that which conveys something about their bodily and biological characteristics. This means, for example, that information about having been conceived using donor gametes will count as bioinformation, insofar as it is understood to speak to the donor-conceived individual's origins as an organism and their genetic relationships, even if the information source is an administrative record rather than a genetic test. Conversely, a mental health diagnosis based on neuroimaging data will count as personal bioinformation when it is derived from data recorded from the individual's brain and has implications for their medical care, even if mental health is not reducible to purely biological states of affairs.

Personal

The 'personal' aspect of bioinformation is intended here to signal that the information has been interpreted as applying to an identifiable individual and purports to reveal something about that person's own health, body, or biological existence. This is not to overlook, however, that some personal bioinformation – most notably, genetic – is inescapably shared with others and that these others may have interests in whether or not it is

---

[44] Taylor 2012.

disclosed and to whom. It also leaves space for recognising that the meaning and significance of particular bioinformation to the information subject may depend – perhaps a great deal – on what it reveals about others and their relationships to the subject, how it might be used to group the subject with or distinguish them from others, or how it might contribute to characterising groups to whom the individual belongs. Furthermore, personal bioinformation may be derived from analysis of data gathered wholly, or in part, from other people. For example, genetic information may be understood as being about a particular individual, even though they themselves have not undergone testing, where its relevance to them can be inferred from family history or tests conducted on close blood relatives. Similarly, with the increasing use of big health data, AI, and machine learning in healthcare and research, it is increasingly likely that personal bioinformation, such as disease susceptibility estimates, will be based upon risk profiles built from data collected from many, perhaps thousands, of other individuals.[45] For the purposes of the following discussion then, being 'personal' does not preclude this information being shared with others, being personal to more than one person, or being derived from data from sources other than the body of the individual in question. What is relevant is that it has been interpreted to be about at least one identifiable individual – whom I shall refer to as the 'information subject' – in a way that is apparent, or easily discoverable, to both whoever currently controls it and the information subject if they were to encounter it. The focus of this enquiry is on the effects of such encounters on information subjects' capacities to develop, understand, and occupy their identities. However it is based neither on an individualistic picture of bioinformation nor on an individualistic conception of identity and identity interests.

Encounters with Bioinformation

The kinds of bioinformation with which this book is concerned include those about an individual's past, present, and possible future health and well-being; their susceptibility to disease and illness; the states, functioning, capacities, and dispositions of their bodies and minds; and their biological relationships to and commonalities with others. These may be generated through healthcare, research, commercial, administrative, or recreational activities. They may be conveyed verbally or in writing.

---

[45] Raghupathi and Raghupathi 2014.

They could comprise text, numerical data, figures, charts, or images – as in the case of brain or body scans. As this suggests, personal bioinformation ranges from the complex, detailed, and technical – such as that conveyed by a magnetic resonance imaging (MRI) scan that requires specialist knowledge and techniques for its generation and interpretation – to that conveyed by bald statements such as 'he is your biological father'. In many cases, these kinds of information will be conveyed by another person. However, the following discussions will also apply to alerts or findings communicated directly to users by devices such as medical implants and wearable health-tracking devices, by mobile device apps, or by the online portals of DTC services.

Of course, the vast majority of the information and knowledge we have of our embodied and biological characteristics are not obtained from other people or devices, and our access to them does not require expert analytical techniques – rather, they are acquired directly from our own senses. To be of interest for this enquiry, personal bioinformation does not necessarily need to uncover what is deeply hidden or convey wholly new insights. Some of it may be confirmatory of, complementary to, or at odds with knowledge we already have about our health or traits. The salient feature is that the bioinformation under scrutiny has an external source, and other actors' choices and agency lie between it and our encounters with it – hence practical, legal, and ethical questions about disclosure and access arising at all. These other actors include those who generate, hold, and manage our bioinformation and those who devise policies about what will be offered and fed back to information subjects. These actors may be individuals operating in their professional or institutional capacity, such as clinicians or health researchers. They might include developers and engineers who design the algorithms and information interfaces that determine what our wearable devices tell us about our sleep, activity, blood oxygen, or mood and in what format. At an institutional and state level, relevant actors might be research ethics committees, professional bodies responsible for – for example – deciding which health screening programmes should be run, or regulators who determine what kinds of tests a DTC genomics company can market. These actors might also include private individuals, for example, a parent who knows that their own carrier status for Huntington's disease means that their children each have a 50 per cent chance of being affected.

The following discussions are concerned to a considerable extent with circumstances in which access is not inevitable or is somehow obstructed – as in the example of Ilana's experience above. But they are no less pertinent to circumstances such as Sam's, in which information is readily or routinely available to its subject. The account of identity-related interests to be developed over the following chapters will look at identity-related reasons both for and against disclosing bioinformation. It will characterise interests that need to be weighed alongside other considerations currently guiding disclosure decisions and require us to think not only about *whether* to disclose but also about *how* information is communicated. The following list provides some examples of the kinds of questions and debates into which the following discussions might feed:

- What is the scope of research data repositories' or researchers' ethical duties to return individually relevant research findings to participants?[46]
- When should genetic screening be offered for conditions that cannot be effectively treated?[47]
- Which factors should healthcare professionals consider when encouraging a patient to inform family members about a shared risk of genetic disease or in deciding when it is acceptable to break the patient's confidence if they refuse?[48]
- Should individuals conceived via mitochondrial replacement therapy be entitled to know the identities of the donor of the egg that provided their healthy mitochondria?[49]
- Which kinds of tests – using which methods and for which conditions and traits – should consumers be able to access through DTC genomics or imaging services?[50]
- When are quantified health, well-being, and behavioural data supplied by wearable personal technologies beneficial or detrimental to their users, and what kinds of user interfaces might influence their value?[51]
- Which categories of patients would be suitable candidates for the use of implanted smart technologies, such as brain-computer interfaces (BCIs) that provide predictive information about the onset of adverse health events such as seizures?[52]
- What are the utilities and risks of digital phenotyping techniques, which use algorithmic analysis of our online activity and behaviours

---

[46] Eckstein et al. 2014
[47] Roberts 2012.
[48] Dove et al. 2019.
[49] Appleby 2018.
[50] Bunnik et al. 2011.
[51] Kreitmair 2019.
[52] Gilbert et al. 2019.

captured by our digital devices to make inferences about, for example, our mental health?[53]

- What concerns might be raised by novel categorisation of people by the algorithms used in, for example, precision medicine or public health surveillance?[54]

This list is indicative, rather than exhaustive. It includes examples of circumstances in which legal and ethical debates about information provision are ongoing, as well as those in which such debates are emerging, or assumed to be long since settled. Some of these debates are ones in which identity impacts are already invoked with greater or less cogency, while identity talk is wholly absent from others. What these questions have in common is that they illustrate contexts in which, I will argue, consideration of clearly and robustly conceptualised identity interests are likely to be critical to ethical information governance. There will not be space to describe in detail the specific implications of my arguments for each of these questions in the following chapters, but they provide indications of the kinds of contexts in which the coming analysis and recommendations are intended to apply. There are, however, three areas in which I will explore the potential impacts and associated identity interests in some depth.

Three Illustrative Examples

In Chapter 5, I will explore in detail information subjects' views and experiences of encountering three kinds of bioinformation – as reported in published empirical studies – to illustrate and sense-test my arguments. These will be the following:

- *Knowledge of having been conceived using donor gametes (sperm and/or eggs).* Donor-assisted conception is used by some intended parents who have been unable to conceive with their own gametes because of infertility or because they are single parents or in same-sex relationships.[55] In the UK this may involve treatment at a licensed fertility clinic or use of privately sourced donor sperm for self-insemination.
- *Results from testing for genetic variants associated with increased susceptibility to serious multifactorial diseases.* Genetic testing

---

[53] Huckvale et al. 2019.

[54] Vayena et al. 2018.

[55] Where single men and gay couples use donor gametes, surrogacy will also be used.

involves the analysis of blood or tissue samples to detect 'the presence or absence of, or alteration in, a particular gene, chromosome or gene product'.[56] Based on this – and often other data such as family history of disease – an individual's susceptibility, typically as lifetime percentage risk, is calculated. These tests are not predictive but provide probabilistic risk estimates. The tests I will focus on are those to detect mutations of the *BRCA* gene, associated with an elevated risk for breast and ovarian cancer, and variants of the *APOE* gene, associated – though less strongly – with elevated risk of late-onset Alzheimer's disease in some populations.

- *Findings from psychiatric applications of neuroimaging.* This concerns research uses and potential clinical applications of neuroimaging to gather data about functional and structural features of participants' brains, from which – in combination with other data sources and using machine learning techniques – researchers hope that predictive, diagnostic, or prognostic inferences to participants' mental health status, relating to conditions including depression, psychosis, and schizophrenia, will be derivable.[57]

In Chapter 5, I will return to describe the characteristics of these three categories of bioinformation further and to outline the extent to which each is currently accessible to information subjects and on what grounds. I have not selected these examples because of their assumed or preeminent identity significance. Rather, they have been chosen to help paint a picture of the diverse nature of identity impacts and how these coincide or differ across different kinds of bioinformation. This will then provide clues to how we might generalise beyond these examples to other kinds of bioinformation and identify the variables on which identity value and significance depend. Before I can engage with questions of identity impacts, however, I need to explain the sense in which 'identity' will be used in this enquiry.

Identity

This book is an interdisciplinary project drawing on arguments, examples, and conceptual frameworks from bioethics, philosophy, law, and the social sciences. Across these disciplines, 'identity' is used in myriad divergent and overlapping ways. Efforts in the literature to

---

[56] Pinto-Basto et al. 2010, p. 33.
[57] Lawrie et al. 2019.

distinguish its various connotations generate taxonomies that themselves lump and split the various uses of the term differently. As Adam Henschke observes in developing his own taxonomy, 'different disciplines will form different ideas when a phrase like "genetic information is necessary for identity formation" is used'.[58]

Amongst these 'different ideas' of identity are several that are perfectly cogent, thought-provoking, and ethically and legally significant in their own way but nevertheless differ from my central focus in this book. Therefore, some disambiguation is needed. Details of the particular 'narrative' conception of identity, on which I will ground my arguments, will receive close attention in Chapter 3. Here I wish to start by drawing some more basic lines of distinction and connection between the understanding of identity that comprises the heart of this project and other prominent senses. The following taxonomy is not intended to be definitive, but it usefully maps the landscape of common usage in medical law and bioethics for my present purposes.

First, I want to set aside two senses of identity that will not be addressed by this book – *species identity* and *public persona* or *image*. Although bioinformation could be potentially implicated by concerns about each of these senses of identity – for example, where genomic analysis is used to help answer questions about the humanness of a human/animal chimeric embryo or where publicity reporting a celebrity's ill health damages their reputation – these concerns are not engaged by an information subject's *own* access to their personal bioinformation and they are not my focus here.

Numerical Identity

Biometric data in a passport is used to identify whether the passenger at the immigration desk is who they claim to be, and a DNA profile may be used to find out whether the suspect held in custody is the person who left a bloodstain at the crime scene. These examples pertain to what is referred to as *numerical identity*, that is, the metaphysical or logical kind of identity concerned with questions of sameness.[59] Here, sameness may be understood in terms of 'persistence' or 'reidentification' – that is, questions about when one thing is the very same entity as that located at a different time or in a different context. It is also used to capture the corresponding idea of 'individuation', which concerns what makes

---

[58] Henschke 2010, p. 450.
[59] Parfit 1984.

something itself and distinct from other things. In the examples above, personal bioinformation is used to ascertain whether the person in the custody cell or at the border check is the very same as the person who was at the crime scene or who is described in their travel documents. Uses and abuses of bioinformation in ascertaining numerical identity are often proper concerns of bioethics and law. However, situations in which someone would have an interest in accessing bioinformation *about themselves* to determine their *own* numerical identity – to answer the question 'was that me?' – are likely to be quite limited. Bioinformation such as distinctive birthmark or DNA analysis might perhaps serve such a purpose when someone wishes to ascertain whether they are the individual captured in an old photograph when records and memories are unable to make this connection.[60] Such examples notwithstanding, matters of strict, logical sameness or difference are not, or at least not directly, my concern here.

Personal Identity

Questions of numerical identity where these apply specifically to *persons*, and particularly to questions about the sameness or reidentification of persons over time and through physical or mental qualitative changes, are commonly termed questions of *personal identity*.[61] Concerns about personal identity in this sense notoriously arise in bioethics and medical law when, for example, we ask questions about the continued validity of consent to treatment or an advanced care directive when someone has lost capacity between the point of giving consent or making their directive and the relevant intervention. These questions arise especially when the person has undergone marked cognitive or personality changes. These kinds of questions are often treated as ones about logical sameness – about when the person-as-entity at an earlier time can be understood as being the very same person-as-entity at a later time.[62] However, the validity of an advanced directive can also be interpreted as a question that relates to a somewhat different sense of personal identity, one closer to that with which I am concerned in this book, as I shall now explain.

Perhaps confusingly, the phrase 'personal identity' is used in both ordinary language and philosophy to capture not only the logical sameness of persons but also the set of qualities that characterise a person,

---

[60] Strictly speaking, this would only reliably confirm personal identity if one adopted a bodily criterion for the persistence of a person.

[61] Schechtman 2014.

[62] Cf. Buchanan 1988.

those that make them who they distinctively are and different from other people. By teasing apart the distinct kinds of logical, practical, and ethical concerns falling under the banner of 'personal identity', Marya Schechtman and Catriona Mackenzie have contributed to reducing the potential for this confusion while shining much-needed light on matters of identity that had been occluded by a focus on numerical identity.[63] In discussing the relevant distinctions, Mackenzie suggests that when we ask questions about, for example, the continued validity of someone's wishes after they have lost competence or undergone a profound change in values, we are usually chiefly interested with what she terms 'practical and evaluative considerations', such as whether the wishes and values of the younger person should bind those of the older, or which treatment option accords with the kind of life the younger person hoped to lead in their later years.[64] These authors argue that it is a mistake to imagine that these questions can be appropriately or wholly addressed by thinking about whether strict conditions for the metaphysical sameness of an entity at two different times are fulfilled. Rather, what we are usually concerned about – and, indeed, what someone writing an advanced directive is themselves likely to be concerned about – is the extent to which the older person remains relevantly like the younger person, shares the same values and hopes, and feels a connection with and understanding of their younger self. We are interested in the extent to which the younger self's imagined projection of their later self's values and priorities was in line with those they in fact come to hold. These kinds of concerns engage what Schechtman's terms the 'characterization question' – that is, the question of which characteristics, beliefs, values, and actions are 'truly attributable' to a person and make them the particular person they are.[65] And as such, Schechtman argues, the answer to whether someone's identity remains the same will admit of degrees and have irreducibly diachronic or evolving aspects that are not captured by trying to see if two frozen 'time slices' or snapshots of a person at different points in their life match.[66] Further explanation of what it means for matters of identity to admit of degrees or have importantly diachronic aspects will have to wait until Chapter 3.

---

[63] Mackenzie 2008a; Schechtman 1996.
[64] Mackenzie 2008a, p. 1.
[65] Schechtman 1996, pp. 74, 76.
[66] Schechtman 1996, p. 77.

Practical Identity

Schechtman's and Mackenzie's analyses serve to bring to light the sense of identity that comprises the heart of my enquiry here. This book is concerned with the impacts of encounters with personal bioinformation on identity understood as *characterisation*. An individual's 'identity' in this sense refers to the constellation of characteristics that are really *theirs*. It captures those characteristics that make them the particular individual that they are, about which we may sensibly ask what role the characteristics play in distinguishing and defining that individual.[67] It is the impacts of encounters with personal bioinformation on identity in the characterisation sense that I will be concerned with in what follows. While detailed discussion of what these impacts look like and why they matter is the subject of the chapters to come, it is possible to get at least a sense here of how personal bioinformation – for example, a diagnosis of diabetes or the revelation that one's father is not one's genetic parent – could shape insights and understandings that feed into how one characterises oneself.

Three features of identity, understood in this characterisation sense, are key to the arguments that I will go on to make. The first two of these are that the narrative account of self-characterisation is of a *normative* and *practical* kind.[68] That is, according to this conception, identity is not merely an inert label or set of descriptors. Rather one's identity provides the foundation for individual perspective on and engagement with the world. It is, in Christine Korsgaard's words, '[the] description under which you value yourself, a description under which you find your life to be worth living and your actions to be worth undertaking'.[69] Our practical identities provide the frameworks for our evaluations of ourselves, our circumstances, and our motives. They provide us with reasons to act in some ways rather than others. And they are themselves constituted, or undermined, to the extent that we do, or do not, act in these ways.[70] As Mackenzie notes, this makes our practical identities 'both a precondition for and a product of our agency'.[71] I will return to explain further what this entails in Chapter 3. The third crucial feature, also to be described further in Chapter 3, is that I will be using 'identity' to refer to a single – albeit a complex and multifaceted – thing, bound together as

---

[67] Schechtman 1996, p. 77.
[68] Korsgaard 1996.
[69] Korsgaard 1996, p. 101.
[70] Korsgaard 2009.
[71] Mackenzie 2008a, p. 11.

a narrative. Someone's identity is to be understood as the totality of who they are and the myriad interacting and intersectional traits and experiences by which they characterise themselves and that make them who they are.

Social Identity

When I talk of 'identity' then, I intend it to be understood in this global sense, rather than to refer to aspects of who someone is or to specific descriptors. As such, it differs from the concept of *social identity*, where this refers to particular social identifiers, group memberships, roles, or markers of belonging and exclusion that we ourselves and others might use to describe, group, or distinguish us – such as gender, ethnicity, sexuality, political affiliation, nationality, social class, or religious faith.[72] Having said this, personal bioinformation will often play a part – for better or worse – in the adoption, affirmation, or allocation of these group and social modes of identification in ways I will go on to describe. And our social identifiers and group memberships are very likely to be amongst the prominent characteristics that make up identity in the practical, multistranded sense with which I am concerned. In distinguishing identity in a global characterisation sense from social identity, then, my intention is not to claim these concepts are wholly unconnected.

Practical Self-characterisation

Why is it that I will focus on identity in this global, practical 'characterisation' sense in this book? The short answer is that – as I will go on to demonstrate – it is this kind of identity that is most plausibly and profoundly impacted by information subjects' own encounters with bioinformation about themselves. And it is with respect to identity understood in this way – what it looks like, how it changes, whether it is sustainable, what it feels like to inhabit, and its role in our practical lives and lived experiences – that our interests are often most plausibly and profoundly engaged. As Schechtman argues, characterisation captures the respect in which 'personal identity matters to us at all'.[73] By this, she means that many of the ethical and practical questions with which questions of identity tend to be concerned – for example, the questions of whether I would still exist following the loss of cognitive capacities or

---

[72] Jenkins 2014.
[73] Schechtman 1996, p. 1.

which of my behaviours I may be held morally responsible for – are properly answered by reference to the degree of continuity and coherence amongst the combination of characteristics that make us who we are.[74] This is what is understood to be in jeopardy and what we are concerned about when we talk about someone having an 'identity crisis' or wishing to express ourselves and act in ways that are 'true to who we are'.[75] We are invested in the qualities that make us the particular individuals we are, in our capacities to maintain or change these, and in our abilities to inhabit and enact them. For these reasons, this is the version of identity where the most plausible, interesting, far-reaching, and ethically pressing questions about our interests in our encounters with bioinformation about our-selves arise. I will argue that personal bioinformation can play a critical part in our abilities to construct, make sense of, and inhabit our own accounts of who we are and what we are like. To be more specific then, this book is concerned with identity in the sense of *self*-characterisation.

Shared and Group Identity

It will be helpful before closing this chapter to clarify some questions that lie outwith the scope of the discussions that follow, including questions pertaining to the relational impacts of bioinformation access. As indi-cated at the start of this chapter, this book is not directly or chiefly concerned with the impacts of *other* people's or institutional access to and (ab)use of personal bioinformation on information subjects' iden-tities. This is not to deny that these impacts are often significant and warrant serious ethical attention. For example, retention on a forensic database of the genetic data of suspects who have never been charged, or uses of biometric data by border forces to 'verify' refugees' countries of origin, could be degrading or alienating and undermine valued modes of self-definition that are core to the information subjects' self-conceptions.[76] Nor will this book address cases in which others' uses of our personal bioinformation could negatively affect group identity as, for example, in the case of genetic research involving the North American Havasupai people. The Havasupai's ancestral origin story and religious beliefs, key foundations of their collective understanding of who they are,

---

[74] In her more recent work, Schechtman's position has evolved. She still holds that our narrative self-characterisations are germane to the phenomenology of selfhood and to practical questions but no longer maintains that they are sufficient to answer all questions about the metaphysical identity of persons. See Schechtman 2014.

[75] DeGrazia 2005.

[76] See, for example, Ajana 2010; Machado and Granja 2020.

were contradicted by non-consensual genetic analyses of blood samples several members had contributed while participating in research purporting to explore the incidence of diabetes.[77] Similarly, I will not directly address ways in which information subjects' access to or uses of their own personal bioinformation might affect the identities of other individuals, or of the groups to which they belong. For example, someone living with a rare genetic disease might agree to participate in research investigating how preimplantation diagnosis could be used to screen for and select against the genetic variant responsible – research that others living with the condition might experience as stigmatising and discriminatory. Each of these (ab)uses of personal bioinformation could have ethically significant consequences for individual or group identities. Other writers have valuably discussed the potential identity threats arising from the kinds of second- and third-person transactions in and uses of personal bioinformation just described. And much of what I will go on to say will have indirect implications for understanding and characterising these kinds of impacts on our individual and shared identities. But it is first-person access and first-person impacts with which I am primarily concerned in this book.

In placing these wider questions outwith the scope of this project, it may seem that I am embarking on an unsatisfactorily and unrealistically individualistic journey. As Heather Widdows observes – with specific reference to genetic information – conceiving of this information as belonging only to us and engaging our interests as discrete individuals risks missing or misrepresenting the shared values and interests at stake, including those relating to identity. As such, it risks failing to provide adequate foundations for the protection of these interests.[78] This is an important objection. And, while it is most obviously pertinent to inherently shared genetic information, uses of big health data and bioinformatics mean that we are all increasingly implicated in the processing and use of each other's data. Potential identity-related interests in the uses of bioinformation are not, therefore, limited or reducible to those of people who act as information sources. For example, as Widdows observes, we risk missing the particular nature and severity of the harm done to the Havasupai people, if we conceive of the harm to their group identity solely in terms of its impacts on individual members.[79] Recognising the

---

[77] Van Assche et al. 2013.
[78] Widdows 2013.
[79] Widdows 2013.

reality and significance of group identity interests, however, does not preclude recognising that there are important, neglected ethical matters to attend to in respect of the identity impacts of information subjects' own encounters with shared categories of bioinformation. And it is the task of this enquiry to draw attention to and address these. However, taking Widdows's warning seriously, if we are to understand the nature and range of these impacts on individuals, we will need to look beyond the individual taken in isolation.

The account of identity to be presented in this project is not an individualistic one. The inherently relational nature of identity development, and the roles played by bioinformation in this, will be central to my argument. Our identities are inextricably bound up with the understandings, knowledge practices, and identities of others and of the groups to which we belong or to which we are assumed to belong by others. By this, I mean at least three things. First – as I will go on to describe – we do not and cannot build our identities in isolation from our relationships with others and the ways they recognise and respond to our own self-conceptions or fail to do so. Second – as will be illustrated in Chapter 5 – how we interpret personal bioinformation and the effects it has on our identities cannot be separated from our relationships, relational roles, and group memberships. Third – as I will describe in Chapter 6 – the interpretations and significance with which others invest particular kinds of personal bioinformation will inform or shape our perceptions of its relevance to our identities and the kinds of impacts it has.

1.3   Guide to the Following Chapters

Over the following chapters, I will develop and defend the argument that because of the possible impacts – both positive and negative – of personal bioinformation on the inhabitability of our identity narratives, we have ethically significant interests in respect of whether and how we are able to access a wide variety of such information. The form and significance of these impacts are shaped by the embodied and socially embedded nature of our lives. I will argue that the identity-related interests characterised by this argument are sufficiently strong to give rise to responsibilities amongst those who hold potentially identity-significant personal bioinformation about us and to be taken into account by information disclosure policies and practices. The strength of these interests and the scope of these responsibilities will vary depending on the type of bioinformation in question, as well as individual, contextual, relational, and institutional factors. Laws, policies, and practices governing information subjects' access to bioinformation will need to remain responsive to this variation. For this reason, the task of specifying precise policy or legal reforms across every context in which decisions about access to and disclosures of personal bioinformation arise lies beyond the capacities of this project. My central aim is to provide the conceptual basis and ethical framework on which any such reforms could be grounded. Without such a foundation, attempts to offer robust, defensible, and non-arbitrary protection for our informational identity interests in policy or law are jeopardised from the start. The following provides a brief roadmap to the chapters that follow.

Chapter 2 establishes the practical, conceptual, and normative gaps that this book seeks to fill by exploring the limited existing opportunities and legal entitlements that information subjects have to access personal bioinformation on explicitly identity-related grounds and the ways that identity interests are reflected in these provisions. This chapter then reviews the extent to which existing theoretical framings of impacts of particular kinds of bioinformation in our self-characterisations are capable of providing satisfactory alternatives to the law's exceptionalist and sometimes essentialist representation of our identity-related interests in bioinformation. It identifies the need for a clear, robust, and non-exceptionalist account of the relationship between identity and personal bioinformation.

Chapter 3 builds on the suggestion, with which Chapter 2 closes, that a conception of identity as self-narrative could provide a promising and plausible basis for understanding the nature and significance of the roles of personal bioinformation in our identities. Following this premise, it reviews the key features of various prominent philosophical accounts of narrative constitution of practical identity. In particular, it highlights the normativity implicit in many of these accounts, setting out both the role that an identity narrative plays in supporting important experiential, evaluative, and practical capacities and also the qualities that an identity-constituting narrative will exhibit if it is to function in this way.

Chapter 4 presents the case that our lives and experiences are inescapably those of embodied beings. As such, it argues that any satisfactory theory of narrative self-constitution must be one that takes account of our embodiment and what this means for the kinds of self-narratives that we construct and that equip us to navigate our lives. This chapter presents the argument at the heart of this book: that personal bioinformation has critical roles to play in helping us to construct self-narratives that are capable not only of remaining coherent, meaningful, and inhabitable in the context of our embodied and socially embedded lives, but also of supporting us in making sense of and navigating our experiences.

Chapter 5 examines in detail information subjects' attitudes to and experiences of encountering three different kinds of personal bioinformation, as reported by a range of empirical social science studies. These three kinds of information are, as described above: disclosures of donor conception; results from genetic tests indicating disease susceptibility; and findings from psychiatric applications of neuroimaging. The aims of looking to empirical accounts are threefold: to illustrate and bring to life my theoretically based claims about identity roles of bioinformation presented in Chapter 4; to sense-test these claims against people's actual experiences; and to refine the claims in light of reported expectations and reactions.

Chapter 6 builds upon my characterisation the nature and strength of our foundational interest in developing inhabitable self-narratives to specify our associated information-related identity interests in whether and how we are able to access personal bioinformation. In doing so, it moves beyond the general picture of the narrative roles of personal bioinformation taken as a broad category to develop a more granular and practically applicable picture of what makes different kinds of bioinformation in different disclosure contexts more or less pertinent, valuable, or detrimental to our identities. It reviews the grounds for recognising the ethical significance of our identity interests in bioinformation, and establishes that these are not coextensive with or reducible to the other interests that currently inform disclosure policies and practices, thus making the case for the need to attend to these interests in their own right.

Chapter 7 spells out the practical implications of the analysis and arguments of the preceding chapters by setting out the basis and extent of the responsibilities of those who generate or hold our personal bioinformation to manage its disclosure to us in ways that take our identity interests seriously. These responsibilities involve recognising and responding to these interests appropriately, whilst weighing them alongside other interests and concerns. This chapter emphasises the necessity of attending to identity impacts not only in decisions about what is disclosed and when but also in planning the context and manner of disclosure.

Chapter 8 concludes this book by indicating what the arguments presented across the preceding chapters could mean for disclosure policies and practices, in general terms and in relation to five select areas in which current debates about the ethics of providing access to or withholding personal bioinformation are particularly live and pressing.

2

Mapping the Landscape

2.1 Introduction

The aim of this chapter is to provide a picture of the practical and theoretical landscape in which the impacts of information subjects' access to bioinformation about themselves are currently recognised and debated. This will give a fuller sense of the practical, conceptual, and normative gaps, introduced briefly in the previous chapter, that this book seeks to address. Here, I will first review the existing areas of law, regulation, and policy that purport to protect information subjects' entitlements to personal bioinformation on identity grounds. This will highlight the narrow scope of these protections, as well as some limitations and unresolved tensions in the way the law currently characterises the relationship between bioinformation in identity. I will explore what this means for clarity about the nature of the interests involved and the efficacy and inclusivity of the available protections. In the later sections of the chapter, I will turn to consider whether, if existing legal protections are lacking, some prominent bioethical and social science treatments of the relationship between personal bioinformation and self-characterisation might offer a more robust and inclusive foundation for conceptualising our identity-related interests. I will argue that while several of these provide valuable signposts to elements of such a foundation, as they stand, they lack the requisite scope and clarity about the normative nature of this relationship.

2.2 Legal Entitlements to Bioinformation

I will start by looking at the extent to which laws and policies that apply in the UK recognise and seek to protect information subjects' identity-related interests in accessing bioinformation, specifically in contexts where it is plausible that identity is intended to mean something like the self-characterisation sense in which I am interested.[1] When it comes to legal entitlements to protection of means of self-characterisation, this is chiefly the domain of international and European human rights law.

International Human Rights Law

At the broadest level, Article 22 of the *Universal Declaration of Human Rights* holds that everyone is entitled to 'the economic, social and cultural rights indispensable for his dignity and the free development of his personality'.[2] However, this makes no explicit connection to information access entitlements. For something approaching this, we can look instead to the *International Declaration on Human Genetic Data*, which holds that '[n]o one should be denied access to his or her own genetic data or proteomic data unless such data are irretrievably unlinked to that person . . . or unless domestic law limits such access in the interest of public health, public order or national security'.[3] This right is associated with the 'special status' of human genetic data, which is held to relate, inter alia, to its predictive capacities and 'cultural significance' in ways that can have a 'significant impact' on individuals, families, and groups.[4] However, this still leaves some inferential leaps to be made if we wish to understand how access to genetic data might impact how one characterises oneself. This right is echoed in provisions under the *European (Oviedo) Convention on Human Rights and Biomedicine*, which has as its core aim the protection of the 'dignity and identity of all human beings'.[5] This convention contains the specific provision that '[e]veryone is entitled to know any information collected about his health. However, the wishes of an individual not to be so

---

[1] I will largely restrict my discussion of law and policy in this book to that which operates in UK jurisdictions. While recognising that entitlements in other jurisdictions will vary, I will take it that the UK provides an illustration that is not markedly anomalous in the protections it offers. The conceptual conclusions of this enquiry are not intended to be jurisdiction-specific but – in principle – universally applicable.

[2] UN General Assembly, 'Universal Declaration of Human Rights' (10 December 1948), 217 A (III).

[3] UNESCO, 'International Declaration on Human Genetic Data' (16 October 2003), Article 13.

[4] UNESCO, 'International Declaration on Human Genetic Data' (16 October 2003), Article 4.

[5] Council of Europe, 'Convention for the Protection of Human Rights and Dignity of the Human Being with Regard to the Application of Biology and Medicine' (4 April 1997), Article 1.

informed shall be observed.'[6] However, again the precise meanings of identity and link to information access remain to be guessed at.

Moving away from instruments specifically concerned with biomedicine, Article 8 of the *United Nations Convention on the Rights of the Child* (UNCRC) recognises a child's right 'to preserve his or her identity, including nationality, name and family relations'.[7] George Stewart argues that this article covers the right to know one's 'biological identity' – itself an inherently ambiguous phrase.[8] Stewart suggests this could include entitlements to medical information, but only insofar as these directly pertain to conditions inherited from one's genetic parents. Meanwhile, Article 7 of the UNCRC protects the right to birth registration, which the UN Committee on the Rights of the Child has interpreted as protecting a child's right to know their genetic parentage.[9] It is not the only human rights provision that has been interpreted in this way, as we will see.

Article 8 and the 'Right to Identity'

The previously cited instruments have distinct limitations when it comes to protecting any putative identity-related interests in accessing bioinformation about oneself. Not only do they leave the relationships between identity and information opaque, but they lack direct enforcement routes – the UK has neither signed nor ratified the Oviedo Convention. In contrast, the 'right to know one's origins' under Article 8 of the European Convention on Human Rights (ECHR) offers the most explicit protection of an identity-based right to information.[10] The rights conferred under the ECHR are given further effect in the UK under the Human Rights Act 1998 (HRA).

The right to know one's origins is situated in the right to identity, itself nested within the Article 8 right to respect for private and family life. The 'right to identity' has been interpreted in a number of ways, including those concerned with public image, the right to retain one's name, and rights

---

[6] Council of Europe, 'Convention for the Protection of Human Rights and Dignity of the Human Being with Regard to the Application of Biology and Medicine' (4 April 1997), Article 10(2). The 2008 Additional Protocol contains a parallel provision for results of genetic testing and that these be in 'comprehensible form'.

[7] UN General Assembly, 'Convention on the Rights of the Child' (20 November 1989), United Nations, Treaty Series, vol. 1577.

[8] Stewart 1992.

[9] Besson 2007.

[10] Council of Europe, 'European Convention for the Protection of Human Rights and Fundamental Freedoms, as Amended by Protocols Nos. 11 and 14' (4 November 1950).

relating to recognition and expression of cultural, religious, gender, and sexual identity.[11] Most pertinently for the current discussion, it has also been invoked with respect to rights to self-knowledge and self-development.[12] These rights have been held to be engaged when applicants have been denied access to information about their early life or parentage – their 'origins'. The European Court of Human Rights (ECtHR) has held that 'everyone should be able to establish details of their identity as individual human beings'[13] and emphasised the importance of being able to 'retrace one's personal history'.[14] As a result, a specific kind of informational right has evolved within the broader right to identity – the 'right to know [one's] origins'[15] or 'the right to know one's parentage'.[16] The vast majority of ECtHR jurisprudence relating to these rights concern applicants' 'vital interest' in knowing, or having confirmed in law, their *genetic* parentage.[17] These rights have been found to be engaged, for example, when children or adults have been denied the opportunity to know or register the identities of their genetic fathers[18] and where domestic law permits mothers to place their babies for adoption anonymously.[19] The ECtHR has described information about genetic parentage as having 'formative implications for [the applicant's] personality'[20] and has held that denying access to this could infringe the 'right to personal development and to self-fulfilment'.[21] It has also held that people have a 'vital interest' in receiving information about genetic parentage as this 'uncover[s] the truth about an important aspect of their personal identity'.[22]

Rights falling under Article 8 of the ECHR are not absolute. Interference with the right to know one's origins may be justified under Article 8(2), where doing so is lawful, necessary to protect a specified suite of other public and private interests, and proportionate. For example, in one of the leading 'origins cases', the privacy interests of

---

[11] Marshall 2014.

[12] *Bensaid* v. *United Kingdom* (no. 44599/98) (2001) ECHR 82.

[13] *Gaskin* v. *United Kingdom* (no. 10454/83) (1989) ECHR 13, [39].

[14] *Odièvre* v. *France* (no. 42326/98) (2003) ECHR 3, Dissenting Opinion, [3].

[15] *Odièvre* v. *France* (no. 42326/98) (2003) ECHR 3, concurring opinion of Judge Ress and Judge Curis, [2].

[16] *Jaggi* v. *Switzerland* (no. 58757/00) (2008) 47 EHRR 30, [37]; Callus 2004.

[17] *Jaggi* v. *Switzerland* (no. 58757/00) (2008) 47 EHRR 30, [38].

[18] *Jaggi* v. *Switzerland* (no. 58757/00) (2008) 47 EHRR 30.

[19] *Odièvre* v. *France* (no. 42326/98) (2003) ECHR 3.

[20] *Mikulic* v. *Croatia* (no. 53176/99) (2002) 2 WLUK 216, [54].

[21] *Odièvre* v. *France* (no. 42326/98) (2003) ECHR 3, Dissenting Opinion, [3].

[22] *Jaggi* v. *Switzerland* (no. 58757/00) (2008) 47 EHRR 30, [38].

the applicant's genetic mother and siblings and the public interest in providing opportunities for anonymous birth were judged to outweigh the applicant's right to know about her genetic mother.[23] Nevertheless, Article 8 operates as a positive right with horizontal effect, meaning that states' obligations extend not only to refraining from obstructing access to information about origins in their own activities but also to taking steps to support citizens in their enjoyment of this right, 'in the sphere of the relations of individuals between themselves'.[24] Moreover, the right to identity is seen as an 'essential feature' 'within the inner core' of the right to respect for private life.[25] Two significant consequences of this are that 'the fairest scrutiny' must be applied in balancing this right against countervailing considerations and in allowing states some local discretion – a 'margin of appreciation' – in discharging their obligations.[26] The ECtHR provides the highest appellate court in Europe and is charged with adjudicating on matters of core human values. What it has to say about the relationship between identity and bioinformation carries significant weight. It not only influences domestic law and policy but also has the capacity to promulgate ethical norms.[27] The sense of identity invoked by the ECtHR in respect of this right does indeed appear to closely resemble self-characterisation. So, at first sight, it looks as if Article 8 could offer broad and robust protection for accessing bioinformation about oneself in the service of the kind of interests with which I am concerned. However, the scope and adequacy of these protections are questionable for a number of reasons.

The first of these reasons is that the relationship between information and identity presented in many of the origins cases is problematic. Jill Marshall argues that the ECtHR jurisprudence reflects a view of identity as preordained rather than self-constructed and that knowledge of genetic origins is presented as essential, not merely useful, for knowing who one is.[28] This is indeed suggested by some of the language used in the judgment in *Mikulic* v. *Croatia*, where information about genetic parentage is described as 'necessary to *uncover the truth* about an important aspect of their personal identity'.[29] And the dissenting

---

[23] *Odièvre* v. *France* (no. 42326/98) (2003) ECHR 3.

[24] *Jaggi* v. *Switzerland* (no. 58757/00) (2008) 47 EHRR 30, [33]; Akandji-Kombe 2007.

[25] *Odièvre* v. *France* (no. 42326/98) (2003) ECHR 3, Dissenting opinion, [11] and [3].

[26] *Odièvre* v. *France* (no. 42326/98) (2003) ECHR 3, Dissenting opinion, [11]; Callus 2004.

[27] Marshall 2014.

[28] Marshall 2014.

[29] *Mikulic* v. *Croatia* (no. 53176/99) (2002) 2 WLUK 216, [54], emphasis added.

judgment in *Odièvre* v. *France* described this information as pertaining to the 'essence' of identity.[30] Marshall argues such an essentialist view is potentially stigmatising – implying that those unaware of their origins have incomplete identities – and restrictive – presenting a picture of identity as 'fixed and unchanging' rather than self-created.[31] The problems inherent to genetic essentialist conceptions of identity are explored further below.

The evidence that the ECtHR invariably treats identity as genetically determined is perhaps more equivocal than Marshall suggests. The jurisprudence refers not only to discovery but also to the developmental and 'formative' value of knowing about one's origins.[32] Furthermore, the ECtHR has not always found the right to identity to be engaged by knowledge of genetic parentage – for example, where the information was sought for inheritance purposes,[33] or when a child's interests were held to lie in not knowing and retaining the undisturbed 'social reality' of their family.[34] These counterexamples to Marshall's critique notwithstanding, the court's view of the relationship between information about genetic parentage and identity is undeniably ambiguous, which is in itself a problem if what we are looking for is clarity about the nature and scope of our identity-related interests.

A second limitation to the protections currently afforded under Article 8 is that there seems to be a mismatch between the 'vital interest' in identity development that it is supposed to protect and the perfunctory remedies recommended by the court. For example, in *Mikulic* v. *Croatia*, it was held that if the assumed genetic father would not comply with genetic testing, then a presumption of parentage by domestic courts would fulfil the appellant's right to identity.[35] This seems strikingly inadequate if, as Richard Blauwhoff suggests, the moral right invoked by the origins cases purports to be something like that 'not to be left to one's own imagination as far as the story surrounding the circumstances at conception and birth'.[36] It is questionable whether a right characterised in this way could be adequately met by the results of a DNA test or mere amendments to administrative records. This highlights an

---

[30] *Odièvre* v. *France* (no. 42326/98) (2003) ECHR 3, Dissenting opinion, [3].
[31] Marshall 2014.
[32] *Mikulic* v. *Croatia* (no. 53176/99) (2002) 2 WLUK 216, [54].
[33] For example, *Haas* v. *the Netherlands* (no. 36983/97) (2004) 1 FCR 147.
[34] For example, *Mizzi* v. *Malta* (no. 26111/02) (2006) 1 FLR 1048.
[35] *Mikulic* v. *Croatia* (no. 53176/99) (2002) 2 WLUK 216.
[36] Blauwhoff 2008, p. 104.

important gap – to which I will return in Chapter 7 – that many debates about information rights focus on the sheer fact of access or 'right to know', whereas the form, manner, and context in which information is conveyed may be just as, if not more, important to how it affects our sense of who we are.

The third limitation to the protections offered by Article 8 – and the most significant, if we are concerned with access to bioinformation *beyond* genetic parentage – is the extremely narrow scope of information recognised as engaging the right to know. This identity-based right originated in a case in which the applicant sought not bioinformation but access to local authority records of his upbringing in care.[37] But subsequent judgments regarding information subjects' right to identity appear not to have extended beyond these kinds of records or information about genetic parentage. Of course, the court can only address the kinds of cases brought before it. But there are instances where the right to identity seems particularly germane, in which it has not been considered. For example, in *KH and Others* v. *Slovakia* – a case concerning Roma women's access to records of their covert, non-consensual sterilisations – the applicants' desire for these records, to help them understand their lives and address their profound loss, echoes the interests in self-understanding and personal development evoked in the genetic origins cases.[38] Yet, while the ECtHR judgment did find the women were entitled to access their health records under Article 8, the right to identity was not raised. Given the instrumental role of information in meeting the more fundamental right to identity, we might expect a range of information to be found as fulfilling this role, perhaps where applicants seek confirmation of genetic relationships to their children or where a right *not* to know is involved.[39] This has not been the case. Such absences lend some weight to Marshall's critique that the ECtHR regards genetic heritage as uniquely and essentially defining who we are.

Regulation of Donor Conception in the UK

The right to identity under Article 8 and the ECtHR's judgments in the origins cases described above have influenced the law governing donor-assisted conception in the UK. The limited entitlements of donor-conceived

---

[37] *Gaskin* v. *United Kingdom* (no. 10454/83) (1989) ECHR 13.

[38] *KH and Others* v. *Slovakia* (no. 32881/04) (2009) ECHR 709.

[39] See, for example, *Mizzi* v. *Malta* and *Anayo* v. *Germany* (no. 20578/07) (2012) 55 EHRR 5.

individuals to access records of their donor conception and details about their gamete donors represent the sole examples of information rights under UK law explicitly rooted in recipients' identity interests. In the 2002 case of *Rose* v. *Secretary of State for Health*, which helped precipitate the end to gamete donor anonymity in the UK, the donor-conceived claimants sought information about their gamete donors.[40] The judge held that this case was 'really an identity case and involves the Claimants' rights to know about their origins'.[41]

The judge found the right to identity under Article 8 of the HRA was engaged but deferred judgment because a UK government consultation on donor anonymity was imminent.[42] Regulations removing donor anonymity subsequently came into force in 2005 and were later incorporated into the Human Fertilisation and Embryology Act 1990 (as amended) (HFE Act).[43] This change in the law means that, provided their parents were treated in a licensed UK clinic using gametes donated after April 2005, donor-conceived individuals can request non-identifying donor information from the UK regulator – the Human Fertilisation and Embryology Authority (HFEA) – once they turn sixteen. They can request identifying information when they turn eighteen. There are also provisions to facilitate mutually consenting contact between adult donor siblings.[44]

Of course, being in a position to request donor information requires knowing, or at least suspecting, that one was donor-conceived. In common with many other jurisdictions that require open-identity donation, disclosure of the use of donor gametes to resulting children is not legally mandated in the UK.[45] However, those eighteen or over are entitled to apply to the HFEA to find out if they are donor-conceived.[46] And, in contrast to the early days of fertility treatment – when professional advice was usually to conceal donor conception – licensed fertility clinics in the UK are now required by law to advise intended parents of the importance of telling their children early in their lives, to offer advice on how to do so, and to provide opportunities to seek counselling.[47] The HFEA and the

---

[40] *Rose* v. *Secretary of State for Health* [2002] EWHC 1593.

[41] *Rose* v. *Secretary of State for Health* [2002] EWHC 1593, [28].

[42] *Rose* v. *Secretary of State for Health* [2002] EWHC 1593; Department of Health 2001.

[43] HFEA (Disclosure of Donor Information) Regulations 2004.

[44] Human Fertilisation and Embryology Act 1990 (as amended) s.31ZA. Identifying information may be more readily available where donors have voluntarily relinquished their anonymity.

[45] Blyth and Frith 2009.

[46] Human Fertlisation and Embryology Act 1990 (as amended) s.31ZA.

[47] Human Fertlisation and Embryology Act 1990 (as amended) s.13; Appleby et al. 2012.

advocacy body the Donor Conception Network recommend that parents begin to talk to children about their donor conception at preschool age.[48] This reflects what Tabitha Freeman describes as 'an emerging consensus in professional and policy discourse in the UK, the USA, Australia and some other Western countries that parental disclosure in early childhood of the fact of donor conception, if not the identity of the donor, is in the best interests of the child'.[49] These interests are sometimes articulated in terms of enhanced psychological well-being or strengthened familial relationships and trust.[50] In some instances, they are also articulated in terms of the benefits to donor-conceived individuals' identities – in particular the benefits to children being able to integrate the information into their developing sense of self.[51] This emerging consensus notwithstanding, it is ultimately left to parents to decide whether to tell.[52]

Where does this leave us with respect to the legal recognition and protection of identity interests? The picture is somewhat equivocal. On one hand, the connection between this information and identity is present in the rationale behind the abolition of donor anonymity and donor-conceived individuals' access entitlements law. The regulatory reforms took place in a context of public, professional, and legal debates in which identity interests were widely invoked.[53] For example, an HFEA policy working paper notes that information about donor origins 'can help people complete a picture of their identity and it is natural to seek it'.[54] On the other hand, parents remain the chief gatekeepers of this knowledge. For diverse reasons, described further in Chapter 5, the majority of parents do not tell their children about their donor conception.[55] And it is still the case that most donor-conceived people do not know about their donor

---

[48] HFEA, 'Talk to Your Child about Their Origins', www.hfea.gov.uk/donation/donor-conceived-people-and-their-parents/talk-to-your-child-about-their-origins/ (accessed 18 July 2021).

[49] Freeman 2014, p. 14.

[50] Ilioi et al. 2017.

[51] Nuffield Council on Bioethics 2013.

[52] Proposals to do so in the United Kingdom have been met with concerns that this is an unwarranted incursion into family privacy and autonomy and risks exclusion and harm in families and communities where donor conception is stigmatising or taboo; see Nuffield Council on Bioethics 2013.

[53] Turkmendag 2012.

[54] HFEA, 'HFEA Paper 485: Opening the Register Policy: A Principled Approach' (21 January 2009).

[55] Nuffield Council on Bioethics 2013; one study found that by the time children in participating families were seven only 29 per cent who had used sperm donors had started to tell (Blake et al. 2014).

origins.[56] While non-disclosure of the use of donor gametes remains commonplace and minimum age limits for consulting the HFEA Register apply, the reality is a rather limited fulfilment of any interests donor-conceived people may have in knowing.

Like the ECtHR jurisprudence, the UK law is also vulnerable to concerns that it reflects, or even promulgates, a geneticised conception of identity. The HFEA's language of identity 'completion' does little to dispel this worry. And this impression is deepened by subsequent legal measures governing donor identifiability in mitochondrial replacement therapy (MRT). MRT involves the use of two eggs from different donors in the in vitro creation of an embryo, with the purpose of avoiding transmission of serious mitochondrial disease. One egg supplies healthy mitochondria; the other provides the nuclear DNA.[57] Under UK law, adults born using MRT can request identifying information about the donors of eggs that supplied the nuclear DNA, but not those that supplied the healthy mitochondria.[58] The UK government's reasoning is that the 'mitochondrial donor does not contribute in any material or significant way to the identity, personal characteristics or traits of the person born'.[59] This betrays the view that whatever identity significance donor information has, this is attributable and limited to only certain kinds of genetic connections and to traits inherited through nuclear DNA. I shall return in Chapter 5 to question this rationale.

Wider Access Entitlements

The sketch thus far of information subjects' legal entitlements to access particular kinds of bioinformation on explicitly self-characterisation-related grounds reveals a picture of conditional access to a markedly narrow tranche of information types, possibly based on problematic conceptions of the relationship between specific kinds of information and identity. What if it were possible to show that we have identity-related interests in accessing other categories of personal bioinformation than those about genetic parentage? For example, where does this leave Ilana and her desire to know about her potential risk of passing degenerative eye disease to her children, or about what her brain scans might reveal about signs of incipient Alzheimer's disease? Perhaps the narrow entitlements set

---

[56] Tallandini et al. 2016.

[57] Appleby 2018.

[58] Human Fertilisation and Embryology Act 1990 (as amended) s.31ZA (2A). The entitlement to non-identifying information includes that about mitochondrial donors.

[59] Department of Health 2014, pp. 29–30.

out above need not be an insurmountable obstacle here. After all, if we do indeed have interests in accessing a wider range of personal bioinformation for the purposes of understanding or developing who we are, there may be other routes open that do not depend on expressly identity-related entitlements. If this is so, it maybe does not matter if identity is not invoked, or its relationship to bioinformation is narrowly conceived. I will briefly look here at the scope of some such alternative routes.

In healthcare contexts, under most circumstances, patients will receive results from medical investigations carried out upon them for the purposes of their own healthcare. If the information is recorded in their medical records, then patients in the UK have a legal entitlement to request access.[60] This is underpinned by subject access provisions in the Data Protection Act 2018 (DPA) and the European General Data Protection Regulation (GDPR). Under UK data protection law, information subjects' entitlements extend – with some conditions and exceptions discussed below – beyond health records to 'personal data', which includes identifiable health, genetic, and biometric data processed for other purposes.[61] Withholding patient information could also constitute a breach of information subjects' right to protection of private life under Article 8, which the ECtHR has held includes 'practical and effective' access to one's health records.[62] And healthcare professionals may be found negligent if they fail to offer information about 'material risks' to those under their care if the recipient could reasonably find these pertinent to their healthcare decision-making and where a failure to do so could result in serious material, physical, or psychological harm.[63]

Being entitled to access the results of medical tests of course does not mean that such tests will be conducted. In healthcare contexts, this will be constrained by, amongst other things, the availability of the necessary licencing, resources, and skills, as well as professional judgements about the appropriateness of testing. For example, the UK National Screening Committee requires that in order to institute a screening programme, there should be, inter alia, an 'effective intervention', 'evidence that intervention at a pre-symptomatic phase leads to better outcomes', and benefits should not be outweighed by risks arising from 'overdiagnosis,

---

[60] British Medical Association 2019.

[61] Data Protection Act 2018, s.45 and s.94.

[62] Eijkholt 2010.

[63] *Montgomery* v. *Lanarkshire Health Board* [2015] UKSC 11, [87]. The law here has developed specifically in relation to information provision in respect of consent to treatment.

overtreatment, false positives, false reassurance, uncertain findings and complications'.[64] Concerns about causing psychological distress in the absence of effective preventative or treatment options are often core to decisions about offering genetic tests.[65] Identity considerations do not yet play an explicit part in such decisions. However, where genetic testing programmes *are* available, clinical geneticists and genetic counsellors will support patients' and family members' decisions about whether to be tested or to receive test results. Genetic counselling is marked by its non-directive nature and is a notable point at which features intimately connected with identity, in the self-characterisation sense, are part of the picture. For example, potential impacts of test results on self-esteem, stigma, familial roles and relationships, and body image may well be raised.[66]

Genetic information about carrier or risk status may also be obtained from the known status of close blood relatives. The idea that genetic information does not belong to just one person but is shared or part of a 'joint account' is widely embraced in genetic counselling and medical ethics.[67] Clinicians and counsellors are likely to advise those who test positive for inherited genetic disorders about the value of discussing the result with their close relatives, though they cannot compel them to do so.[68] When family communication does not happen, professionals' duties of care may be implicated. In 2020, the English High Court ruled that healthcare professionals have a legal duty to conduct a balancing exercise – weighing the opportunity to prevent or mitigate a significant risk of serious harm through disclosure against patients' and publics' interests in respecting patient confidentiality – when deciding whether to disclose patient information to family members with whom they also have close professional relationships.[69] What might count as serious harm under this new duty, and whether this would ever extend to detrimental impacts on identity, remains to be seen. The instant case indicated that it could at least extend beyond the realm of harm to physical or psychological health, to include opportunities for family members to make reproductive decisions, at least where serious monogenic disorders are concerned.[70]

---

[64] UK National Screening Committee 2015.

[65] Parens and Appelbaum 2019.

[66] Esplen et al. 2009; Pinto-Basto et al. 2010.

[67] Parker and Lucassen 2004, p. 165.

[68] Dove et al. 2019.

[69] *ABC* v. *St Georges Healthcare and Others* [2020] EWHC 455 (QB).

[70] The instant case concerned Huntington's disease, a serious, fatal neurological disorder. The patient did not wish his daughter to be told of her risk of inheriting the Huntington's

Turning now to research contexts, a substantial proportion of personal bioinformation is produced by health research, not only by clinical trials but also, increasingly, by data-driven research involving secondary uses of patient data and data repositories and exploratory, rather than hypothesis-driven, enquiries.[71] This markedly increases the quantities of both 'intended' and 'incidental' findings produced about individual information subjects.[72] Feedback of aggregate results at the end of a study, or research phase, is commonplace. But when it comes to identifiable participant-specific findings, communication to participants will depend on the feedback policy of the study in question and participants' agreement to receiving them.[73] Researchers are not subject to a specific legal duty to return individual findings, though it is possible they could be found negligent in not communicating clinically actionable findings of a serious nature.[74] There is, however, a growing consensus that researchers have *ethical* responsibilities, albeit conditional ones, to offer research findings to participants.[75] Guidelines tend to propose responsibilities that extend only to findings that are clinically actionable or inform reproductive decision-making.[76] For example, the Council for International Organizations of Medical Sciences (CIOMS) guidelines state that 'life-saving information and data of immediate clinical utility involving a significant health problem must be offered for disclosure, whereas information of uncertain scientific validity or clinical significance would not qualify for communication to the participant'.[77] Nevertheless, some commentators have suggested that feedback might be warranted where findings have broader 'personal utility' to recipients, which could include identity value.[78] However, the nature of this identity value is not further unpacked, and it is not clear if such recommendations are ever reflected in practice. It does not seem unlikely that – without

gene in case she terminated her pregnancy. The Court found the healthcare team were not negligent as they had conducted a satisfactory balancing exercise.

[71] Eckstein et al. 2014.

[72] 'Intended findings' refer to those that are central to the aims of a study. 'Incidental findings' – secondary or unanticipated findings – are individually relevant observations generated through research, but lying outwith the aims of the study. The practical and ethical relevance of this distinction to feedback policies is increasingly questioned.

[73] Postan 2021.

[74] Johnston and Kaye 2004.

[75] Berkman et al. 2014.

[76] Wolf et al. 2008.

[77] CIOMS 2016, p. 45.

[78] Eckstein et al. 2014.

further clear explanation of its nature and gravity – any professed identity value would be judged insufficient to outweigh concerns about diversion of research resources to validating and communicating individual findings. This is perhaps particularly so in large, long-running studies and those using banked or secondary-use data, where the sheer logistics of reidentifying and contacting participants could be substantial.[79]

This map of the access landscape would be incomplete without noting that consumer technologies, including DTC testing services and personal and wearable self-tracking technologies, are an ever-expanding source of information about our own health, well-being, and non-health-related traits, dispositions, states, behaviours, biomarkers, and genetic relationships.[80] As illustrated by the example of Sam in the previous chapter, alongside welcome insights, users may be assailed by unanticipated information they find distressing.[81] In consumer contexts, it is particularly apparent why ethical concerns might extend not only to what users are able to access but also to whether they are sufficiently protected from potentially harmful information and whether they have adequate interpretive support or counselling to minimise the risk of distress or misinterpretation. In 2013, the US Food and Drug Administration (FDA) sought to limit the availability of several tests offered by online DTC genomics services – including *APOE* and *BRCA* testing for late-onset Alzheimer's disease and cancer risk, respectively – given the risk of 'unreasonable harm' from 'incorrect test results or unsupported clinical interpretations'.[82] While some commentators have raised unease about identity-related impacts of DTC genomics – Anders Nordgren and Eric Juengst refer to the risk of essentialising and distorting user's experience of their identities – these were not apparent amongst the FDA's concerns.[83] Approval to resume marketing these tests in the USA has since been granted.[84] Similar restrictions have not been imposed by UK regulators, and at the time of writing, UK consumers can access DTC genomic tests for

---

[79] Eckstein et al. 2014.

[80] Sharon and Lucivero 2019.

[81] Harper et al. 2016.

[82] US FDA, 'Inspections, Compliance, Enforcement, and Criminal Investigations, Warning Letter to 23&Me, Document Number: Gen1300666' (22 November 2013); Annas and Elias 2014.

[83] Nordgren and Juengst 2009.

[84] US FDA, Press Release, 'FDA Allows Marketing of First Direct-to-Consumer Tests That Provide Genetic Risk Information for Certain Conditions' (6 April 2017).

serious multifactorial conditions including *BRCA*-related cancers and late-onset Alzheimer's.[85]

Where Does This Leave Protection of Identity Interests?

This brief sketch illustrates that the broader landscape of subject access entitlements is unlikely to fill the gaps left by the narrow legal entitlements to personal bioinformation on explicit identity grounds. Each of these entitlements and protections is conditional and includes exceptions. For example, subject access rights under the DPA apply only to 'personal data' as defined by this Act – meaning the data must be identifiable and processed in a structured form – and are subject to exemptions where processing is conducted for research or where disclosure would cause 'serious harm' to the subject's or others' 'physical or mental health' or reveal someone else's data without consent.[86] Similarly, the right to access one's health records under Article 8 must be weighed against conflicting rights, including others' privacy, and can be restricted if it is deemed lawful, necessary, and proportionate to do so.[87] Meanwhile, the success of negligence actions depends on the existence of a duty of care; a causal relationship between denial of information and a relevant category of serious physical, material, or psychiatric harm; and the absence of overriding duties to protect confidentiality.[88] It is of course entirely appropriate that interests other than those in self-characterisation are part of the regulatory landscape and that information subjects' interests in access are weighed against competing considerations. However, if information subject's identity-related interests are not explicitly recognised as part of this landscape they cannot feature in any such weighing. And where their nature and scope are ambiguous or characterised in problematic ways, their relative relevance and gravity cannot be appropriately assessed.

There are two significant implications of this for my line of enquiry. The first is practical – that effective protections currently afforded by the law in the UK to any identity-related interests we might have in accessing personal bioinformation, other than that about genetic origins, are lacking. The second is that existing legal protections, even the relatively

---

[85] 23andMe, '23andMe Genetic Health Risk Reports', www.23andme.com/en-gb/test-info/genetic-health (accessed 18 July 2021).

[86] DPA 2018, s.3, s.45, and Schedule 3, paragraph 2.

[87] HRA 1998, Article 8(2).

[88] See, for example, *ABC* v. *St Georges Healthcare and Others* [2020] EWHC 455 (QB).

well-developed jurisprudence of the ECtHR, do not themselves offer a clear or satisfactory picture of the nature of these interests, due in no small part to the narrow scope of protection offered. Of course, the first of these gaps does not matter – or, rather, is not a gap at all – if our informational identity interests are themselves as narrowly confined as the law seems to suppose. But, while I have yet to provide grounds for persuading sceptics otherwise, I would at least suggest that there is something suspect about the exceptionalism of arguing that our identity interests are uniquely engaged by information about our genetic origins – and only the origins of our nuclear genetics at that. To justify such exceptionalism, it would need to be the case not only that our identities are defined by our genetic parentage – itself a problematic premise – but also that they are *solely* defined by this and, therefore, that knowledge of our biological origins exhausts all our identity-related bioinformation needs. Such contentious assumptions would, at the very least, require further defence than the law currently offers.

The narrow scope and limitations of existing legal protection for our explicitly identity-related interests in accessing personal bioinformation expose the gap that the arguments to be presented in this book aim to fill. For reasons I will explain shortly, I agree with Hauskeller and Marshall that it is indeed problematic if the law or policy instantiates or entrenches a narrow and prescriptive view of identity interests. However, unlike Marshall, I do not wish to hold that recognising and protecting the identity significance of knowledge about genetic parentage – or any other aspect of one's bodily and biological existence – *necessarily* commits one to an essentialist or exclusionary conception of identity. In order to defend this position, it will be necessary for me to address a fundamental question: what is the relationship between bioinformation and identity?

2.3   Seeking Conceptual and Normative Foundations

It is clear from what has been said so far that we cannot look to the law to supply a clear, unambiguous picture of the relationship between the impacts of encounters with personal bioinformation and self-characterisation or of the nature of any interests engaged. In the hunt for such a picture, I turn now to consider instead what the bioethical, philosophical, and social science literature might offer. Here, suggestions – sometimes passing references, sometimes more in-depth treatments – that insights into our bodies, health, or biological relationships could affect our identities are much more plentiful.[89] I cannot hope to capture or do justice to their breadth and variety here, but I will attempt to give a flavour of some prominent themes.

Once again, scholarly claims of the relevance of bioinformation to identity are perhaps most frequently voiced in relation to genetic parentage, extending also to discussions of genetic traits and to disease susceptibility.[90] For example, with respect to knowledge of donor conception, Vardit Ravitsky is just one commentator to articulate a version of the view that '[t]he development of personal identity requires understanding "where you came from"'.[91] This quotation indicates that Ravitsky herself conceptualises knowledge of genetic origins as playing something like a biographical and developmental role in identity. However, more generally, the Nuffield Council on Bioethics has observed that despite the widespread view that not knowing about one's donor conception could cause 'harm to identity', the nature of this harm remains largely unexplained.[92] Moreover, claims to the identity value of knowing, and harms of not knowing, are far from universal. For example, in the case of knowledge of donor origins, there are some who are profoundly sceptical about the intrinsic value of information about genetic origins to our identities.[93] And, as discussed below, others argue that it may be frankly detrimental.[94] What is needed is some way to adjudicate between, or reconcile, these different perspectives.

In some instances, disagreements about value occur because it is unclear, or there is a lack of common ground about, precisely what is meant by identity in assertions of information's value or harm. This is particularly acute in discussions that invoke the concept of 'genetic identity'. This phrase is sometimes used in a way synonymous with genetic parentage, while in other cases it is used to refer to the entire genomic makeup of an individual, the role of genetic markers in picking out numerically distinct people, or to characteristics that are attributable to an individual's genetic inheritance.[95] These have dramatically different implications when it comes to the ethical significance of encounters with genetic information. And only some are

---

[89] My focus here is on discussions of possible effects of information subjects' own encounters with bioinformation about themselves. As mentioned in the previous chapter, there are also ample discussions of how others might use this information to categorise, judge, or manage the information subject, but these do not capture my current focus.

[90] Henschke 2010; Zeiler 2009.

[91] Ravitsky 2010, p. 674.

[92] Nuffield Council on Bioethics 2013, p. 65.

[93] Lillehammer 2014.

[94] de Melo-Martín 2016.

[95] Henschke 2010; Richards 2014.

pertinent to identity understood as self-characterisation. Even when the focus is expressly on self-characterisation, many analyses focus on describing how encounters with bioinformation can contribute new modes of self-description, rather than making explicit claims about the value, or otherwise, of this. For example, there are myriad empirical studies that report ways in which receipt of genetic information may lead recipients to change or adopt new labels – for example, shifting their sense of themselves from 'healthy' to 'unwell', or 'at risk', or 'a cancer survivor'.[96] And much has been written about the rise of the conception of the 'genetic self', with genetic information used as routes to self-understanding or self-description.[97] These analyses provide important clues as to why we might care if someone has the opportunity to (re)describe themselves in particular genetically informed – or other biologically informed – ways. However, taken on their own, they do not yet provide sufficient reasons for understanding the nature and gravity of the harm, benefits, and interests that might be tied up in these means and modes of self-description. In order to provide just such reasons, I will return to explore further examples of these kinds of empirical observations in Chapter 5 and to assess them in light of a particular, normative conception of the relationship between bioinformation and identity. For the roots of this conception though we need to look elsewhere. We might perhaps be tempted to look to a biologically essentialist view of identity for these.

Biological Essentialism

Biologically essentialist views of identity combine determinism – the idea that our defining traits are caused by our genomes, brains, or other aspects of our biological existence – with reductionism – the assumption that these biologically determined characteristics lie at the heart of who we *really* are.[98] One implication of such a view is that access to certain kinds of bioinformation can play a valuable role in our abilities to characterise ourselves because they *reveal* our real, or essential, nature. In seeking to locate possible roots of the value in knowing, it is worth briefly reviewing whether biological essentialism might then provide a satisfactory answer. Before dismissing this possibility as a straw person – it is indeed rare to find allegiance with biologically essentialist views of the self seriously endorsed

---

[96] McGuinness et al. 2010; Zeiler 2009.
[97] Rose 2007; Widdows 2013.
[98] Wachbroit 2002.

in the academic literature – it is worth remembering that essentialist positions are implicit in several of the legal contexts discussed earlier in this chapter. And, as briefly noted in the previous chapter, the idea that our genes determine a wide range of human traits and dispositions – and thus that genetic information can provide direct insights into our identities – has considerable purchase in the popular imagination. As noted above, Nordgren and Juengst document the prominence of genetic-essentialist assumptions in DTC genomics.[99] They observe this not only in the ways that companies market their services as offering windows into users' identities but also in the testimonies of satisfied customers, one of whom they quote as saying, '[k]nowing these traits are the nuclei composition of my DNA puts all the pieces of who I am instinctually into place'.[100] These kinds of claims are not limited to genetic and genomic information. The brain is also widely seen as having special significance to identity, due both to popular views of this organ as the origin of our personalities and to the potentially grave and pervasive implications of its (mal)functioning for our cognition, mood, and sense of self. Indeed, it is sometimes treated as synonymous with the self, as when we talk of a 'depressed brain'.[101] Neuroimaging findings about the structure or activity of the brain are commonly presented as revealing the roots of our motives, personalities, or interpersonal differences and thus as offering insights into what we are 'really like'. For example, Eric Racine and colleagues have observed widespread neuroessentialism in reporting of neuroscientific research in the popular media.[102] This is evidenced by headlines such as 'Long-Term Offenders Have Different Brain Structure, Study Says'.[103] Similarly neuro-reductive views are reflected in fears that if emerging neurotechnologies are able to measure neural activity at sufficiently fine-grained levels, this will permit 'mind-reading' and incursions into 'an unassailable fortress' of our thoughts and true selves.[104] The reflexive corollary of these suggestions – which I will discuss further in Chapter 4 – is that these kinds of findings could potentially provide information subjects themselves with useful correctives to misplaced beliefs about their motives or values.[105] Biologically essentialist views of the self remain tenacious in the popular

[99] Nordgren and Juengst 2009.
[100] Nordgren and Juengst 2009, p. 262.
[101] Dumit 2003, p. 42.
[102] Racine et al. 2010.
[103] Davis 2020.
[104] Ienca and Andorno 2017, p. 1.
[105] Walker 2012

imagination, although some commentators have noted that people's every-day beliefs are often more nuanced and less deterministic than is some-times assumed.[106] Might it be the case that neuro- and genetic essentialisms – perhaps expanded to a more generalised biological essen-tialism grounded in wider assumptions about biological roots of our defining characteristics – could provide the explanation for personal bioinformation's identity value? Is it the case that we need this information if we are to have a full and clear picture of who we really are?

The short answer is no – for several reasons. The first of which is that the central deterministic empirical premise of biological essentialism is true only on rare occasions. Interactions between multiple factors including other aspects of our bodies and our social and physical environments play key roles in the functioning and contents of our minds and – in all but highly penetrant monogenic conditions – on how our genes are expressed.[107] Further empirical grounds for rejecting biological essentialism as a premise for the identity significance of bioinformation are that it certainly appears that all of us manage to have a good sense of who we are without exhaustive knowledge of every aspect of how our bodies and minds work. Indeed, many of us are able to occupy intelligible, satisfying, and functional identities while omit-ting or actively rejecting self-definition in terms of biological character-istics such as our genetic parentage, susceptibility to illness, or the sexed aspects of our bodies.

Additional reasons to reject a biologically essentialist view of the self are that it is not just empirically flawed but conceptually and ethically problematic. Such a view does not admit the possibility that we define ourselves, let alone define ourselves in ways that omit or repudiate aspects of our bodies or biology. More troublingly, essentialist views of the self, when adopted by or imposed upon information subjects, not only limit self-characterisation by framing traits as predetermined and by presenting only a limited pallet of ways in which they may describe and view themselves, they are also potentially oppressive and stigmatising. This is the case, for example, where purported associations are drawn between particular genetic variants, characteristics assumed to have negative social connotations – such as propensity to antisocial behaviour or lower educational attainment – and the prevalence of these variants in populations already living under oppressive conditions – such as

---

[106] Pickersgill et al. 2011; Weiner et al. 2017.
[107] Glannon 2009; Weiner et al. 2017.

indigenous peoples or people of colour.[108] Biological essentialism also implies that those who choose to define themselves in ways that depart from facts about their bodies – for example, rejecting their biological sex or susceptibility to hereditary disease – are in some sense occupying mistaken or inauthentic identities.[109]

These are reasons enough to reject an essentialist explanation of the relationship between personal bioinformation and identity. Moreover, if such an explanation were to be instantiated in policies and laws governing access to this information, this would, as Marshall argues, 'unduly restrain the development of our freedom to be and become our own persons'.[110] Laws of this kind would not only restrict the kinds of information we are entitled to access on identity-related grounds but also – recognising the expressive capacities of laws and rules – communicate and potentially promulgate the view that there are a limited number of correct ways to be and to understand who one is.[111] In suggesting that there is currently a gap in protections for our identity interests in bioinformation governance, my suggestion is emphatically not that we need laws that prescribe what kinds of people we can be. So, again, we need to look elsewhere.

Beyond Biological Essentialism

There is, I would suggest, a tendency at this juncture towards polarisation in debates about the identity significance of personal bioinformation, framing this as a choice between two mutually exclusive options: either our identities are determined by our bodies, brains, and genomes, meaning that personal bioinformation has identity value because it reveals truths about who we are; or we reject this view in favour of the idea that we create who we are, in which case personal bioinformation lacks any particular identity value, being at best an optional extra in this creative process, often irrelevant, and at worst positively harmful. At the more modest end of the scale, Bronwyn Parry and Margaret Lock argue that even though the language of genetics and genetic risk has infiltrated our modes of self-description, contrary to hyperbolic promises that genetic testing and DTC genomics will deliver enhanced self-knowledge, test results actually add little to recipients' existing lay-understandings of

---

[108] Sabatello and Juengst 2019.
[109] de Melo-Martín 2014.
[110] Marshall 2014, p. 125.
[111] Sunstein 1996.

their inherited traits or associated ideas of who they are.[112] Yet more polarised positions are apparent in debates about knowledge of donor origins and uses of personal health-tracking technologies. For example, Sally Haslanger and Inmaculada de Melo-Martín, amongst others, have argued that insistence on, and legal endorsement of, the importance of knowing one's genetic parentage are not only misplaced but run a serious risk of stigmatising those who do not know and placing unwarranted emphasis on genetic relationships and inherited traits at the expense of the social family and chosen identifiers.[113] A parallel dichotomy is apparent in discussions of self-tracking technologies such as Fitbit or sleep monitoring apps. Here, on one side, there are those enthusiastic about possibilities of 'quantifying the self' and associated enhanced understanding of their capacities, health, and well-being. Meanwhile, on the other, there are sceptics who are concerned that – in Deborah Lupton's evocative phrase – the 'optic has come to take pre-eminence over the haptic', and that we rely on quantified data for self-understanding at our peril lest they replace more direct, and the putatively more trustworthy and authentic, evidence of our own senses and phenomenological experience.[114]

I will return in Chapter 3 to address some of these concerns about exclusion and quantification. The assumption I wish to counter here though is that the only available options are that contributions of personal bioinformation to identity are either essential or else trivial, irrelevant, or harmful. I also wish to challenge the assumption that recognising the possibilities of identity value or identity harm depends upon and neatly tracks divergent views of our identities as either discovered or created respectively. Such polarised conceptions are unhelpful to thinking about the relationship between personal bioinformation and identity and the nature and shades of the ethical significance of this relationship. My aim in this book is to offer a perspective from which we may escape this limited polarity. I will explore the possibility that, while we create and develop our identities in ways that may happily depart in many respects from the brute facts of our bodily selves, there are also some tools that we may use in this creation that make our identities more or less inhabitable and suitable as frameworks through which to engage with the world. In the remainder of this chapter, I will briefly survey further potential non-essentialist

---

[112] Lock 2008; Parry 2013.
[113] Haslanger 2009; de Melo-Martín 2014.
[114] Lupton 2013, p. 398; Sharon 2017.

candidates from the literature as to the relationship between various kinds of personal bioinformation and our self-characterisation – broadly understood – and assess their capacities to account satisfactorily for our interests in information access.

I will first briefly review three further, somewhat interconnected, analyses of the ways that bioinformation – chiefly genetic information – may be used in our practices of self-characterisation. The first of these, as described by Christine Hauskeller, involves the use of genetic information to naturalise and reinforce existing social identities or group descriptors – what Hauskeller terms 'intra-species classifications'.[115] While this kind of reinforcing impulse may be based on a geneticised view that the traits and category boundaries in question are determined by genetic distinctions, it is not necessarily a reductive position. The important feature at work is that perceived authority of genetic knowledge lends weight to and thereby entrenches 'prevailing classification patterns of origins, race, ethnicity, or disease'.[116] In this way, genetic information is seen as serving to introduce or cement existing self-descriptors, modes of group identification, and ways of aligning or distinguishing ourselves from others.

Another kind of analysis holds that particular kinds of bioinformation, perhaps particularly those conveying disease susceptibility or diagnoses, introduce *new* means of active, practical identification and self-classification. For example, Ian Hacking has suggested that behavioural and biomarker data associated with developmental or cognitive differences, in conditions such as autism, may seed new 'human kinds' or ways of categorising people. Those living with these conditions are then active in sustaining and modifying these categories through the ways they use and enact these labels.[117] The discovery of the link between mutations to the *BRCA* gene and significantly elevated risk of breast and ovarian cancers may be seen as an example of this. Sahra Gibbon has coined the idea of the 'iconic figure of the *BRCA* carrier', in which the carrier is seen both as burdened with risk and as an activist in their own health protection.[118] This is reflected in press coverage, for example, of the actor Angelina Jolie's *BRCA*-positive status and subsequent double mastectomy.[119] These phenomena may be seen as particular instances

---

[115] Hauskeller 2004, p. 291.
[116] Hauskeller 2004.
[117] Hacking 1995.
[118] Gibbon 2007.
[119] Kamenova et al. 2014.

of wider adoption of novel modes of practical self-characterisation introduced by predictive genetics. One of these modes could be 'being genetically at risk'. Carlos Novas and Nikolas Rose describe a 'risk identity' as 'a grid of perception which informs decisions on how to conduct one's life' and as inextricably bound up with engagement with 'life strategies'.[120] For example, these strategies might include researching one's condition, participating in clinical studies, pursuing therapeutic interventions, or undertaking protective behaviours. Elsewhere Rose uses the phrase 'somatic identity' similarly to capture ways in which genetic information may lead us to think of ourselves in new, biologically defined ways that are closely linked to practical activities of self-constitution.[121] Rose and Joelle Abi-Rached have made parallel observations that advances in the neurosciences present us with novel forms of self-description, providing 'a rich register for narratives of self-fashioning', leading to the emergence of the 'neurobiological self'.[122]

Intersecting with these analyses are those highlighting the role of bioinformation in what Gibbon and Novas term 'biosocial identity-making'.[123] This concept captures the emergence of particular kinds of practical identities, built around and enacted through engagement in collaborative social activities, which themselves coalesce around shared biological traits, such as disease susceptibility, genetic carrier status, or diagnosis. These activities might, for example, include patient activism, membership of online forums dedicated to discussing results from DTC genomic testing, or participation in health research to identify causes of rare diseases. Alondra Nelson has observed biosociality amongst users of DTC genetic geographical ancestry testing services. Nelson uses the phrase 'affiliative self-fashioning' to describe the kinds of self-making practices that she has observed in the course of her research amongst Black British and African American 'root-seekers' who have used DTC services in an effort to trace their ancestral origins to particular African nations or peoples, to find distant relations, and to build connections with those on similar quests.[124]

---

[120] Novas and Rose 2001, pp. 487, 502.

[121] Rose 2007, pp. 186, 187.

[122] Rose and Abi-Rached 2013, p. 220.

[123] Gibbon and Novas 2007, p. 8. The phrase biosociality was coined by Paul Rabinow, see Rabinow 2010.

[124] Nelson 2008, pp. 761, 771.

As will become clear in the picture I will go on to develop, each of the analyses surveyed here could contribute to identifying and explaining some of the ways and reasons why we may have ethically significant interests in accessing personal bioinformation. However, these accounts cannot on their own do all the necessary conceptual and normative work of characterising these interests across a broad spectrum of bioinformation. This is, in part, because the vast majority refer only to genetic information. It is not always clear to what extent they are, or could be, generalisable to other kinds of bioinformation. What is needed is not only grounds for conceptualising the potential identity significance of personal bioinformation in non-essentialist terms, but also ways that are not *exceptionalist*, or at least not arbitrarily so.

The proposed impacts and uses of genetic information sketched in this section do, however, go quite some way towards moving us beyond thinking about bioinformation simply as a conduit for adopting inert labels or precipitating (re)description. They indicate the more active, practical, and relational roles information may play and, in doing so, move us towards a more substantial and normative conception of its potential personal significance. Nevertheless, they do not get us quite far enough along this path. This is because the picture they paint of the identity-related *value* of such uses of bioinformation often remains ambiguous or unresolved. For example, when it comes to Hauskeller's 'intra-species classifications' or engaging in the biosocial activities such as patient activism, genetic information might, at first sight, appear to make positive contributions – perhaps by adding focus or meaning to the information subject's life, or a sense of connection to others. However, the authors highlighting these identity practices are often inclined to more negative assessments, for example, echoing concerns – familiar from the objections to biological essentialism reviewed in the previous section – that tying self-classification to the perceived authority of bio-medical science risks restricting self-definition.[125] More troublingly, Hauskeller suggests, these classifications can be personally and socially harmful where they bind us to retrograde norms relating to gender or health or are used as grounds for exclusion and discrimination.[126] Provocatively, Hauskeller refers to genetically reified classification as a form of racism.[127] Indeed, racism, in its most literal sense, may be

---

[125] Hauskeller 2006; Nordgren and Juengst 2009.
[126] Hauskeller 2006.
[127] Hauskeller 2006.

both motivator and consequence of many attempts to perpetuate the naturalisation of racial distinctions and associated unjust and discriminatory social hierarchies, through abject misuses of genetic science.[128] Such misuses have undeniably serious and far-reaching harms, but we might question whether all biologically informed means of self-classification and affiliation are necessarily and inevitably troubling in the same way.

Displaying similar value ambivalence, Novas and Rose's characterisation of 'risk identity' suggests this might be viewed largely positively in terms of active, engaged self-efficacy in the face of disease risk.[129] However, again there remain suspicions, shared by Novas and Rose, of the colonisation of self by the language and objectives of biosciences.[130] Meanwhile others have observed that managing disease risk may be experienced as a restrictive and distressing obligation rather than as empowering and that responsibilisation for one's health may be accompanied by anxiety and self-blame.[131] To be clear, my reservations about the conceptual and practical limitations of the accounts I have just reviewed rest not on the sheer ambiguity or disagreement about the value of potential impacts of information-led practices of self-characterisation. That there may be a variety of identity impacts, both good and bad, seems highly plausible. What is missing though is a clear and robust picture of what good and bad *mean* and how we can and should adjudicate between competing value claims.

This brings me to the third and most fundamental reason why these otherwise useful and illuminating accounts cannot on their own provide the conceptual and normative basis for thinking about the ethical significance of the impacts of personal bioinformation on our identities. They do not, on their own, provide a clear picture of our *identity-related interests*. This is first because they concern monadic identifiers, largely discussed in isolation from the totality of who someone is. They do not speak to the impacts of bioinformation on identities as multifaceted, intersectional *wholes* or address the question of why it might matter for someone's self-conception, taken in all of its complexity and dynamism, if they were to describe themselves in one way rather than another or to add or subtract particular descriptors, classifications, affiliations, or practical roles. Second, and relatedly, it is not always clear from these analyses

---

[128] Saini 2019.
[129] Novas and Rose 2001.
[130] Rose 2007.
[131] Hallowell 1999; Walker and Rogers 2017.

why particular methods or modes of self-classification or biosocial affiliations might be better or worse for information subjects' identities qua
identities, and not only for reasons of social justice, or for the individual's
emotional well-being or their health – though these other kinds of
impacts may also matter a great deal. What is missing from the pictures
outlined in this section is a global theory of identity that explains the role
and value of these identifiers in identity terms – that is, why having access
to personal bioinformation might make an ethically significant difference
to developing, understanding, and inhabiting an identity that constitutes
the whole of who one is.

Narrative Proposals

I will now turn to introduce a family of arguments that offer a promising
means of addressing the limitations noted in the previous sections. These
are arguments that, in various ways, suggest that a particular category of
personal bioinformation can play an important role in the construction
of our stories of who we are – in our *identity narratives*. It is not
uncommon to encounter claims that personal bioinformation of several
kinds can play a part in our narrative accounts of who we are. For
example, Novas and Rose talk of genetic susceptibility testing giving
rise to 'biographical narration in genetic terms'.[132] Robert Klitzman
talks of individuals trying to fit their test results into 'their previous
understandings of, and narratives about, themselves'.[133] And the language of 'illness narratives' is widespread in the medical humanities,
underpinned by empirical narrative methodologies that aim to capture
the personal, lived experiences of patients.[134] The familiar, vernacular
resonance of 'stories' or 'narratives' and associated ideas as 'disruption'
or 'contribution' lends a kind of an intuitive plausibility to claims about
a narrative role for illness experiences, diagnoses, or risk status.
However, appealing though these framings are, we need to go beyond
evocative metaphor if we are to explain the nature of the relationship
between narrative and identity and the ethical implications of this relationship. 'Contribution' sounds broadly good, and 'disruption' suggests
something undesirable, but is this really so, and why? In order to get

---

[132] Novas and Rose 2001, p. 503.
[133] Klitzman 2009, p. 887.
[134] Riessman 2008.

a better feel for the work that the concept of narrativity could do for us, we need to move beyond metaphor to something more substantial.

Narrative-based arguments for the value – even the necessity – of information about one particular kind of personal bioinformation have been proposed by several writers who return us to the now-familiar topic of knowledge of genetic parentage. Here, however, they do not argue that this knowledge reveals one's true or pre-existing identity. Rather, its value lies in providing a critical tool in actively constructing an 'acceptable' or 'intelligible' account of who one is. Each of these analyses offers a somewhat different picture of the role and value of this knowledge. The most theoretically developed of them is that presented by the philosopher David Velleman.[135] Velleman maintains that direct acquaintance with one's genetic parents – not merely information about one's parentage – is necessary to the development of a worthwhile identity as part of a 'flourishing life'.[136] Velleman's reasons for this are rooted in the particular challenges he believes we face in reconciling our internal experiences of ourselves with our experiences of ourselves as objective things in the world – for example, the person we literally see in the mirror or metaphorically reflected in other's reactions to us – and accommodating these in a single, coherent narrative of who we are.[137] Velleman argues that acquaintance with our genetic parents provides opportunities to observe connections between their psychology and bodies and our own and to witness how they live and cope with their given traits. This, he claims, helps us understand our place, as physical beings, in a chain of heredity and causality and avert alienation from our 'bodily selves'.[138] And this, in turn, allows us to undertake 'the task of identity formation' by understanding how 'someone like me come[s] to be living in a body like this'.[139]

In a similar vein, Jamie Nelson holds that we have an interest in 'perceiving the connections between our lives and the lives of others' and that this not only adds 'depth and richness' to our identity narratives but is also important to our ability to make sense of our lives as cohesive wholes. In Nelson's words, if we lack understanding of the early stages of our biographies, 'we cannot read well what is going on in the part occurring now'.[140] Meanwhile, Sarah Wilson claims a more straightforward

---

[135] Velleman 2005b, 2008.
[136] Velleman 2005b, p. 375.
[137] Velleman 2006.
[138] Velleman 2008, p. 260.
[139] Velleman 2008.
[140] Nelson 1992, p. 81.

epistemic role for genealogical information. She suggests that this information can fill explanatory and interpretive gaps in the identity narratives of adopted, abducted, and donor-conceived individuals, 'alleviat[ing] uncertainty with respect to the past' in a way that supports the accuracy or completeness of their identity narratives.[141] Wilson's proposal is echoed by the empirical work of psychologist Maggie Kirkman, who argues that ignorance of donor conception may lead to the development of a 'misleading' identity narrative.[142]

This family of arguments is considerably more promising as the basis for a robust normative conceptualisation of the relationship between personal bioinformation and identity than the candidates considered in the preceding section for several reasons. They focus on identity not only in the sense of self-characterisation but also in a global sense of an individual's whole self-concept, rather than as a discrete descriptor, social identity, or mode of classification. Moreover, by making claims about the value of information to our identity narratives and offering reasons for this, they provide potential routes to interrogating the nature of the interests involved. As will become clear from what I will go on to say in the chapters to come, my own proposals about the narrative roles of personal bioinformation share elements with, and owe much to, each of the accounts introduced here.

However, as they stand, these accounts are not yet quite sufficient to explain if, when, and why information subjects' access to the varied array of personal bioinformation mentioned in the opening chapter might engage ethically significant, sui generis, identity-related interests. For one thing, these accounts do not speak to the roles of knowledge beyond that about genetic parentage, and they tie its value closely to features specific to this category of knowledge, such as family resemblances and childhood memories. More also remains to be said about why it *matters* if our identities are 'misleading', contain 'uncertainty', or are connected to those of others; what it means for an identity to be 'rich' or 'worthwhile'; how such an identity contributes to a flourishing life; and, crucially, whether bioinformation of other kinds might also contribute to these ends. Furthermore, these accounts focus on the positive contributions of knowledge of genetic parentage to our identities. However, as I shall return to discuss in Chapter 5, it is far from clear that everyone welcomes either this or other kinds of information or experiences these as

---

[141] Wilson 1997, p. 290.
[142] Kirkman 2003, p. 2238.

enhancing their sense of who they are. For example, Jackie Leach Scully has suggested that knowledge of conception using a mitochondrial donor could, in certain circumstances, contribute to a stigmatising self-narrative.[143] And Mary Walker and Wendy Rogers have argued that information conveying diagnoses of asymptomatic disease may precipitate anxiety-inducing narrative adjustments.[144] We may also recall here the distress and confusion experienced by Sam in the fictional vignette at the start of Chapter 1. Any plausible and robust proposal will, therefore, need to address and account for the possibility that some encounters with personal bioinformation are detrimental to our identities.

These are the gaps I seek to fill over the coming chapters. But, before I can do so, I need to establish firm foundations for the precise conception of identity on which my argument will be based. It is not enough to invoke the importance of narrative identity, or the narrative self in claims about the ethics of information disclosures without being transparent about what one understands by these terms and unpacking any implicit normativity. And it is critical that the conception adopted is clear and plausible when held against the mirror of human experience. As Heather Widdows observes:

> Pictures of the self are vitally important. If the picture of the self is wrong so too are the legal ethical and social structures which are built upon it. What matters to human beings is that key goods are protected and that possibilities of flourishing and wellbeing are ensured.[145]

In the next two chapters, I shall establish this picture. It is one grounded in philosophical theories in which our identities – our practical self-characterisations of the particular individuals we are – are constituted by self-constructed narratives. This conception provides ways of understanding both why being able to develop and inhabit one's self-narrative plays a foundational role in a full and fulfilling human life and the conditions on which serving such a role depends. I will propose that this picture of the self, once recognised as an inescapably embodied and relational one, also offers persuasive grounds for recognising the ethically significant nature of the impacts that personal bioinformation may have on our self-conceptions.

---

[143] Scully 2017. I return to discuss this further in Chapter 6.
[144] Walker and Rogers 2017.
[145] Widdows 2013, p. 6.

3

Narrative Self-Constitution

3.1 Introduction

Over the coming chapters, I will argue that thinking of our identities as narratives provides a compelling way of understanding both the roles that personal bioinformation can play in the development of our identities and our significant identity-related interests in whether and how we encounter this information. These arguments, however, are not the focus of this chapter. The aim here is to establish the picture of identity on which they will be based. This picture will draw on philosophical accounts of narrative identity, specifically ones that hold that our identities – understood as practically oriented self-characterisations – are constituted by our own first-person accounts of who we are. I will not seek here to provide a fresh or unassailable defence of this particular way of conceiving of identity but to lay the groundwork for my arguments to come. Existing philosophical theories of narrative self-constitution do not themselves claim a particular role for personal bioinformation as I have defined it. The task of this chapter is to outline the key features of these theories that will provide the conceptual and normative foundations for my own subsequent claims about the ethical significance of information access. The tasks at hand here are, first, to establish what an identity narrative is; second, to explore what makes a narrative self-constituting; and third, to make clear what is at stake in being able to construct such a narrative.

Narrative theories of identity are found in a number of disciplines, including philosophy, psychology,[1] and sociology.[2] My own arguments will be grounded in a family of conceptions of narrative self-constitution discussed in the philosophical and bioethics literature. This overview draws principally on the work of Marya Schechtman – most prominently

---

[1] For example, Gergen and Gergen 1988; Hardcastle 2008.
[2] For example, Giddens 1991; Somers 1994.

the arguments developed in her 1996 monograph *The Constitution of Selves* – and Catriona Mackenzie and her co-authors, including Kim Atkins, Jacqui Poltera, and Mary Walker.[3] It also owes much to arguments developed by David de Grazia, Hilde Lindemann, Alasdair Macintyre, Charles Taylor, and David Velleman, amongst others.[4] These accounts variously build upon insights from, amongst other sources, philosophy, psychology, neuroscience, cultural studies, feminist theory, and personal memoir. And they are distinctive amongst much philosophical writing on identity in that they are chiefly concerned with the ethical, social, and practical implications of what makes us who we are. They are notable for focusing upon why identity matters to us from a first-person perspective, rather than with abstract metaphysical questions relating to numerical identity and the reidentification and persistence of persons. They emphasise the evaluative and interpretive parts played by our identity narratives in our lives, agency, and experiences and the qualities exhibited by narratives that are best equipped to play these parts. As such, they offer the kind of theoretically detailed and, crucially, *normative* conceptions that are well-equipped to contribute to a robust explanatory and critical framework for interrogating the nature and scope of our interests in constructing our identities. The authors whose work I discuss below inevitably diverge in their views on some specifics of what makes a narrative one that constitutes an identity and what role such a narrative plays in our lives. It will not be possible to resolve these disagreements here, and I will not seek to do so. My aim is to capture core commonalities, highlight relevant divergences where they are salient to my later arguments, and address questions and concerns insofar as this is needed to establish firm foundations for my proposals in subsequent chapters.

3.2 Identity Narratives

What, then, is 'an identity narrative' according to the accounts to be reviewed here? The first thing to recall from previous chapters is that in this enquiry I am concerned with identity understood in the

---

[3] Schechtman 1996 and other works as cited below. In her more recent work, Schechtman has offered a more circumscribed role for self-narrative than she does in *The Constitution of Selves*, allowing that it still serves to illuminate practical and ethical questions about selfhood but less so questions about personhood and the numerical identity of persons, see Schechtman 2014.

[4] These authors' publications are cited in context below.

characterisation sense, as that which captures someone's qualities as a particular individual – what they are like and which features make them *them*.[5] This sense of identity is associated with the idea of selfhood and I shall use the language of self and identity interchangeably in what follows. As noted in the previous chapter, the conception of identity to be explored here is not merely concerned with monadic, inert descriptions or classifications. I shall use 'identity' to refer to the whole of who someone is, in all their multifaceted complexity and through changes occurring over the course of their lives. I am interested in the ways that issues of identity engage our first-person concerns – that is, where it matters to us what we are like, who we have been, and what we will come to be, and where we have something at stake in how well our identities serve us in helping us to make sense of and navigate our lives. Self-characterisation in this context is also intimately connected to our practical and moral existence. Our identities are implicated in 'practical and evaluative' aspects of our lives: the judgements we make; the reasons we have for doing or feeling one thing rather than another; and determinations of which behaviours are expressive of who we are and which actions we may appropriately be held responsible for.[6] These practical and evaluative aspects will be key to the implicit normativity of the particular conception of narrative identity to be described below.

As the phrase 'narrative self-constitution' suggests, narrative theories do not hold that our identities are preordained, awaiting discovery. One's self-narrative does not merely describe who one already or essentially is. Rather, we constitute, or *create*, our identities through developing and revising our own interpretive accounts of who we are and by enacting these accounts.[7] The answer to the question of what makes me *me* lies in the contents of and particular perspective supplied by my own narrative of who I am. And my characteristics are *mine* because, and to the degree to which, they contribute to and shape this narrative. Schechtman expresses the core contention of her account as follows, '[o]n this view a person's identity (in the sense at issue in the characterization question) is constituted by the content of her self-narrative, and the traits, actions and experiences included in it are, by virtue of that inclusion, hers'.[8] And Mackenzie elucidates a related conception when she says that '[f]rom the person's perspective they not only define who she is, what she stands for,

---

[5] Schechtman 1996.
[6] Mackenzie 2007, p. 264.
[7] Schechtman 1996.
[8] Schechtman 1996, p. 94.

and what makes her life meaningful, but they also shape the interpretive framework in terms of which she understands and engages with the world'.[9]

Perspectives differ on the extent to which our identity-constituting self-narratives can be understood as our 'life stories'.[10] However, these narratives are emphatically not intended to be understood as straightforward, comprehensive catalogues of everything that happens to us. Instead, narrative is the form in which we understand who we are and the means by which we interpret, prioritise, and bind together the constituent parts of our lives.[11] Narrative is the means by which we ascribe intelligibility, meaning, and significance to these constituents. This binding together and meaning-making takes place across two dimensions: between the various aspects of an individual's characteristics at any one time and over the course of our lives.[12] With respect to the latter, Mackenzie explains that, '[b]y appropriating our past, anticipating our future actions and experiences, and identifying or distancing ourselves from certain characteristics, emotions, desires and values, we develop a self-conception that brings about the integration of the self over time'.[13]

These processes of synchronic and longitudinal appropriation and integration are the means by which one's identity narrative is constructed. I will take it in what follows that there is a one-to-one correspondence between someone's identity and their self-narrative.[14] If there is a sharp enough and irrevocable bifurcation – not merely change or evolution – in someone's account of who they are, such that they cannot make sense of or access one part from the perspective of another, this might be taken to be a breakdown of identity for practical, psychological, and ethical purposes, if not metaphysical ones.[15] I will return below to examine the matter of narrative integration and coherence more closely.

---

[9] Mackenzie 2007, p. 267.

[10] Cf. MacIntyre 1985.

[11] Schechtman 1996.

[12] Mackenzie 2007.

[13] Mackenzie 2008a, p. 12.

[14] This one-to-one correspondence is not universally accepted. For example, Hilde Lindemann argues instead that we have a 'tissue' of narratives (Lindemann 2001) and Velleman holds that our lives are made up of many episodic stories, not one long extended account (Velleman 2005a). However, the absence of interactions between these successive or parallel accounts presents some challenges in making sense of the practical roles these authors suggest they fulfil.

[15] Schechtman 1996.

First, I want to look at more basic questions, including those concerning what populates our identity narratives, and how they come about.

Narrative Contents

I will look first to the 'contents' or threads from which a self-narrative is constructed. Schechtman refers to these collectively as our 'characteristics' – they are the narrative constituents that characterise us.[16] Schechtman describes these as comprising our 'actions, experiences, beliefs, values, desires, character traits … [and] other psychological features'.[17] Mackenzie widens this list to include 'certain commitments, cares, beliefs, motivations, values, principles … religious beliefs, political convictions … and personal attachments'.[18] We may unpack further items implied by this list, so that it includes relationships to others; the social, professional, and relational roles that we occupy, such as being a parent, a friend, or a teacher; and the social groups to which we recognise ourselves as belonging, such as our gender, ethnicity, faith, profession, nationality, or class. Crucially, each of the characteristics listed here is only part of someone's identity to the extent that it is included in and contributes to their self-narrative, not just because it occurs in the course of their life or because – or not solely because – other people ascribe these to them.[19] In the next chapter, I will argue that the absence from many existing theories of explicit mention of traits and experiences relating to our bodies, (dis)abilities, cognitive and physical capacities and dispositions, and health represents a notable omission from these lists of narrative contents and underestimates the extent to which our narratives are those of inescapably embodied beings.

Narrative Construction

This brings me to perhaps the most distinctive feature of identity-constituting narratives – they are not comprehensive or 'crude, literal

---

[16] Schechtman 1996, p. 73.

[17] Schechtman 1996, p. 73.

[18] Mackenzie 2007, p. 266.

[19] There are different views about whether traits or motives that the subject herself does not acknowledge are part of her identity-constituting narrative. For example, in *The Constitution of Selves*, Schechtman has suggested that they are not. Meanwhile, Mackenzie and Poltera have suggested that characteristics that comprise part of our identities (which may include unacknowledged ones that give rise to characteristic patterns of behaviour) can be distinguished from those with respect to which we are not autonomous (Mackenzie and Poltera 2010).

reproductions' of everything that one does and experiences.[20] Nor are they just descriptions of ready-structured proto-narratives presented to us by the world. In Schechtman's terminology, they are not cut from 'wholecloth'.[21] Instead, our self-narratives are constructed from disparate, chosen, and mutually informing components. They are *selective and interpretive*. As authors of our narratives, we edit their contents by 'appropriating' or excluding characteristics and experiences.[22] These are not merely collated but organised and modified by the interpretive activity of narrativity itself. The construction of a self-narrative is a practice of meaning-making – or attempted meaning-making – amongst the bewildering richness of our experiences and attributes. It is an attempt to integrate constituent elements into a more or less intelligible whole.[23] The individual's existing, remembered, and projected account of who they are provides the interpretive framework or 'lens' through which they judge the meaning and relevance of potential narrative contents.[24] The interpretive and integrative nature of self-narratives may be seen as operating in three directions: drawing together the contemporaneous experience of self at any one time, while also interpreting past behaviours and experiences retrospectively, and anticipating future plans and experiences prospectively. As Schechtman says, 'creating an autobiographical narrative is not simply composing a story of one's life – it is organizing and processing one's experience in a way that presupposes an implicit understanding of oneself as an evolving protagonist'.[25]

Schechtman suggests that an apt metaphor here is one of cooking, rather than compiling. The meaning and significance of narrative elements are flavoured and shaped by their role in the overall narrative of which they become a part. One key implication of this is that the 'same' characteristics will play different roles in each of our identities depending on the rest of our narrative. A second implication is that not all of our characteristics occupy equally pronounced or enduring positions in our own narratives. Their prominence admits of degrees, and the extent to which we are identifiable with particular characteristics varies accordingly.[26]

---

[20] Schechtman 1996, p. 125.
[21] Schechtman 2012, p. 75.
[22] Schechtman 1996, p. 125.
[23] Walker 2019.
[24] Schechtman 1996, p. 142.
[25] Schechtman 1996, p. 142.
[26] Schechtman 1996, p. 142.

Recognising these interpretive and prioritising aspects of our self-narratives helps explain the concern expressed in the previous chapter – that we are at risk of missing something important if we conceive of identity and identity-related interests solely in terms of discrete self-descriptors, rather than as related parts of a wider story.

As this suggests, an identity narrative is something that an individual *does* – that they create, sustain, modify, inhabit, and enact through their interpretations, choices, and actions – not just a cluster of 'static and passive features' that they *have*.[27] Emphases differ, however, as to whether 'narrative' refers solely to a reflective and interpretive activity or includes the evolving product of such an approach.[28] In what is to come, I will sometimes refer to it as a product. There are perhaps sound reasons to avoid this construal, to the extent that this might erroneously imply that our identities are metaphysically distinct entities, separable from our activities of making sense of ourselves or that our self-narratives can in some sense be 'completed'. The role and integration of particular elements within our narratives are never more than conditional, responding to and changing with new experiences and priorities.[29] Our identities evolve and change accordingly. In what is to come, I will follow Genevieve Lloyd in recognising that narrativity entails the 'perpetual weaving of fresh threads'[30] and Charles Taylor in holding that 'our condition can never be exhausted for us by what we *are*, because we are always changing and *becoming*'.[31] Nevertheless, the distinction between activity and entity should not be overstated. Recognising the intertwined nature of these two aspects will prove useful when I come to consider how bioinformation may be a tool in the activity of narrative self-constitution without necessarily ending up as *part* of someone's identity.

Relational Narrativity

Our identity narratives are not developed through solo introspection. They are inescapably socially and culturally embedded. We do not and cannot work out who we are in isolation from others and the stories they tell about us and about themselves and third parties. There are several interlinking senses in which this is the case with respect to both the

---

[27] Schechtman 1996, pp. 142, 117.
[28] Cf. Velleman 2005.
[29] Mackenzie 2008a.
[30] Lloyd 2003, p. 144.
[31] Taylor 1989, p. 47 (emphasis in source).

practice and skills of self-constitution and the contributing materials. Perhaps, most obviously, our relationships and relational roles are likely to supply features and plot lines to our accounts of who we are.[32] Then, at a more fundamental level, the norms and evaluative standards we use to make sense of ourselves are relationally developed, as are the conceptual frameworks of selfhood.[33] Taylor describes our communities as supplying a 'common language' with which to reflect upon and articulate what it means to have an identity, what we value, and what kind of selves we want to be.[34] Similarly, Schechtman holds that self-constitution entails the adoption of a culturally shared – and perhaps culturally specific – template of what it is to live 'the life of a person'.[35]

When it comes to 'colouring in' this template, Lindemann suggests we draw, for better and worse, on shared, culturally pervasive tropes or 'master narratives' containing 'stock plots and character types'.[36] These inform our understanding of the kinds of people it is possible to be. Macintyre, meanwhile, observes that 'the story of my life is always embedded in the story of those communities from which I derive my identity', and that 'asking for and giving of accounts itself plays an important part in constituting narratives'.[37] This is echoed by Taylor's characterisation of self-constitution as 'fundamentally *dialogical*'.[38] We cannot work out who we are by introspection alone. Lindemann and others suggest that those close to us may play a role in helping 'hold' us in our identities, by recognising our stories or helping us piece them together when our own capacities to do so falter.[39]

The stories others tell about who we are can then have a significant impact on our own. They can reflect and reinforce those we tell about ourselves, but they can also constrain or undermine them. Taylor observes that we 'define [ourselves] always in dialogue with and some-times in struggle against the identities our significant others want to recognise in us'.[40] As Lindemann pithily puts it, 'who I am depends to

---

[32] Mackenzie 2007.

[33] MacIntyre 1985. Parallels may be observed here with relational views of autonomy, in which it is argued that socialisation and personal relationships are necessary in order to develop the competencies for being autonomous. See, for example, Barclay 2000.

[34] Taylor 1989, p. 35.

[35] Schechtman 1996, p. 95.

[36] Lindemann 2001, p. 72.

[37] MacIntyre 1985, pp. 221, 218.

[38] Taylor 1992, p. 33.

[39] Lindemann 2016; Mackenzie and Poltera 2010.

[40] Taylor 1992, p. 33.

some extent on who other people will let me be'.[41] Others may reject particular aspects of our own stories – perhaps refusing to recognise that we are chronically unwell when our illness is not readily visible. They may even reject our story as an intelligible account of a person's life altogether – for example, by refusing to recognise the possibility of non-binary gender identity. Non-recognition of identity can be seen as a harm in itself. It is not merely a form of disrespect.[42] If we are prevented from enacting our self-characterisations, our abilities to claim and feel at home in these and to continue to constitute them through our commitments and conduct are likely to be seriously hindered.[43]

First-Personal Narration

In what follows, I will take it that our identities are constituted by our own, subjective narratives.[44] This emphasis on first-personal narration stands in contrast to, for example, suggestions that our own stories have no greater claim to authority in defining who we are than those of others. Not all narrative identity theorists prioritise the first-person perspective. For example, Françoise Baylis holds that our identity lies at a point of 'equilibrium' between how we see ourselves and how others see us.[45] The view of self-constitution I will adopt recognises that our narratives are inescapably relationally forged in all the ways described above. Moreover, if we are to comfortably inhabit our self-conceptions in a social world, these must, in Schechtman's terms, be 'in synch with the view of one held by others' and to some extent recognisable and intelligible to them.[46]

Nevertheless, allowing for these important provisos, I will take it that a first-person perspective is needed to fulfil the kinds of evaluative and perspectival functions noted above. This perspective best captures the phenomenology – the 'what it is like' – of selfhood and of 'living a human life from the inside'.[47] Furthermore, we ourselves are usually best positioned to capture the kinds of experiences and traits that are core to who

---

[41] Lindemann 2001, p. 99.

[42] Taylor 1992.

[43] Lindemann 2001.

[44] DeGrazia 2005.

[45] Baylis 2012, p. 118. Hilde Lindemann argues that our own stories of what we are like carrying greater weight but do not *necessarily* have precedence over those others tell about us. The legitimacy of each must be adjudicated by external 'credibility' criteria (Lindemann 2001).

[46] Schechtman 1996, p. 95.

[47] Mackenzie 2008a, p. 14.

we are, that motivate us, and without which we would feel alienated. This does not mean we cannot be mistaken about which of our characteristics are most typical or prominent – but other people are no less likely to be biased or fallible in this regard. It is also important to resist too great a concession to the role of others' perspectives in identity constitution given that these perspectives could be oppressive or harmful.[48] As Lindemann suggests, we have most at stake in making the best of who we are.[49] Perhaps, most importantly, the construction of a self-narrative is, as described above, an interpretive undertaking in which the roles and significance of the various constituents of our stories are understood in relation to the whole and each other. As Mary Walker explains, '[c]haracteristics are part of the same narrative when they are mutually influential and interdependent, each contributing to the context through which the others are interpreted'.[50] Interpretation of this kind requires a perspective from which these connections can be understood, felt, and made – the perspective of the subject who experiences them all.[51] And, if our identity-constituting narratives are to provide the foundations for our practical judgements and agency, then they must be accessible and intelligible *to us,* the people who judge and act.

3.3 Two Objections

I will turn shortly to consider further features that are considered necessary if a narrative is to be identity-constituting. Before doing so, I want to address two possible lines of objection to the picture outlined so far. The first of these is the charge that this picture reflects neither most people's experiences of self nor their approaches to self-understanding. For example, Jonathan Glover observes, '[m]ost of us do not spend our lives on endless landscape-gardening of the self'.[52] John Christman raises the more pointed objection that the requirement that our identities have a narrative structure – particularly where this entails exhibiting thematic unity and an orientation towards a particular goal – is both implausible and too demanding for many people.[53] Meanwhile, Galen Strawson asserts that it is simply empirically false to assert that everyone

---

[48] Christman 2015.
[49] Lindemann 2001.
[50] Walker 2019, p. 82.
[51] DeGrazia 2005.
[52] Glover1988, p. 132.
[53] Christman 2004.

experiences their lives or thinks of themselves in the form of a continuing, thematically linked narrative. He himself professes instead to have only discrete short-lived 'episodic' self-experiences,[54] maintaining that 'I have absolutely no sense of my life as a narrative with a form, or indeed as a narrative without a form .... Nor do I have any great or special interest in my past. Nor do I have a great deal of concern for my future.'[55] These kinds of objections suggest that narrative theories paint an unattractive and unrealistically rationalist, onerous, or self-absorbed picture of self-constitution, one that depends on the privilege of time and leisure for self-examination, as well as a particular kind of psychological disposition.

These lines of critique would be serious if they met their mark, but there are several reasons to see them as misplaced.[56] Chief amongst these is that they set too high and literal a threshold for what counts as a self-narrative, imagining that these must resemble polished literary texts.[57] Narrativity in the present context involves something less formal and less teleological than the construction of a novel with a well-defined plot or achieving the neat arc of a conventional memoir. It is better understood in terms of the pursuit of connections and meaning in one's life, making sense of its multiple threads as part of a whole, and experiencing one's self as extended over time and through change. I will return below to consider what might be made of Strawson's purported episodic experiences. However, as noted above, identity development is, crucially, not about isolated navel-gazing or self-absorption. And the selection and interpretation involved need not be – and is perhaps only rarely – an entirely conscious or rationalised endeavour. It does not entail that we constantly mull over our pasts, nor think of our identities as stories. Rather, identity development takes place through the business of living, feeling, and acting. The connections we forge between the parts of our stories are rooted as much, if not more, in felt significance, practical concerns, emotional resonance, and how we act and interact with others than in intellectual analysis.[58] As Schechtman explains, '[narrative] is the lens

---

[54] Strawson 2008, p. 430.

[55] Strawson 2008, p. 433.

[56] There is insufficient space here to do justice to the detail of the responses of narrative identity to these kinds of objections. For further discussion, see Mackenzie and Poltera 2010 and Schechtman 2007.

[57] Mackenzie and Poltera 2010.

[58] Mackenzie 2008a.

through which we filter our experiences and plan for actions, not a way we think about ourselves in reflective hours'.[59]

A second line of objection, also lodged by Strawson, is that composing experiences and characteristics into a narrative allows for the wholesale invention of fictitious or confected identities and militates against, rather than promotes, the development of an authentic or reliable account of who one is.[60] Several interconnected responses may be made here. First, it is not obvious how we could make sense of all the different aspects of our lives *without* prioritisation and interpretation.[61] Excessive inclusivity and richness of detail or lack of an interpretive overlay would preclude rather than support clarity of self-understanding and the development of a useful interpretive framework. Second, if we understand our narratives as *constituting* our identities rather than as describing us, then we simply do not have more basic, or more 'true' pre-existing identities with respect to which our self-narratives could be found inauthentic.[62] It is, of course, possible that we can be fantasists, self-deceiving, or mistaken about or oblivious to which characteristics are prominent in our lives. Narrative theories recognise this and incorporate constraints that preclude identity narratives from incorporating unfettered invention, misappropriations, and misinterpretations, or at least preclude them from being self-constituting. These are not arbitrary limits but ones that are required if identity is not just to be something we *have* but something that functions as part of our practical lives. I will turn to consider these limits now.

3.4 Limits on Identity-Constituting Narratives

Schechtman proposes two 'constraints' on identity-constituting narratives. The first is that we must be capable of articulating them. The second is that they must 'cohere with reality'.[63] The 'articulation constraint' requires that we are able to explain the connections between our self-narratives and their constituent parts in ways that are intelligible to ourselves and to others. This does not mean that we must perpetually and self-consciously recount stories of who we are or that every detail must always be transparently present to our consciousness.[64] But the

---

[59] Schechtman 1996, p. 113.
[60] Strawson 2008.
[61] Mackenzie and Poltera 2010.
[62] Schechtman 2012.
[63] Schechtman 1996, p. 119.
[64] Schechtman 1996, p. 114.

connections between our experiences, actions, beliefs, and values, and their places in our narratives must at least be *amenable* to 'local articulation'.[65] That is, we must be able to explain why in a given circumstance we feel or act as we do and how these elements fit into 'an intelligible life story with a comprehensible and well-drawn subject as its protagonist'.[66] Schechtman's justification for the articulation constraint is grounded in the fact that being able to understand the roles played by the characteristics that comprise our narratives in the context of our wider story is key to our abilities to make sense of who we are, what we care about, and the motives from which we act. For these reasons, as described further below, this kind of intelligibility is key to realising the capacities and experiences of practically and morally engaged beings.

The second constraint is that our self-narratives 'cohere with the basic contours of reality'.[67] The reality in question here is not facts about identities or selves – this would be circular – but about the world, including facts about ourselves as organisms and actors. Specifically, it requires that our narratives do not seriously depart from events and states of affairs as others experience them. The grounds for this constraint are that such departures would make it difficult to maintain accounts of who we are that are intelligible to and recognisable by others and thus hinder our abilities to operate in the world, particularly the social world. Schechtman argues that '[t]he failure to be tuned into basic facts about the world one inhabits – and hence the failure to inhabit a world in common with one's fellows – interferes with the capacities and activities that define the lives of persons'.[68]

A realistic self-narrative does not, however, entail comprehensive inclusion of all such facts. And departures from reality that threaten identity can be distinguished from those that may reasonably be accommodated in a functioning identity. In the first category are gross and 'recalcitrant' mistakes about matters of fact or interpretations of facts, such as the belief that one is immortal, or delusions about being under surveillance.[69] Minor errors of observation or memory that we could readily revise, if brought to our attention, do not compromise our identities. Similarly, Schechtman suggests that minor interpretive differences – for example, seeing life through an optimistic lens – far from being obstacles to intelligibility, are

---

[65] Schechtman 1996, p. 114.
[66] Schechtman 1996, p. 114.
[67] Schechtman 1996, p. 123.
[68] Schechtman 1996, p. 122.
[69] Schechtman 1996, p. 123.

intrinsic to the idiosyncratic interpretive nature of our narrative endeavours.[70]

These two constraints are, in one form or another, broadly endorsed by many proponents of a narrative conception of identity. And they, or a version of them, will play a central part in what I will say later about the role of personal bioinformation in contributing to identity narratives that remain coherent and intelligible in the context of our lives, which are not only socially embedded but also inescapably *embodied*. In the literature, these constraints are joined by a varying selection of cognate qualities, which are also variously proposed as hallmarks or necessary features of identity-constituting narratives. For example, Schechtman herself requires that identity-constituting narratives are integrated and internally consistent such that they 'hang together' in a way that makes them intelligible.[71] Mackenzie invokes the idea of 'stability'.[72] She also, in common with Walker and Poltera, emphasises the importance of the 'unity' and 'integration' of our self-narratives and the requirement that they exhibit some degree of 'coherence' while also displaying – from our own and others' perspectives – 'intelligibility'.[73] Lindemann, meanwhile, holds that our identity narratives must be 'credible'.[74] Of course, neither in everyday usage nor in the narrative identity literature do articulability, unity, integration, intelligibility, stability, realism, credibility, and coherence mean precisely the same thing or carry the same connotations. I cannot do justice to every possible nuance and point of departure between the various uses of these terms by the authors whose accounts I draw on here. Instead, I will sketch out the cluster of qualities that will be pertinent to what I go on to say about the role of personal bioinformation in our narratives, before turning to address the crucial question of *why* these qualities are important.

Narrative Coherence

I will take it that an identity-constituting self-narrative is one that is intelligible as a whole to the person to whom it belongs, even if it is not immediately readable and intelligibility takes some work. Our narratives must also be relatively coherent and integrated, not in the sense of being

---

a neat, locked-in tessellation of parts but in the sense that these different parts inform and shape each other. This then implies a kind of unity. Unification involves more than a cluster of characteristics that happen to be subsumed within a single life story but less than an insistence on a perfectly homogeneous whole. Unity requires that many threads contribute to one story. The meaning and significance of these threads are defined by their role in that single story and their relationships to each other, even as these threads are gained and lost and these relationships shift. The intelligibility, integration, and unity of an identity-constituting narrative hold both through time and synchronically.

In the discussions to follow, I shall take it that – all being well – an individual's identity is constituted by a single temporally extended narrative, albeit one with myriad interwoven and shifting threads and characteristics. Echoing the ideas of articulability and realism, the requirements for integration and intelligibility are held to apply both internally to an identity narrative on its own terms and externally with respect to the world. In Velleman's words, our self-narratives must be 'both consonant with the facts [of one's life] and sufficiently consonant with itself'.[75] To avoid repeating the full list of adjectives denoting these qualities each time in the remainder of this book, I will often use 'coherence' as shorthand. While this risks sacrificing some nuance, it allows me to exploit the dual hermeneutic and structural connotations of coherence, capturing the importance of a self-narrative being both something that we can make sense of and something that is integrated, rather than made up of discrete parts. In the following section, I will look at why coherence matters at all, before examining what *degree* of coherence is required for a practical, identity-constituting narrative.

3.5 Practical and Evaluative Capacities

The requirement for identity-constituting narratives to exhibit some degree of coherence – and the associated qualities above – is neither an arbitrary nor merely an aesthetic stipulation. To appreciate this, we must recall that the conception of identity outlined in this chapter is more than a mere description of who someone is, it is a *normative* and *practical* one. It is the framework through which we interpret our experiences, navigate the world and our relationships with others, and make choices about what to do. The value to the individual of developing and maintaining

---

[75] Velleman 2005, p. 67.

a coherent self-narrative lies in the kind of engaged, practical, evaluative life that it supports. In Schechtman's terms, this is the 'life of a person'.[76] 'Person' here should be understood as describing the subject of particular kinds of self-conscious, reflective, and evaluative capacities and first-person experiences, rather than referring to the ascription of moral status and determinations of whose lives and interests warrant protection.[77] The coherence of our self-narratives is held to be a critical – though not a sufficient – quality for self-narratives that are capable of providing the foundations for a range of experiences and practical capacities that contribute in no small way to the richness of our lives and our well-being. These claims need to be unpacked a little further.

Perhaps the most basic – and self-evident – of the capacities under-pinned by coherent self-narratives is that of being able to make sense of who we are. As Mackenzie and Walker describe it, '[b]ecause self-narratives are selective and interpretive, they enable us to make psycho-logical and evaluative sense of our selves, forging patterns of coherence and psychological intelligibility in response to the changing and frag-mentary nature of our lived experience'.[78] As Walker notes, a unified narrative offers a kind of 'epistemological strength' – the opportunity to make sense of ourselves and our experiences and explain why we acted as we did or why we value particular things.[79] Unification allows us to think of our lives as a whole and to interpret our experiences in light of the wider context of who we are. It helps us locate our 'central qualities' within the bewildering array accrued over a life course.[80] It also makes readable the connections between our past, present, and future, thus, for example, allowing us to understand how the 'me' in the past is continu-ous with the present 'me', despite having undergone perhaps quite significant changes.[81] This grounds our investment in our survival and 'self-interested concern' for what will happen to us in the future.[82] This, in turn, supports the kinds of long-term commitments, such as friend-ships, political allegiances, and life-long projects, that take time to develop and whose worth lies in part in their longevity.[83] Jeanette

---

[76] Schechtman 1996, p. 95.
[77] Schechtman 2014.
[78] Mackenzie and Walker 2015, p. 380.
[79] Walker 2012, p. 64.
[80] DeGrazia 2005, p. 83.
[81] Walker 2019.
[82] Schechtman 1996, p. 136.
[83] DeGrazia 2005.

Kennett and Steve Matthews highlight the particular kinds of well-being and rewards that come from being able to achieve and sustain enduring commitments and bonds like these.[84]

An integrated and intelligible self-narrative can also be recognised as central to our capacities for autonomy and our identities as moral agents. Autonomy here is intended in the 'thick' sense of the capacity of a person to be the author of their own actions, rather than merely the property of isolated 'free choice'. On many accounts, a condition for being an autonomous agent is that one's motives are the product of critical reflection on one's goals, commitments, and values.[85] This requires the capacity for what Charles Taylor calls 'strong evaluation'.[86] Taylor holds that while the autonomy in the thin sense of 'simply weighing' options in an ad hoc fashion could be exhibited by someone who does not have a clear sense of who they are, autonomy in the thick sense is reliant on a reasonably coherent self-narrative that provides the framework through which they can interpret their experiences, work out what they value, and determine what a worthwhile life looks like for them. Our self-narratives provide the foundations from which we can develop and articulate what Schechtman refers to as the 'stable pattern of value, desires, goals and character traits' that makes autonomous agency possible and the kind of self-trust that allows us to act from this.[87] As I shall explore shortly, *perfect* coherence may be an unobtainable or even undesirable goal. However, less dogmatic – though perhaps no less demanding – is the more plausible assertion that the ongoing pursuit of integration, accompanied by what Diana Meyers terms 'emergent intelligibility', provides the context in which to decide whether we identify with one value or course of action rather than another and to reflect upon and try to resolve tensions between multiple motives.[88] None of this entails an individualistic conception of autonomy or isolation from external influence and support. On the contrary, as already discussed, the narrative foundations and reflective activities on which our strong evaluations are based depend on and are shaped through dialogue and relationships with others.

The significance of knowing who one is and where one stands on matters of value is not, however, reducible solely to supporting our

---

[84] Kenett and Matthews 2008.
[85] Christman 1991; Dworkin 1988.
[86] Taylor 1989, p. 42.
[87] Schechtman 1996, p. 159.
[88] Meyers 2000, p. 173.

agency and autonomy. As Iris Murdoch observes, our moral characters are constituted not only by the exercise of what we do but also by our attitudes and ways of attending to and seeing the world and other people.[89] Integrated, intelligible self-narratives provide the foundation for our moral outlook and the interpretive frameworks through which we attend to the moral character of situations and the needs of others.[90] Taylor meanwhile reminds us that '[t]o know who I am is a species of knowing where I stand' and that '[o]ur identity is what allows us to define what is important to us and what is not'.[91] Mackenzie further suggests that being able to make sense of who we are and what we value fosters what she terms 'internal goods', such as confidence and self-esteem, as well as virtuous traits such as compassion and generosity.[92]

Our abilities to make strong evaluations; to act, feel, and judge in concert with these; and to engage in enduring commitments are not only the *products* of our self-narratives but also the *means* by which we select and enact the components of our self-narratives and thereby shape their evolving course into the future. The ability to make sense of who we are and exercise autonomy is critical to our ability to continue to develop who we are and to consolidate or reassess the constitutive characteristics we value. And, as noted in Chapter 1, the nature of our practical identities and the characteristics that comprise them are not separable from how we act. Our roles and self-descriptors are constituted by what we do and undermined by behaviours that cannot be intelligibly integrated with them. In other words, we cannot include characteristics in our self-narratives if we never act on them without reasonable and intelligible reasons for failing to do so. Narrative identity development is inherently reflexive – the creator and created are the same, existing in a cycle of self-constitution.[93] As DeGrazia neatly describes it, 'self-creation projects flow from narrative identity and, as they do so, continue to write and often edit the narratives from which they flow'.[94]

The picture outlined here captures the essentially normative nature of the version of narrative self-constitution on which my later arguments will be based. This normativity has two aspects. First, there is something personally and ethically important at stake in being in a position to

---

[89] Murdoch 2013.
[90] Mackenzie 2007, p. 267.
[91] Taylor 1989, pp. 27, 30.
[92] Mackenzie 2008a, p. 16.
[93] Velleman 2005.
[94] DeGrazia 2005, p. 106.

develop and maintain an identity-constituting narrative. At stake is the ability to realise the kinds of experiences and practical and evaluative capabilities just described. I shall take it that these capacities are valuable because they contribute to our well-being and to rich, meaningful, and practically engaged lives. Mackenzie describes them as the 'goods that flow from a coherent practical identity'.[95] This brings in the second normative aspect. Realisation of these capacities or 'goods' is not inevitable. It is contingent, in part, upon our developing or pursuing a particular kind of self-narrative, one that is integrated and intelligible, both on its own terms and with respect to our own and others' experiences; one that is, in short, coherent. And this, again, is not inevitable. A number of factors – as I go on to describe below and in subsequent chapters – mean that the pursuit of a coherent identity narrative can go better or worse. The two normative aspects just described are key to the picture I will paint in Chapter 4 of the nature of our identity interests and the potential roles of personal bioinformation in serving these interests.

3.6   The Trouble with Coherence

It is not uncontroversial to propose that we need to have an integrated and intelligible sense of our lives and characteristics in order to lead a full, practically engaged human existence, given the groups of people who are potentially excluded by this requirement. So, at this point, I want to address a further pair of possible concerns about the normative conception of narrative self-constitution offered above. The first of these is rooted in scepticism about whether narrative coherence is actually necessary for a fulfilling, morally engaged life. The second is the worry that the requirement for coherence excludes those who do not lead neat, conventional, secure existences from having identity-constituting narratives.

The Value of Coherence

As evidence of the superfluity of an integrated narrative experience of self, Strawson cites his own facility for commitment and friendship despite – as noted above – having only discrete episodic experiences of self, rather than temporarily extended, unified ones.[96] Meanwhile, John Christman observes that even people who live under oppressive

---

[95] Mackenzie 2008a, p. 17.
[96] Strawson 2008.

conditions that preclude the construction of neatly structured self-narratives that are straightforwardly intelligible to others are nevertheless capable of having practical identities and being autonomous agents.[97] As with objections to the foundational claims of narrative self-constitution considered above, one response to these objections is that they are addressing a straw person by setting too high a bar for what counts as a coherent narrative capable of supporting valuable, practical aspects of our lives.[98] Mackenzie and Poltera suggest that Strawson reports sufficient connectivity between his experiences to meet conditions of narrativity less caricatured than those he erroneously imagines are required.[99] A second, more trenchant response to those, such as Strawson, who question the value of narrative integration altogether is to consider the challenges of living without a reasonably unified and intelligible foundation from which to interpret our experiences, to judge, decide, act, and navigate our lives. As Jonathan Glover describes it, '[o]ur inner story lets us get our bearings when we act. Without it, all decisions would be like steering at sea without a map or compass.'[100]

As a stark illustration of this sense of being adrift, Mackenzie and Poltera discuss the example of Elyn Saks, who recounts in her memoir her experiences of living with schizophrenic psychosis. Saks recalls how her illness removed any 'vantage point' or 'core' from which she was able to organise or interpret her experiences or locate herself amongst them.[101] Mackenzie and Poltera offer this as an example of the 'loss of agency' and 'real suffering' caused by a disintegrated and disrupted self-conception and experienced by Saks not only during her periods of psychosis but also as she struggled to make sense of her experiences and decide how to characterise herself in between these episodes.[102] Mackenzie and Poltera suggest that Saks's rehabilitation was dependent on her ability to reconstruct a narrative that incorporated acknowledgement of her illness as a means of making sense of its place in – and destructive effects on – the totality of who she is. This is undoubtedly an extreme example, but it indicates how a fragmented self may place the kinds of practical and evaluative capacities cited above largely beyond someone's reach – even if in many cases it is only for limited periods. For

---

[97] Christman 2015.
[98] Mackenzie and Poltera 2011.
[99] Mackenzie and Poltera 2011.
[100] Glover 1988, p. 152.
[101] Saks 2007, p. 12, cited in Mackenzie and Poltera 2010.
[102] Mackenzie and Poltera 2010, p. 32.

example, we may imagine the experience of undergoing an 'identity crisis' following the loss of a job, during which one loses the parameters within which one is able to determine who one is or what one values. Self-understanding and autonomy may also be hindered by the kinds of decisional paralysis or self-alienation that accompany deep compartmentalisation or irresoluble conflict between commitments and values. As Diana Meyers argues, 'if one cannot decide what one really wants, one cannot do what one really wants – one cannot be "true to oneself".[103]

Setting the Bar Too High

This brings me to the second line of concern. All of us have lives made up of diverse, sometimes contrasting, characteristics that change, often dramatically, over the course of our lives. Tensions between our self-descriptors, commitments, and what is required of us under our diverse roles are almost inevitable. If the bar for narrative coherence is set so high that it is attainable only by the very few, this would threaten the plausibility of the normative conception of identity set out above. The first thing to note in response to this concern is that narrative (in)coherence and (un)intelligibility are not all-or-nothing but admit of degrees and can be more, or less, pervasive and enduring. For example, the inability to recognise oneself or work out what really matters after losing a job to which one has dedicated one's life may unsettle almost every part of one's self-narrative but be resoluble over time. Meanwhile, an inability to reconcile one's sexuality with the teachings of a faith that is central to one's family and cultural life may sow deep and enduring conflict in some areas, but not all dimensions of one's self-narrative. Authors differ on how much coherence is required for a self-narrative to be identity-constituting and to support the kinds of practical and evaluative capacities and experiences discussed above. Schechtman acknowledges that 'perfect intelligibility' is an unattainable ideal but still insists on a 'high degree'.[104] Many, though, see this as too demanding. For example, Meyers points out that all of us have intersectional identities, comprising multiple group affiliations or social identifiers, such as class, gender, or ethnicity, which may variously be sources of estrangement or empowerment, mutually compounding or in tension with each other.[105] For this

---

[103] Meyers 2000, p. 158.
[104] Schechtman 1996, pp. 97–98.
[105] Meyers 2000.

reason, Meyers insists, the notion of a 'transparent' or 'homogeneous' self is a hyperbolic distortion.[106]

An Achievable Pursuit

The picture of identity narratives outlined above does not depend on unattainable ideals of transparency or homogeneity. Mackenzie and Poltera suggest that an identity-constituting narrative needs only be 'relatively integrated'.[107] What matters is that it is 'meaningful' or 'satisfying', with constituent elements that make sense as parts of a whole story that is 'psychologically intelligible' to us, even if – or perhaps especially when – it is a story containing multiple threads and plot twists.[108] Simply possessing a mix of diverse characteristics is not in itself antithetical to developing and inhabiting a functioning and fulfilling practical identity. The very concept of narrativity is one that entails trying to make sense of precisely the kinds of complexity, diversity, and changes in our traits, experiences, and roles that typify most of our lives. And the intelligibility of the constituent characteristics comes not from these taken in isolation but their situation in the wider story. Crucially, the requirement for coherence should not be understood to require a neat or rigid structure, the immutability or preservation of characteristics at all costs, or the linear pursuit of a single goal. Our narratives must adapt and respond to new experiences, so any coherence is only ever 'dynamic and provisional'.[109] As Mackenzie says, 'part of what is involved in constituting oneself as a persisting subject is to create an identity that has *a degree of* permanence and coherence. This identity takes the form of character or a set of *relatively* stable and integrated traits, habits, dispositions, and emotional attitudes.'[110]

Nevertheless, concerns might persist that even a qualified and precarious degree of coherence could still be beyond the reach of many. It seems to exclude those without the cognitive capacities that would allow them to make interpretive connections between different threads of their lives, such as the very young or those with profound learning disabilities or dementia. It also potentially excludes those whose lives and characteristics do not conform to, or do not find echoes in, the master narratives that

---

[106] Meyers 2000, p. 152.
[107] Mackenzie and Poltera 2010, p. 33.
[108] Mackenzie 2008a, p. 12; Mackenzie and Poltera 2010, p. 47.
[109] Mackenzie and Walker 2015, p. 381.
[110] Mackenzie 2009, p. 107 (emphasis added).

are available to them in the cultures in which they live – those whose modes of self-characterisations are disparaged, unrecognised, or regarded as profoundly internally incompatible. Here, we might think, for example, of a young woman who chooses to pursue higher education when no one in her family or community have done so, or a trans man whose desire to be identified as 'father' to his child is not reinforced by others or the law.

In such cases – which are perhaps not at all uncommon – it has been suggested that a relative degree of integration and internal intelligibility is attainable but requires effort. Mackenzie and Poltera describe narrative coherence as 'an achievement', and a fragile one at that, only ever attained provisionally.[111] Meyers similarly talks about the ongoing, 'open-ended' endeavour of forging integration and intelligibility amongst the facets of our intersectional selves.[112] While himself eschewing the language of narrativity, Christman allows that a practical identity may be achievable even under oppressive conditions, provided one is able to be 'a reflecting subject whose self-interpretations make enough sense of those events that a consistent character can be seen at their center'.[113] Walker, meanwhile, describes how intelligibility and unity may be achievable within a life that contains seismic changes in values, outlook, behaviour, and traits – such as that which might be precipitated by wholesale religious conversion in adulthood – through reflecting upon and accounting for the ways in which the disparate, even conflicting, parts of one's life fit together. Here, coherence consists not in stability or permanence but in the ability of the individual to *explain* how their conversion came about and to *understand* their former beliefs and behaviours and their current ones in light of each other.[114] What matters is not a neat fit between the different parts of the individual's life but their mutual interpretive accessibility. In some circumstances, this kind of explanation and accommodation may be 'fraught' and a struggle.[115] Meyers maintains that this struggle requires frank acknowledgement by the individual themselves of the diversity of descriptors and conflict between them, as well as any internalised subjugation or privilege that comes with these. She also echoes Lindemann in suggesting that recognition by others and collective efforts to foster alternative, more explanatory or enabling 'emancipatory group images' – in Lindemann's

---

[111] Mackenzie and Poltera 2010, p. 38.
[112] Meyers 2000, p. 168.
[113] Christman 2004, p. 710.
[114] Walker 2019.
[115] Mackenzie and Poltera 2010, p. 48.

terminology, 'counterstories' – may be of assistance here.[116] As this suggests, our interpretive and reconciliatory efforts are not pursued alone or solely through introspection and independent resolve. Communication, allegiance with others, and shared narrative tools – for example, wide recognition of trans fatherhood, or increased visibility of working-class female academics – can help us make sense of who we are.

The language of 'achievement' introduced above implies that developing and maintaining a coherent sense of self is a product of our agency. It is worth noting, however, that while this is partially true, coherence is by no means wholly within our control. Circumstances over which we have little or no power shape the contexts in which our narratives and self-descriptors are invested with or denied particular meanings. And events such as job loss, bereavement, or parenthood disrupt formerly well-integrated narratives or derail their anticipated future trajectories. Also, instrumental are the ways that others behave towards us, their recognition, rejection, or contradiction of our own self-conceptions and the social structures and norms that imbue particular roles or characteristics with esteem or disrespect or worse. As I shall go on to discuss in detail over the coming chapters, prominent amongst the kinds of characteristics, events, and experiences that may jeopardise the coherence of our self-conceptions, while lying largely beyond our control, are those arising from our bodies and our physical and mental health.

It is not inevitable that efforts to attain or retain even a realistically tempered level of provisional narrative integration and intelligibility will be successful. What then should be said about the state of someone's identity? Again, views on the specific hierarchy of consequences following various degrees of (in)coherence vary. Mackenzie and Poltera, for example, suggest the coherence conditions for preserving a sense of who we are may be less demanding than those for autonomy.[117] Schechtman, meanwhile, holds that our sense of connection to our past may be more resilient than our subjective sense of self.[118] What matters for the discussions to come in this book – and what I will say about the impacts of denials or disclosures of personal bioinformation in particular – is that narrative integration and intelligibility admit of degrees, and incoherence that stops short of a wholesale and catastrophic inability to recognise or locate oneself is neither uncommon nor need obviate our identities

---

[116] Meyers 2000, p. 167; Lindemann 2001, p. 150.
[117] Mackenzie and Poltera 2010.
[118] Schechtman 1996.

entirely. However, as I shall demonstrate, consequences falling short of identity loss nevertheless carry personal and ethical significance.

It is also important to recognise that narrative coherence is not necessarily an unalloyed good. To illustrate this, Mary Walker and Wendy Rogers consider potential responses to receiving unexpected diagnoses of asymptomatic disease. These authors suggest that in their urge to restore coherence to their self-narratives, to reconcile their diagnosis with apparent experiences of being healthy, people receiving such diagnosis may be led to mistrust or reinterpret their bodily experiences, to become over-vigilant, or to experience anxiety.[119] As I will introduce below and explore further in later chapters, coherence is not the only valuable quality of an inhabitable, identity-constituting self-narrative, and its achievement must be balanced against other qualities. I shall further suggest that coherence constructed around partially apprehended insights, or in the absence of interpretive support, may be of questionable value.

Even if narrative coherence may not be *sufficient* for a fulfilling and practically engaged life, is it *necessary*? Schechtman stops short of saying that the life of someone with the practical capacities listed above is objectively better than that of someone without them. However, she argues that when we do have these capacities, we care about retaining them.[120] I will broadly follow Schechtman in this regard. The life of someone who lacks the cognitive capabilities, freedom, time, or means to achieve a realistic level of relative narrative integration and intelligibility could be a happy one, valued by the individual themselves and by those with whom they share their lives. And the life and well-being of such a person would certainly be no less worthy of respect, recognition, and protection by others. But, for those who are in a position to achieve or lose the kinds of practical and experiential capacities listed above, I will take it that these really are valuable. This assertion echoes familiar claims that the foundations of our well-being can be understood in terms of particular kinds of core capabilities. In Martha Nussbaum's rendition of these capabilities, she includes the capabilities for '[b]eing able to have attachments to things and people outside ourselves', '[b]eing able to form a conception of the good and to engage in critical reflection about the planning of one's life' and '[b]eing able to live with and toward others, to recognize and show

---

[119] Walker and Rogers 2017.
[120] Schechtman 1996.

concern for other human beings, to engage in various forms of social interaction'.[121] As with this subset of capabilities identified by Nussbaum, the capacities and experiences enabled by a coherent self-narrative may not be sufficient on their own for a happy, rich, or fulfilling life, and they require an enabling and supportive environment for their realisation. Nevertheless, lacking them has non-trivial and undesirable impacts on the trajectories of our lives and relationships with others, and on our abilities to flourish, to make sense of who we are, and to interpret and navigate the world. In other words, it carries consequences that do not comprise and need not be described as wholesale identity loss but are nonetheless real identity harms.

3.7 Beyond Coherence

The preceding discussion invites the question of whether narrative coherence is the only factor relevant to achieving an identity that supports a rich and fulfilling practical identity or whether the nature of the narrative's contents is equally important. I will return to discuss this question in greater detail in Chapter 6, but it will be useful briefly to review here what narrative identity theorists have said on this subject.

Narrative theories tend to be clear about the 'structural conditions' for practical identity narratives – how the constituent parts fit together and fit with the world – but less prescriptive when it comes to the qualities of their substantive contents. Schechtman's account, for example, is notably quiet about the qualities of the characteristics that make up identity-constituting narratives, except insofar as these are relevant to meeting the articulation and reality constraints described above. However, narrativity is often seen as inextricably bound up with the pursuit of meaning. And it is common to find claims that the pursuit of *value* provides the necessary organising and motivating principle for the development of our practical identities. For example, Taylor argues that an identity built solely upon individualistic or ephemeral concerns, divorced from social engagement and contexts, would be a limited and impoverished one.[122] And engagement in long-term projects and deep commitments are often seen as part of what grounds our sense of self and propels us into the future.[123] Paul Ricoeur, meanwhile, sets the

---

[121] Nussbaum 2006, p. 76–77.
[122] Taylor 1992.
[123] Calhoun 2000.

rather modest condition that requires our self-narratives to be 'bearable', although this too is connected to the pursuit of meaning.[124]

These kinds of claims do not set explicit objective criteria for what counts as meaningful or worthwhile narrative contents.[125] Much like Nussbaum's capabilities approach, they are neutral as to the particular characteristics, priorities, and pursuits that make up our practical identities. What matters is that *we ourselves* experience our identities as meaningful and worthwhile. This relative value-neutrality contributes to the appeal and plausibility of narrative identity theory. However, it is vital to recognise that the contents and tenor of a person's narrative, how comfortable someone feels occupying and 'owning-up' to their identity, are often critical to their well-being and to how their life and projects of self-constitution go. Lindemann, for example, draws attention to the ways that our identities can be damaged by the adoption of oppressive master narratives – such as those that embody racist or transphobic attitudes.[126] These kinds of oppression may not only cause distress or shame but also limit the scope of our lives and our opportunities to act and define ourselves beyond stereotypes. As such, they undermine precisely the kinds of valued capacities described above, including those for agency, self-respect, and self-constitution.

Accordingly, in the discussions to come I shall not adopt a wholly neutral view of the kinds of templates, characteristics, and commitments that make up inhabitable self-narratives. We cannot overlook that some kinds of narrative contents may be oppressive or destructive and bad for us. It is also worth noting that these kinds of damaging master narratives or modes of self-description – if sufficiently internalised and socially pervasive – could be consistent with a relatively coherent self-narrative. And, while it is possible to recognise a multiplicity of contents that contribute to desirable self-narratives, it is also important to acknowledge that we benefit when our identities are meaningful and worthwhile to us. Recalling Christine Korsgaard's words noted in Chapter 1, a practical identity is a 'description under which you value yourself, a description under which you find your life to be worth living and your actions to be worth undertaking'.[127] I will follow many of the accounts discussed above

---

[124] Ricoeur 1992, p. 158.

[125] Not all such theories are quite so neutral. Macintyre and Taylor, for example, each hold that identity-constituting narratives are defined by a 'quest' for a morally good life – though this is not a position I shall adopt here (MacIntyre 1985; Taylor 1989).

[126] Lindemann 2001.

[127] Korsgaard 1996, p. 101.

in proposing that it *is* important to be in a position to develop and maintain reasonable narrative coherence. This brings an interpretive framework and binding logic to our myriad, diverse characteristics, activities, and experiences, such that these comprise an intelligible, temporally extended practical identity, albeit one that involves complexity and change. However coherence is not all that matters for inhabitable identities that support us in pursuing fulfilling and practically engaged lives, and it is not an unequivocal good. I will go on to substantiate these claims further in the coming chapters.

3.8   A Practical, Normative Conception of Identity

At the close of the last chapter, I outlined several reasons why a narrative conception of self-constitution offers a promising way of thinking about our identity-related interests and the role of personal bioinformation in fulfilling these. These included the fact that conceptualising identity in narrative terms allows us to think of identity in a holistic, interconnected way, which highlights the ways that changes to our defining characteristics may have wider-reaching, more entangled, and more significant implications for our sense of who we are and our lives than mere edits to discrete self-descriptors. A narrative conception, I submit, also reflects the phenomenology of what it is like to make sense of ourselves and the belief that we create rather than discover who we are. As such, it allows us to move away from implausible essentialist or prescriptive conceptions of what substantive contents a flourishing or 'authentic' identity must contain. It also leaves ample room for recognising, respecting, and supporting diverse ways of characterising ourselves. This chapter has sought not only to fill out the picture of what an identity narrative looks like but also to make plain the inherent normativity of narrative accounts of practical identity constitution and to set out *what is at stake* in constructing such a narrative. It allows us to understand how our identities may fare better or worse and support us more or less effectively in understanding ourselves, living amongst others, and navigating the world. This normativity is key to the case I shall build for the nature and weight of our interests in accessing personal bioinformation. As I will go on to explain, it accounts for the ethically significant roles that personal bioinformation may play in our identities, without recourse to biologically essentialist conceptions of the self. It also illuminates how a wide range of different kinds of bioinformation may play these roles, to different extents, without falling into arbitrary exceptionalism.

4

Bioinformation in Embodied Identity Narratives

4.1 Introduction

The previous chapter outlined the key features of the conception of narrative identity constitution that will provide the foundations for the analysis and arguments that follow. Those discussions set out not only the self-constructed, interpretive, and selective nature of our identity narratives but also their normativity – the valuable practical and evaluative capacities that they sustain and the qualities that allow them to do so. I now turn to address the relationship between our self-narratives and the kinds of information about our health, bodies, and biology that I have grouped under the heading of personal bioinformation. I will propose not only that personal bioinformation plays a number of roles in our self-narratives but also that there is something personally and ethically important at stake when it does so. This argument provides the basis for my motivating claim in this book – that our identity-related interests in accessing bioinformation about ourselves warrant serious ethical attention in the law, policies, and practices governing whether and how we are able to access it.

The previous chapter highlighted the social and relational aspects of our self-narratives. In this chapter, I will argue that it is also necessary to recognise the comparable significance of their *embodied* nature – a feature that has not always been given due regard by prominent narrative identity theories. I will then set out my central argument: that personal bioinformation can contribute in ethically significant ways to the construction of coherent and inhabitable embodied identity narratives. In doing so, I will respond to concerns that invoking a role for bioinformation in our identities reignites an implausible biologically essentialist conception of self or erroneously conflates the objective biological body with the phenomenological lived body. The analysis and claims of this chapter are intended to apply to personal bioinformation taken as a broad, inclusive category, which does not mean that they

89

will apply universally or equally to each type or token of information in practice. I will return to address the factors that help shape and differentiate the specific identity roles and varying value of encounters with specific instances and kinds of personal bioinformation in Chapter 6, drawing on findings from empirical studies to be explored in Chapter 5.

4.2   Embodied Lives, Embodied Selves

I will begin setting the context for my argument by briefly stepping back from the specifics of narrative self-constitution to examine in broader terms why we have good grounds for recognising that our lives and our identities are necessarily those of embodied beings. I will take this to mean that our experiences of ourselves and of the world, our relationships to others, and the ways we interact with and navigate our environment are all shaped by the fact that we exist as material beings with particular bodily attributes. Claims about the nature and significance of the role of embodiment in our lives arise in diverse disciplines including neuroscience, philosophy, bioethics, and social theory. Different approaches place different emphases on our bodies' roles in enabling and mediating cognition and feeling, the fact of our objective materiality, and the subjective lived experience of living as a body.[1] I take each of these aspects to be relevant to what I will go on to say and I will offer a brief flavour of this spread of views here.

To embrace an embodied conception of human existence is, at its most basic, to reject dualist conceptions of persons, according to which our experiences, cognitive faculties, and sense of self are seen as solely the product of our minds. Dualism relegates our bodies to no more than the fleshy housing in which our minds just happen to be located, or the mere instruments through which mental processes are enacted and our identities are expressed.[2] In contrast, accounts that emphasise the embodied nature of cognition hold that 'the mind is always embodied, it is generated through the corporeal and sensory relations of the body to its world'.[3] The claim here is that consciousness and thought are made possible by and organised according to schema that are shaped by our bodily functions and the ways we encounter the world as material bodies operating in space.[4] Similarly, the ways we perceive the world and

---

[1]   Lennon 2019.
[2]   Shildrick 2005.
[3]   Mackenzie and Scully 2007, p. 342.
[4]   Wilson 2002.

interpret our perceptions are determined by how our senses work, our physiology, and mobility. For example, we literally see the world in a particular way because of the position of our eyes and the kind of vision we have.[5] Our affective responses and emotions are also bound up with our visceral reactions and their physical manifestations in, for example, a racing pulse or laughter.[6]

Philosophers working in the phenomenological tradition hold that embodiment 'is our mode of being-in-the-world' and the 'condition for the possibility of perception and action'.[7] As embodied beings, we are inescapably located in our physical environment and perceive, think, feel, and interact with this environment through our bodies. For example, Maurice Merleau-Ponty holds that '[t]he body is the vehicle of being in the world, and having a body is, for a living creature, to be intervolved in a definite environment, to identify oneself with certain projects and be continually committed to them'.[8] As this suggests, theories of embodiment are concerned not just with the embodiment of consciousness or thought but also with the ways that our perspective on the world – our subjectivity – and sense of self are embedded in and shaped by our materiality and the particular form it takes. In Margrit Shildrick's words, 'the subject's very being – or more accurately, becoming – is dependent on the body. It is not simply a matter of having or owning a body, or of using it as an instrument, where the subject might yet be seen as a controlling overseer, but one in which embodiment is the condition of being a self at all.'[9] Phenomenologists tend to distinguish the *lived* body, encountered from a first-person perspective, from the objective body as seen by others and treated as the subject of scientific study and medicine.[10] However, we may recognise that our material bodies themselves – not only our experiences of and through them – frequently shape and constrain our lives, how we behave, and who we can be. Recent years have seen a 'material turn' in sociological and feminist theories of self – one that seeks to (re)assert 'the way material aspects of our embodiment condition our lived subjectivity'.[11] Assertions of these kinds do not claim that the material body wholly determines who we are

---

[5] Gallagher 2006.
[6] Niedenthal 2007.
[7] Carel 2016, p. 27.
[8] Merleau-Ponty 1962, p. 94.
[9] Shildrick 2005, p. 6.
[10] Lennon et al. 2012.
[11] Lennon et al. 2012, p. 1; Witz 2000.

but rather that our bodies and biology are an irreducible part of our ongoing development as particular kinds of selves. As Stacy Alaimo and Susan Hekman observe, our bodies and biology exert both 'active' and 'recalcitrant' forces upon our lives that serve to shape, enable, and place limits upon what we are able to do and how we are able to define ourselves.[12] Some features of our bodies present opportunities – for example, only people with particular kinds of bodies can become pregnant, and an especially wide handspan may provide additional dexterity as a pianist. Others can impose limitations – for example, someone with chronic obstructive pulmonary disease may struggle with activities involving physical exertion. And many features, including parenthood and (dis)abilities, present a mixture of positive and negative influences – colouring our experiences, influencing our behaviours and expectations, and altering our sense of what is valuable, in myriad subtle or more prominent ways.

Embodied theories of self challenge, for example, the cogency of thought experiments that ask one to imagine being *precisely the same* person while existing as a disembodied brain in a tank or occupying a body radically different than one's own. They also provide the basis for ethical and epistemological enquiries about the ways that, for example, sex, (dis)ability, or illness affect our ways of being in, and navigating, the world.[13] Differences between our bodies, their forms, functions, and capacities can result in divergent experiences of the world and differences in the patterns of meaning we bring to these experiences. As such, we should be cautious about making too ready assumptions that others' experiences and interpretations are the same as our own, or that our own will remain stable.[14] As aspects of our own bodies and health change, as they inevitably do, so might our outlook and way of being. For example, Havi Carel – drawing on phenomenological theory and her own experiences of living with chronic respiratory illness – argues that the manner in which our particular embodiments shape our ways of being is brought into sharp focus when illness disrupts former certainties and replaces these with 'bodily doubt', which threatens our abilities to make sense of the world and find meaning in our lives.[15] And Shildrick suggests that the impacts of our bodies on our sense of self are not limited to features such as serious illness that we might most immediately think

---

[12]   Alaimo and Hekman 2008, pp. 3–4.
[13]   Mackenzie and Scully 2007.
[14]   Mackenzie and Scully 2007.
[15]   Carel 2016, p. 92.

of as life-changing.[16] Navigating life with a relatively minor and temporary injury such as a broken ankle might be no less instrumental in changing the way we perceive the world and our place in it. To say that our embodiment shapes our perspectives and sense of self is not, of course, the same as saying that everyone who shares similar bodily attributes shares the same embodied perspective. It is important to recognise that the impacts and meaning of different intersecting aspects of our embodied and social existences – for example, our sex, skin colour, and socio-economic status – will mediate each other in shifting permutations, modifying and diversifying our experiences accordingly.[17]

As this suggests, our embodied nature is closely entwined with the social and relational aspects of our lives.[18] Our materiality unavoidably connects us to others and renders us dependent upon, responsible for, and vulnerable to them. This is perhaps most readily recognised with respect to our genetic, sexual, and family relationships. It is also true of more formal relationships, such as those with healthcare professionals or colleagues. Our bodies and bodily traits play a further key role in our sense of who we are to the extent that they shape how other people respond to us. For example, when others fail to recognise our 'invisible' chronic pain or make assumptions about our personalities from our weight, this can affect not only the significance and meaning these attributes have for us and our sense of who we are but also how these inform our engagement with the world. What was said above about the brute, material ways that our bodies can affect us notwithstanding, the meaning and significance we invest in aspects of our material bodies, and the roles these play in our lives are rarely, if ever, inherent or universal but rather socially constructed and socially inscribed to a greater or lesser extent. This highlights a further respect in which the bodily and social are enmeshed – where 'there is an entanglement of nature/culture, matter and meaning'.[19] As Iris Marion Young observes, differential experiences of embodiment and our embodied capacities are often not due to features of our anatomy per se, or not solely to these, but rather to what these features are taken to mean in particular social circumstances.[20] I shall return to these themes in discussing the differential identity significance afforded to different kinds of personal bioinformation in Chapter 6.

---

[16] Shildrick 2005.
[17] Shildrick 2005.
[18] Baylis 2012.
[19] Lennon 2019.
[20] Young 2005.

The core lesson I wish to take forward from these various perspectives into the arguments to come is that, in Quassim Cassam's neat turn of phrase, 'the fantasy of the disembodied self is just that: a fantasy'.[21] Any adequate theory of identity must reflect: the phenomenology, the 'what it is like', of biological, material human existence; the embodied perspective from which we construct our sense of who we are; and the entanglement of bodily opportunities and constraints within which we do so. These factors require that we acknowledge the significance of embodiment to the stories we can meaningfully and sustainably construct about who we are.

4.3   Bodies in Narrative Identity Theory

Given what has just been said, it is striking that many of the prominent theories of narrative self-constitution cited in the previous chapter have little to say about the relevance of our embodied and biological existence to our identity-constituting narratives and our roles as narrators.[22] The influential accounts developed by Marya Schechtman in *The Constitution of Selves* and by Charles Taylor and Alasdair MacIntyre can seem peculiarly rationalist or dualist in the ways they construe self-narrative. They paint a picture of self-constitution that takes place in the mind, while the body is relegated to the vehicle through which we happen to enact our stories of who we are, or perhaps at most, the source of practical limits on the kinds of narratives we can construct. For example, MacIntyre merely notes that birth and death inevitably bookend our self-narratives.[23] Schechtman makes only a little more space for the body in noting that 'the life of a person' – which in her account marks the minimal requirement for the shape of an identity constituting narrative – is an embodied one.[24] Beyond this, however, Schechtman restricts the relevance of our human bodies to their role in allowing *others* to (re)identify us. As such, she admits an indirect significance for the body in self-constitution, inasmuch as others' capacities to recognise us are important as a precondition for the kinds of social interactions that contribute to the development of a practical narrative identity.[25]

---

[21] Cassam 2011, p. 154.

[22] MacIntyre 1985; Schechtman 1996; Taylor 1989.

[23] MacIntyre 1985.

[24] Schechtman 1996.

[25] In her more recent work, Schechtman recognises that our bodies and physical attributes play a role in what constitutes us as persons for the purposes of reidentification and

As Catriona Mackenzie points out, abstracted views of identity which locate the business of self-characterisation solely in our psychology overlook 'the first-personal significance of the body in the constitution of identity'.[26] However, not all theories of narrative identity marginalise the body in this way. Several influential accounts, including Mackenzie's own, place the lived experience of our bodies at the heart of narrative self-constitution.[27] Here, I shall review what this 'first-personal significance' amounts to.

Asserting that our practical, narrative self-characterisations are inescapably embodied does not mean that our narratives are reducible to or wholly populated by our bodily and biological attributes. Rather, it involves recognising that because we exist as material beings and our cognition, feelings, and experiences of ourselves and of the world are – in all the ways described above – framed by our particular embodied perspective, the context in which we construct our narratives is a necessarily embodied one.[28] Perhaps the most readily appreciated way in which our bodies contribute to and shape our identity narratives is by providing some of the palette and scope of characteristics with which we can practically, intelligibly, and sustainably define ourselves.[29] Many of our bodily attributes inform, even if they do not determine, the nature and mix of self-descriptors we weave into our narratives. For example, these might include our sex, skin colour, height, physical fitness, or health. Many of these embodied attributes also affect the ways in which others characterise us. For example, as Françoise Baylis argues, aspects of our bodies such as the colour of our skin 'influence who we are and how we can be in the world'.[30] This is in no small part because the stories others tell about us inform – and sometimes problematically limit – the stories we are able intelligibly to tell about ourselves, tying them to some degree to the stories that others are prepared to recognise and permit us to enact.

Our material embodiment is also the unavoidable context within which self-constitution takes place. As noted above, our bodies, their

survival and in the relationships of recognition that support personhood in the absence of self-conscious self-narration. See Schechtman 2014.

[26] Mackenzie 2009, p. 103.

[27] For example, Atkins 2008; Baylis 2012; Mackenzie 2009; Ricoeur 1992; and Velleman 2006. In other respects, several of these treatments – most notably Mackenzie's and Atkins's – share core features with Schechtman's analysis.

[28] Mackenzie 2009.

[29] Mackenzie 2008b.

[30] Baylis 2012, p. 112.

states, and functions operate as both 'active' and 'recalcitrant' forces in our capacities to act and define ourselves. As such, they are a source of opportunities for, and boundaries upon, self-creation. As Ian Hacking observes, '[w]e push our lives through a thicket in which the stern trunks of determinism are entangled in the twisting vines of chance'.[31] One need not subscribe to Hacking's language of determinism for his metaphor to remain apt. No matter how strongly we adhere to the idea that we create our own identities, we must nevertheless recognise that in doing so we are constrained to a degree by our environment, which includes the environment of our own bodies and biology. Embodiment impinges on who we are and who we can be because it has real, concrete consequences for us. In constituting ourselves, we will inevitably bump up against, become ensnared by, or must find ways around the capacities and limits of our material selves. This is just as true of the less visible aspects of our embodiment, such as our reproductive and cognitive capacities, as it is of the kinds of characteristics that are readily visible to others. And, as I shall go on to explore below, the resilience of the accounts we are able to give of who we are, and our ability to comfortably inhabit these accounts, are also vulnerable to aspects of our biological lives about which we might not (yet) be directly aware, such as the latent risk of a serious inherited disease.

Our bodies not only contribute to the contents and scope of our self-narratives but also shape our perspective as narrators and indeed make narration possible at all. For example, they enable the cognitive skills that allow us to interpret and arrange our experiences into a meaningful account of who we are. Mackenzie further holds that our experiences of our 'bodies as lived' and sense of our continuous material embodiment provide reference points for our sense of self and anchor the unity of our self-narratives.[32] In the previous chapter, I introduced the idea that our self-narratives provide each of our particular, idiosyncratic, interpretive frameworks through which we make sense of experiences and continue to constitute ourselves. Mackenzie supplements this by highlighting the irreducible role of the body in these frameworks, which she describes as providing our 'bodily perspectives'.[33] We approach the world as beings whose interests and interest perspectives are bound up with our bodily needs and vulnerabilities and whose agency is realised through bodies

---

[31] Hacking 2004, p. 282.
[32] Mackenzie 2009.
[33] Mackenzie 2009, p. 103.

with particular capacities and dispositions. In Atkins's pithy phrase, 'the first person perspective is corporeal'.[34] And, as Mackenzie asserts, 'making sense of oneself involves making sense of one's embodied subjectivity'.[35] Priscilla Brandon, meanwhile, underlines the reflexive nature of narrative self-constitution by observing not only that our embodiment influences our accounts of who we are but also that these accounts can in turn affect our bodies, for example, by informing how we hold, use, care for, or modify them.[36] This serves as a valuable reminder that our self-narratives are not epiphenomenal. They do more than just describe what we are like. They play a practical role in how we make sense of, engage with, and conduct ourselves in the world, in how we view and act upon our bodies, and in who we become.

As narrators, we cannot ignore our materiality. And it may be no less true that, as material beings, identity construction requires a narrative approach. Atkins – reflecting on the work of Paul Ricoeur – argues that narrative, with its inherently interpretative and diachronic nature, is the form that our self-conceptions must take if we are to be capable of unifying and making sense of the complexity and temporal dimensions of our biological bodies and lives in all their messy, changing natures and mortality.[37] She holds that in constructing narrative accounts of who we are, we have the opportunity to square our lived experiences with the objective chronology of our material existence and to make causal and explanatory connections between bodily events and experiences. Thinking about identity in terms of narrative helps explain why the beginnings and ends of our lives may be significant to our self-conceptions. It also provides clues as to why it might matter if there are abrupt changes in our bodies or explanatory gaps in understanding how they work or why they are like they are – for example, why we have particular symptoms or look the way we do – and why we might value being able to anticipate biological events that lie in our futures. Atkins emphasises the importance of narrativity in permitting us to integrate and, as far as possible, reconcile multiple perspectives on who and what we are, perspectives that include our internal experiences of ourselves, our own 'as-if third-personal' encounters with ourselves as objects in the world, and other people's reactions to us.[38] This incorporation and

---

[34] Atkins 2008, p. 80.
[35] Mackenzie 2009, p. 118.
[36] Brandon 2016.
[37] Atkins 2008; Ricoeur 1992.
[38] Atkins 2008.

accommodation is not automatic. Atkins argues for the necessity of a kind of self-attribution or endorsement of the bodily and biological features that we take to characterise who we are.[39] Constructing stories and finding meaning when our bodies undergo sudden or major changes, for example, following serious illness, injury, ageing, or childbirth, may also offer a way of averting alienation from aspects of our material selves.

Atkins recognises that while an embodied view of narrative self-constitution treats bodily features as legitimate elements of our identities, their inclusion – as with all narrative elements – is still a matter of selection and meaning-making. This underscores the claim introduced in the previous chapter: that the development and maintenance of a coherent, inhabitable identity narrative are, in Atkins's words, 'something I must achieve, something that I have to integrate, recuperate, and finally attest to'.[40] As such, we may be more, or less, successful in these endeavours. Our bodily characteristics and perspectives are not static; they evolve and shift with changes in our bodies and biology. This affects the self-narratives that they constrain, enable, and inform. This in turn brings the constant possibility of fresh interpretive frameworks and gains and losses in terms of narrative integration, intelligibility, and meaning. And where these changes are dramatic or unanticipated – such as at the acute onset of serious disease – the tone and coherence of our embodied narratives may be abruptly altered or disrupted. These changes matter. They have personal and ethical significance because – as described in the previous chapter – of the practical, experiential, and evaluative capacities that depend on the structural and substantive qualities of our self-narratives. As Mackenzie asserts, 'developing an integrated and ongoing narrative of one's embodied subjectivity is central to the activity of self-constitution'.[41] These moves towards placing embodiment at the heart of theories of narrative self-constitution are central to my own argument for the narrative role of personal bioinformation – as I shall now describe.

4.4   Personal Bioinformation as a Narrative Tool

The preceding discussion leads me to my reasons for holding that personal bioinformation – taken as a broad category – can play a number of ethically significant roles in narrative self-constitution.

---

[39] See also Velleman 2006.
[40] Atkins 2008, p. 91.
[41] Mackenzie 2009, p. 103.

The argument presented in the remainder of this chapter will focus chiefly on the conceptual grounds for these claims. I will return in Chapter 5 to consider detailed illustrative examples of what these roles might look like in practice.

Existing theoretical accounts of narrative identity – with a few exceptions to which I will return – are notably silent on the potential identity significance of bioinformation that comes from 'external sources' – for example, medical tests or research findings – rather than from our own senses.[42] This is perhaps unsurprising when it comes to the more disembodied theories like Schechtman's, but it is also evident amongst those that place considerable emphasis on the bodily perspective. Sometimes, this is simply because it lies beyond their scope of interest. However, it could also be attributable to perceptions that positing a narrative role for objective or technical sources confuses information that is merely relevant to us as human organisms, with the kinds of experiential input that is relevant to our *identities* as embodied persons.[43] As such, it might appear that proposing the identity significance of personal information rests on a basic misunderstanding of the central premises of embodied views of identity, wrongly conflating these views with reductive materialism. To make clear why this concern is misplaced, I want to consider the roles that personal bioinformation could play in helping us develop self-narratives that are integrated, intelligible, and meaningful when occupied in the context of embodied existence, and also equipped to support us in navigating the vagaries of this existence.

Offering Contents

First, I want to suggest that, by conveying insights into, for example, our health and susceptibilities to disease, our physical, cognitive, or affective traits, previous events that have assailed our bodies, when and how our stories began and might end, our relationships, and the traits we share with others, personal bioinformation can contribute the characteristics, contents, and plotlines that populate our self-narratives.[44] This may seem

---

[42] Exceptions include the claims made for narrative roles for knowledge of genetic parentage introduced in Chapter 2. Most such analyses focus on single categories of information. Mary Walker has notably offered critical views of the potential narrative roles of both neuro information and diagnoses of asymptomatic disease, as discussed further below.

[43] Ajana 2010.

[44] These uses of bioinformation may occur irrespective of whether these 'insights' are reliable. What I say here is premised on the assumption that they are and I return to discuss the consequences if they are not, below.

almost too obvious. After all, conveying these kinds of insights is integral to the very definition of personal bioinformation established in Chapter 1. However, as noted in the last chapter, the inclusion of these kinds of characteristics as paradigm narrative constituents is not a given. My intention here is to highlight that once we appreciate the embodied nature of our lives, it is virtually impossible to imagine our identity narratives – with which we organise our defining traits and experiences and make sense of who we are – without the inclusion of health-related, biological, and bodily characteristics. These are the kinds of identity stories we tell because of the kinds of beings we are. Moreover, the materials we use to compose these stories are likely to include bioinformation about ourselves generated or revealed by others. In this respect, self-understanding and self-interpretation are no different from other epistemic or hermeneutic endeavours in that these rely not only on our direct experiences but also on the observations and testimonies of others and on propositional, qualitative, quantitative, or graphical information. For example, an individual may come to characterise themselves as someone at risk of colon cancer because they have experienced a familial history of this disease. Alternatively they may do so following receipt of test results revealing genetic mutations associated with Lynch syndrome. Or someone may think of themselves as physically fit in part because of the ease with which they can complete a five-kilometre run but also because their wearable fitness tracker records a healthy heart rate while they do so.

No doubt, insights into and understanding of our bodies derived from externally received bioinformation are likely to differ qualitatively – for example, in perspective, immediacy, complexity, and, perhaps, reliability – from those gained from direct experience.[45] However, I would suggest that these differences influence, but do not necessarily obviate, the contributions of bioinformation to the plot and content of our identity narratives. Moreover, I want to suggest that it is precisely the relationship and interaction between our direct experiences of our bodies and our identities that signals a further, perhaps less obvious, narrative role for bioinformation, as I will now explain.

Providing Interpretive Context

According to the theories outlined in the previous chapter, narrativity is an intrinsically interpretive endeavour. The appropriation of characteristics,

---

[45] I return in Chapter 6 to discuss the relevance of these qualitative differences.

locating their place and priority within our accounts of who we are, the mutual reconciliation of narrative elements, and the unification of these elements within a broadly intelligible and coherent self-conception, all involve selection, shaping, and meaning-making. My second core claim, then, is that personal bioinformation provides not only potential raw building blocks of identity – 'I am someone at risk of colon cancer' – but also the *interpretive* tools for making sense of and constructing one's wider account of who one is in light of beliefs about an elevated risk of cancer. It can play useful roles in contextualising, explaining, or connecting our disparate experiences and other sources of understanding or insight. For example, receiving a long-sought diagnosis may help explain not only symptoms of concern but also other experiences that the individual had perhaps attributed to other causes, as well as other more broadly connected aspects of their lives and biographies, such as a family history of illness. These interpretive roles may also extend beyond explanation to include alteration of the connotations and significance of particular embodied experiences or characteristics, by supplying comparators, filters, or lenses. For example, receiving a diagnosis may cast someone's symptoms in a fresh light, perhaps making them a source of anxiety that dominates their self-conception, or leading them to feel new commonality with a similarly affected parent.

These examples concern the interpretation of prior or existing experiences. However, it is just as likely that personal bioinformation could play a part in drawing attention to or providing an interpretive context for processes or events of which we are not (yet) directly aware. For example, a diagnosis of Asperger's syndrome might provide someone with a means of reading future social and professional encounters and appreciating that others do not necessarily share their experiences of particular situations as easy or stressful. Bioinformation can also help us anticipate the ways that our bodies and embodied experiences may yet come to impinge in significant ways on our self-narratives. For example, learning that one has early warning signs of rheumatoid arthritis could throw someone's existing self-conception of themselves as athletic or an adventurous traveller into disarray, upending several of roles and projects with which they closely identify. However, it could also allow them to reconfigure their expectations of how their narratives could unfold and how this informs how they currently see themselves.

In each of the examples outlined here, the interpretive roles played by personal bioinformation can be seen as operating across several planes – connecting contemporary experiences, explaining past ones, casting existing self-descriptors in a new light, flagging future narrative disruption, or instigating a review of projected storylines in anticipation of things yet to come. It is possible that the impacts of encountering some information could extend across all of these dimensions. And, importantly, while it might be the case that this involves the reframing of a single descriptor or experience, it seems much more likely, given the interconnected and mutually informing nature of the strands of our identity narratives, that the impacts of encountering bioinformation will ripple wider and will serve to knit together or unpick multiple experiences, beliefs, descriptors, and themes in different ways.

Fulfilling Normative Roles

What I have said so far aims to explain why personal bioinformation might play a part in the narratives that comprise our identities, why it might change their content or configuration, and why it might fulfil expository, interpretive, contextualising, or prognostic roles. But the hypothesis with which I began this enquiry was that having access to personal bioinformation, and thus the opportunity to reflect on and use it in the construction of one's self-narrative, engages *ethically significant interests*. And it might not yet be clear why this stronger claim is justified. Why might access to this information have sufficient impact on what is important in our lives and engage interests strong enough to warrant the attention of, let alone action on the part of, those who hold this information about us?

The answer to this question is located in the inherent normativity of theories of narrative self-constitution, as described in the previous chapter. A self-narrative is not simply someone's life story; it is a selective and interpretive account that is constitutive of their practical identity. And maintaining, sustaining, and inhabiting a reasonably coherent and comfortable identity-constituting narrative has important consequences in that it provides the foundations for a number of valuable practical and evaluative capacities and experiences. I wish to suggest that personal bioinformation – by contributing to the scope and tenor of the contents and plotlines of our self-narratives and by providing interpretive and contextual tools for making sense of and configuring these narratives in the context of our embodied lives – may play all or any of the following four closely entwined roles.

The first way that personal bioinformation may contribute in normatively significant ways to our self-narratives is by providing a means of developing, maintaining, or restoring their internal coherence and intelligibility as we are confronted by the realities and vagaries of embodied life. I have suggested that many of the characteristics that make up our identities will themselves be derived from our embodied perspectives and characteristics. Given this, bioinformation has the capacity to support internal narrative coherence – or, to use Schechtman's terminology, 'articulability' – by informing our selection, prioritisation, and interpretation of the health-related, physical, cognitive, or behavioural traits, and biological relationships that contribute to our self-conceptions, and by enhancing the explicability of these in relation to each other and our overall sense of who we are.[46] For example, a blood test that reveals an overactive thyroid may help someone reinterpret their recent sleeplessness, work-related anxiety, and shortness of temper at home, attribute this to excess thyroxine, and, thus, understand how their experiences are reconcilable with their sense of themselves as a relatively calm and patient person, with a good aptitude for their job, and loving family relationships.

Internal intelligibility is not all that matters to the practical aspects of our identities. If our self-narratives are to support us in functioning as evaluators, planners, and agents, they also need to be intelligible with respect to our engagement with the world. Personal bioinformation can assist in this regard too by supplying insights that help us construct identities that are responsive to the realities of our own biology and materiality, or at least not vulnerable to being rendered incoherent when confronted by these. For example, an implanted device that provides early warning of the onset of epileptic seizures, allowing the user to take appropriate action, may help them inhabit an account of themselves as an active and self-reliant person capable of recognising and managing the risks posed by unexpected seizures. Or learning of a medical cause of infertility may help someone understand their difficulties in conceiving, somewhat alleviate their feelings of confusion or self-blame, and rethink the ways they may wish to fulfil the role of parent in which they invest great value. This support for 'external coherence' is the second normatively significant role that, I want to suggest, personal bioinformation can play.

The suggestion that bioinformation can help us maintain narratives that are broadly intelligible in light of objective bodily facts echoes Schechtman's 'reality constraint' as described in the previous chapter.

---

[46] Schechtman 1996.

To recap, according to Schechtman this constraint requires that our narratives are reasonably consistent with the contours of reality because we cannot function effectively in *social* contexts if our self-characterisations are unintelligible to other people.[47] I do not want to reject Schechtman's premise or its applicability to the narrative roles of bioinformation. It may well be the case that personal bioinformation can help us construct self-narratives that accord with other people's understandings of our particular embodied qualities in ways that help us function comfortably in social contexts and avoid the risk that our self-conceptions are not recognised by others. This is not a trivial benefit and may account for some of bioinformation's utility. However, Schechtman's characterisation of the reality constraint is silent on other reasons why a degree of external consistency might be valuable to us. My suggestion is that, because our identities are not only socially embedded and relationally constituted but also those of embodied, biological beings who operate in a material world, it also matters to us that the intelligibility and inhabitability of our self-narratives are not jeopardised by being at odds with *our own* encounters with our bodies, biology, and health. Our own abilities to make sense of our self-narratives and to function practically within them when confronted by our materiality matter at least as much, perhaps more, than their social plausibility. My suggestion then is that personal bioinformation plays a valuable role in supporting us in developing, maintaining, or restoring identity narratives that are reasonably consistent with, and intelligible and sustainable in light of, the material realities of our embodied lives. And it does so to the extent it offers *reliable* insights into the biological and bodily contexts, causes, and implications of our embodied encounters, capabilities, and experiences.

To be clear, the 'coherence value' of personal bioinformation appealed to here is not just about making our *bodies* more intelligible to us but also about making our *identities* and their constituent parts intelligible and resilient when faced with the vagaries and onslaught of embodied existence. In this respect, it is perhaps artificial to separate, as I have done above, the contributions of bioinformation to the internal and external coherence of our self-conceptions. Furthermore, the pursuit of (reasonable) coherence should be thought of as operating both synchronically and over time. For example, it matters not only that our identities are intelligible now but also that they are – as far as this is possible – not easily or imminently vulnerable to being rendered unintelligible and fractured

---

[47] Schechtman 1996.

by future bodily events or encounters.[48] While the sheer preservation of one's identity in an unchanging form is neither realistic nor desirable – by their very nature self-narratives do and must evolve in response to changing circumstances – abrupt and far-reaching disruptions may be distressing and disorienting and take considerable effort to resolve. Access to personal bioinformation could enhance the resilience of the coherence and sustainability of our self-conceptions over time by alerting us to how our capabilities or experiences may change. Avoiding such prospective jeopardy is important to comfortably and sustainably inhabiting who we are.

The normative roles played by personal bioinformation in the construction of our identities are not restricted solely to 'structural' features – that is, those supporting the internal, external, or future coherence of our self-narratives. The third way in which personal bioinformation may make an ethically significant, not merely a qualitative, difference to our identity-constituting narratives rests on the fact that our identity narratives provide the interpretive frameworks, or 'bodily perspectives', through which we encounter the world. My contention here is that bioinformation can play a valuable role in informing self-narratives that provide suitable interpretive frameworks with which to make sense of the material world, and seaworthy vessels within which to navigate, and conduct ourselves as embodied beings. Bioinformation can help us construct identities that are responsive to and developed in 'dialogue' with our biological and bodily lives. It does so by providing insights beyond our inevitably limited direct experiences. It thereby helps us understand and negotiate some – though undoubtedly not all – of our 'recalcitrant' materiality by alerting us to the whereabouts of some of the 'stern trunks' and 'twisting vines' that our bodily and biological form places in our path. It can help us anticipate these features of the landscape and embrace, tackle, or steer around them. For example, blood tests revealing high levels of antibodies consistent with early stages of rheumatoid arthritis may allow someone to build the risk of disease into their self-narrative, to anticipate and make sense of experiences of pain and reduced mobility as these emerge, and to map their future narrative with the prospect of this illness on their horizon.

---

[48] Hallvard Lillehammer makes a parallel suggestion with respect to the value of knowledge of genetic parentage to our identities. While Lillehammer is sceptical that this knowledge is valuable in itself, he allows that *erroneous* beliefs about our parentage could set one's identity up to be 'subverted' by the later discovery of the truth in ways that are detrimental to our well-being (Lillehammer 2014).

We should not be surprised that as embodied beings our self-narratives and our needs and capacities as narrators are enabled and limited by our physical and mental strengths and vulnerabilities and by the arc of our biological biographies that are bounded by conception and death and waymarked by – amongst many other things – growth, strength, illness, reproduction, and dependency. As such, we are the kinds of beings for whom insights into our bodily states and functions, our health, and our relationships to others can impact upon and colour how we characterise ourselves. This brings me to the fourth way in which bioinformation can make a normatively significant contribution to our identities. This one is more equivocal, or double-edged, than the previous three, in that it more obviously entails detrimental as well as positive impacts. It quite simply involves the contribution made by personal bioinformation of fresh or reconfigured descriptors, contents, and plot-lines in which we either invest value or take no pleasure. These may include features that help make our narratives meaningful and add to their detail and texture and those that, in contrast, introduce burden-some, demeaning, frightening, or limiting contents. The fact that these impacts on the tone, comfort, and qualities of our narratives may be positive *or* negative – which is not to say that they need be either – does not detract from their potential significance. Either way, they affect the inhabitability and meaning of our identities in non-trivial ways.

Though Mackenzie does not herself explicitly discuss a role for exter-nally sourced personal bioinformation in identity construction, the various narrative roles that I am proposing here echo her position that '[m]aking sense of who we are, and making sense of our lived embodi-ment, involves constructing an identity that is shaped by, and responsive to, biological realities'.[49] My contention, as set out above, is that personal bioinformation has several important, interconnected roles to play in achieving this sense-making and responsiveness. Something important – to the individual in question – is at stake in these roles being filled. At stake are, as described in Chapter 3, our abilities to make sense of who we are, to engage in practical and evaluative ways with the world, to be active and critical in our ongoing self-constitution, to sustain enduring projects and commitments, and to have a reasonably stable and useful interpret-ive perspective through which to make sense of our experiences and navigate the world. These are experiences and capacities that we have strong interests in cultivating and exercising because they contribute to

---

[49] Mackenzie 2009, p. 121.

the quality and richness of our lives. But being in a position to cultivate and exercise them is not inevitable. As I have suggested, these practical and evaluative capacities depend not simply on a reasonably intelligible, integrated, and resilient self-narrative but also on one that is capable of exhibiting and maintaining these features and supporting us in the context of embodied existence and as particular selves with our own particular forms of embodiment. This is the basis for my claim that personal bioinformation – taken as a wide category – has a number of important normative roles to play in the composition of our identities. I will return in subsequent chapters to discuss when and why particular kinds and instances of information may or may not fulfil these roles in the same ways or to the same extent.

The claims made above resonate with aspects of those concerning the narrative roles of knowledge of genetic parents introduced at the end of Chapter 2 – for example, Sarah Wilson's proposal that this knowledge plays an explanatory role and can contribute to 'alleviation of uncertainty with respect to the past'[50] and Jamie Nelson's claim that knowledge of our origins fills a gap by supplying the opening pages of our biographies, 'without which we cannot read well what is going on in the part occurring now'.[51] My position also shares features with Velleman's argument that acquaintance with our genetic parents provides tools to make sense of our particular form of embodiment and the ways our particular physicality and psychology contribute to and constrain who we are.[52] The arguments made by these three authors point us in a fruitful direction. However, my proposals go further. First, they posit epistemic and hermeneutic roles for bioinformation that extend beyond filling in gaps about our past or averting alienation from our materiality. Second, the suggestions I have made here encompass far more than information about genetic parentage, to embrace any kinds of personal bioinformation that help us make sense of who we are in the context of our embodied lives. But my claims are also more conservative, in not assuming that knowledge of genetic parentage will invariably fulfil these roles – I shall return in Chapter 5 to interrogate the narrative roles played by this specific category of information. And finally, while the idea that self-narratives – like novels and memoirs – are better for having clear beginnings and lacking gaps has intuitive metaphorical appeal, metaphor alone

---

[50] Wilson 1997, p. 285.
[51] Nelson 1992, p. 81.
[52] Velleman 2005.

is not enough. It is not enough to explain why access to information that fulfils these functions. We also need to know why this *matters* in ways that engage important interests and deserve ethical attention. Over the preceding sections, I have offered a set of pictures that seek to explain the potential value of personal bioinformation to our narrative undertakings and thus to our identities. This includes its potential explanatory value, but also derives from its selecting, evaluating, contextualising, interpretive, prognostic, and enriching roles. And I have grounded this value in the normativity inherent to narrative constitution of embodied, practical identity. The account I have offered above helps us appreciate why there are important capacities and experiences at stake in being able to develop and maintain an identity narrative that remains reasonably coherent, intelligible, and inhabitable in the context of our embodied, relational, and temporally extended lives.

Constituting, Not Revealing Identity

Before turning to consider some possible concerns that might arise in response to the claims I have made above, I want to differentiate my position from a line of reasoning to which it may initially appear similar. This is the proposition that some kinds of insights into the functions of our brains or psychology can supply vital correctives to our self-narratives, revealing the truth about who we are and what we are really like. For example, Mary Walker examines the possibility that findings from neuroscience and cognitive psychology – which, for example, purport to indicate that our effective motives differ from our acknowledged ones, our memories are unreliable, or our self-descriptions are biased – challenge the 'truth' of our self-narratives by revealing where our 'real' identities depart from the stories we tell about them.[53] Walker herself is sceptical about the cogency of this hypothesis and adopts a critical stance to the conception of objective truth at its heart. However, Lisa Bortolotti is more optimistic that findings from psychological research which purport to provide 'knowledge of [our] own mind[s]' and to reveal our 'behavioural dispositions', 'biases in deliberation', and 'attitudes' could be essential to constructing coherent identity narratives that align with our 'real motives' and support our autonomy.[54]

---

[53] Walker 2012.
[54] Bortolotti 2013, pp. 687–688.

The prima facie similarity between these kinds of claims and my own is that they each appear to hold that personal bioinformation – albeit of narrowly specific kinds – is of value to our identities because it can help us develop identity narratives that are more consistent with the ways our brains and minds actually work. My position, however, is not that bioinformation's value lies in its role as a *corrective* revealing the 'real' nature of our identities. There are two reasons for rejecting a corrective model. First, according to a narrative conception, our identities are *constituted* by our self-narratives. It therefore is not cogent to hold that scientific investigation can reveal what Schechtman terms 'prenarrative truth about the self', as there is no such truth.[55] This means that Bortolotti's contention that 'knowledge of the self matters to accurate and coherent narratives' is circular.[56] Second, the suggestion that neurological or behavioural data alone reveal the true nature of our motives and attitudes, let alone our identities, rests on a misplaced view of what accounts for this 'true nature'. Motives and attitudes are not discrete neurological or behavioural events, separable from the stories we tell about who we are. It is with reference to their place in the contents and arc of our embodied, relational self-narratives that these features of our evaluative and practical lives acquire their meaning and become explicable. This is not to say that we can never be confused or self-deluding about what characterises us. And according to the account I have given above, findings of causal or contributory factors in our traits or behaviours could lead us to revisit our self-characterisations. However, this is not because these findings *reveal* our real identities. It is rather because they offer contextual insights that may assist us in the interpretive activity of identity construction. Furthermore, contrary to Bortolotti's claims that bioinformation about our minds and motives are unique amongst personal bioinformation in playing a valuable role in self-understanding and self-determination – while, for example, information about genetic disease risks can only make cosmetic alterations to narrative contents – my position is that the interpretive and reconciliatory capabilities of bioinformation extend much wider. These capabilities may be fulfilled not only by neurological information, but also by genetic and many other kinds of information about our bodies and biology. And the contributions they can make are far from merely cosmetic.

[55] Schechtman 2012, p. 75.
[56] Bortolotti 2013, p. 687.

4.5   The Suitability of Bioinformation: Responding to Concerns

Having drawn these important distinctions, in this final section of this chapter I wish to address some concerns or objections that might be invited by the proposals I have made above. These fall into two categories. The first is that despite earlier protestations, my argument is based on a biologically essentialist premise after all. The second concern questions the suitability of personal bioinformation for fulfilling the epistemological and hermeneutic roles I have proposed. I shall take these in turn.

Biological Essentialism Revisited

Accounts that propose an ethically significant role for information of one's health, body, or biology in identity are often viewed with suspicion as they are assumed to cleave to a view of identity as reducible to and ready-defined by our biology rather than created by its subject.[57] The presumption seems to be that any claim to value must be based on the premise that this information is necessary for revealing or bringing to fruition a pre-existing essential self. As noted in Chapter 2, there are both empirical and ethical reasons for resisting the idea that our identities are defined and determined by our bodies and our biology. The argument I have presented above, however, does not commit me to a biologically reductionist or biologically essentialist conception of identity. The first thing to say is that focus on *bio*information in this book should not be taken as signalling that this – out of all possible sources of narrative materials and interpretations – makes, or should make, an unparalleled contribution to our identities. It is only one amongst many possible constitutive, epistemic, or hermeneutic tools in identity development – albeit an important one. My focus on the 'bio' here is motivated instead by the roots of this enquiry, which lie in bioethical and policy debates about which interests should inform policies and practices governing the disclosure of bioinformation in clinical, health research, and consumer contexts. And my claim is not that unfettered access to personal bioinformation would be sufficient for the construction of a coherent, inhabitable self-narrative. Our narratives will inevitably and appropriately also be woven from strands that have nothing to do with our bodies or biology. To this extent, I concur with Hallvard Lillehammer, who, in expressing his scepticism about the universal value of knowing one's

---

[57] For example, Marshall 2014.

genetic parentage, observes, '[t]here are many things that could make more of a difference to how I think of myself than facts that determine how I was constituted as a biological entity'.[58] Furthermore, as I have emphasised, my account takes bioinformation to be a potential source of insights into aspects of our health, bodies, or biology, not into our *identities* themselves. So, in positing, for example, that someone could have an identity-related interest in accessing genetic test results, my suggestion is not that these will reveal what that person is really like but rather that the results might provide material they could use, or not, in developing and enacting their sense of who they are. Bioinformation is relevant and valuable to identity in a *potential* and *instrumental* sense rather than in an inevitable and essential one.

These responses notwithstanding, it might still be a source of concern that my position emphasises the desirability of coherence between someone's self-narrative and their material, biological attributes. This might look like a capitulation to a requirement that we define ourselves in close accordance with our biological attributes on pain of a debilitating, or at least an unhelpful, lack of intelligibility. Yet many of us actively exclude aspects of our bodies and health from our self-definitions or characterise ourselves in ways that run contrary to our embodied forms and biological traits. Even where some aspects of our embodiment are part of our self-conceptions, we may perhaps resent this or reject the implication that this is the most important aspect of who we are. And, in countless cases, we will simply omit aspects of our health or biology from our self-narratives because we are unaware of them or see them as incidental. It would be problematic, therefore, if my analysis implied that any of these circumstances represent a necessary barrier to developing and occupying a meaningful and intelligible practical identity. However, this is not the implication of my claims.

My argument does not preclude refusing to be defined by particular aspects of our bodily existence – for example, phenotypic sex or chronic illness – or defining oneself in opposition to these. Active rejection of aspects of our embodiment from our identities need not jeopardise narrative coherence or intelligibility. To understand how this can be so, we can return to the useful analysis of dramatic personal changes offered by Mary Walker, which I briefly mentioned in Chapter 3. Walker explains how someone can retain a unified and intelligible self-narrative through an experience like a dramatic religious conversion.

---

[58] Lillehammer 2014, p. 103.

She proposes that this continuity requires that the individual is able reflectively to access, respond to, and explain their former now repudiated values and behaviours in the light of their conversion and current characteristics, with the result that they can still make sense of themselves as someone who was once 'that' and is now 'this'.[59] Under a similar principle – and one that may apply to synchronous complexities no less than it does to change over time – it is possible that particular bodily or biological characteristics may inform our identity narratives without becoming *defining parts* of us. This is the case when we are able to offer meaningful accounts of who we are that exclude unwanted traits or minimise their role, while also being able – in principle – to explain the relationship or journey between these and our defining characteristics and to anticipate and account for the ways these rejected traits may sometimes impinge upon our embodied lives.[60]

These kinds of selection, prioritisation, and mutual explicability of narrative threads are inherent to the concept of narrativity. And one of the key conceptual strengths of a narrative-based account of the relationship between identity and personal bioinformation is that it allows us to understand that bioinformation can play a valuable *instrumental* role, as a tool of identity development, without itself directly supplying the substantive building blocks and self-descriptors of our self-characterisations. In such cases, it may fulfil interpretive or editorial functions that help restore or preserve intelligibility amongst diverse experiences and traits. These functions might involve, for example, relegating aspects of one's health to the status of brute bodily states of affairs rather than parts of one's identity, charting the submerged boulders of biology to be navigated around, or providing the point of tension against which one can build a counter-story that allows one to make sense of one's embodied experiences. For example, learning that they are at high risk of hereditary colorectal cancer may help someone relegate this risk to serious but a largely pragmatic matter to be clinically managed, so that it impinges on their self-conception as little as possible rather than defining them.

As to the sheer omission of details about our bodies and biology from our self-narratives, this is inevitable and is not in itself a threat to the

---

[59] Walker 2019.

[60] Walker herself makes a slightly different argument about the place of illness in our self-narratives, holding that while they cannot be 'regarded as expressions of one's characteristics ... we can still integrate them into our narratives' through reflecting on and responding to them (Walker 2019, p. 87).

intelligibility and integrity of our identities. Indeed, any attempt at factual completism is more likely to militate against intelligibility and our abilities to discern which features are key to shaping our priorities and values. My contention that personal bioinformation can provide valuable explanatory, interpretive, or contextualising tools does not mean that any *particular* aspect of our embodiment, or any particular kind of personal bioinformation, is universally essential or invariably valuable to the development of our practical identities. However, there is a critical distinction to be made here between a mere lack of bioinformation or rejection of its proffered descriptors, as contrasted with the unwitting incorporation of frankly false beliefs. Lillehammer captures this in observing that:

> It is one thing to develop a virtuous practical identity in conditions where facts about one's genealogical origins play little or no role while being aware that there are significant gaps in one's knowledge of those facts. It is quite another to develop such an identity in the false belief that one's knowledge of these origins is accurate or complete.[61]

Lillehammer's concession – with which I concur and would extend to bioinformation beyond 'genealogical origins' – is that the former situation is often innocuous, whereas the latter could harm one's identity and interfere with its capacity to support a flourishing life. The narrative-based account I have offered in this chapter suggests that this harm could take two forms. First, false beliefs could render one's self-narrative vulnerable to being undermined when one stubs one's toe against biological reality. And, second, such misconceptions make one's self-narrative an unreliable foundation from which to navigate and make sense of one's experiences of embodiment because these are then premised on false assumptions. Misapprehensions of aspects of our bodies, biology, or health are not necessarily problematic in themselves, but they could be insofar as they foster self-characterisations that we struggle to make sense of or sustain. I will return to the threats posed by false and unreliable information in the next chapter.

Epistemic Suitability

Turning now to the second set of concerns: those that question the suitability of personal bioinformation – perhaps especially that generated

---

[61] Lillehammer 2014, p. 106.

by the biomedical sciences – to fulfil the roles I have proposed. These concerns are grounded in scepticism that objective, quantified, and theory-laden bioinformation does not reveal the truth about our bodies and biology and, even if it does, it is not an appropriate tool for interpreting the phenomenology of embodied existence. I shall respond to each of these in turn.

What I have said so far takes as its unspoken assumption that personal bioinformation can make valuable contributions to the coherence and interpretive capacities of our identities because it delivers relevant reliable knowledge of our health, bodies, and biology. However, anti-realist perspectives call into question – for diverse reasons – the assumption that science provides knowledge of the world 'as it really is'.[62] If this is so, then it is not obvious that the information biomedical sciences and technologies supply could help us construct narratives that are more intelligible in light of, or better for negotiating, our materiality. It is not possible to engage with the detail of debates about scientific antirealism here.[63] It is sufficient to note that my argument does not depend on a naïve realism that assumes '[t]he picture which science gives us of the world is a true one, faithful in its details'.[64] This would be unwise, particularly given the relative youth and rapid developments of some of the disciplines and techniques, such as machine-learning-driven association studies in genomics or neuroimaging, with which this project is concerned. It is also the case that some personal bioinformation will incorporate constructed categories such as 'depressive illness' that do not correspond to neatly defined biological categories.[65] This does not, however, obviate the potential interpretive utility of personal bioinformation. It is sufficient for my purposes that the biomedical sciences can provide the kind of 'empirically adequate' theories that generate findings that broadly accord with the world as we experience it.[66] It is enough that personal bioinformation offers reasonably reliable instrumental knowledge about how observable phenomena are likely to behave, in which, in Bas van Fraassen's phrase, our actual experiences can 'find a home'.[67] This leaves space for recognising that we may yet find better and more reliable and

---

[62] For example, Kuhn 2012; Latour and Woolgar 1979.

[63] For discussion, see Rowbottom 2019.

[64] Van Fraassen 1980, pp. 6–7.

[65] It is possible to recognise that labels such as this are social constructions, without conceding that the states of affairs to which they refer are not real (see Hacking 1999).

[66] Van Fraassen 1980, p. 12.

[67] Van Fraassen 1980, p. 86.

explanatory ways to, for example, identify and categorise diseases, while allowing that current observations and inferences retain utility for now. Of course, not all bioinformation will confer equally useful or reliable means for interpreting embodied existence. Some of it may be frankly false or otherwise unsound or misleading because of unsuitable or immature analytic methods. And much of it will deal not in certainties but instead in broad probabilistic claims. I will return in Chapter 6 to interrogate the limits of particular kinds of bioinformation as useful epistemic and hermeneutic tools.

The second category of concern I want to address is that even if one is sympathetic to the idea that we have an interest in constructing and making sense of an embodied identity narrative, one might imagine that this entails a self-conception woven from first-personal, subjective, experiential material, not one built from the kinds of third-personal propositional, quantified, and technical information generated by medicine, health research, or biotechnologies. In suggesting that biomedical information has a role to play in our embodied identity narratives, I may seem to have committed a category mistake by conflating the biological body with the 'body as lived'. It may appear that I have incorrectly elided the kinds of information pertinent to numerical identity – as concerned with sameness and brute facts about us as organisms – with those pertinent to identity in the sense of characterisation and practical selfhood.[68] Or it might appear that I have overlooked the lack of equivalence between objective symptoms of disease and our experiences of illness. These concerns are rooted in doubts that personal bioinformation – as I have defined it – captures the phenomenology of the bodily states of affairs or ill-health to which they pertain.[69] This might mean, at the very least, that bioinformation is not well-suited to providing the kinds of explanatory and interpretative tools for embodied identity development that I have suggested. More pessimistically, it could be objected that reliance on 'external' information over our own direct experiences of ourselves and our characteristics is to the serious detriment of our well-being and understandings of who we are. For example, as noted in the last chapter, Mary Walker and Wendy Rogers have proposed that when the advent of unexpected bioinformation – their example is a diagnosis of asymptomatic disease – does not correspond with the recipients' experiences, the urge to restore narrative coherence

---

[68] See Ajana 2010.
[69] Carel 2011.

may force them to distort other aspects of their self-conceptions. They may, for example, start to habitually doubt their own perceptions of their health.[70] Deborah Lupton and others have raised related concerns that objective, quantified data supplied by consumer health technologies such as sleep-monitoring apps might unhelpfully replace more 'authentic' phenomenological experiences of self.[71]

My responses to these concerns about epistemic suitability and usurped phenomenology are twofold. First, as Mackenzie argues, it is a mistake to conflate characteristics with respect to which we are non-autonomous – for example, our inherited genetic traits – with characteristics that have no relevance to our identities.[72] Even though our biological and bodily states and capacities are 'given', they – and, by association, information about them – may nonetheless be pertinent to our subjective experiences of self, our abilities to construct our self-narratives, and the particular shape and nature of our resultant identities, in all the ways described above. Second, my claim for the identity value of personal bioinformation relies neither on assumptions that it invariably provides the correct or complete story of someone's embodied existence – with all the personal, experiential nuances this entails – nor the contention that it ought to replace our own experiences in the construction of our identities. Lupton's anxiety might indeed be justified if quantified bioinformation were wholly to usurp embodied experience in narrative self-constitution. But here Michael Loughlin and his co-authors offer a useful distinction, observing that 'there is a difference between saying that looking at the world in a certain way can help you understand *aspects of* the truth about your predicament, and saying that looking at the world in a particular way, understood through the lens of scientism, provides the only truth'.[73] With due caution about the reference to 'truth' here, the former claim in this passage is close to the view I wish to defend. It is undeniable that externally sourced personal bioinformation will usually be qualitatively and functionally different from that delivered by our experiences and senses. My suggestion, however, is that it is a mutually informing combination of our experiences and bioinformation that provides the fruitful material for our self-narratives. For example, findings about structural neurological explanations for psychiatric illness,

---

[70] Walker and Rogers 2017.

[71] Lupton 2013; Kreitmair and Cho 2017. I do not myself use the language of authenticity in this discussion because of its ambiguity and unwanted associations with both individualistic and essentialist conceptions of identity.

[72] Mackenzie 2009.

[73] Loughlin et al. 2013, p. 143 (emphasis added).

taken in isolation, are unlikely to equip someone with everything they need to understand or navigate their illness experiences. However, this does not mean that these findings could not be of use in helping them make sense of the onset of their recent symptoms and how these have affected their personality and relationships.

While drawing attention to precisely the differences between the experience of one's own ill body and clinical knowledge that motivates the above concern, Carel notes that it is nevertheless an advantage to a patient to have access to both. As she says, '[t]he claim here is that the unique ability to oscillate between the two perspectives gives the patient a deeper understanding of the illness experience and potentially to the dual nature of the body'.[74] The combination of experience and information allows the patient to know both the 'how' and the 'that' of their body or illness. Carel's position echoes the position of some narrative identity theorists that, because we are embodied beings, identity construction entails a dialogue or reconciliation between the contrasting viewpoints of our bodies as objects in the world and our subjective experiences of them 'from the inside'.[75] For example, we can recall here Velleman's suggestion that observing family resemblances can help us identify with our objective materiality, to 'com[e] to terms with our bodily selves'.[76] Developing our embodied accounts of who we are may require external epistemic and hermeneutic resources beyond our phenomenological experiences to help us interpret these and work out whether and how they feature in our stories of who we are. In this way these external resources may help make our stories inhabitable and recognisably our own.

Nevertheless, Walker and Roger's warning about the risks of distortion is an important one. Not only does it remind us that pursuit of narrative coherence above all else may be neither an unalloyed good nor valuable at any cost. It also flags the possibility that personal bioinformation could, for various reasons, carry a greater gravitational pull – greater than other epistemic and hermeneutic tools and perhaps greater than its contributions warrant – when it comes to recipients' pursuit of coherence. And this may come at the expense of the comfort or sustainability of their sense of who they are. I will return in Chapter 6 to consider the relationships between the qualities of narrative coherence and comfort.

---

[74] Carel 2016, p. 50. See also Sharon 2017.
[75] See, for example, Atkins 2008; Ricoeur 1992; Velleman 1996.
[76] Velleman 2008, p. 260.

Whether particular information generated by medicine, health research, or biotechnologies does in fact offer useful interpretive tools for navigating embodied existence and experience will vary between information types, disclosure contexts, and recipients. The possibility remains that some bioinformation will just not be very good at fulfilling these roles. Some might even be detrimental to our efforts to construct coherent, inhabitable self-characterisations. Over the coming chapters, I will explore in greater detail the diversity of information's effects on recipients' self-conceptions, how we might identify when these are likely to be beneficial or detrimental, and what might be done to manage the proportionate influence of bioinformation and to achieve a helpful dialogue and accommodation between diverse narrative contributions and interpretive tools.

4.6 Moving Beyond Theory

In this chapter I have outlined my central contention that personal bioinformation, taken as a broad category, can play a number of vital roles in helping us construct self-narratives that are responsive to the vagaries, limitations, and opportunities of embodied existence. My claim is that personal bioinformation is important to our identities because our material, biological, vulnerable, and capable bodies frame our subjective experiences and play an active part in shaping 'how our lives go'. Therefore they can play key roles in the contents, scope, and context of the narratives that constitute our lived, practical identities. This information supports us in constructing self-narratives that not only make sense when confronted by our embodied experiences but also provide the foundations from which we are able to interpret and navigate our embodied lives. It does so by acting as a contributory and interpretive tool, not necessarily by straightforwardly installing self-descriptors but by assisting us in the task of meaning-making across the threads that make up the stories of who we are. In fulfilling these roles, personal bioinformation helps us develop, maintain, or restore the kind of narrative integration, intelligibility, and inhabitability that are necessary if our identities are to ground our capacities to have a strong sense of who we are, provide a solid foundation from which to make judgements and commitments, and support us in being the authors of our own actions and ongoing self-creation. As established in the previous chapter, I take these capacities to be central to leading a rich, fulfilling, and practically engaged life. On these grounds, I submit, we may understand why access to personal bioinformation could engage ethically significant interests that warrant attention by those who hold this information when they make decisions about whether to disclose it to us. I will specify the nature of these interests in Chapter 6, having refined my account in light of the illustrative examples to come.

If this account of the relationship between personal bioinformation and identity is to provide a sound foundation for practical ethical decision-making, if it is to inform policies and practices governing disclosure of personal bioinformation to information subjects, then it is vital that it remains plausible when held up to people's actual experiences of encountering this information and is responsive to the kinds of factors that affect the nature of these encounters. To these ends, my next step is to turn to the empirical social science literature for examples of information subjects' attitudes and reactions to receiving three different kinds of personal bioinformation. My intention is to check that the conceptual and ethical analysis I have presented here is at least congruent with people's experiences. These examples will also serve to bring to life and further refine the claims I have made so far. I shall describe these illustrative examples and my approach to them in detail in the next chapter.

5

Encounters with Bioinformation: Three Examples

5.1 Introduction

At this point in the discussion, I want to step back from theory a little, to examine how the proposition offered in the last chapter – that personal bioinformation has potentially important epistemic and hermeneutic roles to play in embodied narrative self-constitution – stands up when considered in light of people's experiences of encountering bioinformation about themselves. To this end, in this chapter I will examine findings from empirical studies that have gathered data on people's expectations of and reactions to receiving – or, in some cases, not receiving – information relating to their health, bodies, and biological relationships.

To be clear, the objective here is not one of *proving* my hypothesis about the roles played by bioinformation in our self-constituting narratives, much less proving that a narrative conception of identity is an appropriate one. It is not clear that empirical proof of a conceptual and normative picture such as this would be possible. Furthermore, the empirical findings I will draw upon have not been selected in a theory-neutral way, so cannot provide a non-question-begging verification of my hypothesis. Having said this, if the account offered in this book is to make a useful contribution to practical, ethical frameworks that can guide information governance, it must be responsive to, and plausible in light of, the available evidence of how people respond to and use personal bioinformation. So, although this project does not itself use empirical methods, it shares some of the concerns motivating the so-called empirical turn in bioethics. That is, if bioethical arguments are to be relevant and of concrete value in informing disclosure practices, policy, and law, they need to engage with findings from the empirical social sciences about the realities of people's experiences and practices.[1]

---

[1] For further discussion of approaches to empirical bioethics, see Borry et al. (2004); Hedgecoe (2004).

The aims of this chapter reflect aspects of what has been termed a 'theorist approach' to empirical bioethics, in which the locus of normative authority lies in the theoretical premises of the enquiry, while empirical evidence is used to sense-check and refine factually based elements of the normative argument.[2]

My first aim in this chapter is to demonstrate that my theory-based position is, at the very least, congruent with people's lived experiences. It is to check that what we know of these experiences supports, or at least does not undermine, the cogency and credibility of the arguments presented in the previous chapter. In order to do so, it must indicate that people do indeed use personal bioinformation to construct or make sense of who they are in ways that are not trivial, wildly anomalous, or vanishingly rare. My second objective is to bring to life and illustrate my central claims about the critical instrumental roles of bioinformation in building our accounts of who we are. Examples from the empirical literature will add texture and detail, moving these claims beyond abstractions. Third, I will use evidence from empirical studies to refine the proposals I have made so far, with the aim of arriving at a more nuanced picture of the extent and nature of impacts of different kinds of information, on different people, and under different circumstances. This, in turn, will also allow me to move beyond discussing personal bioinformation in general terms as a single undifferentiated class, which it plainly is not, by looking at how different kinds and instances of bioinformation may vary in the ways and degrees to which they affect our identities. This will not only allow for greater specificity in what can be said about the narrative roles of personal bioinformation and the normative significance of these roles but also offer insights into reasons for these differences. Each will be key when considering, in the coming chapters, how identity impacts might be addressed in practice.

As introduced in Chapter 1, I will explore findings relating to three categories of bioinformation. These are: information conveying the fact of having been conceived using donor gametes; results from tests for genetic susceptibility to common complex disorders; and neuroimaging findings that purport to provide predictive, diagnostic, or prognostic insights into mental illness. I have selected these examples for a number of reasons. First, on purely pragmatic grounds, these choices have been influenced by the availability of high-quality empirical studies that provide insights into information subjects' attitudes and reactions. Second, these three

---

[2] Molewijk et al. (2004).

examples are not confined to one kind of information, and each kind differs in the extent to which it conveys reliable or meaningful insights into subjects' health, bodies, or minds. Third, they represent information encountered in different contexts – some are generated in healthcare, some may be available to information subjects in research or commercial contexts, and others may not yet be readily accessible. Finally, each kind of bioinformation has been subject to diverse assertions or repudiations of identity significance. For example, claims about the identity relevance of genetic relatedness and genetic test results have attracted significant scholarly attention in recent years. And, although the potential identity value of knowledge of donor conception is now reflected to some extent in UK law, the reality and nature of this value remain a disputed topic. In contrast, findings derived from psychiatric neuroimaging have attracted markedly fewer discussions of identity impacts. This variety of examples will help us understand not only the possible ways identity impacts may vary but also where all three share common features that may then be generalisable beyond these particular examples.

The findings discussed below are sourced from published empirical social science research. This includes qualitative and quantitative studies, of various sizes and methodologies, encompassing, for example, large multiphased longitudinal studies and small ethnographic projects, as well as systematic reviews. The unifying feature is that they report individuals' expectations of and reactions to receiving, or being denied, bioinformation that pertains to them. In some cases, these studies report the views of other parties, for example, clinicians or parents, where their views reflect or anticipate how information subjects might react. The studies discussed exhibit some limitations and are not representative of all possible information recipients. They are chiefly conducted in the UK, Western Europe, North America, and Australasia, and white and more highly educated participants are often over-represented. And further issues arise from self-selection in some studies, where participants with a particular interest in, for example, undergoing genetic testing are over-represented. These limitations are flagged further below and must be taken into account when considering the generalisability of the findings.

What follows here is not a comprehensive or systematic review and it does not need to be in order to serve the purposes described above. I have drawn upon findings that plausibly speak to the possible impacts of receiving bioinformation – or, in some cases, lacking or being denied it – on individuals' self-narratives. In some studies, though by no means all, investigators have collected or interpreted these findings with the express research aim of examining effects on recipients' identities. My approach here will be neither to unquestioningly adopt these existing analyses nor to limit my focus to those impacts that investigators or research participants explicitly characterise as identity-significant. Doing so risks tying this inquiry to narrower, or simply different, senses of identity than the narratively-constituted conception with which I am concerned – a conception that, I am suggesting, offers distinct advantages in terms of normative and conceptual robustness and practical applicability. According to the picture outlined in the preceding chapters, our identity narratives are woven from many diverse experiences, characteristics, and activities. Casting the net to include a range of reported reactions, unrestricted by researchers' and – to a lesser extent – participants' different conceptions of what 'identity' means, makes space for a more holistic picture of identity and allows for consideration of the ways that our identities may be significantly affected by shifts in diverse constituent threads. However, I have not taken this as a licence to include every reported fleeting impression or to play fast and loose with participants' own depictions of their experiences. To count as having a potential narrative impact, and thus be included in the illustrative examples below, participants' accounts must imply effects with a degree of stickiness and weight, such that it is reasonable to consider that the information encounter somehow alters, contributes to, or detracts from their account of who they are. As this suggests, the approach taken here to identifying relevant studies and findings is theory-led and purposive, involving the strategic selection of illustrative material, and my analysis of the findings is inferential and interpretive.[3] While this approach entails some circularity, it reflects the reflexive and mutually informing nature of the relationship between what is inferred from evidence of people's responses and the theoretical framing of these in this inquiry.[4]

The remainder of this chapter is divided into four parts. The first three will present findings relating to each of the three different categories of bioinformation in turn and explore each through the lens of a narrative conception of identity. The fourth will draw these analyses together to take stock of what may be gleaned about the diverse ways that different personal bioinformation may contribute to or impact upon our stories of who we are, the variety of roles it may play, and how these observations might lend weight to or require refinement of the picture I have offered so

---

[3] Bryman 2016.
[4] Chan et al. 2020.

far. The first category of bioinformation to which I will turn is the one that sparked my curiosity and initiated the central enquiry of this book – information about donor conception.

5.2   Illustrative Example I: Encounters with Donor Origins

What Kind of Bioinformation?

The empirical findings to be explored in this section are those reporting people's experiences of learning of and living with the knowledge that they were conceived using donated gametes – that is, sperm or eggs from someone other than one or both of their parents.[5] The personal bioinformation under scrutiny here chiefly concerns the fact of donor-conception, rather than details about the donor.[6] As noted in the opening chapters, donor-conceived individuals' interests – particularly their identity-related interests – in knowing about their 'genetic parentage' has been a topic that has animated academic, legal, policy, and public debates in recent decades.[7] The view that it is in the interests of donor-conceived individuals to be told of their donor origins is now widely, if not universally, held.[8] Nevertheless, as observed in Chapter 2, despite the fact that UK law reflects some recognition of these interests by requiring donor identifiability, scholarly debate continues about the nature and extent of the benefits of knowing to donor-conceived individuals' identities, whether not knowing really leads to harm, and what such harm might amount to.[9]

Before turning to look at the experiences of those who have learned that they were conceived using donor gametes, it will be useful to expand a little on what was said in Chapter 2 about when and how donor-conceived individuals conceived in the UK are currently able to come

---

[5] Information about donor conception counts as 'personal bioinformation' under the definition set out in Chapter 1 because it is interpreted as being about the origins of an individual's biological existence and their genetic relationships (it has a biological 'interpretive pedigree'), rather than because it is necessarily derived from analysis of biological material or processes.

[6] In various sources, 'information about donor origins' may be used to refer to information about the sheer fact of donor-assisted conception or to descriptive and identifying information about gamete donors themselves. Here, I will concentrate on research relating to the former.

[7] Nuffield Council on Bioethics 2013.

[8] Nuffield Council on Bioethics 2013.

[9] For a dissenting view, see Pennings 2017, and for responses to this view, see Letters to the Editor (2017) *Human Reproduction* 32 (7), 1532–1536.

by this knowledge. As previously mentioned, the identities of donors of gametes used in licensed treatment in the UK are required by law to be recorded and accessible to donor-conceived individuals on request once they turn eighteen.[10] However, making such a request clearly requires knowing, or suspecting, that one was donor conceived. Parents in the UK are not legally obliged to tell their children about their conception, and there is no indication of donor conception on birth certificates as required in some other jurisdictions.[11] Licensed fertility clinics are, however, required by law to advise parents of the importance of telling children early in their lives and to offer parents support in doing so.[12] This follows recommendations of many leading researchers in the field that it is in the interests of children's psychosocial well-being and family relationships if parents begin to talk to children about their donor conception at a preschool age.[13] Public and professional attitudes about the benefits of openness are changing, in line with emerging evidence from social research and social trends towards investing significance in genetic heritage.[14] Nevertheless, it is ultimately left to parents to decide whether and when to tell, and while they are increasingly telling their children, the majority of parents still do not do so.[15] Not all share the view that disclosure is in their children's interests.[16] Many parents report finding it difficult to do so.[17] And stigma associated with infertility and donor conception, as well as concerns about damaging family relationships, are cited as reasons why some families do not disclose.[18] Same-sex and single parents are more likely to tell than heterosexual couples.[19]

Parents are of course not the only possible source of this information. People may find out from other family members or friends, or reach their own inferences, for example by observing differing family traits or when

[10] Human Fertilisation and Embryology Act 1990 (as amended)

[11] Blyth and Frith 2009. In the Australian State of Victoria, birth certificates indicate that further information is held on the register.

[12] Human Fertilisation and Embryology Act 1990 (as amended) s.13(6) and (6c). *HFEA Code of Practice (9th Edition)* (Human Fertilisation and Embryology Authority).

[13] Ilioi et al. 2017; Nuffield Council on Bioethics 2013.

[14] Freeman 2014.

[15] Nuffield Council on Bioethics 2013. As an indication of the proportion of families that disclose, one 2014 study found that by the time children in the participating families were seven, only 29 per cent who had used sperm donors and 41 per cent who had used egg donors had started the process of disclosure (Blake et al. 2014).

[16] Readings et al. 2011.

[17] Readings et al. 2011.

[18] Crawshaw and Daniels 2019; Nuffield Council on Bioethics 2013.

[19] Beeson et al. 2011.

asked for their family medical history.[20] Events such as divorce or bereavement can prompt revelations, and late and unplanned disclosures are not uncommon.[21] Increasingly, unsuspecting individuals are discovering they are donor-conceived accidentally through their own or close relatives' uses of DTC genomic testing services, many of which offer the means to ascertain genetic relatedness or connect with genetic relatives.[22] Individuals with suspicions can also take matters into their own hands by using these DTC services. And the UK Donor Conceived Register provides a route for people to undergo voluntary genetic testing for the purposes of connecting with donors or donor-siblings.[23] Once they reach eighteen, people are entitled to apply to the HFEA to find out if they are donor-conceived.[24] However, for those conceived outwith licensed UK clinics, for example via private arrangements or treatment in other countries, the HFEA will not hold these records. Research and surveys indicate that most donor-conceived people do not know about their donor origins.[25]

Though many of the findings considered below are from studies conducted in the UK, and thus in the disclosure context outlined above, some predate 2005 changes in UK law that required donor identifiability and encouraged parental openness. And some of the studies took place in other jurisdictions with different disclosure policies, including the USA and Australia. Many of the findings are from two prominent longitudinal projects, the European Study of Assisted Reproduction Families and the UK Longitudinal Study of Assisted Reproduction Families, both led by the Centre for Family Research at the University of Cambridge.[26] These studies investigate children's psychological well-being and quality of family relationships at intervals between infancy and adolescence, offering insights into how experiences change with age. Other studies drawn on below include smaller ethnographies, some of which expressly set out to explore identity-related

---

[20] Frith et al. 2018b.

[21] Daniels et al. 2011; Kirkman 2003.

[22] Harper et al. 2016.

[23] Donor Conceived Register website, www.donorconceivedregister.co.uk/ (accessed 18 July 2021).

[24] Human Fertilisation and Embryology Act 1990 (as amended) s.31.

[25] Tallandini et al. 2016; '2020 We Are Donor Conceived Survey Report' www.wearedonorconceived.com/2020-survey-top/2020-we-are-donor-conceived-survey/ (accessed 18 July 2021).

[26] University of Cambridge Centre for Family Research website 'New Families Research Group', www.cfr.cam.ac.uk/groups/ntf (accessed 18 July 2021).

impacts. Rich though these findings are, they exhibit two limitations relevant to the present inquiry. First, there are inevitable practical and ethical obstacles to capturing the experiences of individuals who are unaware they are donor-conceived. Second, studies in this field often draw participants from networks that facilitate contact between donor-relatives, meaning those particularly invested in understanding their origins may be over-represented.[27]

Information Subjects' Experiences

The following sections highlight findings from the empirical research literature that potentially speak to the roles played by knowledge of their conception in donor-conceived individuals' identity narratives. In order to tease apart potentially different impacts of *discovering* and *knowing* that one is donor-conceived, I will divide these findings according to three epistemic states: those of *not* knowing about one's donor origins; discovering one's donor origins; and living with this knowledge.

What Is It Like Not to Know?

Despite the inherent methodological difficulties of ascertaining the effects of 'not knowing' on donor-conceived individuals, observational studies comparing disclosing and non-disclosing families offer one possible source of insights, and individuals' reflections on their experiences prior to learning of their donor conception are another. The two longitudinal studies mentioned above have, at the time of writing, followed children up to fourteen years old and have found no significant differences in children's psychological well-being or quality of family relationships between disclosing and non-disclosing families.[28] When it comes to retrospective reflections from those who now know, it is not uncommon for participants to report that, before they found out, they felt 'different' from other family members in appearance or character traits or as if their parents were hiding something.[29] For example, one individual reports, 'I'd always known that something wasn't quite right that there was something different about me but I just didn't know what.'[30] Another

---

[27] Those conceived using donor eggs or embryos may be less well represented in current research. Freeman 2015.

[28] Ilioi and Golombok 2015; Ilioi et al. 2017.

[29] Frith et al. 2018, p. 177; Kirkman 2003; Schrijvers et al. 2019.

[30] Nuffield Council on Bioethics 2013, p. 87.

recalls 'huge parts of my life which seemed somehow wrong but I had no idea why'.[31]

It has been posited that concealing donor conception can itself cause family tensions or affect parents' behaviours in ways that are palpable to their children.[32] For example, one donor-conceived individual reports that this 'created a "shroud of secrecy" and a "sense of shame" something I could sense, but of what I had no real knowledge'.[33] And another reports, 'I sensed that my social father wasn't my biological father and I began asking questions'.[34] Some describe a sense of disconnection blighting their lives or damaging their self-esteem.[35] Others report having experienced a 'disjointed' sense of self.[36] It is possible that some of these recollections are coloured by hindsight or by difficult experiences of discovery.[37] However, these kinds of findings appear consistent across a number of studies, and they cannot be easily dismissed.

What Is It Like to Find Out?

Even if not knowing is not itself experienced as problematic, it leaves open the likelihood of late or unplanned discovery. Reactions to discovery tend to vary markedly by the age at which this happens and the ways in which people find out.[38] The two are often linked, with earlier telling generally managed by parents in planned and incremental ways, while later disclosures are often accidental, revealed by third parties, or precipitated by family crises.[39]

It is not uncommon for parents to report fearing that disclosure will confuse young children or cause psychological problems, but the most common reactions observed amongst those told before reaching school-age are indifference, pleasure, or curiosity.[40] For many, the experience is one of 'always having known'.[41] One teenager remembering being told says, 'I don't think I really minded … to be honest …

---

[31]   Frith et al. 2018a, p. 176.
[32]   Golombok et al. 2002.
[33]   Turner and Coyle 2000.
[34]   Hewitt 2002, p. 3.
[35]   Frith et al. 2018a.
[36]   Frith et al. 2018a, p. 176.
[37]   Nuffield Council on Bioethics 2013.
[38]   Ilioi and Golombok 2015.
[39]   Nuffield Council on Bioethics 2013.
[40]   Ilioi et al. 2017.
[41]   Freeman 2015.

I still don't really care'.[42] Research indicates that, generally speaking, the older someone is, the more difficult the experience of discovery tends to be, and that discovery later in life may cause psychological harm.[43] Those who find out during adolescence or adulthood are more likely to react with shock, anger, distress, or confusion.[44] Participants in several studies report a sense of betrayal that they had been lied to by those close to them, as illustrated by the words of one interviewee who recalls '[s]hock, absolute disbelief, felt I'd been betrayed and lied to all my life'.[45] While another recalls feeling that their 'entire life [had been] based on a lie'.[46]

Sometimes, this shock is related to a perceived loss of family relationships. For example, one participant, who found out when she was forty, says, '[i]t rocked my foundation, it was completely unbelievable. Couldn't believe how naive I'd been for so long. Suddenly I have a void where I used to have a family history and relatives.'[47] Another reports being forced, abruptly and involuntarily, to relinquish her self-conception as the 'biological product of both her parents'.[48] And others describe revelations during medical consultations when it transpired family medical histories did not apply to them.[49] Some describe their experiences explicitly in the language of identity. One individual recalls being 'shocked and surprised. The knowledge presented a whole new way of viewing myself in terms of identity.'[50] Some describe becoming depressed having 'discovered' they were no longer 'the person I thought I was'[51] or being angry because they no longer knew who they were.[52] Others talk of challenges in making sense of their own characteristics. For example, one person expresses the regret, 'I don't know who my dad is, who I am when I look in the mirror, where my son got his cleft chin from'.[53]

---

[42] Zadeh et al. 2018, p. 1101.

[43] Golombok 2017. Cf. Mahlstedt et al. 2010 found no straightforward correlation between age and experience of discovery. Lucy Frith and her co-authors have also suggested that early disclosure does not necessarily eradicate all difficulties people have in adjusting to the knowledge (Frith et al. 2018a).

[44] Beeson et al. 2011; Turner and Coyle 2000.

[45] Frith et al. 2018b, p. 194.

[46] Turner and Coyle 2000, p. 2045.

[47] Frith et al. 2018a, p. 177.

[48] Turner and Coyle 2000, p. 2045.

[49] Frith et al. 2018b.

[50] Frith et al. 2018a, p. 177.

[51] Kirkman 2003, p. 2229.

[52] Hewitt 2002, p. 3.

[53] Frith et al. 2018a, p. 177.

Not all experiences of disclosure in adolescence or adulthood are negative. Some individuals report curiosity or joy upon learning of their donor conception.[54] Some are excited to gain a new living 'parent'.[55] And, many welcome what they see as explanations for differences in familial characteristics, feelings of non-belonging, or family tensions – of the kinds described above.[56] For example, one individual says that it 'explained so many unanswered questions I had [and] resolved a fog of confusion'.[57] Another one recalls that '[t]he shock made me extremely emotional and I cried a lot. I also felt relief in knowing that I was not imagining things when I felt as though I were different from my parents.'[58] As this illustrates, it is not uncommon for those who learn of their donor origins in their teens or adulthood to describe a mixture of positive and negative reactions – often shock and disorientation upon discovery, followed by feeling 'liberated' or 'relieved'.[59] Here too, participants frequently talk in terms of identity. Several participants in one study describe having to 'reappraise' their identities, framing this as a positive opportunity.[60] A participant in another study describes '[t]he sense of relief of finally having an answer to questions I hadn't vocalised was very welcome'.[61] As we will see in the next subsection, it is often necessary to distinguish between the initial experiences and impacts of learning new information and subsequent experiences of living with the knowledge.

What Is It Like to Live with the Knowledge?

As already noted, longitudinal studies have found no differences in psychological well-being or adjustment between children and young adolescents in disclosing and non-disclosing families, leading researchers to conclude that sheer fact of being, and knowing about being, donor-conceived 'does not create significant difficulties' in these age groups.[62] However, some 'consistent and meaningful' differences emerge when comparisons are made by age of discovery.[63] Disclosure during

---

[54] Hewitt 2002; Nuffield Council on Bioethics 2013.
[55] Jadva et al. 2009; Kirkman 2003.
[56] Blyth 2012.
[57] Kirkman 2003, p. 2229.
[58] Frith et al. 2018a, p. 177.
[59] Kirkman 2003; Turner and Coyle 2000, pp. 2044, 2045.
[60] Turner and Coyle 2000, p. 2045.
[61] Frith et al. 2018a, pp. 176–7.
[62] Freeman and Golombok 2012, p. 202; Ilioi et al. 2017.
[63] Ilioi et al. 2017, p. 322.

childhood is generally followed by unproblematic accommodation of the knowledge.[64] Parents report children being 'comfortable' or 'unfazed'.[65] Those told before they were seven display higher levels of well-being, often associated with better family relationships.[66] And most adolescents in the UK Longitudinal Study of Assisted Reproduction Families reported feeling indifferent about being donor-conceived, though some found it 'cool' or 'interesting'.[67]

For those that learn of their donor origins for the first time in adolescence or adulthood, anger or confusion may persist, even after any initial shock has passed.[68] For some, this involves negative feelings about *being* donor-conceived.[69] For example, one participant refers to it as a 'shameful secret', albeit one they have come to terms with.[70] And another says that they 'felt like a commodity that has been commissioned ... I genuinely felt that I am different to other people'.[71] For some, their donor conception is central to how they define themselves, marking them out in positive ways, or making them feel 'special'.[72] As one research participant who 'always knew' her origins explains, '[m]y conception is who I am, it is who I will always be, it will never change. ... My hair is black, my parents divorced when I was three, I am an only child, and I was conceived through DI [donor insemination].'[73] However, donor conception sometimes plays no part in someone's self-characterisation, as is the case for the individual who reports, 'I am no different than any other person. How we are born does not make us who we are. I do not define myself by that trait.'[74]

Some kinds of reported identity impacts may be distinguished from the bald adoption or loss of particular labels. Several studies observe that later discovery can precipitate a kind of 'identity crisis', challenging or replacing someone's existing sense of themselves or leaving them feeling as if their identities are incomplete or now contain irreconcilable

---

[64] Ilioi et al. 2017.
[65] Nuffield Council on Bioethics 2013, p. 56.
[66] Ilioi et al. 2017.
[67] Zadeh et al. 2018, p. 1101.
[68] Beeson et al. 2011.
[69] Jadva et al. 2009.
[70] Frith et al. 2018b, p. 194.
[71] Hewitt 2002, p. 4.
[72] Hewitt 2002, p. 3; Nuffield Council on Bioethics 2013.
[73] Kirkman 2003, p. 2238.
[74] Jadva et al. 2009, p. 1913.

elements.[75] Maggie Kirkman notes that some participants in her study report difficulties reconstructing a satisfying sense of who they are.[76] Lucy Frith and her co-authors encounter similar findings, with participants recalling that they 'found it very hard to come to terms with. It's like a whole half of who I am and my history is just missing', or that '[t]he knowledge presented a whole new way of viewing myself in terms of identity, now having to incorporate the fact that one half of my genetic background was unknown to me'.[77]

However, Frith and colleagues also report a contrasting experience of discovering donor-conception, in which participants describe this knowledge as bringing together disparate parts of their biographies, 'enabling a more coherent narrative to be formed'.[78] Even when discovery is disruptive or distressing, many individuals nevertheless report welcoming the information because it provides a 'better sense' of who they are or explains disparities in appearances or family tensions.[79] This is illustrated by one respondent who explains, '[i]t made sense of my life so far. I was aware that things had not always made sense before I was told. So decisions my parents had made became understandable. It hugely impacted my sense of my own identity and my feelings of self-worth.'[80] And another says, 'I feel that this explained huge parts of my life which seemed somehow wrong but I had no idea why … [it was] a huge adjustment in my personal feeling of identity, overall positive'.[81]

For many, the significance of knowing about their donor conception lies in the impact it has on their family relationships. Reconfigured family relationships are experienced in both positive and negative ways. For some, knowing about their conception helps them locate their own beginnings in the circumstances and choices of their parents and gamete donors and understand how their own story began. This is illustrated by a Donor Sibling Registry member who says, 'who wants to start a book on Chapter 2? I want Chapter 1, the Introduction and the Prologue as well!'[82]

Several studies have observed that openness about donor conception can enhance relationships, for example, by cementing trust or by

---

[75] Frith et al. 2018b, p. 194; Turner and Coyle 2000.
[76] Kirkman 2003.
[77] Frith et al. 2018a, p. 177.
[78] Frith et al. 2018a, p. 176.
[79] Blyth 2012; Frith et al. 2018a, pp. 176, 178; Kirkman 2003.
[80] Frith et al. 2018a, p. 176.
[81] Frith et al. 2018a, pp. 176–8.
[82] Ravelingien et al. 2013, p. 259.

providing a 'special bond' in ways that bring a family closer together.[83] In contrast, enduring anger amongst individuals who learn they are donor-conceived in their later teens or adulthood is sometimes directed at parents who are regarded as having lied or prioritised other family members' needs.[84] Some describe their relationships with their parents as permanently damaged.[85] Trust between parents and offspring may be a casualty of later disclosure.[86] Mothers attract a considerable proportion of blame and mistrust, often being viewed, perhaps unfairly, as being chiefly responsible for concealing, disclosing, and discussing this information.[87]

Several studies report participants' feelings of loss and grief at having to relinquish previously assumed relationships or heritage,[88] as illustrated by the respondent quoted above who talks of 'a void' where family connections had once been.[89] However, others describe relief upon learning that they are not genetically related to a parent towards whom they feel antipathy or disconnection.[90] For example, one individual recalls, '[m]y father and I never had a bond really ... In some ways I got some closure from learning the truth because I could finally see that we didn't have a bond for a reason and not because of something I had done wrong.'[91]

Relationships with extended family may also suffer for a number of reasons, including donor-conceived individuals' fears of rejection.[92] Some also inherit the burden of concealing their conception, as illustrated by a research participant who says, '[i]t made me feel distanced from my father's family as I wasn't sure if they would still think of me in the same way if they knew that we weren't genetically related'.[93] These dilemmas and concerns may have intergenerational reverberations – as one respondent reports, 'I feel sorry for my children because they are deprived of a grandparent. I'm also reluctant to discuss my genetic background with them and that perpetuates the secrecy of my

---

[83] Hewitt 2002, p. 3; Ilioi et al. 2017; Scheib et al. 2003.
[84] Frith et al. 2018b.
[85] Hewitt 2002; Kirkman 2003.
[86] Blyth 2012; Turner and Coyle 2000.
[87] Frith et al. 2018b.
[88] Beeson et al. 2011; Blyth 2012.
[89] Blyth 2012; Frith et al. 2018, p. 177.
[90] Beeson et al. 2011; Jadva et al. 2009; Turner and Coyle 2000.
[91] Frith et al. 2018a, p. 180.
[92] Frith et al. 2018a, p. 180.
[93] Frith et al. 2018a, pp. 180, 181.

origins.'[94] Individuals' views about family secrets may offer glimpses of their own feelings about what donor conception means for their identity, as with the respondent who says, 'I think they should know the truth (then they can care about me for me and not just the person they think I am)'.[95]

Knowing that one is donor-conceived also opens up the possibility of identifying donor relations. Some do not wish to take up this opportunity. But many donor-conceived individuals express excitement at the prospect of meeting, learning more about, or building relationships with their gamete donors or donor siblings.[96] For some, donors may be imagined as 'fantasy parents'; one individual recalls, 'I also felt excited, because it meant I might have a living "father" (my social father died when I was quite young), and half-siblings as well'.[97] Some report positive contact experiences, such as the participant who says, 'I now understand myself a lot better and I feel my four daughters have also gained a great deal from finding members of their biological grandfather's family'.[98]

The ways that individuals interpret and respond to knowledge of donor conception are themselves influenced – for better and worse – by new and changed relationships that follow discovery. Kirkman observes that parents can be important collaborators in helping donor-conceived individuals make sense of what their conception might mean for their identities.[99] However, loss of trust, damaged relationships, fears of rejection, and parents' further unwillingness to talk following disclosure may close-off precisely these kinds of collaborative opportunities.[100] It has also been suggested that having a chance to meet donors or to learn more about them can be a factor in how well donor-conceived individuals are able to reconcile knowledge of their conception with their identities.[101] Similarly, people report valuing opportunities to share experiences with donor siblings.[102] However, for regulatory, practical, or personal reasons, hopes of contacting donors or donor siblings may not always be realisable. And contact is not always a positive experience.[103]

---

[94] Frith et al. 2018a, pp. 180, 181, 198.
[95] Frith et al. 2018b, p. 196.
[96] Zadeh et al. 2018.
[97] Jadva et al. 2009, p. 1913.
[98] Frith et al. 2018a, p. 182.
[99] Kirkman 2003.
[100] Kirkman 2003.
[101] Blyth 2012; Ravelingien et al. 2013.
[102] Kirkman 2004.
[103] Freeman 2015.

Despite the varied, deeply personal, and sometimes distressing nature of the experiences described above, one finding is particularly striking – several studies indicate a widespread *preference for knowing* that is not straightforwardly correlated with positive experiences of disclosure. For example, in one relatively large study, only 1 per cent of participants said that they wished that they had not found out.[104] Another smaller study found that '[w]ithout exception participants who are adult offspring of donor-assisted conception argued the necessity of developing an identity that accurately reflected their conception'.[105] One such participant reports that despite having to 'redevelop' her sense of identity, she is glad to have found out because 'truth is always better'.[106] And participants in several studies conducted with people who found out in their teens or adult years say they wish they had found our earlier.[107] The widespread importance of knowing – and the specific relevance of this knowledge to identity – is borne out by the Nuffield Council on Bioethics' observation from their 2013 review of evidence and testimony of donor-conceived people that,

> [S]ome have expressed very strongly the view that knowledge of their biological origins, in the sense both of the truth about the circumstances of their conception and of the knowledge of their donor, is essential to both their sense of self and to their social identity: their understanding of 'who they are' and of where they fit in the world.[108]

Through the Lens of Narrative Self-constitution

What inferences can be drawn from these diverse and complex experiences to the possible roles that knowledge of donor conception might play in individuals' narratives of who they are? And what light might this shed on debates about the identity-significance of this particular kind of personal bioinformation? Over the next few paragraphs, I will start to investigate these questions, before bringing them together with lessons from two further illustrative examples at the end of this chapter.

The views reported above indicate that for many donor-conceived individuals, knowledge of their conception has marked impacts on

---

[104] Jadva et al. 2009. This study had 164 participants, recruited from a network facilitating donor and sibling contact, so those invested in knowing may be overrepresented.
[105] Kirkman 2003, p. 2238.
[106] Kirkman 2003, pp. 2229, 2230, 2238.
[107] Frith et al. 2018a; Hewitt 2002.
[108] Nuffield Council on Bioethics 2013, p. 89.

their understanding of who they are. However, they also demonstrate that these impacts are not inevitable and are not always positive. If we then look closer to examine the specific nature of these impacts, there are some signs that learning of donor-conception can instigate the acquisition or loss of particular *labels* – for example, where recipients come to think of themselves as 'being donor-conceived'. However, perhaps contrary to what one might assume, reports of straightforwad (re)labelling are not prominent amongst participants' recollections. Instead, two of the strongest themes are, first, the ways in which learning of and living with the knowledge of donor conception offers new explanatory or interpretive contexts for experiences of family life, relationships, and traits; and second, the ways that disclosure affects the relational aspects of people's accounts of who they are.

When it comes to the second of these themes, knowledge of donor conception is widely experienced as unpicking or adding new threads to the stories that individuals tell about who they are – for example, with respect to their family heritage, who they are related to, and the qualities of their relationships to others, as well as shifting the range of supporting actors and contributing editors that feature in these stories. Altered relationships are experienced as significant in their own right – as when lost heritage is mourned – but often also play a role in making recipients identity stories more or less intelligible and comfortable to inhabit and enact – for example, by explaining difficult family relationships or by making their own past appear founded on untruths. Changing relationships, such as loss of trust in parents or subsequent contact with donor siblings, are experienced as having consequent effects upon individuals' abilities to make sense of who they are, by removing or introducing opportunities to discuss and reconcile their feelings with significant others. This then often plays into their onward relational and dialogical construction of comfortable, coherent self-narratives in which the fact of their donor-conception may variously play a significant part, or little or no part.

These indications of the relational construction of more – or less – intelligible and comfortable self-narratives point to the wider (re)interpretive and explanatory roles that knowledge of donor conception can play. Here, we may recall the cluster of claims about the narrative importance of knowing about one's genetic parentage introduced in Chapter 2. Several of the personal experiences cited above, particularly with respect to explanations of anomalous traits or feelings of not-belonging, lend weight to Sarah Wilson's suggestion that information about genetic parentage is valuable when it helps with 'alleviation of uncertainty with respect to the past'.[109] However, the empirical findings indicate that this knowledge does not only fulfil retrospective interpretive roles but can also help make sense of contemporary occurrences and relationships. As Jamie Nelson says, understanding the 'earlier chapters of our lives' can help us 'read well what is going on in the part occurring now'.[110] The empirical findings described above similarly lend some support to David Velleman's claim that recognising similarities between ourselves and close genetic relatives can be valuable for making sense of aspects of our physical embodiment.[111] However, here again, the experiences reported indicate a wider case can be made that it is not only *acquaintance* with donor relatives that can be helpful. Simply knowing about donor conception can sometimes allow individuals to locate themselves in their embodied and relational history. For example, knowledge of donor origins can be useful when it helps fill in the beginnings of recipients' biographies as biological beings and as members of their families, thus helping them (re)conceptualise where they stand within relationships, parental decisions about family-making, and wider family narratives. The empirical literature also provides illustrations of the roles that knowledge of donor origins can play in helping individuals align their own self-narratives with those of their parents and with their families' view of them, and to understand why these accounts have diverged. In other cases, however, these new insights may instead hinder mutual understanding and shared perspectives.

Where these explanatory, grounding, and aligning roles contribute to the internal and external coherence, comfort, and sustainability of recipients' stories of who they are, this may equip recipients better to understand and navigate their embodied lives and relationships and to engage in continued relational self-constitution. As Nelson says, seeing how our lives connect with those of others can bring 'depth and richness to the continuing story in which we participate'.[112] However, it is equally clear that for many donor-conceived individuals – particularly those who discover after childhood – knowledge of donor conception has the opposite effect. Rather than bringing coherence or richness, it upends previously valued and relatively settled or intelligible self-conceptions, resulting in what Eric Blyth calls 'disjunctions in [recipients']

---

[109] Wilson 1997, p. 285.
[110] Nelson 1992, p. 81.
[111] Velleman 2008.
[112] Nelson 1992, p. 81.

biographies'.[113] As Frith and her co-authors observe of some of their participants, 'the knowledge they were donor-conceived came as a complete surprise and did not fit any previous sense of biography and therefore challenged their sense of identity'.[114] The 'challenge' here may take a number of forms including loss of previously valued threads of self-characterisation, or the introduction of a 'competing' narrative in which central beliefs have been replaced with new, unfamiliar, or unwelcome ones.[115] The above recollections also indicate the particular distress that can arise from occupying a self-narrative that is at odds with others' views of who one is – for example, family members who do not know about one's conception. Thinking about these harms in narrative terms – as arising from disjunction and external incoherence – is consistent with indications that disclosure is less likely to cause distress when it occurs in early childhood, when individuals have the opportunity to develop identity narratives consistent with their donor origins from the start and in ways that are also in harmony with wider family narratives.[116]

It is apparent that the disruptive impacts of late disclosure can have serious and enduring impacts, with some individuals reporting that they have been unable to reconstruct a satisfying account of who they are.[117] These negative consequences must be taken seriously. We cannot assume that personal bioinformation is always beneficial to our self-narratives. However, the experiences reported in the empirical literature, coupled with a narrative analysis, also offer a valuable insight into the possibility that distressing identity *disruption* and identity *detriment* are not necessarily synonymous or coextensive. Freeman, who has herself conducted research with donor-conceived individuals, cautions that '[a]n absence of evidence of psychological "harm" should not be equated with an absence of evidence of psychological "wrong". Conversely, a negative outcome cannot necessarily be equated with a "wrong".'[118] We could substitute 'identity' for 'psychological' here while also further characterising the nature of the wrong involved. When identity is seen as constituted by a responsive, evolving, diachronic narrative, we can understand how the possibilities for identity impacts extend beyond the bald options of preservation or destruction. We can also appreciate why it is important

---

[113] Blyth 2012, p. 10.
[114] Frith et al. 2018a, p. 177.
[115] Frith et al. 2018a, p.177.
[116] Freeman 2014.
[117] Kirkman 2003.
[118] Freeman 2015, p. 60.

to distinguish between experiences of *discovery* and those of living with or without the information. A narrative perspective allows us to recognise that initial disruption, even of a profound and painful kind, may sometimes be resolved into – or even serve – a longer-term identity benefit in terms of narrative intelligibility and resilience. For example, this may be the case where, despite initial distress, someone comes to value the opportunity to re-evaluate and adjust their account of who they are, now equipped with fresh insights into their parents' choices or inherited traits. Conversely, we can understand how non-disclosure could place the *future* comfort and coherence of someone's self-narrative in a vulnerable position of probable, non-trivial jeopardy from late discovery, even when the prior state of 'not knowing' is not itself distressing.

I want to suggest that the kind of latent harm characterised in this last scenario lies in the construction of what Kirkman terms a 'misleading identity', based on ignorance of donor origins.[119] It might reasonably be objected that there are infinite facts about our lives of which we are unaware without being *misled* about who we are.[120] However, in this respect, ignorance of donor conception differs – not because this knowledge is intrinsically essential to our identities but because, where it is the norm for one's social parents also to be one's genetic ones, and in the absence of information to the contrary, most people would assume this is true of their family.[121] In the case of donor-conceived individuals, this assumption would be, at least partly, false. And, as noted in the previous chapter, it is the risk of building one's identity around an unrecognised false belief, rather than the omission of particular facts, that is the relevant potential source of identity harm here.[122] The ethical dimension of this difference comes into sharp focus when we think of our identity narratives as the interpretive frameworks on which we depend for making sense of and navigating our practical lives, frameworks that could serve us poorly if premised on falsehoods.

Before closing this exploration of reported experiences through the lens of narrativity, I want briefly to return to respond to worries that the kind of identity significance I am positing here is after all synonymous with an essentialised view of identity. My intention here is not to claim that knowledge of our genetic parentage is essential to a 'complete' or

---

[119] Kirkman 2003, p. 2238.
[120] de Melo-Martín 2014.
[121] Shaw 2006.
[122] Lillehammer 2014.

'true' identity. As the Nuffield Council is careful to point out, when donor-conceived individuals invest knowledge of their conception with identity significance, this cannot automatically be read in geneticised terms, '[i]t should be understood, rather, much more broadly in terms of their own story, including their biography, background and family connections'.[123] This highlights an important and subtle point – that a useful and necessary distinction can be drawn between identity-significance that *tracks* genetic connections and identity-significance that is *reducible* to genetic heritage. For example, when research participants report welcoming knowledge of their conception because it allows them to make sense of discrepancies between family traits, this does not necessarily mean that they take inherited characteristics as wholly defining who they are. Rather, it may signal that they welcome the opportunity to understand how these traits fit into a story that starts in a particular way and incorporates various kinds of relationships to and commonalities with others. They value the fresh perspective, on their lives and characteristics, provided by this knowledge and the ways in which, in Velleman's terms, this 'encode[s] one's appreciation of meaning in the events of one's life'.[124] As Maggie Kirkman observes, in applying a narrative framing to the findings from her own empirical research, '[f]amily stories of birth and conception, stories of "how our family came to be", are fundamental to the idea of narrative identity'.[125]

As to the many expressions of a desire to know 'the truth' – some participants might indeed mean the truth about 'who they really are', with all the genetic essentialism this implies. However, again, such a desire need not be intended or interpreted in this way, but rather as a wish to understand the circumstances in which their life and family relationships came to be, or the wish not be left in the dark – much less deceived – about these aspects of their biography. Interpretation of donor-conceived individuals' experiences through the lens of narrative self-constitution can help us make sense of this significance without recourse to essentialism. We need neither assume essentialism is present in the attitudes of donor-conceived individuals nor utilise this as an explanatory tool ourselves. Before I can attempt to draw wider conclusions about the generalisability of the analysis offered here to other categories of personal bioinformation, or consider which refinements

---

[123]   Nuffield Council on Bioethics 2013, p. 14.
[124]   Velleman 2005, p. 375.
[125]   Kirkman 2003, p. 2231.

might be required to the conceptual and normative picture drawn in the previous chapter, I want to look to two further illustrative examples.

5.3 Illustrative Example II: Encounters with Genetic Risk

What Kind of Bioinformation?

This second illustrative example looks at findings from empirical studies reporting individuals' expectations of and reactions to receiving results from genetic testing for susceptibility to serious, complex disorders. The two kinds of tests to be looked at here are those for variants of the Apolipoprotein E (*APOE*) gene associated with an elevated risk of late-onset Alzheimer's disease and tests for genetic mutations on the *BRCA1* and *BRCA2* genes associated with higher risks of breast and ovarian cancers. The E4 variant of the *APOE* gene is believed to be a 'robust risk factor' for late-onset Alzheimer's disease in some populations.[126] The *BRCA* mutations are responsible for significantly elevated lifetime risk of developing hereditary forms of breast and ovarian cancer in female carriers and breast and prostate cancer in men.[127] Both late-onset Alzheimer's disease and breast and ovarian cancers are multifactorial disorders, meaning they are not caused by a single gene but by inter-actions between multiple genetic and environmental factors. They may also occur in the absence of the genetic variants in question. So a 'positive' result – indicating that the person tested is a carrier of the variant associated with higher susceptibility – provides an estimate of an indi-vidual's predisposition to the disease, rather than being straightforwardly predictive.[128] And a negative test result does not rule out risk. As in the previous example, before turning to people's experiences, I will review the current availability of *APOE* and *BRCA* testing in the UK, bearing in mind that this sits within the wider landscape of access entitlements reviewed in Chapter 2.

---

[126] Having one copy Ɛ4 variant of the *APOE* gene is thought to increase the risk of Alzheimer's disease to about three times that of the general population, while two copies increase the risk between eight and thirty times. There is variation in the association between the Ɛ4 allele and late-onset Alzheimer's in different ethnic groups (Farrer et al., 1997).

[127] A previously unaffected woman testing positive as a carrier of the *BRCA1* mutation has a 60–90 per cent lifetime risk of developing breast cancer and a 40–60 per cent lifetime risk of developing ovarian cancer, compared with a general population risk of 12.5 per cent for breast and 2 per cent for ovarian cancer (The Royal Marsden NHS Foundation Trust, 2016).

[128] A *BRCA*-positive result is more strongly predictive than one for relevant *APOE* variants.

There are ongoing clinical and ethical debates about the relative harms and benefits of – and thus justifications for – offering genetic testing for serious multifactorial conditions, particularly if there are no effective preventative or therapeutic options or where there are risks of over-diagnosis. These debates have traditionally focused on clinical action-ability as the chief desideratum. And there are long-standing assumptions that uncertainty – for example, arising from probabilistic findings or unclear prognoses – is likely to cause psychological distress, which may be both greater and harder to justify in the absence of therapeutic options.[129] A central aim of this project is to demonstrate that treating the ethical considerations relevant to such decisions solely in terms of a balance between clinical utility, physical harm, and psycho-logical distress is to work with an incomplete ethical palette. This second illustrative example offers an opportunity to explore whether identity should be part of the picture when instituting genetic screening policies – not only part of subsequent approaches in genetic counselling – and also to contribute to the conceptual and ethical debates about the identity-related impacts of genetic testing introduced in Chapter 2.

In accordance with National Institute for Health and Care Excellence (NICE) guidelines, *BRCA* screening in the UK is offered only to adults with a family history of breast or ovarian cancer and a genetic relative who has tested positive for a *BRCA* mutation.[130] These cancers are sometimes treatable, and surveillance and preventative interventions, such as prophy-lactic surgery, may be available to those testing positive.[131] By comparison, *APOE* testing has relatively low predictive strength, and there are no effective preventative measures or treatments available for Alzheimer's disease.[132] Clinicians and Alzheimer's advocacy groups, therefore, recom-mend against provision of *APOE* testing altogether.[133] However, as noted

---

[129] Parens and Appelbaum 2019.

[130] *Guidelines: Familial Breast Cancer: Classification and Care of People at Risk of Familial Breast Cancer and Management of Breast Cancer and Related Risks in People with a Family History of Breast Cancer (Cg164)* (National Institute for Health and Care Excellence, 2013, updated 2019).

[131] *Guidelines: Familial Breast Cancer: Classification and Care of People at Risk of Familial Breast Cancer and Management of Breast Cancer and Related Risks in People with a Family History of Breast Cancer (Cg164)* (National Institute for Health and Care Excellence, 2013, updated 2019).

[132] Atkins and Panegyres 2011.

[133] Alzheimer's Research UK, 'Genes and Dementia' (2014); Alzheimer's Society website, 'Genetic Testing', www.alzheimers.org.uk/info/20091/what_we_think/153/genetic_test ing (accessed 18 July 2021).

in Chapter 2, tests for both *APOE* and *BRCA* mutations are available, without restriction, through DTC genomic services.[134] Two further key routes by which someone might find out their carrier status for particular genetic variants are through individual findings from genomic research or from the status of close genetic relatives. Clinical actionability and the seriousness of the condition are likely to be key to professional and legal decisions about the requirement to communicate risk findings in each of these circumstances. So, while it is not possible to say definitively, it is somewhat more likely that someone might learn of *BRCA*-positive status than of *APOE*-related Alzheimer's risk in research contexts or from family members. Of course those tested may share their results with family members without this being a legal obligation or on the advice of a clinician.

The views discussed below are drawn from published social science studies that used a range of methodologies to investigate the attitudes and reactions of individuals to the prospect or experience of receiving susceptibility estimates based on genetic testing. Most of these studies collected data on some combination of psychological, social, and behavioural effects. The views of *APOE* testing for Alzheimer's susceptibility discussed below are chiefly drawn from the US-based REVEAL study.[135] The phases of this large, longitudinal study discussed here comprised a series of randomised clinical trials involving asymptomatic adults with first-degree relatives with late-onset Alzheimer's disease.[136] The study aimed, inter alia, to investigate the psychological and behavioural effects of receiving genetics-based risk estimates for Alzheimer's from tests conducted as part of the study and the effectiveness of different genetic counselling approaches.[137] The findings relating to *BRCA* testing for susceptibility to breast and ovarian cancer discussed here come from a wider range of, often smaller, studies and from systematic reviews. All the participants were women, some with prior cancer diagnoses, who had undergone *BRCA* testing in clinical settings. Most of these studies did not set out to investigate identity-related effects directly. Limitations of these sources for my current purposes include over-representation amongst participants of people willing to undergo testing and a lack of socio-economic and ethnic diversity.[138] There are also possible pitfalls in

---

[134] See, for example, '23andMe Genetic Health Risk Reports: What you should know' www .23andme.com/en-gb/test-info/genetic-health (accessed 18 July 2021).

[135] Roberts et al. 2005.

[136] Roberts 2012.

[137] Roberts et al. 2011.

[138] Roberts et al. 2011.

attempting to generalise from findings relating to particular tests for susceptibility to conditions with particular characteristics.[139] The inclusion of views about both *APOE* and *BRCA* testing will go some way to mapping possible points of commonality and divergence.

Information Subjects' Experiences

In the following sections, I bring together findings that plausibly speak to the impacts of test results on recipients' identity narratives, dividing the findings into two parts. The first will look at the expectations and motivations of participants who have not yet received test results or are recalling their feelings prior to receipt. The second will review reactions to encounters with test results and subsequent experiences and behaviours. This division will allow reflection on the extent to which actual impacts of tests results match people's expectations. I will return in the next chapter to consider the reasons behind divergences in people's attitudes and reactions to different types of testing.

Motivations and Expectations

Many participants in REVEAL report that their motivation for taking part in the study was a bald desire to know their risk status and many felt broadly positive about this prospect.[140] All REVEAL participants had a family history of Alzheimer's.[141] Several report that because of their family history, they were 'scared to death' that they were 'already doomed' to a future with the disease or feared they were already exhibiting signs of impaired memory.[142] Many view genetic testing as a possible means of coping with or taking control of a suspected, though unquantified, risk of inherited disease by confirming or dispelling such fears.[143] One motive commonly cited is to 'put my mind at ease'.[144] Others report the hope that knowledge will equip them with a kind of power, even in the absence of effective preventative or treatment options.[145] For some, the sheer act of participating in the REVEAL study offers a sense of purpose and way of dealing with

---

[139] Wade2019.
[140] Hurley et al. 2005.
[141] Roberts et al. 2005.
[142] Hurley et al. 2005, p. 379.
[143] Lock 2008.
[144] Christensen et al. 2011, p. 412.
[145] Gooding et al. 2006.

uncertainty.[146] Mitigating uncertainty similarly emerges as a common theme amongst motivations for *BRCA* testing, with participants in one study reporting that 'knowing gives you more control', and 'the more I know, the more I can help myself'.[147] A participant in another study, who had a history of breast cancer but had not had prophylactic surgery, explains that 'obviously I hope I'm negative. But I'd much rather live with the knowledge of knowing that I'm positive and that I'm doing everything I can to give myself the best chance, than to live with uncertainty.'[148] It has been suggested that even when someone knows they have a family history of cancer or Alzheimer's, they may nevertheless look to genetic testing for a source of 'credible' information, with the authority to overturn or confirm their assumptions.[149] However, as we will see below, reality may be more complicated than this.

Many participants in REVEAL anticipate that their personal risk estimates will be of practical use.[150] Some of this anticipated utility is directly health-related, for example where it was hoped that test results will open avenues to specialist health advice or act as incentives to take up behaviours purported to be protective.[151] And some want to be prepared in case genuinely effective preventive or therapeutic interventions for Alzheimer's become available.[152] Practical motivations also extend beyond health protection. REVEAL participants talk in terms of 'getting things in order', where these 'things' include personal and financial affairs, for example purchasing long-term care insurance.[153] Holly Gooding and her co-authors report that the most common reason given by participants for pursuing genetic testing was to 'better plan for other problem-focused coping efforts, like financial planning and completing advance directives. This focus on taking concrete actions may help people exert some sense of control over an uncontrollable disease like AD.'[154]

Some REVEAL participants cite less specific, but nonetheless future-focused, reasons. One participant says if she was to learn that she was at high risk of Alzheimer's, '[t]here are some things that I haven't done that

---

[146] Hurley et al. 2005; Lynch et al. 2006.

[147] d'Agincourt-Canning 2006, pp. 104–105.

[148] Hallowell et al. 2004, p. 558.

[149] Roberts and Uhlmann 2013, p. 1225.

[150] Hurley et al. 2005.

[151] Hurley et al. 2005.

[152] Roberts et al. 2003.

[153] Gooding et al. 2006, p. 264; Hurley et al. 2005.

[154] Gooding et al. 2006, p. 265. AD refers here to Alzheimer's disease.

I might want to start doing'.[155] Meanwhile, others are motivated by opportunities for reflection or reprioritisation. For example, one participant reports that the information could be useful for 'see[ing] where I am at', and another wonders, 'maybe it will make me look at my life in a different way'.[156] Nina Hallowell and her co-authors observe, that for the most part, participants in their study with existing cancer diagnoses were less motivated by planning for their future health than understanding their past.[157] A substantial number report seeking testing to obtain 'an explanation for why they had developed cancer'.[158]

Another prominent theme amongst participants' motivations is obtaining susceptibility information for the direct benefit of others or to inform their own other-affecting decisions. Many in the REVEAL study report seeking *APOE* testing because of their feelings of responsibility for or commonality with family members who had experienced Alzheimer's or who could be at risk.[159] The desire to prepare family members for future caring responsibilities and financial burdens was another significant motivator amongst REVEAL participants.[160] It has been suggested that female participants were more likely to want to know their susceptibility because of their experiences of caring for affected relatives.[161]

Similar altruistic or relational aims were evident in the context of *BRCA* testing, where individuals talk about seeking testing to help close relatives or to contribute to research.[162] Lori d'Agincourt-Canning notes that participants in her own study 'did not view their decision to seek [*BRCA*] testing in isolation from everyone else. Rather, obtaining genetic information allowed them to express their identity as embodied selves as well as selves-in-relation.'[163] Hallowell and her co-authors observe that all thirty participants in their study said that they sought testing to provide family members with information to help plan their futures. Enactment of relational roles and concerns is also indicated by the age at which *BRCA* testing is sought, with one study finding that participants were more likely to seek testing around the age their mothers were

---

155   Hurley et al. 2005, p. 378.
156   Hurley et al. 2005, p. 378.
157   Hallowell et al. 2004.
158   Hallowell et al. 2004, p. 558.
159   Lock 2008.
160   Chilibeck et al. 2011.
161   Roberts et al. 2003.
162   Foster et al. 2009; Hallowell et al. 2003.
163   d'Agincourt-Canning 2006, p. 113.

diagnosed.[164] This study also found that being a parent was associated with earlier testing.[165] Responsibility for relatives is similarly present in choices *not* to be tested, with participants worried that their own positive result might make their family members feel, in one participant's words, 'almost like a person who's been diagnosed'.[166]

A wish to contribute to Alzheimer's research emerges strongly amongst REVEAL interviewees, with many citing the desire to reciprocate indirectly for the care that their relatives had received or to express solidarity with other affected families as their reasons for participating.[167] Similar motivations have been observed in those undergoing *BRCA* testing. D'Agincourt Canning argues that decisions about being tested are not motivated by solipsistic concerns but rather call upon the individual to exercise the moral aspects of their identity.[168] These observations echo findings about motivations for taking part in medical research more generally, in which individuals may characterise participation as an expression of their moral values, where the values expressed might include, for example, concern for the wellbeing of specific family members or the desire to support scientific knowledge as a broader, public good.[169]

The nature of the studies reviewed here means that they disproportionately represent the views of those willing, even keen, to be tested. However, less enthusiastic attitudes do also emerge. Some REVEAL participants declined to be tested on the grounds they believed they would not benefit from or cope well with the findings. For example, one participant worries that the test results would drive them 'crazy' and that 'sometimes a little knowledge is too much'.[170] While another says, 'I don't want any more bad information. This is all I can handle. And I'm healthy, so I'm all set.'[171] Similar reasons for declining testing are also evident in *BRCA*-focused studies.[172] For example, one participant worries 'cancer [would then become] this consuming thing in your life'.[173] In

---

[164] Hesse-Biber and An 2016.
[165] Hesse-Biber and An 2016.
[166] d'Agincourt-Canning 2006, p.111.
[167] Christensen et al. 2011; Hurley et al. 2005.
[168] d'Agincourt-Canning 2006.
[169] See Hallowell et al. 2010.
[170] Gooding et al. 2006, p. 264.
[171] Gooding et al. 2006, p. 264.
[172] d'Agincourt-Canning 2006.
[173] d'Agincourt-Canning 2006, p. 110.

another study, participants were sceptical that available clinical options would compensate for the anxiety of being tested.[174]

Reactions and Responses

Between being asked about their motivations and receiving their test results, REVEAL participants underwent counselling and education about *APOE* testing that highlighted the weak predictive strength of the tests and the multifactorial nature of Alzheimer's risk.[175] This may partially explain a prominent finding of a 'slight discordance' between how participants expected they would respond to learning of their risk of Alzheimer's and how they actually reacted.[176] The most noted aspect of this discrepancy is that in many cases – contrary to participants' expectations – test results failed to supplant their prior perceptions of their inherited risk or to provide an end to uncertainty.[177] Some participants discounted the evidence of their low risk estimates. For example, one interviewee is reported as saying, '[s]o technically I should feel better. But I don't believe it.'[178] Some who had received high risk estimates reacted with equanimity, viewing their results as 'nothing new' to worry about.[179] Accurate recall of results was also patchy. Even where participants could recall which *APOE* variant they carried, many could not explain its risk significance.[180] The educational materials and counselling received by REVEAL participants are thought to have contributed to tempering reactions to results.[181] In addition, Gillian Chilibeck and colleagues suggest recipients' lay beliefs about the causes and nature of Alzheimer's were often 'actively mobilized' to help make sense of the science.[182] As Margaret Lock describes it, '[r]isk estimates provided in the REVEAL study rarely displace "lay knowledge" that participants bring with them ….. Rather this "scientific" information is either nested into pre-existing knowledge, simply forgotten, or even actively rejected.'[183]

---

[174] Esplen et al. 2009.

[175] Christensen et al. 2011. Participants were divided into groups, each of which received counselling and education materials of varying degrees of detail.

[176] Christensen et al. 2011, p. 413.

[177] Lock et al. 2006.

[178] Lock et al. 2006, p. 292.

[179] Lock et al. 2006, p. 292.

[180] Eckert et al. 2006. For example, only around half of the participants remembered the general gist of their risk estimate after a year.

[181] Christensen et al. 2011.

[182] Chilibeck et al. 2011, p. 1771.

[183] Lock 2008, p. 75.

The personal significance of the *APOE*-based risk estimates was not, however, totally obviated, as discussed below.[184]

There are similar indications that existing beliefs about cancer risk can prove resistant to new information. For example, some recipients' presumptions of being at high risk persisted despite negative *BRCA* results.[185] And others continued to feel vulnerable in their liminal 'lower risk' status – neither eligible for follow-up screening nor wholly free from risk.[186] Hallowell and her co-authors report that amongst most of their participants, all of whom had existing diagnoses, *BRCA* test results had little impact on perception of their risk or existing sense of fatalism about future health.[187] These authors also observe that 'the majority of women in [our] study were able to accommodate the information that they are/may be at genetic risk of cancer into their biography and maintain their forward trajectory'.[188]

When it comes to practical and behavioural responses to receiving test results, REVEAL participants again described making fewer changes than they had anticipated.[189] Results indicating elevated risk did prompt some to purchase or change their long-term care insurance or adopt what they perceived to be protective health behaviours.[190] In contrast – perhaps unsurprisingly, given greater availability of risk-reducing interventions – receipt of positive *BRCA* tests often led to behavioural changes including increased uptake of prophylactic surgery and screening or lifestyle adjustments, such as changed diet or smoking cessation.[191] Perhaps more surprisingly, these changes were not limited to those found to be *BRCA*-positive.[192] One study found that variability amongst women choosing to pursue screening or surgery depended more on personal circumstances, such as feelings of guilt or vulnerability and availability of social support, than on sheer facts about their health.[193]

One of the headline conclusions from the REVEAL study is that the long-held assumption that probabilistic susceptibility testing will cause distress and anxiety, particularly in the absence of clinical options, was

---

[184] Christensen et al. 2011.
[185] Roberts 2012.
[186] Scott et al. 2005.
[187] Hallowell et al. 2004.
[188] Hallowell et al. 2004, p. 560.
[189] Christensen et al. 2011.
[190] Gooding et al. 2006; Roberts 2012.
[191] Lim et al. 2004; Lynch et al. 2006.
[192] Heshka et al. 2008.
[193] Hesse-Biber and An 2016, p. 987.

not substantiated by the findings.[194] Many participants – not only those at low risk of Alzheimer's – reported relief and reduced distress.[195] Studies looking at *BRCA* testing have reported similar findings. For example, one found 'a generally low level of potential distress' and an 'overwhelming positive attitude toward genetic testing'.[196] Perhaps surprisingly, several studies have noted a lack of straightforward correlations between positive test results for *BRCA* and distress, or negative results and relief.[197] Though increased levels of distress or anxiety and 'turmoil' were commonly observed at the time of *APOE* and *BRCA* testing itself, this was seen to dissipate, with few suffering enduring psychological harm.[198] One large review looking at the psychological impacts of receiving genetic information about diverse kinds of disease risk concludes that negative reactions are, on the whole, minor and transient, while nevertheless cautioning that more serious negative psychological reactions, though rare, should not be ignored.[199]

It would be a mistake to assume that all notable reactions to test results can be reduced solely to either practical risk management or distress. Many report broader changes in attitude or outlook, and often positive ones. For example, mutation-positive *BRCA* tests are described by some as 'life-changing' or leading to a 're-evaluation of priorities'.[200] Some participants are glad to know so that they can undertake 'important and positive life changes' or prepare emotionally for future changes in their health.[201] Several studies report participants who received negative *BRCA* results as experiencing relief or a 'renewed appreciation for life', or as feeling like they were finally being 'part of the normal population'.[202] Similarly, *APOE* testing was often found to facilitate what REVEAL researchers refer to as 'emotion-focused coping strategies', helping participants address uncertainty and make plans in awareness of possible risk.[203] Echoing the views expressed by donor-conceived individuals, genetic test results are frequently welcomed for the sheer knowledge they convey or are perceived as conveying. For example, one

---

[194] Roberts 2012.
[195] Christensen et al. 2020; Lock et al. 2007.
[196] Lynch et al. 2006, p. 95.
[197] Hallowell et al. 2004; Mella et al. 2017.
[198] Bemelmans et al. 2016; Lim et al. 2004, p. 129.
[199] Wade 2019.
[200] Esplen et al. 2009, p. 1217.
[201] Esplen et al. 2009, p. 1217; Lim et al. 2004, p. 129.
[202] Butow et al. 2003; Esplen et al. 2009, p. 1217; Lim et al. 2004, p. 122.
[203] Gooding et al. 2006, p. 265.

individual undergoing *BRCA* testing reported simply wanting to know 'what's going on with my body'.[204] Meanwhile, a REVEAL participant expresses the view, '[k]nowledge is power … I don't think you can necessarily change your destiny, but certainly to go through life with your eyes only half open doesn't help you at all'.[205]

However, more negative reactions are also seen. Some receiving negative *BRCA* results report feeling numb, dislocated, or guilty about having 'escaped' a threat faced by family members.[206] Meanwhile, others who had not previously considered a genetic dimension to their cancer react to positive results as if receiving a new diagnosis, finding it hard to imagine their future or come to terms with their risk status.[207] One such participant regretfully reports, 'I would much rather not know that I had the gene …. It's part of your life all the time with the gene.'[208] The researchers suggest that in these cases, 'the risks of unknown cancers are perceived as presenting an explicit threat to self'.[209] One participant in another study reports, '[s]ometimes I think of myself as *healthy, but doomed.* I don't think of myself as sick, or as a mutant, but as healthy, but on the edge, *healthy, but with a curse.* ….. It's unpleasant. It doesn't enter into everything I do – all of my functioning or everyday life – but just sort of hangs there.'[210] This kind of reaction takes on a notably concrete dimension in the context of *APOE* testing. In one study, researchers observed that despite being informed of the predictive limitations of *APOE* testing, participants who knew they had tested positive for the *APOE* genotype associated with increased risk of Alzheimer's not only underestimated their performance in memory tests but actually performed worse in them.[211]

Amongst the long-recognised, detrimental effects of receiving a positive *BRCA* test result are negative self-perceptions and stigma.[212] Some carriers report feelings of alienation or of being 'different' as a result of learning they had 'a defective or altered gene'.[213] A participant on one study describes how they feel as if '[t]here's something wrong with me that's not even physical – it's like my body or the

[204] d'Agincourt-Canning 2006, p. 106.
[205] Lock et al. 2006, p. 290.
[206] Esplen et al. 2009; Lim et al. 2004.
[207] Hallowell et al. 2004.
[208] Hallowell et al. 2004, p. 561.
[209] Hallowell et al. 2004, p. 561.
[210] Klitzman 2009, p. 884 (italics in source).
[211] Lineweaver et al. 2014.
[212] Vodermaier et al. 2010.
[213] Vodermaier et al. 2010, p. 10.

blueprints of my body don't work well'.[214] These feelings can extend to recipients' body image by, for example, undermining their confidence and trust in their bodies, causing them to see themselves as 'mutants', 'damaged goods', or reproductively 'impaired'.[215] Stigma and fatalism are not, however, universal amongst those who learn they are *BRCA* positive. For example, one research participant says, 'I don't feel I'm a "sick person". I feel I'm very healthy. I know women who say, "I have cancer". I never thought like that. I don't look at myself as being sick. I go for my check-ups, but it definitely doesn't affect my everyday life.'[216]

Recognition of the need to capture the kinds of impacts just described led one group of Canadian researchers to develop 'The *BRCA* Self-Concept Scale', a validated, evidence-based tool to be used in counselling and research that measures effects of *BRCA* testing across a number of dimensions, including self-esteem and stigma.[217] Studies using this scale are able to go beyond observations of distress amongst those testing positive to deliver more nuanced findings. For example, one study found that higher existing levels of 'self-esteem' and 'self-mastery' were associated with less anxiety upon receiving results, and that feelings of stigma were closely correlated with distress, with younger carriers experiencing higher levels of both.[218] The authors speculate this finding may be attributable to younger recipients experiencing a positive test result as derailing unrealised life goals.

Impacts on familial roles and responsibilities emerge strongly in the *BRCA*-related research, as do the parts played by familial roles in shaping the personal significance of test results. As noted above, for many, seeking testing represents a way of enacting care and responsibility for close relatives. However, for others, positive results are experienced as undermining precisely these roles.[219] For example, because of the risk of passing on the mutation, some parents felt guilt upon testing positive or as though they had failed to fulfil the role of a parent as protector of their children's well-being.[220] The effects of surgery and feelings of 'impairment' following a positive result can also impact negatively on people's feelings about parenting and reproductive choices.[221] In some contrast, researchers on

---

[214] Klitzman 2009, p. 885.
[215] Esplen et al. 2009, p. 1217; Klitzman 2009, p. 886.
[216] Klitzman 2009, p. 883.
[217] Esplen et al. 2009.
[218] Vodermaier et al. 2010.
[219] Underhill et al. 2012.
[220] Lynch et al. 2006; McConkie-Rosell and DeVellis 2000.
[221] Vodermaier et al. 2010.

the REVEAL study have suggested that genetic tests with relatively low predictive power, such as *APOE* testing, can reinforce family connections.[222] For example, some participants found it helpful to gain what they felt was an explanation of their parents' dementia.[223] And several reported being pleased that they and their children now knew 'where they stood'.[224] Others were concerned about what their future illness could mean for the caring responsibilities of family members.[225]

The contribution of positive test results to feelings of commonality with others beyond immediate family has been observed in relation to *BRCA* testing. For example, Robert Klitzman reports one participant in his study as saying, '[h]aving this gene makes me feel more female. Women have to deal with special things: having this biological clock, bleeding every month, menopause. It's not a self-pity thing, but an added female thing.'[226] Meanwhile, another says, 'I do hotline work. I don't do the Walk-a-thon, but do cancer runs – for cancer research in general, not just BC [breast cancer]. I don't look at myself as "gene-positive person". I always say "I'm a BrCa-1 carrier". I would say I'm outgoing, athletic, enjoy people, and am sensitive.'[227] Several of the participants in Klitzman's study were clear that their risk status is only 'a piece of who I am'.[228] Indeed, the reactions cited above illustrate how recipients' varied responses to their results join a constellation of interwoven characteristics which extend far beyond their health.

I will now turn to take stock of what inferences might be drawn from the attitudes and experiences described above to the possible roles played by this category of personal bioinformation in recipients' narrative accounts of who they are.

Through the Lens of Narrative Identity

Due to the nature of genetic disease, experiences of living through family illness and awareness or expectations of their own disease risk already feature prominently in the stories many of the above participants tell

---

[222] Chilibeck et al. 2011. Monica Konrad (2005) has noted that where family members learn they do not share the same risk of developing the highly penetrative, monogenic condition Huntington's disease, this can be a new source of familial divisions.

[223] Lock et al. 2006.

[224] Lock et al. 2005, p. 59.

[225] Ashida et al. 2010.

[226] Klitzman 2009, p. 886.

[227] Klitzman 2009, pp. 884, 886.

[228] Klitzman 2009, pp. 884, 886, 887.

about themselves. This means that the effects of new susceptibility information on their identities are not always immediately obvious or dramatic. That is, they do not generally involve wholesale revision of narrative contents or direction, or the imposition of specific new labels or self-descriptors. However, there are clear indications of the ways in which learning of risk status serves to cast both past and anticipated future chapters of recipients' narratives in a new interpretive light. Even when results are probabilistic and uncertain, they can help recipients make sense of their past experiences – for example, of their own illness or of caring for affected family members. And even when test results do not remove uncertainty in the ways recipients hoped they would, they often still provide recipients with impetus and assistance in thinking about how their future self-narratives might look and how they might exercise some degree of control over this. This control might involve taking steps to protect their health or their material security, preparing for health challenges to come, or rethinking their plans, priorities, and outlook.

It is clear that the impacts of test results on identity-constituting narratives are not always welcome or constructive. For some, positive test results disrupt their sense of themselves as healthy, or how they envisioned their stories would unfold. The risk of genetic disease may be experienced as threatening self-defining projects, roles, or relationships, or exacerbating uncertainty about their futures and future health. Learning they are a carrier can also change recipients' relationships with their bodies, making them feel alien or unreliable, sometimes leading to stigmatised self-conceptions or loss of a sense of agency. However, as with knowledge of donor conception, there are also indications that we should not assume that initial distress or disruption of self-perceptions always translates into longer-term identity harms. Some recipients come to accommodate their risk status in, or exclude it from, their accounts of who they are. It is also notable that it is not possible to draw a neat correlation between the ostensibly bad news of a positive test result and negative impacts on the recipients' sense of who they are. The value of susceptibility estimates often appears to lie in the explanatory power and sense of, albeit limited, control that they offer, the changes in outlook and priorities that they make possible, and their influence on the tone and comfort of recipients' self-conceptions.

As the above examples indicate, the ethically significant effects of test results on people's lives are not necessarily tied to clinical actionability or practical planning. However, it is also a mistake to think of practical undertakings as wholly separate from the business of identity development. Practical activities – for example, planning for the future security of our families – are often themselves identity-constituting, particularly where these are expressive of the values, plans, and commitments by which we characterise ourselves. Our stories of who we are constructed by what we do, not just by how we think of ourselves.

As with the discovery of donor conception, genetic susceptibility test results often affect the narrative threads comprising recipients' relationships to and concern for others. Unwelcome or unexpected results can be sources of family tensions or bonds. And familial and social responsibilities provide motivations for seeking testing. More specifically, testing and test results appear to play important parts in constituting the particular familial or social roles that make up people's stories of who they are. For example, being tested may be a way of enacting care and concern for relatives. And learning of shared, inherited genetic risk can affect the recipients' feelings about their abilities to meet behavioural and moral norms associated with fulfilling the roles of a loving parent or a responsible member of an at-risk family or community. As d'Agincourt Canning observes, 'within genetics, people might see their selves inscribed onto the lives of others'.[229]

The responses cited above also hint at the role of positive risk status in engagement with self-constituting 'biosocial' activities – those centred on biological connections and experiences of embodied commonality with others.[230] Sahra Gibbon has noted that hereditary breast cancer and being a *BRCA* carrier are particularly associated with biosociality and patient activism, such as fundraising for research or seeking to increase awareness of the disease.[231] *BRCA* activism may also intersect with other shared modes of self-definition, for example gender or ethnic identifiers. *BRCA*-related cancers occur with particular frequency in Ashkenazi Jewish populations.[232] It has been suggested that being a carrier – and what this is taken to imply about a shared history of oppression and migration – may be experienced as connecting members of Ashkenazi communities and as a 'reiteration of Jewish identity'.[233] It is not uncommon for *BRCA* campaign groups to link awareness-raising activities to shared community identity.[234]

---

[229] d'Agincourt-Canning 2006, p. 111.
[230] Rabinow 2010.
[231] Gibbon 2007.
[232] Levy-Lahad et al. 1997.
[233] Mozersky and Joseph 2010.
[234] See, for example, the Sharsheret campaign in the US https://sharsheret.org/who-we-are/ (accessed 18 July 2021).

The analysis offered over the preceding paragraphs stands in contrast to the sceptical perspective that probabilistic susceptibility testing – when contrasted with strongly predictive tests for single-gene disorders – has few, if any, noteworthy impacts on individuals' identities. This kind of view is emphatically expressed by Margaret Lock and her co-authors in their analysis of the REVEAL findings. They conclude that REVEAL participants did not experience 'anything remotely approaching a profound personal or identity change based on the test results'[235] and that 'little if any significant changes take place with respect to [their] sense of identity'.[236] I wish to suggest that these claims are not wholly borne out by findings relating to *APOE* testing, much less *BRCA* testing.

The studies discussed above do indeed indicate that distress – particularly of a clinically significant kind – is much less in evidence than it has long been assumed. It is also apparent that receipt of genetic risk information – whether positive or negative – does not necessarily lead recipients to make wholesale revisions to their prior beliefs about their susceptibility.[237] And while there are some examples of recipients adopting their risk status as a specific self-descriptor, there is little evidence that this is universal, or that it necessarily involves adoption of the kind of encompassing, illness-vigilant, responsibilised selfhood that Carlos Novas and Nikolas Rose have termed a 'risk identity'.[238] So, while it is perhaps true that those tested rarely experience seismic or wholesale changes in how they describe and present themselves, I would argue that we absolutely cannot conclude from this that genetic susceptibility testing has *no* significant identity impacts. To do so would be to adopt too narrow a conception of identity and of the kinds of identity changes that might make a difference to our lives and well-being. One of the conclusions from the REVEAL study is that information about Alzheimer's risk informed by *APOE* testing can have 'personal value' for those tested.[239] And a recent overview of systematic reviews of impacts of genetic susceptibility testing concludes that 'there are enough data showing that people are influenced by such testing, even if more subtly than is detected with many general, validated measures',[240] and that 'qualitative findings clearly demonstrate that genetic and genomic testing results can

---

[235] Lock et al. 2005, p. 58. See also, Parry 2013.
[236] Lock 2008, p. 72.
[237] Lock 2008, p. 72.
[238] Novas and Rose 2001.
[239] Roberts 2012, p. 142.
[240] Wade 2019, p. S95.

change peoples' inner lives'.[241] My suggestion is that some of this 'personal value', 'influence', and 'change' – and not only to recipients' *inner* lives but also to their *practical, moral,* and *relational* lives – can be understood in terms of the contribution of test results to recipients' identity narratives. These contributions include enhancing the coherence and depth of meaning of these narratives, for example by better equipping recipients to make sense of prior experiences of family illness or to deal with the prospect of personal, relational, and health challenges, or by leading them to feel solidarity with others similarly affected. These narrative contributions do not involve wholesale revisions or adoption of brand new social identities. Rather, they exemplify precisely the kind of interpretive and selective digestion of information that is integral to the narrative-building endeavour. And when these kinds of assimilation, adjustment, and perspectival shifts change how the recipient understands themselves, interprets the world, weighs up what matters to them, and projects themselves into their own future, they are far from trivial.

A number of researchers, working both on REVEAL and *BRCA*-related studies, note that the personal meaning and significance of test results to recipients are shaped by their family history, existing diagnoses and illness experiences, and their familial roles.[242] These observations highlight the ways in which identity development is neither linear nor monadic. It involves the weaving and reweaving of multiple threads – some of which are contributed by existing experiences and characteristics, and others of which are contributed by externally sourced information about our bodies. The reconciliation and mutual interpretation of these threads are no less important to the business of identity construction, and our interests in being able to develop and inhabit the identities we construct, than dramatic reinvention.

It should be clear that the picture of the identity significance of genetic test results offered here in no way rests upon the premise that our genetic inheritance defines who we 'really' are. As with knowledge of donor conception, we might wonder, however, whether any identity significance invested by *recipients themselves* depends on their holding geneticised beliefs about what constitutes their identities. Commentators are divided on the extent to which essentialist attitudes are evident in research participants' responses.[243] Discussing *BRCA* testing, d'Agincourt-Canning suggests that

---

[241] Wade 2019, pp. S93, S95.
[242] Chilibeck et al. 2011; d'Agincourt-Canning 2006; Hallowell et al. 2004.
[243] Parens and Appelbaum 2019.

many people's views sit somewhere between belief in the unassailable authority of genetic tests and a more 'pragmatic' perspective that recognises the limitations of these tests but also sees them as their best hope for taking control of their epistemic insecurity in the face of risk.[244] The experiences discussed above reflect this mixed picture. Some degree of deterministic thinking may be signalled by participants who report feeling doomed or like 'mutants'. However, many reject determinism – for example, by refusing to be defined by their risk or by embracing measures to take some control of their health and futures. This signals that biologically essentialist assumptions are neither prerequisite for nor a necessary consequence of experiencing test results as having identity-significance. I will return in the next chapter to consider the kinds of factors that do affect differential attributions of identity-significance. Before doing so, I will turn to my third and final illustrative example.

5.4   Illustrative Example III: Encounters with Psychiatric Neuroimaging

What Kind of Bioinformation?

With this third and final illustrative example, I move beyond genetic information to look at research participants' actual and anticipated reactions to findings derived from neuroimaging data about functional and structural features of their brains. These are findings that purport to provide insights into information subjects' mental health status. The kinds of mental health status in question here include probabilistic future risk of developing conditions such as major depressive disorder (MDD), bipolar disorder, psychosis, and schizophrenia, diagnosis of these conditions, and likely responsiveness to particular treatments or interventions.

The attitudes and experiences explored below relate chiefly to uses, or prospective uses, of data about regions of metabolic activity in the brain – treated as a proxy for brain function – obtained from functional magnetic resonance imaging (fMRI) or, in some cases, positron emission tomography or single-photon emission computed tomography. Some of the studies also relate to uses of MRI to examine subjects' brain structures. The following discussion will refer to findings generated 'from neuroimaging'. However, in many cases, conclusions drawn about individuals' mental health status will be the product of algorithmic analyses of their

---

[244] d'Agincourt-Canning 2006, p. 113.

neuroimaging data in combination with other data gathered from them – for example, about family disease history – and compared with data collected from large groups of research participants with and without mental health diagnoses.[245]

At the time of writing, neuroimaging is only used for limited purposes in clinical psychiatric and mental healthcare, chiefly to identify targets for surgery and to rule out structural anomalies as causes of psychiatric symptoms.[246] These uses are not my focus here. Instead, I will examine attitudes to predictive, diagnostic, or prognostic applications that are currently chiefly restricted to research contexts, research that is often aimed at clinical translation.[247] There is enthusiasm in some quarters about the prospects of this field of inquiry delivering ways of identifying pre-symptomatic risk, more precise and robust diagnoses than those that currently rely substantially on clinicians' judgements, and better targeted treatments.[248] However, there is also widespread scepticism about the value of neuroimaging-based techniques over existing practices for three key reasons.[249] First, at the time of writing, several aspects of the methodologies used – particularly in fMRI studies – are insufficiently standardised or well-developed to deliver reliable and sensitive results at an individual patient level.[250] Second, the equipment, expertise, and resources needed to conduct fMRI scanning in routine clinical practice are currently prohibitive.[251] These two practical limitations may be resoluble as methods and technologies develop.[252] However, a third, concern arises from more fundamental disagreement about the validity of biological models of mental illness and may not be so readily overcome. It is not necessary to adopt a wholly anti-biological view of mental illness to recognise that neural biomarkers are rarely unique to or neatly aligned with existing psychiatric diagnostic categories, or to be concerned that neurobiological methodologies may lead to embodied, social, or environmental causes of and therapies for mental illness being sidelined.[253] For these reasons, there remains doubt about whether neuroimaging could ever provide suitable predictive, diagnostic, or

---

[245] Kellmeyer 2021.
[246] Staudt et al. 2019.
[247] Cooper et al. 2013.
[248] Farah and Gillihan 2012; Rose et al. 2015.
[249] For further discussion, see Etkin 2019.
[250] Lawrie et al. 2019.
[251] Lawrie et al. 2019.
[252] Kellmeyer 2017.
[253] Pickersgill 2011; Ramos 2012.

prognostic methods in mental healthcare.[254] Despite these limitations, there are two reasons for selecting this as my third illustrative example. First, I want to take steps to make sure that any conclusions I draw are not only applicable to genetic information. Second, brain data represent a category of bioinformation about which questions of identity significance seem likely to become more ubiquitous and pressing as neuroscience and data-driven healthcare advance.

As with the previous examples, it will be helpful to review the current availability of this kind of bioinformation to information subjects. For the reasons given above, patients are currently very unlikely to receive diagnostic or prognostic neuroimaging-based findings in mental healthcare. And because of the questionable reliability of individual research findings, it also remains unlikely that participants would receive findings about their mental health as part of the feedback policies of research studies.[255] If patients or participants were to receive such findings, these would not necessarily take the form of literal brain *images*. They would perhaps be more likely to receive verbal advice about diagnoses, percentage risk estimates of susceptibility to a particular illness, or guidance on more effective treatment regimes. It is not, however, impossible that they could receive images. In one ethnographic study, discussed further below, psychiatric patients were given structural MRI scan images of their brains, as hard copies or digital files, by investigators as an 'enticement' or 'thank you' for taking part in neurological research.[256] This was despite the neurologists describing these images as 'mere window dressing', displaying no visible markers of the participant's illness, when discussing them with the researcher.[257] At present, the most likely – though still not widespread – source of purported mental health 'diagnoses' using neuroimaging are probably DTC imaging services and consumer devices that are marketed with the promise of allowing users to monitor their own states of, for example, focus, anxiety, or relaxation.[258] Concerns noted above about

---

[254] Giordano 2012.

[255] Lawrie et al. 2019. Depending on the research protocol, participants might receive feedback on incidental findings raising serious clinical concerns. Considerations informing feedback policies are discussed in Chapter 2.

[256] Cohn 2010, pp. 67, 74. A further route by which participants may obtain images is if serious incidental findings are observed and image files are sent to their NHS patient record – in which case the participant could submit a request to view these (see Littlejohns et al. 2020).

[257] Cohn 2010, p. 74.

[258] Alpert 2012; Hickey et al. 2021.

methodological reliability are magnified considerably in the context of DTC neuroimaging.[259]

The following discussion draws on findings from the empirical literature that provide insights into information subjects' attitudes to receiving various kinds of neuroimaging-based information relating to their mental health. As with the previous two examples, these studies broadly investigate psychosocial effects, though several set out explicitly to explore potential identity impacts in some form.[260] Unsurprising, given the current state of the art, there are very few studies involving participants who have actually received neuroimaging-based mental health information. The majority of those discussed below report instead how participants – many with existing mental health diagnoses, some without – anticipate how they would react to hypothetical receipt of neuroimaging findings. Some of the studies report clinicians', researchers', and parents' views about how patients would be likely to react. The few exceptions to these hypothetical enquiries are those that report of experiences of those who have used DTC imaging services[261] or who have received neuroimaging findings through participating in research.[262] This means that the limitations to note with respect to these findings include the caveat that attitudes and expectations reported are often speculative or based on third-person assumptions and they are usually predicated on the hypothetical counterfactual that neuroimaging would deliver robust and reliable mental health insights.[263] In addition to this many of the studies are relatively small, with several comprising part of interconnected projects with overlapping groups of participants.

Information Subjects' Experiences

Perhaps the most immediately striking indication from the studies looked at here is that the majority of participants are enthusiastic – sometimes cautiously, sometimes more fulsomely – about what neuroimaging results could offer in terms of their own treatment, care, self-perceptions, and

---

[259] Thom and Farrell 2019.

[260] Buchman et al. 2013; Dumit 2003, 2004.

[261] Anderson et al. 2013.

[262] Cohn 2010; Dumit 2003.

[263] As indicated by attitudes to genetic susceptibility testing above, expectations and hypothetical reactions may diverge from what people actually feel or do once they receive the information. I discuss the possible implications of the epistemic limitations of this information below.

wider lives. For example, in one survey of the general public – none of whom had psychiatric diagnoses – the vast majority said they would be prepared to have a brain scan if it could safely and reliably predict an illness such as depression or schizophrenia.[264] Amenability to predictive scanning extends also to those with known diagnoses or risk factors.[265] Not all patients or members of the public have such positive expectations or experiences, though, as described further below.

One of the reasons many participants with existing psychiatric diagnoses give for their enthusiasm is that they see neuroimaging as potentially providing authoritative and reliable insights into the nature or cause of their mental illness – implicitly more dependable than subjective clinical judgements of mental health professionals. Participants in several studies said that neuroimaging-based assessment would provide, or had provided them with a more 'clear and objective', 'certain', or 'concrete' diagnosis.[266] Another study found that the majority of participants believed neuroimaging results would help them accept their condition and understand its biology.[267]

Several studies note beliefs amongst patients and healthcare professionals that – because of their perceived objectivity and authority – neuroimaging-based diagnoses would deliver therapeutic benefits by encouraging improved access to, uptake of, or compliance with health-protective behaviours and treatment.[268] However, in counterpoint to these hopes, some clinicians and commentators voiced concerns that biologised, brain-based explanations of mental illness might encourage patients to be pessimistic about treatment or recovery or to rely more heavily on psychopharmaceuticals to the exclusion of other therapeutic strategies.[269] While some patients expressed concerns that neuroimaging-based diagnoses could increase their worry about their illness, for the most part, professionals' concerns about fatalism or 'prognostic pessimism' are not borne out by patients' own responses.[270] Indeed, the majority of participants in one study – who had diagnoses of MDD – reported that a neuroimaging-based diagnosis would make them more likely to undertake psychotherapy.[271] Participants with

---

[264] Lawrie et al. 2019.

[265] Anderson et al. 2013; Illes et al. 2008; Lawrie et al. 2019.

[266] Anderson et al. 2013, p. 7; Buchman et al. 2013, p. 74.

[267] Illes et al. 2008

[268] Anderson et al. 2013; Borgelt et al. 2011; Buchman et al. 2013.

[269] Borgelt et al. 2011; Lebowitz 2014.

[270] Buchman et al. 2013; Illes et al. 2008.

[271] Illes et al. 2008.

schizophrenia in another study welcomed the prospect of neuroimaging if it could help tailor individual treatment more effectively.[272] And amongst a group who had used commercial neuroimaging services, most said they felt more positive and in control of their health, with only a few reporting decreased hope.[273]

Another common reason given by those with existing diagnoses for welcoming neuroimaging-based diagnoses is that these could help explain or legitimise their experiences of mental illness.[274] For example, Daniel Buchman and colleagues describe one participant's hope that neuroimaging will offer a way to 'reconfigure the meaning of his experience [of illness]'.[275] While another reports that he would welcome neuroimaging as 'acknowledgement of what I am going through' and proof that he is not 'just crazy'.[276] Meanwhile a participant in Simon Cohn's study recalls, 'I did think to myself, "would it show up on the scan? Which part of the brain is it that is causing the depression?" You know, can you just point to something and say, "That's your depression?"'[277] This optimism is echoed by some participating mental healthcare professionals, who hope that neuroimaging could provide their patients with 'existential relief' by offering biological reasons, 'a physical basis', and 'meaningful explanation' for their suffering.[278] Cohn, whose participants had been gifted brain images after taking part in neurological research, observes that some found these images 'comforting', carrying them in their wallets or displaying them in their homes.[279] Joseph Dumit similarly notes that, in contrast to the hostile ways patients with genetic disease have been observed to respond to gene images, in his experience patients with mental illness often react to neuroimages with care and concern, indicating that they see these images as representing their suffering, rather than its external cause.[280]

Several studies report patients' hopes that neuroimaging-based findings would also legitimise their experiences of mental illness in others' eyes – including family and friends – by communicating the illness's 'reality'. Dumit observes that putatively diagnostic neuroimages carry

---

[272] Rose et al. 2015.
[273] Anderson et al. 2013.
[274] Illes et al. 2008.
[275] Buchman et al. 2013, p. 74.
[276] Buchman et al. 2013, p. 74.
[277] Cohn 2010, p. 75.
[278] Borgelt et al. 2011, pp. 9–10; Cohn 2010, p. 74.
[279] Cohn 2010, p. 77.
[280] Dumit 2003.

medical and scientific authority that makes them a valued resource for accounting for oneself in social contexts and a basis for finding commonality with others and for engagement in patient activism.[281] Cohn notes the particular importance of the material, portable nature of the printed brain image in communicating illness experiences.[282] He suggests that physical images offer a means for patients to engage others and 'convey private subjective suffering within the social world'.[283] For example, one individual with schizophrenia describes such an image as providing 'proof now about my schizophrenia .... It's there on the scan, no one needs question it any more.'[284]

Cohn's findings, however, also highlight the risk that friends and family will not always interpret neuroimages in the ways that participants hope, for example by failing to be persuaded that the images convey evidence of an 'ordinary' physical illness.[285] Indeed, neuroimaging researchers and health professionals participating in another study raised concerns that neurobiological explanations of psychosis might lead to conflict or paternalistic behaviour within families.[286] Not all participants living with mental illness invested neuroimaging findings with the authority or insight to explain or legitimise their experiences. Dumit quotes an individual with a diagnosis of bipolar disorder, who sees images representing their brain function as 'genuinely exciting' but then goes on to say, these 'do not explain my madness nor do they guide me in what I can do about it'.[287] Similarly, others regard neuroimaging as a 'crude limitation' of what their illness means for them.[288]

The optimistic expectations for explanation, validation, and health benefits noted above must be viewed in light of the current limitations in the reliability, accuracy, and appropriateness of neuroimaging-based psychiatric diagnosis and risk estimates, as well as misplaced assumptions about their objectivity. Images representing functional brain data look like cross-sections of a human brain and are often vividly coloured to indicate areas of greater or less activity. A number of authors note the compelling but potentially misleading nature of their seductive visual

---

[281] Dumit 2003.

[282] Cohn 2010.

[283] Cohn 2010, p. 79.

[284] Cohn 2010, p. 76.

[285] Cohn 2010, p. 76.

[286] Corsico 2021.

[287] Dumit 2003, p. 43.

[288] Cohn 2010, p. 77.

form and the apparent simplicity and objectivity of the insights they are taken to convey about the brain and mental health.[289] For example, Dumit describes neuroimages as 'potent objects'.[290] Neuroimages are not, however, literal photographs of the brain but graphical representations of statistical analyses of highly processed data sets and the product of researchers' choices and machine learning processes.[291] Cohn suggests that by giving scan images as 'thanks', the neuroscientists in his study may be – albeit inadvertently – colluding in patients' interpretations of these as literal pictures of disease and in their need for these images to validate their illness.[292] In contrast to patients and the public, healthcare professionals and neuroscience researchers are more cautious or sceptical about the current clinical or personal value of psychiatric neuroimaging to individual patients.[293] Many of the anticipated therapeutic and personal benefits discussed here would be undermined, or even commuted into harms, if neuroimaging technologies were to provide misdiagnoses and false reassurance or to misdirect care pathways.[294] I will return below to discuss how a parallel risk may play out with respect to anticipated identity benefits.

When it comes to explicit discussion of the relationship between mental illness and identity, a number of studies report that people living with psychiatric disorders hoped that neuroimaging findings would help them to attribute their disorder to faults or features of their brains rather than part of 'who they are'; in some cases this was reflected in people's experiences.[295] Cohn observes that amongst his participants, 'the scans are frequently used to endorse a categorical separation from their disease' and offer a means by which patients cease to regard themselves as 'intrinsically ill'.[296] As he describes it, seeing – or imagining that they see – the location of their disease in a brain scan image allows some living with serious psychiatric illness to view their disease as an external, physical 'thing', 'something particular, bounded', or 'an alien pathological entity', separate from the self.[297] Dumit too suggests that some people may use neuroimaging findings as a source of impartial facts from which to

---

[289] Dumit 2004; Joyce 2005.

[290] Dumit 2004, p. 133; see also Roskies 2008.

[291] Kellmeyer 2017. For further discussion, see Farah 2014.

[292] Cohn 2010.

[293] Anderson and Illes 2012; Borgelt et al. 2012.

[294] Kellmeyer 2017.

[295] Buchman et al. 2013; Dumit 2004; Illes et al. 2008.

[296] Cohn 2010, pp. 74, 79.

[297] Cohn 2010, pp. 74, 75, 79.

construct what he calls an 'objective self' – a mere biological object-in-the-world.[298] So, for example, someone may talk of their 'depressed self' as separable from their 'true self' and distance themselves from particular behaviours, as expressed in disavowals such as 'the illness is speaking not me'.[299] A further, hoped-for benefit of this kind of separation – cited by both patients and clinicians alike – is that by demonstrating that mental illness is a 'banal physical disease' like any other, neuroimaging could help alleviate feelings of self-blame for illness and moral responsibility for recovery.[300] Judy Illes and her co-authors report that the majority of their participants who reported feeling self-blame for their depression expected that a diagnostic brain scan would significantly mitigate these feelings.[301] Similarly, in another study, participants with diagnoses of MDD echoed hopes commonly voiced by mental health advocates that neuroimaging-based diagnoses could reduce the stigma and fear often associated with mental illness.[302]

Some participating health professionals, however, worry that rather than facilitating a separation between identity and illness, neuroimaging-derived information about mental health could have the opposite effect, leading patients to see their disorder as an intrinsic, permanent brain 'defect' or 'an error in them' as a person.[303] These concerns may not be without foundation. For example, some studies suggest that receipt of neuroimaging findings could lead recipients to define themselves as 'a depressed person' or someone with 'defective brain chemistry'.[304] Dumit cites a biographical account of living with depression in which the author questions the very possibility of disassociating *who* she is from her 'sick brain', given its role in her experience and agency.[305] And Cohn's observation – that friends or family members may fail to invest neuroimages with the explanatory or exculpatory power that patients hope for – also indicates that stigma may be recalcitrant.[306] Indeed, researchers have observed that invoking *genetic* causal factors in psychiatric disorders can

---

[298] Dumit 2003, p. 35.

[299] Dumit 2003, pp. 35, 45.

[300] Buchman et al. 2013; Cohn 2010, p. 67; Dumit 2004, p. 37.

[301] Illes et al. 2008.

[302] Buchman et al. 2013.

[303] Buchman et al. 2013; Borgelt et al. 2011, p. 6.

[304] Buchman et al. 2013; Dumit 2004.

[305] Here, Dumit cites the experiences of depression described by journalist Tracy Thompson in her memoir of illness *The Beast: A Reckoning with Depression* (New York: G. P. Putnam's Sons, 1995) discussed in Dumit 2004.

[306] Cohn 2010.

actually increase associated fear and prejudice.[307] Insofar as this is attributable to perceptions that biological causes make these disorders more serious or intractable, similarly negative attitudes might extend to evidence of neurobiological factors.

As these diverse findings indicate, the perceptions of the relationship between brain, mental illness, and identity – and the ways that these then shape or are shaped by real or hypothetical encounters with neuroimaging-based risk estimates or diagnoses – are far from straightforward. Neuroscience researchers and health professionals in one study report that perceptions of the connection between mental illness and the self varied widely amongst patients and that neuroessentialist views are not as widespread as might be assumed.[308] Patients themselves hold ambivalent views about the connection between brain and self. For example, Cohn observes that his participants ascribed 'complex and multiple' meanings to their scan images.[309] Dumit too suggests that seeing oneself as having a depressed 'brain-type' may be experienced in simultaneously objective *and* subjective ways, 'lived by the person as well as against the person'.[310] Similarly, Buchman and his co-authors note that their empirical findings reflect 'the complex and sometimes contradictory ways in which people integrate notions of a disordered brain into a concept of self that at once *has* a brain and *is* a brain'.[311] This tension or vacillation has also been observed in empirical studies addressing the wider relationship between neuroscience and self-conceptions.[312] For example, Martyn Pickersgill and his co-authors conclude that while people are drawn to neuroscientific accounts of the self, they also often continue to view their brains not as a 'magnificent epicentre of subjectivity' but as 'an object of mundane significance'.[313]

Through the Lens of Narrative Identity

The findings discussed above indicate that neuroimaging-derived information purporting to provide insights into mental health status often do feed into the ways individuals characterise themselves. And

---

[307] Read 2007.
[308] Corsico 2021.
[309] Cohn 2010.
[310] Dumit 2004, p. 45.
[311] Buchman et al. 2013, p. 73 (emphasis in source).
[312] Martin 2010.
[313] Pickersgill et al. 2011, p. 361.

it seems likely that it might do so more widely if this kind of bioinformation were to become generally available in care or consumer settings. Citing a view prominent amongst the research and clinical professionals that he interviewed, Paolo Corsico concludes that 'information around genomic and brain correlates of psychosis, as well as information around psychosis risk status and illness susceptibility is a powerful tool in the process through which research participants and care recipients define their identity'.[314] As with the two previous illustrative examples, the ways and extent to which this category of personal bioinformation is likely to affect recipients' identity narratives will vary between individuals and circumstances and these effects may manifest in negative as well as positive ways.

Given that many of the views described above are voiced by people with existing mental health diagnoses or family histories of mental illness, it is perhaps unsurprising that – much as with genetic susceptibility testing – there are no widespread indications that neuroimaging-derived information would introduce wholly new categories of contents to information subjects' accounts of who they are. Instead, for many, this information is seen as offering opportunities to adjust the self-descriptors that already contribute to their self-narratives – for example, by confirming a diagnosis or by allowing them to think of themselves as having a disease rather than being 'crazy'. And the most notable anticipated impacts lie in the potential for neuroimaging findings to provide fresh interpretive tools with which people are able to reframe their lived experiences, reinterpret the meaning of mental illness, and find a place for it within – or outwith – their accounts of who they are. If, however, neuroimaging were to be used to identify the pre-symptomatic risk of serious disease in those without a known family history of mental illness, we might perhaps anticipate different reactions – perhaps ones more akin to the narrative disruption experienced upon late discovery of donor-conception.

The (re)interpretive opportunities offered by neuroimaging-based information are often welcomed, as exemplified by people's relief, or anticipated relief, at having authoritative, external verification of their subjective experiences of illness or at acquiring grounds for seeing themselves as having a real, concrete disease. The specifically narrative advantage of this kind of interpretative facility may be seen in the opportunity to make sense of distressing experiences resulting from mental illness and

---

[314] Corsico 2021, p. 10.

to construct a more intelligible or resilient self-narrative around understanding that these experiences are symptoms of a disorder. Serious mental illness can itself have profound impacts on sufferers' identities. Psychiatric diagnoses may be viewed as markers of difference and otherness and are often sources of stigma.[315] And where distress, confusion, or delusions are amongst the symptoms, illness may be experienced as disruption to identity or loss of self.[316] It is not uncommon for accounts of these kinds of identity impacts to be characterised in narrative terms. For example, David Roe and Larry Davidson describe the onset of a serious mental illness such as schizophrenia as a bifurcation of the individual's self-narrative.[317] And – as discussed in Chapter 3 – Catriona Mackenzie and Jacqui Poltera characterise Elyn Saks's experiences of living with schizophrenia as a fragmentation of self and inability to construct a narrative that hangs together in any intelligible way.[318] Mackenzie and Poltera suggest that by 'appropriating her illness as part of herself', Saks has been able to understand the fragmenting effects of psychosis on her sense of identity, pursue treatment, and bring some coherence to her self-narrative in ways that 'enable her to be the self she wants to be'.[319] This reflects psychological research that suggests that those living with psychosis may benefit from constructing 'recovery narratives', incorporating acknowledgement of their illness into rebuilding their sense of who they are.[320] Neither Saks's experience nor the literature on recovery narratives relate to neuroimaging specifically. Nevertheless, the empirical findings outlined above offer some ways of imagining how the perceived reliability and objectivity of neuroimaging-based findings might support (re)construction of intelligible narratives. Meanwhile self-narratives incorporating illness insights may, in turn, support individuals in accounting for and weathering distressing experiences and periods of 'loss of self' that accompany some forms of mental illness.

As highlighted in the previous illustrative example, it is important not to reduce all significant effects of encountering bioinformation solely to the information's clinical utility or its emotional impacts. However, it is equally important not to assume that clinical utility is

---

[315] Read 2007.

[316] Wisdom et al. 2008.

[317] Roe and Davidson 2005.

[318] Mackenzie and Poltera 2010.

[319] Mackenzie and Poltera 2010, p. 40.

[320] Ben-David and Kealy 2020; Roe and Davidson 2005.

unrelated to identity development. If hopes that neuroimaging-based insights could open doors to more effective therapies and treatment compliance were to be vindicated, these insights could contribute to patients' identities insofar as they help patients to manage symptoms that interfere with their capacities to make sense of their experiences and identities. And some of the therapeutic approaches adopted, such as talking therapies, might be precisely the kinds of practices that deal in storytelling and self-understanding. Beyond this, it is clear that psychiatric neuroimaging could offer new ways of thinking about the origins and nature of the mental illness, potentially – provided that disclosure is appropriately managed – recasting it in a less stigmatising light and helping alleviate shame and self-blame. If neuroimaging findings were able to reliably fill these practical and reinterpretive roles, they could make positive contributions to information subjects' identities to the extent that they could support the development of self-narratives that are more intelligible and comfortable to inhabit.

If our identity narratives are to be inhabitable and sustainable and allow us to function in the world, however, it is not enough that they are rendered intelligible in our own eyes. They also need to be recognised and respected as such – at least to some degree – by the people we live amongst. The findings above indicate that, for some people, psychiatric neuroimaging findings could be of considerable value in bearing witness to their suffering and the reality of their disease and thus – they hope – in persuading those around them of the veracity of their self-characterisations and the role of mental illness in – or separate from – their identity. Having said this, the experiences recounted above indicate that this hoped-for recognition could be elusive or fragile. It is at the mercy of what others understand neuroimages to convey and the extent to which these match information subjects' own interpretations. Findings from the empirical literature also illustrate ways in which neuroimaging-derived risk estimates or diagnoses could encourage stigma or fatalism, rather than supporting resilience. This could, in turn, engender self-narratives that are experienced as oppressive or limiting. Corsico notes that the neuroscientists and clinicians participating in his study are divided on whether neuroimaging-based diagnoses would exacerbate or ameliorate essentialist thinking, stigma, or prognostic pessimism.[321] Importantly, these professionals place considerable

---

[321] Corsico 2021.

emphasis on the manner in which findings are disclosed in shaping whether they are received as stigmatising and whether they foster resilience or hopelessness. In the words of one participant, 'it's all about delivery!'[322] I will return in Chapter 7 to consider the ways in which delivery might be able to avert some identity harms and cultivate benefits.

As in the previous two examples, the kinds of impacts on narrative identity indicated by the views reviewed above do not depend on information subjects adopting neuroessentialist views of self. Even when participants welcome the objectivity and authority of neuroimaging findings, this does not automatically signal a biologised view of their *identities*, even if it is rooted in a biological view of mental illness. This decoupling is evidenced in a number of places. For example, it is apparent that some individuals embrace neuroimaging as a way of communicating the reality of their illness but do not seek to reduce the nature of this 'reality' to something solely biological or innate. And it is yet more explicit in instances where neuroimaging findings are valued for identity development precisely because they allow, or would allow, the individual to exclude mental illness from their story of who they are, reframing it as an 'ordinary' physical disease, rather than part of what defines them. This notwithstanding, healthcare professionals' concerns that some patients might take neuroimaging-derived risk estimates or diagnoses to mean that they are inherently defective need to be taken seriously, particularly if this could reinforce or seed oppressive or limiting neuroessentialist views of the self.

This brings me to a crucial rider to what has been said thus far about the possible narrative roles of this category of bioinformation, particularly where these carry the prospect of making self-narratives more coherent or bearable. Here, the current, potentially surmountable, practical and methodological barriers to its reliability and clinical utility, as well as less tractable concerns about reducing mental illness to brain states or functions, cannot be ignored. The most obvious potentially detrimental effects of these epistemic limitations are health-related, for example where they lead to inappropriate diagnosis or care. And, as noted above, this is not unrelated to the maintenance of a reasonably inhabitable and coherent self-narrative, insofar as maintenance may be contingent upon effective symptom management. However, more direct threats to identity detriment may also be appreciated when the roles of neuroimaging findings are viewed in narrative terms. False or misleading

[322] Corsico 2021, p. 11.

findings, including those that obscure social and environmental contributions to mental illness, could lead recipients to misinterpret or misapply the meaning of their experiences of illness in their self-narratives. As discussed in the context of donor conception, this may lead to the development of an unsustainable identity narrative that provides a poor interpretive framework for lived experience. For example, misdiagnosis might poorly prepare someone to anticipate or tackle the way that symptoms of psychosis or depression influence their sense of who they are. And a welcome 'meaningful explanation' of one's illness is no explanation at all if it is inaccurate or misleading. Indeed, it is possible that embracing such an explanation could jeopardise the current or future intelligibility of someone's sense of themselves if it comes to occupy a role in their self-narrative to the occlusion of other factors more relevant to a more meaningful and intelligible story. Although the threats of these kinds of narrative jeopardy may still be remote while neuroimaging is not yet used in clinical psychiatry, they pose more immediate challenges if and when neuroimaging findings are made available in research or supplied in DTC settings.

This concludes the third and last of my illustrative examples. My suggestion here is that as with the previous two examples, findings from empirical studies offer compelling illustrations of how this category of personal bioinformation could play a range of both welcome and unwelcome, but nonetheless non-trivial, roles in the identity narratives of those to whom it pertains. However – and this is no small caveat – many of the potential narrative roles noted above are premised on the counterfactual reliability and accuracy of psychiatric applications of neuroimaging.

Before turning, in the next chapter, to focus on the specific nature of our identity-related interests and the variables that contribute to particular kinds of bioinformation meeting these interests, I want to take stock of where all three illustrative examples taken together leave my central proposition, that personal bioinformation can play important contributory, epistemic, and hermeneutic roles in the ongoing development of our narrative identities.

5.5   Narrativity across the Three Examples

As noted at the start of this chapter, my aims in exploring the three illustrative examples are threefold: to sense-test my core proposition – that personal bioinformation can play key roles in the construction of embodied narratives with the qualities that constitute and support our practical identities – against accounts of people's real experiences of encountering various kinds of bioinformation; to illustrate and bring this proposition to life; and to further refine it in light of information subjects' views and experiences. In this final section of the chapter, I will take stock of where we are in respect of these aims. In doing so, I will identify common themes amongst the narrative roles of these categories of bioinformation based on my interpretation of the findings discussed above. This will provide clues to the kinds of narrative roles that might be similarly filled by categories of bioinformation other than those examined here. From this, we can begin to extrapolate beyond these examples and establish a more broadly applicable picture of the nature of identity-related interests and responsibilities in respect of bioinformation disclosure in a range of contexts. The seeds sown here will be developed further in the coming chapters.

The first, broad observation I wish to make is that the expectations and reactions described in this chapter certainly seem to indicate that information subjects' encounters with all three categories of personal bioinformation can – or could – contribute to, or otherwise alter, their accounts of who they are as particular individuals with particular characteristics, outlooks, commitments, and needs. These impacts take different forms and vary in pervasiveness and gravity. And none of these categories of personal bioinformation is universally experienced as having identity significance or value by all recipients in all circumstances. Indeed, disclosures are variously experienced as welcome, unwelcome, beneficial, and disruptive. And, sometimes, they have little or no obvious or contemporaneous effects on recipients' identities at all. This variation notwithstanding, illustrations of how encounters with these three categories of personal bioinformation affect information subjects' understanding of their own characterising traits, behaviours, and experiences are by no means anomalous. And where this occurs, the effects are often experienced as initiating non-trivial changes in both their sense of who they are and the framework through which they interpret and engage with the world. Furthermore, while variation amongst impacts is undeniable, the extent to which reactions across the three broad bioinformation types echo each other is striking. Where there are variations in the degree and nature of these impacts, these chiefly lie between different people, in different circumstances and contexts, receiving ostensibly similar kinds of bioinformation. I will return to examine what kinds of factors may account for these differences in the next chapter.

It is of course the case that narrative identity, particularly the normative, embodied conception I have set out in the preceding chapters, is not the only lens through which the experiences reviewed above could be interpreted. However, I would suggest that it is both a plausible and illuminating one. It serves to highlight that there is no single effect, mechanism, or phenomenon that is '*the* identity role of personal bioinformation'. It is also clear that recognising the identity significance of personal bioinformation does not depend on either information subjects themselves or us adopting a biologically essentialised view of identity. The distinction drawn above with respect to knowledge of donor conception – that the identity significance and narrative roles of personal bioinformation may track biology without being reducible to it – holds no less true for the effects of learning of genetic disease susceptibility or mental health status. A narrative analysis also demonstrates that identity impacts are by no means limited to adding or replacing discrete, unitary labels or identifiers. While self-labelling and classification by 'person type' may sometimes be a consequence of receiving new bioinformation, it is worth noting how infrequently this is cited as the most notable consequences of disclosure. Indeed, new labels are often expressly rejected. The lens of narrativity also draws attention to the fact that bioinformation-instigated shifts in someone's understanding of their body, mind, relationships, or health do not need to be dramatic or involve wholesale reinvention to be keenly felt and make a meaningful difference to their identities. Below, I will map what I see to be the spread and intersections of what emerge as the most substantial and widely experienced parts played by personal bioinformation on recipients' self-constituting narratives, as evidenced by the accounts above.

Diverse Narrative Roles

Perhaps most straightforwardly, the three examples illustrate ways in which diverse kinds of personal bioinformation may introduce or remove contents or plotlines of recipients' self-narratives. For example, a recipient of a positive *APOE* test may start a regime of intellectual stimulation hoping to defer the effects of dementia or plan to embark on a long-deferred personal project – commitments and activities that then become part of how they describe themselves. And while one donor-conceived individual may acquire a painful storyline of themselves as someone with a difficult relationship with their mother, another may throw themselves into a rewarding and consuming search for donor-siblings. Receipt of bioinformation is just as likely to entail the removal or editing of existing self-descriptors as to add new ones. This is apparent in cases in which perceptions of being a strong or indomitable person are challenged by unexpected genetic susceptibility or when valued family relationships are damaged by reproductive revelations.

Another conspicuous cluster of narrative roles illustrated by all three examples relate to the introduction of fresh context or perspectives from which the recipient is able to re-evaluate or make sense of aspects of their embodied and relational memories and experiences and to interpret and adjust their self-narrative in light of these. These memories and experiences might include, for example, those of their own behaviour or that of others towards them; periods of ill health, changing mood, or impaired thinking; sensations and emotions; awareness of family illness; or manifestations of particular traits. The views related above illustrate ways in which bioinformation can cast these in a new light, change their meaning or significance, address uncertainties, or help account for tensions, anomalies, and gaps. For example, donor-conceived individuals may welcome learning of their donor conception because it helps resolve questions and confusion about family resemblances. And a neuroimaging-based diagnosis may help someone to make sense of distressing symptoms and to reconceive themselves as suffering from a disease rather than being 'crazy'.

This is not the same as suggesting that bioinformation provides the *truth* about who someone is or that it functions as a bald corrective to mistaken beliefs about what they thought or experienced.[323] Rather, the claim here is that it provides them with the opportunity, interpretive context, and perhaps impetus to reappraise the contents – and relations between the contents – of their existing self-narrative in light of fresh insights into their biological, bodily states. This may then facilitate the repositioning, weaving-in, or exclusion of threads from the individual's own account of who they are. This, in turn, offers the possibility of arriving at an account that is more intelligible, satisfying, or sustainable given wider lived experiences and other narrative threads. It is also clear, however, that bioinformation is not always useful or successful in fulfilling these kinds of reinterpretive or explanatory roles. For example, a discovery of donor conception during adulthood, which coincides with the death of a parent who could have supported them in making sense of this knowledge, may leave someone's self-narrative less readable and inhabitable than it was before. And unexpected identification of a risk

---

[323] Cf. Walker 2012.

of serious physical or mental illness may be experienced as disorienting and existentially threatening.

The stories we construct about who we are shaped not only by what has already happened to us but also by our anticipation of what is to come. The diachronic nature of narrativity allows us to recognise how bioinformation's explanatory and interpretive capacities can also function prospectively. Insights and knowledge gained now may support someone in making sense of, accommodating, or excluding future experiences of changing embodiment, relationships, or ill health from their accounts of who they are. While this – by the very nature of its future orientation – is less explicitly illustrated by the examples considered here than retrospective explanatory potential, it is signalled by the regret of donor-conceived individuals who wish they had been given the means to make sense of family anomalies earlier, and by those who talk of welcoming genetic susceptibility testing so that they can 'get things in order' or 'rethink their priorities'. Again, it would be a mistake to assume that personal bioinformation invariably usefully fulfils this prospective narrative role. For example, the weakly predictive nature of an *APOE* test result might fail to deliver hoped-for certainty about dementia risk, leaving the recipient's future self-narrative as foggy and unreadable as it was before.

The examples above also illustrate the role of bioinformation in initiating practical planning and behavioural changes. A narrative lens allows us to recognise that where bioinformation instigates steps such as embarking on treatment or searching for donor siblings, these activities are not necessarily distinct from identity development just because they are practical. They may themselves provide narrative contents or plotlines in their own right. They could, as previously noted, also be part of the individual's efforts to gain some understanding and control over the way their self-narrative might unfurl in the future and to adjust their current behaviours or priorities accordingly. These activities and undertakings should not automatically be assumed to separate from the business of self-constitution. According to the practical conception of identity described in the preceding chapters, the roles and traits that contribute to the self-narratives that constitute our identities are not mere inert descriptors. They supply our motives and evaluative frameworks, and they are true self-characterisations to the extent that they are expressed and enacted in appropriate circumstances. For example, sharing genetic test results with family members or undertaking financial planning in anticipation of future incapacity may be inherent to what it means to someone to be a responsible parent and a loving spouse. Conversely, a positive test result could threaten someone's self-conception as a responsible parent when they view protection of their children's safety and well-being as integral to fulfilling this descriptor.

Having said this, it is apparent that a practical response to a diagnosis or identification of disease risk is sometimes just this – an opportunity for the recipient to undertake, for example, the appropriate preventative steps and relegate the matter to a brute fact of their biological existence, rather than something that defines them. Conversely, the experiences recounted above indicate that receipt of information does not need to result in action or behavioural changes to be experienced as making a significant difference to the recipient's sense of who they are. Findings relating to all three examples suggest that bioinformation is often experienced as adding context or explanations, precipitating changes in outlook, setting expectations, or shifting relationships and roles in ways that make meaningful, non-trivial differences to recipients' characteristics and experiences of the world, despite not being manifest in contemporaneous activity. For example, being alerted to disease susceptibility can allow someone to 'see where they stand', or knowledge of donor conception can lead to feelings of being cut adrift from a family, even – or perhaps especially – when there are few opportunities to express or discuss these feelings.

In Chapter 4, I hypothesised that personal bioinformation derives identity value from its contribution to the coherence and interpretive capacities of our *embodied* self-narratives. It is apparent that the same may be said of the *relational* nature of these narratives. The three examples examined here serve to underline the ways in which the embodied and the relational aspects of our self-narratives are often closely entwined and mutually constituting, with neither wholly reducible to the other. This is manifest in a number of ways. For example, encounters with bioinformation can reinforce or undermine particular relationships and the way these feature in people's stories of who they are. Reasons for seeking, and subsequent reactions to receiving, genetic risk information may also play a part in constituting or undermining relational roles of care and responsibility for parents, siblings, and children. And people's desires for information, and subsequent responses to it, often spring from and feed into the ways they see their self-narratives as entwined with those of particular others and with shared familial or community narratives. For example, REVEAL participants' reasons for undergoing genetic testing and their responses to their results reflect their sense of already being characterised by the membership of families marked by Alzheimer's disease and by wanting to contribute to research that could help others in the same position. As previously noted, the intertwining of self-constitution, biology, and social connections has been observed by Sahra Gibbon in the activism coalescing around *BRCA* carrier status, and by Alondra Nelson amongst African American and Black British users of DTC ancestry tracing services hoping to find their ancestral African roots.[324] Nelson's phrase 'affiliative self-fashioning' captures the role that these kinds of biosocial activities play not only in adding plot lines but also in providing the kinds of dialogical contexts in which narrative meaning-making and construction take place.[325] Finally, it is apparent that the meaning and significance that particular personal bioinformation holds for recipients and the ways in which it affects their self-narratives are shaped by the meaning it holds for those close to them – for example, whether these people also see donor conception as a source of shame or mental illness as sufficiently explained by an image of brain functioning. I shall return in the next chapter to consider the part played by socially ascribed meanings in shaping the identity-significance of particular kinds of findings and insights.

It is critical to note here that alongside the potential for personal bioinformation to be welcome, exciting, explanatory, reassuring, or enabling lies the possibility that it is instead disruptive, stigmatising, oppressive, or uncomfortable. The conceptual picture I advanced in Chapter 4 paid too little attention to the prospect for identity harms. It is apparent that negative narrative impacts can take several forms. These may involve the introduction of unwanted or hurtful self-descriptors and narrative contents – as when genetic test results cause recipients to feel as if they are 'marked' or 'damaged goods' – or the severing of cherished narrative threads – for example where someone's self-characterisation as a future parent is threatened. It is also possible that bioinformation could be experienced as unprecedented and shattering – as in cases of a late revelation of donor conception and consequently damaged relationships – to the extent that it undermines the recipient's ability to recognise themselves or to see their self-narrative continuing in any recognisable or desirable form. This indicates the third dimension of identity harm brought to light by a narrative framing. This is the particular threat to the sustainability and future coherence of someone's narrative posed by the active or implicit communication of misleading or false information.

---

[324] Gibbon 2007; Nelson 2008.
[325] Nelson 2008, p. 771.

While it is crucial that we recognise that personal bioinformation is not always sought or happily received, it is also important not to lose sight of just how widespread the desire is to receive, or not to be denied, information is across all three examples. While mindful of the potentially self-selecting participation of 'information enthusiasts' in the studies reviewed above, it is still striking that where there are quantified findings, the vast majority skew towards 'wanting to know'. In the qualitative findings, this is manifest in phrases such as 'to go through life with your eyes only half open doesn't help you at all'[326] and 'truth is always better'.[327] These kinds of attitudes are present even when people know that test results could reveal susceptibility to serious disease and amongst those who have had distressing experiences of discovery. Personal testimonies indicate that many information subjects really do value the insights and explanations, the interpretive tools, and the foresight that personal bioinformation offers to them when making sense of who they are in light of their health, bodies, biology, and relationships, and when (re)building a self-conception that 'fits' their past, present, and future experiences.

These observations point towards a third important area for refinement of the conceptual picture set out in Chapter 4 – the need to explore the complex relationship between identity-related impacts that are experienced as beneficial or detrimental. The illustrative examples indicate that there may not always be straightforward dichotomies or correlations between 'beneficial' and 'harmful', 'welcome' and 'unwelcome' bioinformation – where 'beneficial' and 'harmful' refer to the relative utility and suitability of bioinformation for the development and maintenance of coherent, meaningful, and inhabitable self-narratives. As illustrated by accounts of discovery of donor origins, initially shocking and identity-disrupting revelations may eventually come to be valued when they help the individual make sense of their previous experiences of familial discord and reconstruct a fresh, satisfying account of who they are. And it is plausible that the converse may also be true – for example, eagerly sought and welcomed neuroimaging results from a DTC clinic may be so inaccurate as to provide false reassurance to the client about their mental health and constitute a precarious basis for imagining their future and navigating emerging symptoms. I will return in the next chapter to further unpick the nature of narrative identity value and detriment and the complex relationships between their various dimensions.

---

[326] Lock et al. 2006, p. 290.
[327] Kirkman 2003, pp. 2229–2230.

A Dynamic, Multistranded Whole

The possibility that personal bioinformation may be upsetting but also welcome, or initially comforting but ultimately treacherous, is an important reminder that our identities are not inert, with the only prospects being preservation – where this is assumed to be a virtue – or disruption – which is commonly assumed to be harmful. Characterisations of identity impacts that reduce identity value to the absence of distress or dogged retention of our existing stories are too simplistic. Our identities are perpetually evolving and responding to our experiences and circumstances, and this may go better or worse, aided or undermined by myriad factors, including encounters with personal bioinformation. Furthermore, our identities are not homogeneous or monadic but complex, multistranded wholes in which the different constitutive threads bend and colour each other and are bent and coloured by their interpretive environment. As such, ethically significant impacts on our identities extend far beyond labelling or classification. A narrative framing highlights that it is not only the bald addition or removal of contents from our self-narratives that makes a difference to our identities but also the ways these are interpreted, woven together in different permutations, and enacted. The experiences and views detailed above support the contention that, rather than using insights into our bodies to create – in Dumit's terms – 'objective selves' that are separate from our phenomenal, lived identities, our *subjective* accounts of who we are are richly embroidered by our insights into our biological characteristics and relationships.[328] Personal bioinformation provides new threads, as well as ways of reinforcing, redirecting, or unpicking old ones, and fresh lights in which to view the whole. A narrative conception allows us to appreciate that a mutually interpretive interweaving of experience and externally sourced data, which with varying degrees of success brings together the material and phenomenological, permits the construction of a lived and liveable embodied and relational identity. Recognising the diachronic, dynamic, and multistranded nature of our identities and the multiple roles that personal bioinformation may play in them is essential to grounding a robust and properly conceived picture of our identity interests in our encounters with this information. It is the precise nature of these interests and how they can be met to which I turn in the next chapter.

[328] Dumit 2003.

6

Locating Identity Interests

6.1 Introduction

In this chapter, I will draw together the various elements of the preceding discussions to set out what I take to be the nature and scope of our identity-related interests in accessing personal bioinformation. These are the interests that, I wish to argue, need to be taken into account by those who generate and manage our personal bioinformation when making decisions or developing laws and policies about disclosing this information to us, the subjects of this information. The characterisation of identity interests that follows is supported by three pillars. The first of these is the normative conception of a narrative self-constitution set out in Chapters 3 and 4. This entails that an identity narrative is not just something inert that we have by default but something that may fare better or worse and serve us better or worse. The second is the fact that we lead inescapably embodied and social existences that shape our experiences, the kinds of stories we can and do tell about ourselves, and the context in which we inhabit and enact these stories. The third pillar is provided by the insights provided by the three illustrative examples explored in the previous chapter. In what follows I will first set out the underlying interest in narrative self-constitution and its various facets, before specifying three information-related interests that are predicated upon and serve this more basic one. I will then unpack several features that are relevant to the practical application of these interests, including the qualities of the particular kinds of bioinformation that are likely to serve them. This chapter concludes by reviewing the ways in which the appropriate character-isation and recognition of these identity interests add an important and unmet dimension to the ethical landscape of bioinformation governance.

6.2 Our Identity Interests

To say someone has an interest in a particular state of affairs or outcome is to say that they have something at stake in it; they have something to

181

lose or gain depending on whether it comes to pass or how it goes.[1] They are harmed if their interests are not met, though the way and degree to which this is so will depend on the nature and strength of the interests in question. Our interests and desires will frequently overlap. However, in what I go on to say, I will take it that an interest is not precisely the same as a desire or preference insofar as many of our interests, particularly those predicated on the conditions for our basic survival and functioning, hold irrespective of particular wishes. Interests can be of different strengths. And they may be ephemeral or life-long, vital or trivial. We may have interests that are specific to particular roles or situations – for example, a clinical trial participant with an unmet treatment need has an interest in being assigned to the group receiving the active therapy rather than the placebo control. We may also have those that apply to everyone simply by virtue of being human, for example, the interest in being mentally and physically healthy. As this suggests, some interests are more fundamental than others. And the fulfilment of some context-specific interests – for example, that in being assigned to the active arm of a trial – may serve other more basic ones – such as being healthy – and gain their ethical significance from this more basic interest. At this more fundamental end of the spectrum, interests shade into 'vital interests' or 'needs', which must be fulfilled if we are to survive.

I will take it that the identity interests described below are ones held by everyone in virtue of the kinds of embodied, social beings we are and that they are ethically significant because of their connection to the development and exercise of the kinds of experiential, evaluative, and practical capacities that contribute rich, fulfilling, and engaged lives, as described in Chapter 3. As such, I will argue they are not as strong as the vital interests related to basic survival, such as those for food or shelter. However, their fulfilment is core to our well-being, to leading a flourishing life, and to pursuing other important interests and goals.

What I have just said might suggest that the language of rights would be appropriate here. However, I will not talk in terms of identity rights for three reasons. First, I take it that interests are conceptually prior to rights. Characterising the nature of interests is, therefore, the more immediate and illuminating task. It is where the values, objects of value, activities, or relationships at stake are unpacked and described. Second, rights talk brings with it a kind of endgame inflexibility that implies stand-offs between putatively competing rights and can obscure

---

[1] Feinberg 1984.

the importance of the ways in which they are fulfilled. Third, rights imply inevitable correlated duties. While I will argue in the next chapter that our information-related identity interests are often sufficiently strong to create responsibilities for others to meet them, I do not want to short-circuit the discussion of why and when these responsibilities obtain by using the language of entitlement.

Fundamental Identity Interest

Before I can characterise our specifically information-related interests, it is necessary first to establish the more basic interest in narrative self-constitution that they serve. On the basis of the picture developed over the preceding chapters, my claim is that we each have *a fundamental interest in developing and maintaining an inhabitable self-narrative, that is, one that is coherent, sustainable, meaningful, and comfortable when occupied and enacted in the course of our embodied and socially embedded lives.*

I take it that each of the four adjectives – coherent, sustainable, meaningful, and comfortable – signals a distinctively important quality, but that these are also interdependent such that it may not be possible to realise any to a satisfactory degree in the complete absence of others. At the same time, they also place limits on each other in ways discussed further below. Collectively, they comprise the quality I will refer to as 'inhabitability'. I will say a little more here about what is entailed by each of these qualities.

The first of these – *coherence* – was addressed in detail in Chapters 3 and 4, and I will not rehearse all of those discussions here. To recap, it may be recalled that I am using coherence to encompass connotations of both integration and intelligibility. These qualities matter because our self-narratives provide the perspective from which we view and navigate the world and the foundation for working out who we are and what matters to us. The importance of narrative coherence is illustrated across all three illustrative examples in the previous chapter, where it is captured, for example, by the welcome explicability of family memories and relationships, reconciliation of symptoms with self-descriptors, management of uncertainty, and validation or bearing witness to the suffering of mental illness. Achieving narrative coherence does not require a neat structuring of contents, homogeneity, or total transparency. Perfect coherence is not required, probably not attainable, and may not always be desirable where it entails ignoring the tensions that may accompany intersectionality or forcing a fit between contrasting experiences. But a realistic and valuable level of coherence does require that different aspects of our narratives should have interpretive access to each other and be reasonably explicable in light of our experiences of our own embodiment and environment. We also benefit to the extent that our self-characterisations are intelligible to others, as this allows us to occupy and sustain them in our relationships and interactions. However, given that others may refuse or lack the imagination or tools to recognise our self-narratives, our own capacities to make sense of them in the light of our experiences is generally of principal importance.

Closely related to this is the requirement that our self-narratives are *sustainable*. By this, I mean that they should be resilient and – as far as possible – equipped to maintain or regain their integrity and intelligibility when confronted by our experiences, including experiences of, and mediated by, our health and bodies. Identity narratives suffer when they are built on precarious foundations, for example when they include fundamental misconceptions about the basis or nature of the characteristics core to our stories, which render them vulnerable to extensive disturbance by lived experiences. However, sustainability does not require that our identities remain rigidly unchanging. On the contrary, to remain coherent and intelligible and useful frameworks for interpreting and navigating our lives, they must respond to our experiences and evolve accordingly. Sudden or big changes in our lives, such as the onset of serious illness, may precipitate dramatic changes in our self-narratives. These disruptions – particularly when they sever threads that are bound deeply and widely into the fabric of our self-conceptions – may render our existing narratives unintelligible or hard to inhabit. And this damage may be disabling or challenging to resolve. However, narrative disruption is not necessarily unwelcome or irresoluble, as illustrated by some individuals' evolving experiences of learning of their donor origins or of elevated risk of serious disease. What matters is that we have access to the resources – within ourselves or in the form of personal, epistemic, and hermeneutic support – to restore a reasonable degree of coherence, meaning, and comfort following disruption.

Our self-narratives best support our experiential, practical, and evaluative capacities and allow us to locate ourselves in our past and project ourselves into own futures when they contain characteristics, roles, and experiences that we find *meaningful* or *worthwhile*. This does not mean they have to be wholly concerned with highbrow or other-regarding concerns. But we benefit when our narrative 'contents' motivate us and provide us with a sense of what we value. These kinds of contents contribute to the kind of self-esteem that equips us with the drive and confidence to be able to enact and develop our values and life projects in ways that permit continuing identity development. They also support the kinds of enduring commitments – to people, projects, or causes – that are not only valuable in themselves but also help support narrative coherence and sustainability over time. The examples in the previous chapter illustrate self-descriptors and relational roles that provide meaning, shape, and direction to people's self-conceptions that are grounded in, often shared, biological traits – those of being a parent, a member of a family affected by Alzheimer's, or *BRCA* activist. If someone is frustrated in their enactment of meaningful narrative contents, or if valued roles and descriptors are threatened or undermined by new information or circumstances, then something important is lost.

Meaningfulness is important, but it would be artificial and set the bar unreasonably high to demand that all aspects of our identity narratives are a source of joy and pride. As Mary Walker and Wendy Rogers note, '[e]lements of one's self-conception are not, however, necessarily things one endorses or even approves of'.[2] This signals the importance of a *comfortable* self-narrative. As with meaningfulness, there will be substantial variation in what a 'comfortable' narrative looks like to each of us. Nevertheless, I want to suggest that stigmatising, alienating, distressing, frightening, or oppressive characteristics, roles, and experiences are antithetical to narrative comfort. For example, we are unlikely to be comfortable in self-descriptors or roles that we are ashamed to lay claim to or enact because we experience them as having negative or stigmatising associations – for example, those of being 'a mutant' carrier of a disease-causing gene, 'doomed' by genetic risks, or a 'commodity' traded through a surrogacy contract. Similarly, we may feel alienated from descriptors in which we do not recognise ourselves but that are imposed on us – for example, 'crazy' or 'illegitimate'. Comfortable self-narratives will be enhanced by characteristics that are rewarding and cause us little friction in our daily lives – for example, those of being a much-wanted child, a responsible parent, or a contributor to vital health research. However, there will also be characteristics that we strongly embrace and would like to experience as a source of pride that we nevertheless find challenging to occupy and enact, perhaps because others do not recognise them as 'real' or respect-worthy. For example, in

---

[2] Walker and Rogers 2017, p. 314.

some contexts, this might include being a person of colour, a trans father, or a competent professional living with schizophrenia. In proposing that narrative comfort matters, it is important to leave space for recognising the value of sustaining valued narrative threads such as these that nevertheless face disrespect or lack of recognition by others.

I will collectively refer to the interactive combination of the four qualities described above as comprising an *inhabitable* self-narrative. A fractured, unintelligible, unsustainable self-narrative, populated chiefly by characteristics and experiences that we find alienating, trivial, or unwelcome, is unlikely to be one that we are comfortable occupying, or one that provides a supportive and useful framework though which to interpret and navigate our lives. An inhabitable self-narrative need not be an unremittingly joyous story in which we take unalloyed pleasure and pride. Ricoeur's description of the necessity of having a 'bearable' identity narrative is closer to the mark, though perhaps rather too downbeat.[3] 'Inhabitability' here is intended to capture the achievable ideal of a self-narrative with realistically welcome and desirable contents given what we are able, and unable, to control about our lives and the meanings attaching to our experiences and characteristics. An inhabitable narrative is one that accommodates diversity amongst intersecting characteristics and reflects the light and shade of real life.

My claim is that our interest in achieving and maintaining an inhabitable self-narrative is a fundamental and ethically significant one, shared by each of us to the extent we have, or can be supported in having, the cognitive and affective and relational capacities to construct such an account. The strength of this interest is attributable to the importance of the narrative qualities of coherence, sustainability, meaning, and comfort for realising and exercising our experiential, evaluative, and practical capacities for self-understanding and ongoing self-creation; interpreting and evaluating our experiences; and developing autonomous agency, long-term commitments, and our own critical outlook and style of attention.

Information-related Interests

I now want to turn to the specific information-related interests that serve the more fundamental interest in narrative self-constitution just

---

[3] Ricoeur 1992, p. 158.

described. I will set out here what I take to be our three principal information-related interests.[4]

Our first information-related identity interest is that in *being able to access personal bioinformation that would contribute to developing and maintaining an inhabitable self-narrative that is coherent, sustainable, meaningful, and comfortable when occupied and enacted in the course of an embodied and socially embedded life*. Or, more pithily, *we each have an interest in accessing personal bioinformation that would contribute to an inhabitable self-narrative*.

The second information-related identity interest is that in *not being exposed to personal bioinformation that would threaten an inhabitable self-narrative*.

However, it is not simply by supplying or withholding bioinformation that harms to the inhabitability of our self-narratives may be averted or mitigated, and not all disclosures will support inhabitability equally effectively. These outcomes are also influenced by the *manner* in which information is offered and disclosed. This brings me to a crucial third information-related identity interest – that in *being offered, and potentially given, personal bioinformation in a way that supports the development and maintenance of an inhabitable self-narrative in the course of an embodied and socially embedded life*.

In a purely conceptual sense it is not surprising that, if we have interests connected to our encounters with and uses of bioinformation, then the manner and context in which this information is conveyed also becomes crucially relevant. This is because, according to the definition of information presented in Chapter 1, the communication context can contribute in no small way to the explanatory and interpretive framework that shapes the semantic content or meaning of the information, thus producing what should – strictly speaking – be thought of as *new* information.[5] For example, when a doctor conveys the results from a biopsy, the information the patient receives is not identical with that written in their patient records, nor yet with the doctor's own interpretation of the results. It is shaped by the patient's circumstances, how the doctor conveys the result, and the wider explanatory and interpretive context in which communication takes place. Furthermore, according to

---

[4] In proposing these interests, I am neither suggesting that they necessarily take precedence over other interests nor that they entail imposing or withholding personal bioinformation against the information subject's wishes. I will return to consider the responsibilities of others to meet and weigh such interests in Chapter 7.

[5] Floridi 2019.

the picture I have developed over the preceding chapters, narrativity is itself an interpretive and meaning-making endeavour. So, if we are concerned with managing the effects of people's encounters with particular bioinformation on their self-narratives, it follows that this concern will extend to the factors that shape how the information is understood by the recipient and the ways in which it subsequently informs their self-narrative. Prominent amongst these factors are the ways that the information is presented and explained at the point of communication and receipt.

The experiences discussed in the previous chapter offer vivid illustrations of the ways in which disclosure context can make significant differences to how recipients' underlying identity interests are affected. For example, the UK regulator and leading researchers in the field recommend introducing the topic of donor conception to donor-conceived children early and in incremental, age-appropriate ways, allowing them to assimilate it gradually.[6] And family members' willingness to discuss the meaning and significance of donor conception, as well as the availability of further information about gamete donors, have both been observed to make a difference to how well adult recipients respond to discovery of their conception and whether they are able to restore a satisfying and coherent sense of who they are.[7] The importance of interpretive context also emerges from the REVEAL study investigating genetic testing for Alzheimer's risk. REVEAL researchers attributed participants' relative lack of distress and fatalism in response to their risk estimates to prior receipt of educational materials that emphasised the probabilistic and conditional nature of these estimates and the complex, multifactorial nature of late-onset Alzheimer's disease.[8] In contrast, the visual nature of brain images has been observed to lend them an apparent immediacy and objectivity that makes them a particularly 'potent' and persuasive communication medium and heightens the personal significance of what they seem to convey.[9]

My focus in this chapter and the next is on describing the nature of our identity interests and how these might be met. The three information-related interests listed above are held by individual information subjects

---

[6] Human Fertilisation and Embryology Authority, *Talk to your child about their origins*, https://www.hfea.gov.uk/donation/donor-conceived-people-and-their-parents/talk-to-your-child-about-their-origins/ (accessed 18 July 2021); Golombok 2017.

[7] Blyth 2012; Freeman and Golombok 2012; Ravelingien et al. 2013.

[8] Christensen et al. 2011.

[9] Dumit 2004, p. 109.

by virtue of being authors of their own identity-constituting self-narratives. However, meeting these interests requires recognising that they are often interdependent or in tension with the needs and interests of others. As noted in earlier chapters, we do not and cannot build our identities in isolation. And, as I shall go on to discuss below, the ways in which particular bioinformation engages and impacts upon the information subject's fundamental identity interest are not separable from how others around them understand and use this information or from how disclosure affects other people and the recipient's relationships with them.

It is also important to recognise that the fulfilment of our fundamental interest in developing and maintaining an inhabitable self-narrative is not all-or-nothing nor a once-and-for-all achievement. The coherence of an identity narrative admits of degrees. The same is true of its meaningfulness, sustainability, and comfort. Failure to fulfil all the dimensions of the overarching inhabitability of one's self-narrative to a perfect degree is inevitable in the course of any recognisably human life. And this does not necessarily entail a *loss of identity*. But such a catastrophic outcome is not necessary for our underlying identity interest to be engaged and for legitimate ethical concerns to arise. Similarly, contributions towards enhancing or supporting narrative coherence, meaningfulness, sustainability, and comfort are valuable and worthy of attention, even when these would not achieve perfect inhabitability or avert total disintegration. That is to say, incremental losses and gains in the various dimensions of inhabitability can make ethically significant differences that still demand our attention. The development of an inhabitable self-narrative is a constant work in progress, frequently progressing and regressing, and subject to external influence and impacts, re-evaluations, and reinterpretations. These factors mean that our associated information-related identity interests are ever-present and may be engaged in different ways at different times.

These, then, are the central qualities of the three information-related interests which, I propose, should comprise a central and routine part of ethical frameworks that govern bioinformation disclosure practices and policies in healthcare, research, consumer, administrative, and interpersonal contexts. Before moving on to map the shape of the ethical and practical gap that would be filled by recognising and responding to these identity-focused interests, I want first to examine more closely the factors that influence when particular kinds or instances of bioinformation might fulfil or undermine them. Understanding these factors and knowing how to recognise them are essential steps in making protection of information-related identity interests a realistic and practicable prospect.

6.3 Sources of Identity Significance

I have argued over the preceding chapters that personal bioinformation, taken as a broad and inclusive class, has the potential to contribute to the inhabitability of our identity-constituting self-narratives. However, it is clear that not all kinds or instances do so to the same extent, or on all occasions. Some may indeed threaten inhabitability. I want to look more closely at the kinds of factors that shape when and why these differences occur. The first step in doing this is to examine what accounts for the quality of 'identity significance'.

I take identity significance to be the quality of a particular instance of bioinformation, without which it would not have a noteworthy effect on someone's identity – either good or bad. In practice, it seems most likely that information's identity significance and its positive or negative impacts will be experienced in tandem rather than sequentially, each bound together in subjects' perceptions of its value or detriment to their account of who they are. But it is worth decoupling them for the purposes of this stage of the enquiry, as identity significance may be attributable to some reasonably discernible and predictable factors, even when the precise positive or negative qualities of the effects on narrative inhabit-ability are less readily predicted. With some possible exceptions dis-cussed below, it seems most plausible – given the variety of experiences reviewed in the previous chapter – that the matter of whether any particular type of personal bioinformation in any particular circumstance is experienced as having identity significance and then, further to this, whether it serves or threatens the information recipient's basic identity interest is not inherent to the information itself. Instead, it is largely a contingent matter, dependent on a cluster of factors that we might think of as embodied context, communication context, social context, and narrative context.

Embodied Context

Turning to the first of these, it seems likely that the nature of the health, biological, or bodily state of affairs conveyed by particular bioinforma-tion will often be a considerable contributory factor in its perceived identity significance – even if it is not determined by this alone. Specifically, the greater the gravity, scale, or pervasiveness of the effects of particular kinds of bodily states, functions, and susceptibilities on the lives, experiences, and well-being of embodied beings – given, for example, the ways we use our senses, our physical and mental capacities and vulnerabilities, our reproductive capabilities, and our lifespan – the greater the likelihood that these will impinge on our self-narratives. And, by the same reasoning, bioinformation conveying insights into these 'weighty' biological or bodily states of affairs – such as diagnosis of serious chronic illness – seems particularly likely to be experienced as having identity significance. For example, it has been observed that people's reactions to results from genetic susceptibility testing tend to vary relative to the severity and nature of the condition tested for, including its age of onset, amenability to treatment, the severity of its symptoms, or whether it affects mental capacities.[10] This is not to claim that all bioinformation with marked health or functional implications will inevitably be seen as identity-significant, or be significant in the same ways to different people. Observations of the 'disability paradox' – in which the quality of life reported by those living with disabilities is often considerably higher than imagined by able-bodied people – provide a clear warning against assuming that people's experiences of different forms of embodiment are universal or straightforwardly predictable.[11] We may also witness disparities in the connotations of apparently similar information in the ways in which carrier status for the *BRCA* mutations linked to breast and ovarian cancer are often seen as particularly frightening and closely associated with patient activism – associations that are perhaps not as widely shared by genetic susceptibility to hereditary bowel cancer, despite these diseases having comparably severe health risks.[12]

Communication and Social Context

This last example points towards the extent to which bodily states of affairs – while perhaps presenting as brute matters of fact – are nevertheless susceptible to being shaped by the stories we tell about them and the interpretations and associations we invest in them. As Iris Marion Young, Donna Haraway, and others have observed, the meaning and

---

[10] Roberts et al. 2003.
[11] Scully 2008, p. 56.
[12] Lock 2008, p. 73.

significance of features of our material bodies are often neither inherent nor wholly socially constructed but rather the result of entwined 'nature/culture'.[13] I have indicated above how the immediate communication environment can influence the meaning of particular bioinformation and its roles in recipients' self-narratives. It is no less important to recognise that the wider social contexts in which the disclosure takes place – in which I include cultural, medical, political, institutional, and legal environments and structures – can have similar effects by contributing further layers to the interpretive frameworks within which the identity relevance, or lack thereof, of particular kinds of bioinformation are viewed.

It is not possible to explore here in depth the many means by which this entanglement of biology and social context can come about. However, over the previous chapters, we have encountered several examples in which it is manifest. For example, it has been suggested that it is not possible fully to understand the significance of knowledge of donor conception to donor-conceived individuals in abstraction from the importance assigned to genetic relatedness, infertility, or marital fidelity in the cultures into which these individuals were born.[14] Indeed, Tabitha Freeman and others have posited that gamete donation policies that require donor identifiability could themselves contribute to a feedback loop, reinforcing the perception that knowledge of genetic parentage is important to donor-conceived individuals' self-understanding.[15] Further indications are supplied by research findings that suggest that individuals conceived using donor sperm tend to invest more importance in knowing about their donors than those conceived using donor eggs.[16] Freeman and her co-authors surmise that this could be due to culturally prevalent perceptions that fatherhood is conferred at conception, while motherhood is constituted by gestation and care.[17] The attitudes examined in the previous chapter suggest that beliefs about the particular authority, objectivity, and reliability of particular kinds of bioinformation – for example, findings generated by genomics or neuroimaging – can also make a substantial difference to whether information subjects treat these findings as relevant to their accounts of who they are. These 'entanglements of meaning' may occur at the point

---

[13] Haraway 2006, p. 128; Young 2005.
[14] Freeman 2014.
[15] Freeman 2015.
[16] Freeman et al. 2014.
[17] Freeman et al. 2014.

of disclosure – for instance, introduced by the disclosers' apparent expertise and authority – as well as being woven in the wider communication environment. For example, commonplace beliefs that functional neuroimaging can provides robust insights into our character traits and behaviours might be explained in part by the prominence in the public realm – including popular media and social policy – of neuroscientific explanations for differences between people and their characteristics.[18] And perceptions of the divergent identity significance of different kinds of bioinformation may extend to yet more concrete social and cultural factors. For example, diagnosis of a serious disease may take on a very different narrative complexion in settings where treatment is provided by a tax-payer funded health service and one in which healthcare provision is sparse or treatment is prohibitively expensive.

Narrative Context

In light of the examples just outlined, it is possible to see how information about our bodies, health, or biological relationships may arrive ready-packaged with value judgements and attributions of identity significance. However, while recognising this, it is crucial that we do not overlook or afford too little weight to the role of the interpretive framework supplied by the individual subject's own identity narrative. The contents and connections of their existing narrative will be instrumental in shaping whether particular personal bioinformation is experienced by them as being relevant to who they are, or when it is seen as supporting or threatening the coherence, sustainability, meaning, and comfort of their identity. In Marya Schechtman's words, a self-narrative is the 'lens through which we filter our experience and plan for actions'.[19] To this list we may add that it is also the lens through which we interpret new incoming information. What a particular item of personal bioinformation means to us will be dependent on the ways we already characterise ourselves; the relative priorities and accommodation we have previously forged between different intertwined and intersecting aspects of ourselves; and the priorities, concerns, and values arising from these. The role played by this narrative lens is perhaps most obvious where bioinformation gains significance through corroborating or posing a direct threat to existing, valued narrative contents. But it also operates as

---

[18] O'Connor and Joffe 2013.
[19] Schechtman 1996, p. 113.

a broader interpretive framework. For example, the experiences explored in Chapter 5 demonstrated that it is not possible to understand the significance of a *BRCA* test result to a recipient without understanding their family's history of cancer, their existing beliefs about their risk, and how they imagine serious illness or treatment will impact the projects, roles, and relationships that sustain and define them.

My suggestion is that our own identity narratives are the ultimate – though neither the sole nor necessarily the dominant – factor shaping the significance and identity value or detrimental character of personal bioinformation. This is in no way to underestimate the parts played by communication and cultural contexts. These 'external' factors may contribute aspects – sometimes really substantial aspects – of the meaning of the features, group memberships, susceptibilities, diagnoses, or relationships that bioinformation conveys. And, sometimes, their influence may be hard to resist and doing so may demand substantial personal and social resources.[20] However, potential self-descriptors are rarely if ever – in Diana Meyers's vivid phraseology – 'implanted' as ready-made 'trait nuggets ... as if our psyches swallowed social inputs whole and never metabolized them'.[21] The relationship between identity and bioinformation is best understood as a bidirectional process, whereby our self-narratives should be seen both as being shaped by bioinformation and also as being the prism through which this information passes, bending and colouring the eventual roles information plays in our self-conceptions. These roles may be substantive – adding or subtracting contents and descriptors – or interpretive – adjusting the relationships between existing contents and descriptors. The edits made may be prominent or trivial, and sometimes, the information will be excluded altogether.

The Reality of Constructed Significance

One possible line of critique warrants addressing at this point. It is sometimes implied that if the identity significance and consequent value of particular kinds of personal bioinformation are not intrinsic to the information but rather contingent – constructed by, amongst other things, changeable social norms and personal idiosyncrasies – then any supposed identity-based interests attached to receiving it are artefactual

---

[20] Lindemann 2001.
[21] Meyers 2000, p. 163.

and of questionable ethical importance. For example, Inmaculada de Melo-Martín argues that, because perceptions of the identity significance of knowing one's donor origins are the product of 'culturally dominant narratives' and these perceptions carry the risk of stigmatising those who do not know their genetic parentage, it would be better to resist the contingent significance of this knowledge than to recognise it and give it credence and influence.[22] However, objections of this kind are, I want to suggest, based on a misunderstanding about *what* is contingent in this picture. Our information-related identity interests are no less real and significant for being contingently engaged in any particular instance. This is because if and when particular bioinformation *does* substantially enhance the inhabitability of the recipient's self-identity, it fulfils a particular, non-fungible role in the complex, interwoven whole and particularity of that individual's self-narrative given the particularities of their existing narrative, their embodied and relational circumstances, and the cultural and social context in which they live. And, in doing so, it contributes to meeting a fundamental interest. This is no less true of bioinformation that is not inherently identity-significant. Only under a strangely individualistic and inert conception of narrative self-constitution, in which the forms our self-narratives take must be untouched by external influences and play no role in shaping the meaning of incoming information, would the sheer operation of partially socially constructed significance undermine the reality of the information's identity value to its recipient, or make its value to some more suspect than its stigmatising impacts on others.

Similarly, the socially constructed aspects of identity significance should not be seen as obviating the selective, interpretive authorship of information subject. Undoubtedly, authorial and interpretive control over our identities will sometimes be constrained or involve a struggle. For example, this might be the case when others refuse to recognise our own accounts of who we are, or when bioinformation conveys health news associated with particularly oppressive or stigmatising tropes. However, these real and serious possibilities do not mean that we are *always* powerless in how we respond to external influences on identity significance. The diverse accounts of rejecting or reconfiguring the results of genetic tests or neuroimaging findings discussed in the previous chapter indicate that, despite the perceived objectivity and authority of the source material, bioinformation may still be reinterpreted and shaped

---

[22] de Melo-Martín 2014, p. 33.

by recipients' exiting narratives. Alondra Nelson observed just such practices amongst users of DTC genomic ancestry tracing services.[23] Participants in her study hoped that the findings supplied by these services would provide insights into their ancestral roots in Africa. Nelson notes that these 'roots seekers' 'actively draw together and evaluate many sources of genealogical information (genetic and otherwise) and from these weave their own ancestry narratives'.[24] The perceived authority and objectivity of this information and its profound significance to these peoples' lives did not obviate their role as authors of their own identities.

Not only do we have the capacity to reflect upon, resist, or subvert socially constructed identity significance, I would suggest that it is also a mistake to assume that we can be effective, intelligible narrators *without* access to shared cultural storytelling tools. As discussed in Chapter 3, our self-narratives are constructed in dialogue with others. And this necessarily involves using shared language and modes of self-understanding, including those about the range of forms that we imagine human lives can take and the kinds of characteristics that can populate the stories of these lives. Some of the templates or 'master narratives' available in our communities may be restrictive and challenging to resist, such as Hilde Lindemann's example in which female nurses are habitually seen and treated as 'Earth Mother[s] with the Bedpan'.[25] However, many other templates are enabling. For example, shared accounts of what it is like to be a teenager may help young people understand that their feelings of frustration and alienation are, usually, not moral failings or signs of mental ill health but widely shared and useful parts of developing independence. Or it might be hoped that increasing visibility of non-binary ways of living and characterising oneself will support people who do not feel gendered along traditional lines to feel more able to develop and inhabit their own accounts of who they are.

Lindemann is sympathetic to Diana Meyers's view that, '[t]o some extent, people are captives of their culture's repertory of figurations'.[26] However, she points out that it is 'neither possible nor desirable' to extricate ourselves from or eschew these shared figurations and understandings altogether.[27] In her words,

[23] Nelson 2008.
[24] Nelson 2008, p. 762.
[25] Lindemann 2001, pp. 3, 6.
[26] Meyers 2000, p. 239.
[27] Lindemann 2001, p. 85.

> '[t]hese understandings are narrative understandings, made up of the stories and fragments of stories that circulate widely in the community and that allow us to make sense not only of ourselves but also of those around us .... In our found communities there exists not only what besieges, deprives and violates us but also our moral good: a considerable portion of the richness and variety of life lies in the given.'[28]

Without the shared tools of narration, we struggle to construct our identities at all, to recognise or find meaning in them, or to have them recognised and understood by others. For example, Jackie Leach Scully suggests that one of the challenges that might face the first generation of people conceived using MRT – a reproductive technique described in Chapter 2 that uses eggs from two women to create an embryo – is the absence of 'a vocabulary to match some crucial areas of her experience that arise out of the special way she was conceived, and a story that enables her to make sense of those aspects of her life and eventually to describe and account for them to others'.[29] Here, we might call to mind Marian Wright Edelman's maxim that 'it is hard to be what you cannot see'.[30] Edelman is speaking to the importance of role models, but her words also resonate with the importance of being able to reach for positive, publicly available templates for the stories we can and want to tell about who we are. Scully emphasises that we hold collective responsibilities for generating positive, enabling, and recognisable master narratives – in Lindemann's terms 'counterstories' – that children conceived using MRT could use, to avert the risk that the void is instead filled by stories in which they are seen as 'so unusual as to be morally suspect, possibly even "monstrous"'.[31] This imperative clearly applies far beyond our obligations to those conceived using MRT.

6.4 Filling a Conceptual and Normative Gap

In Chapter 2, I undertook the first steps towards identifying the conceptual and practical gaps in the landscape of explicit regulatory protections and prevalent bioethical characterisations of our identity-related interests in accessing bioinformation about ourselves. I noted that, in the current landscape, the precise nature of the relationship between bioinformation and identity, and the normative dimensions of this relationship, often

---

[28] Lindemann 2001, p. 187.
[29] Scully 2017, p. 42
[30] Edelman 2015.
[31] Lindemann 2001, p. 6; Scully 2017, p. 44.

remain ambiguous, exceptionalist, or reliant on biologically essentialist views of identity. Having developed a picture of the nature and strength of our information-related identity interests I want now to take stock of what recognition of these interests would add to the ethical landscape and why it is crucial that we attend to identity interests in their own right.

Widening the Aperture

I have sought to demonstrate over this and the preceding chapter that our identity-related interests in our encounters with personal bioinformation are real, ethically significant, and engaged by a range of different kinds of bioinformation. Recognising the roles played by bioinformation in enhancing or undermining our capacities to develop and maintain inhabitable identity-constituting narratives offers a useful and plausible perspective that – I suggest – does not do violence to the reported experiences of information subjects. It not only introduces a clear basis for understanding the ethical significance of bioinformation's impacts on and roles in our identities but also widens the scope of what these impacts and roles might look like. Not least – as the illustrative examples in the previous chapter indicate – it suggests that it is necessary to be alert to effects that might not already be recognised and labelled as 'identity related' by information subjects, those who manage our bioinformation, or academic commentators. Similarly, it highlights that the kinds of effects that warrant serious ethical attention can include, but also extend far beyond, many of the most commonplace tropes associated in the literature with 'identity impacts' of health-related or genetic information – namely disruption, labelling, or the adoption of biologised or geneticised self-conceptions. Shifts in information recipients' understanding of their identities instigated by encounters with bioinformation do not need to adhere to these tropes, much less entail wholesale personal reinvention, to be keenly felt and make meaningful differences to values, outlook, and engagement with the world.

Adopting a narrative lens makes insights into this wider nature of identity impacts possible because this lens refocuses our attention on the experiences of living with identities that are complex, multifaceted, intersectional wholes, with crucially interpretive, diachronic, and evolving natures. Our identities are not just loose bundles of discrete identifiers. Nor are they monolithic entities simply to be preserved or lost. And the kinds of impacts that warrant ethical attention are not limited to 'identity loss' or to the addition and replacement of labels and contents.

Just as important are the advent and loss of interpretive tools that help us make sense of or reframe existing characteristics and the relationships between these characteristics and our experiences. Even where labels or characteristics are acquired or revised, this is rarely an isolated event or best thought of in this way. Rather, a narrative conception of identity allows us to recognise that it is part of reciprocal shaping and meaning-making amongst the many intersecting threads that make up the fabric of someone's story of who they are. For example, diagnostic testing may lead someone to newly describe themselves as 'diabetic', but this may also, in turn, shape, what it means for them to be 'a father', 'healthy', 'a long-distance cyclist', and 'much like my grandfather'. Because of this wider network of interpretive and sense-making effects and the associated consequences for the intelligibility and inhabitability of the *whole* of the information subject's identity, we are able to recognise why changes to aspects of someone's self-characterisation *matter*. They are neither merely aesthetic nor simply about preserving a preferred persona. They go deeper and wider. When personal bioinformation supports someone in developing, understanding, occupying, and enacting who they are as an entire person, and thus in enabling them to realise and exercise their experiential, practical, and evaluative capacities, it engages ethically significant interests and has real value.

Foreseeable Identity Harms

In addition to allowing us to recognise the nature and scope of *valuable* identity roles played by bioinformation, a narrative conception also shines a light on the possibility of real identity *harms*. As noted above, the identity significance, value, and detriment of particular information encounters are not intrinsic qualities, but rather are dependent on a range of variables, several of which arise from the interpretive framework supplied by the communication context and specific self-narrative of the individual recipient. It therefore may not be at all straightforward reliably to predict a priori whether or to what extent particular personal bioinformation will prove valuable to a particular individual. As I shall explore in the next chapter, this presents challenges, though not necessarily insurmountable ones, to meeting identity interests in practice. However, I want to suggest that there are at least two circumstances in which the likelihood of non-trivial identity *harm* may be reliably foreseen. These circumstances involve the communication of misleading information and the communication of information that would introduce oppressive or degrading narrative threads.

Misleading Information

The picture of identity interests I have presented above has implications for the epistemic qualities of the kinds of bioinformation that are likely to serve us well. By 'epistemic qualities', I mean those relating to information's fit with the world and its 'adequacy for the practical purposes for which [it] is used'.[32] The practical purpose here is the construction of an inhabitable identity. This undertaking entails interpretation and navigation of a material, biological, relational life. For this reason, I want to suggest that the identity value of bioinformation – its capacity to fulfil our basic identity interest – depends to a great extent on it providing us with *dependable* insights into our past, present, or (likely) future health, bodily states or functions, and biological relationships. Information that would fail to meet this criterion is not limited to that which is straightforwardly false. It includes ambiguous and misleading information, for example estimates of disease risk with high percentages of false positives and negatives; vague or under-contextualised prognoses; test results that draw unwarrantedly deterministic conclusions about complex multifactorial traits; and 'findings' that are incapable of speaking meaningfully to the state of affairs they purport to.

To illustrate the problem with misleading information, we can imagine someone who uses a novel automated blood testing service offered by their high-street pharmacist, a test which fraudulently purports to be able to detect a range of health-related biomarkers when it is actually unable to do so with any reliability or accuracy.[33] We can further imagine that this customer receives false positive results for, amongst other things, syphilis antibodies and an overactive thyroid. Consequently, they experience distress about their health and a sense of unfamiliarity and loss of confidence in their own body. They come to mistrust their partner and their own judgement and feel ashamed. They had been seeing a counsellor to address mood swings and sleeplessness but now believe these are most likely to be symptoms of hyperthyroidism, so decide not to continue with counselling. And they had been trying to get pregnant but can no longer imagine parenthood as part of their future.

---

[32] De Winter 2016, p. 79.

[33] This example is based on tests offered by the now discredited Theranos's 'Edison machine' that was used in-store in Walgreens pharmacists in the USA. See Topol 2018.

I would suggest that the suite of effects just described could constitute non-trivial identity harms. Anders Nordgren and Eric Juengst raise a similar concern about provision by DTC genetic testing services of misleading, 'inadequate' information about health risks or ancestral heritage. They suggest that such information may 'distort rather than clarify [their] clients' subjective experience of their identities'.[34] This is a valuable insight. But I want to suggest that it is not just the individual's 'subjective experience' of identity that is distorted by vague and under-contextualised DTC genomic tests or by the inaccurate blood test described above. More fundamentally, it is the coherence, intelligibility, and sustainability of recipients' identity narratives that suffer. This threat has four dimensions.[35] First, there is the possibility of unnecessary stigma, alienation, and hopelessness in response to erroneous results. Second is the, also unnecessary and potentially distressing, work of narrative reconfiguration and reinterpretation by the recipient. Third, the resulting misconceptions about their health, bodily states of affairs, or relationships may render the recipient's self-narrative an unreliable foundation from which to live and act in the world and through which to continue to interpret and constitute who they are. In the above example, they have withdrawn from plans and commitments that provided meaning and sustenance to their sense of self. Fourth, the self-narrative they come to occupy is premised on misleading beliefs about their health, body, and relationships. This renders it vulnerable to being further undermined when they run up against their own embodied experiences and others' conceptions of the world. For example, the person in the above vignette is now liable to misattribute future episodes of poor mental health and fail to address these in suitable ways. And if further tests reveal they were never infected with syphilis, their sense of themselves as betrayed and principled may be abruptly replaced by an uncomfortable picture of themselves as untrusting and judgemental.[36]

The depth and severity of identity detriment in cases such as this will depend on how central the newly acquired, precariously founded characteristics and reinterpretations are to the recipient's self-conception.

---

[34] Nordgren and Juengst 2009, p. 166.

[35] Adam Henschke argues that a self-characterisation based on falsehoods is no less worthy of respect. I will return to consider whether this is so in relation to others' responsibilities to enable such a characterisation in the next chapter, Henschke 2017.

[36] While, as noted in this and the preceding chapter, not all narrative disruptions are detrimental, they are often undesirable, particularly if the path to reconstruction is painful or overwhelming.

And it is clear that what matters is not solely the epistemic limitations of the information itself, but these coupled with the recipient's lack of awareness of these limitations and their uncritical accommodation of the information as presented.

To be clear, I am not seeking to claim here that simply being *true* is *sufficient* for personal bioinformation to be relevant or valuable to our self-narratives. Much of it, no matter how robust, will be irrelevant, superfluous, or unwelcome. Rather, my suggestion is that only under very limited circumstances could it be in our identity interests to receive false, unreliable, or meaningless bioinformation. Furthermore, the narrative harms associated with misleading bioinformation may obtain even, and perhaps especially, if this information is welcome and keenly sought. This possibility is only revealed if we appreciate – as a narrative lens allows us to do – the importance of the structure and interpretive features of our identities alongside the desirability of their 'contents'. I will return to examine possible tensions between desired yet structurally problematic narrative contributions shortly.

Damaging Narrative Contents

Whether particular kinds of bioinformation contribute meaningful or comfortable narrative contents will – for all the reasons described above – vary between individuals and circumstances. However, might it be possible to say something, if not wholly a priori then at least widely applicable, about some kinds of information that would invariably make for *less* inhabitable and practically enabling self-narratives?

I want to suggest that there are two further sets of potentially overlapping circumstances in which this would be the case. The first concerns bioinformation that is uncritically presented to the information subject as deterministic or revealing who they essentially are. Even if, for example, a disease prognosis or revelation of a genetic relationship is true as far as biological matters of fact are concerned, these matters of fact do not, at least without further narrative work, define the subject's identity. When they are presented by others as doing so, however, they risk not only constraining the individual's self-authorship but could also sow seeds of narrative factures and discomfort. This is illustrated, for example, by donor-conceived individuals who remain uncomfortable with the knowledge of their origins, distressed that their wider family does not know who they 'really are'.

The second set of predictably identity-damaging circumstances are those in which bioinformation arrives ready-invested with stigmatising, demeaning, or oppressive connotations. These may be connotations that are derived from the wider social and institutional environment or the immediate communication context. For example, some traits or conditions – such as those relating to particular disabilities or those marking departures from sex, gender, cognitive, or aesthetic norms – may, due to racism, ableism, or other kinds of prejudice, be associated with negative stereotypes. We might think here of the potentially stigmatising connotations of schizophrenia, differences in sex development (DSD),[37] or the ways in which the language of genetic 'mutations' to describe test results might contribute to negative self-image to those receiving diagnoses or positive test results.[38] Where the negative associations of such traits are sufficiently evident in others' reactions or prominent in public debate or cultural representations, these may be incorporated into recipients' self-narratives alongside the purported 'bio' state of affairs reported by the information.

When we experience bioinformation as contributing stigmatising or degrading self-descriptors or interpretive lenses that colour wider narrative threads, this not only threatens the comfort or desirability of our identities.[39] It can also undermine our abilities to make sense of or sustain our own experiences of, and beliefs about, who we are and what we are like, where these are at odds with the associated negative stereotype, or where these stereotypes undermine our self-esteem or authorial control.[40] As Catriona Mackenzie notes, oppressive social forces, non-recognition of our chosen self-descriptors, and lack of self-worth undermine our confidence and capacity to be authors of our own identities, not least by 'curtail[ing] our imaginative explorations of alternative possibilities of action, emotion, belief, and desire'.[41]

Information subjects may sometimes have the personal and interpretive resources to resist the narrative harms invited by bioinformation that carries particularly stigmatising or degrading associations. And it may be possible for others to help avert or ameliorate such harms by using particular communication strategies or offering interpretive support.

---

[37] DSDs include, for example, having physiology, genitals, or internal sexual organs more commonly found in people of a different chromosomal sex.

[38] Esplen et al. 2009.

[39] Mackenzie 2000.

[40] It is not only the identities of *recipients* of bioinformation with demeaning or oppressive associations that will be affected by these associations but potentially anyone who shares the same traits or counts themselves, or is counted by others, as belonging to the relevantly same group.

[41] Mackenzie 2000, p. 144.

However, more troubling, and potentially less tractable, identity harms may arise where the bioinformation plays into, or itself purports to convey, intersections between biomarkers associated with stigmatising or otherwise negatively perceived traits or conditions and membership of populations that already face prejudice and social injustice. Here, the risk is that these intersections compound the narrative harms of existing oppressive forces. Encounters with bioinformation that introduce harmful identity contents or negative interpretive lenses may be particularly damaging for those whose self-narratives already contend with negative stereotypes and discrimination. For example, an unexpected diagnosis of sickle cell disease or psychosis may disturb anyone's account of who they are. However, these diagnoses may take on particular significance and potential for harm for recipients of African or Caribbean heritage, where the diagnoses occur in a context of racialised assumptions about the incidence of these conditions amongst people of colour, and where they compound the narrative impacts of multiple intersecting sources of oppression, including racism, underserved health needs, and epistemic injustices in which recipients' own accounts of their experiences and priorities go unheard or are given less credence.[42]

Health research involving large-scale association studies, such as those used in genomics or behavioural neuroscience, further extend the scope for negative stereotyping, where these methods – either inadvertently or motivated by problematic or vicious assumptions and hypotheses – purport not only to identify biomarkers associated with particular negatively associated traits such as low educational attainment or propensity to antisocial behaviour but also make claims about the prevalence of these traits amongst particular population groups.[43] For example, at the start if this century, researchers claimed to have identified a now widely criticised connection between being a carrier of variants of the *MAOA* gene – variants often observed in Maori populations – and a propensity to aggression.[44] Institutional information practices outside healthcare and health research may be no less implicated in contributing to the degrading, damaging connotations of certain kinds of bioinformation. For example, controversial practices of racial or ethnic profiling for forensic purposes using data held in DNA databases, such as have been used in the UK, risk stigmatising particular populations by falsely

---

[42] Bulgin et al. 2018; Nazroo et al. 2020.
[43] Saini 2019.
[44] Henschke 2010.

imputing connections between criminality, membership of particular racial or ethnic groups, and genetic inheritance.[45] The connections between biomarkers, negatively associated traits, and memberships of particular groups do not need to be true or based in sound science to shape the normative frameworks within which personal bioinformation is conveyed, received, and narratively deployed. Indeed, much of their harm lies precisely in their falsehood and the unthinking or malign uses for which they are employed. Narrative harms associated with bioinformation that introduces stigmatising or oppressive narrative tools may not be inevitable but they will often be predictable given our understanding of contributory factors such as prevalent prejudices and sources of oppression. This predictability has important implications for responsibilities and practices associated with disclosure, as will be explored in the next chapter.

6.5   Relationships between Structure and Contents

The conception of identity interest I have proposed above emphasises the importance of both the structure of our identities – their coherence, integration, intelligibility, and sustainability – and the qualities of their contents – how comfortable, welcome, and meaningful these are. Recognising these two dimensions poses a challenge when it comes to determining the identity value of information that seems to contribute to one dimension while detracting from the other. What should we say about bioinformation that is fervently sought but unreliable, or true but painful?

To explore the first of these permutations, we might imagine someone who receives a 'diagnosis' of attention-deficit hyperactivity disorder (ADHD) from a private, commercial neuroimaging clinic. They are delighted to receive this, unaware of the lack of validity or reliability of the diagnostic techniques used. In their eyes, it validates their existing beliefs about their impulsive and distracted behaviour and appears to counter friends' suggestions that they are prone to being emotionally immature and thoughtless. Does receipt of these results serve, or undermine, their identity interests?

Any assessment of the identity value of results, such as those just described and those detailed below, will of course depend on the

---

[45] Racial profiling involves conducting searches for genetic markers associated with a family membership, shared ancestry, or particular inherited traits. See Skinner 2020.

context and manner in which they are communicated and the existing self-narrative of the recipient. And none of what I say here is intended to second-guess the perspectives and wishes of actual recipients, but rather to illustrate the complex and variable relationship between the veracity, desirability, and identity value of personal bioinformation. Allowing for this, I would suggest that in the example above, the 'contents' value of the ADHD diagnosis is unlikely to outweigh the structural deficiencies it introduces. This is in part because its perceived value is dependent on its truth and would presumably dissolve if its falsity were exposed. It is also because the risks, that a narrative built around this misleading diagnosis will be undermined by future experiences and provide a poor basis for the recipient's management and interpretation of their behaviours and traits, are neither unlikely nor trivial. If this is so, the diagnosis, while welcome, at the very least fails to serve the recipient's identity interests and it could well threaten them.

However, if we look at another example of welcome but unreliable findings, the balance of identity benefit to harm might look quite different. In this instance, let us imagine someone who uses a DTC genomic ancestry tracing service to find out where their enslaved ancestors were trafficked from. This person embraces their results, which report a high proportion of genomic markers associated with Ghanaian ancestry. They experience the opportunity to discover Ghanaian roots, to honour the suffering and survival of their forebears, and to make connections with others who share this heritage as contributing valued meaning and purpose to their sense of who they are and as helping to fill in the missing history and self-descriptors that slavery and colonialism have denied them.[46] However, these results trace only the maternal line in each generation, so account for a tiny fraction of the individual's heritage, they rely on markers also present in populations of other countries, and they cannot account for population movements prior to trans-Atlantic slavery.[47] Let us also imagine the recipient is not made adequately aware of how partial and unreliable their results are.

---

[46] This example is borrowed, with some adjustments and simplification, from the experiences reported by participants in Alondra Nelson's research with 'roots seekers'. For a more detailed discussion of participants' experiences and Nelson's own nuanced interpretation of the identity role of this information, see Nelson 2008.

[47] Given population movement and limitations in the genomic markers and reference data sets used by DTC genomic ancestry services, they are generally unable to provide

Here, the likelihood of overall identity benefit might be somewhat greater than in the previous example, though not inevitable. This is in part because – in this imagined example – the 'contents value' to the recipient of being able to build Ghanaian heritage into their identity narrative is so substantial. A narrative constructed around misplaced beliefs about ancestry is also less likely to be easily falsified by, or present obstacles to navigating, everyday experiences. Furthermore, these beliefs may not wholly replace others the recipient has about their ancestry. As noted above, Nelson observes that many people in circumstances like those imagined here do not build their identities on the reports supplied by the DTC ancestry tracing services alone, but rather compare and combine genomic results with other genealogical information.[48] However, *if* the substantial personal and identity value invested by the recipient were to be premised wholly on the veracity of the genomic ancestry tracing, the risk of serious narrative harm may well be substantial.

What then of instances in which personal bioinformation is reliable but unwelcome and distressing? Here again, much will depend on the specifics of the situation. So, on one hand, we might say that an individual's identity interests are served overall by an authoritative diagnosis of type 1 diabetes because of the benefits for their health and also in terms of being able to construct a narrative that anticipates and accommodates experiences of and ill health and ways of planning for and managing these. This overall value may plausibly be sustained despite the diagnosis also bringing unwelcome stigma, a sense of vulnerability, anxiety, the daily burden of blood-sugar monitoring and insulin injections, and loss of the valued characteristics of being a long-distance cyclist and an invulnerable partner and father. However, overall identity value is less plausibly sustained in other circumstances. For example, we might imagine an athlete who is required to undergo genetic testing for so-called sex verification purposes to determine their eligibility to compete in women's elite athletics.[49] Here, likely narrative harms include distressing disruption of the individual's characterisation of their sex and gender, the stigma of being marked out as someone who is not 'female enough', implied doubt about the legitimacy of their athletic achievements, and being obstructed from competing in a sport that gives their life meaning.

---

meaningful insights into ancestral geographical origins at an individual level. For discussion of the limitations of genetic ancestry tracing, see Royal et al. 2010.

[48] Nelson 2008.

[49] See, for example, Camporesi 2019.

It is not hard to imagine these identity harms being so great as to be too high a price to pay for any potential interpretive benefits of accounting for particular traits associated with a diagnosis of a difference in sex development or of being able to seek medical advice and support for any health or reproductive implications of living with this condition.[50]

The first thing I want to take from these four examples is that there is no rigid rule about whether bioinformation that contributes to the coherence of our self-narratives is more valuable than that which contributes to its comfort. However, these examples also indicate the difficulties of conceiving of lives in which an identity narrative is alienating but still largely coherent, or unintelligible but nevertheless truly comfortable. Here, we may recall Walker and Rogers's observation that, when seeking to make sense of and restore narrative coherence following unexpected diagnoses of asymptomatic illness, some people experience anxiety or become uncomfortably hypervigilant about their health.[51] This observation and the imagined examples above suggest that we should think of the 'structural' and 'contents' dimensions of our self-narratives as deeply intertwined and mutually limiting aspects of their inhabitability not as separable features. Bioinformation that affects one dimension of inhabitability for the worse is unlikely to leave other dimensions wholly undiminished. So, while coherence and comfort may sometimes exist in tension, the impacts of bioinformation on each cannot be considered in isolation.

6.6 Distinguishing Identity from Other Interests

Having closely examined the nature of our information-related identity interests I now want to turn to address the question of what being able to recognise and appreciate the strength of these interests adds to the ethical landscape of bioinformation governance. It is all very well characterising the strength of our information-related identity interests and the circumstances in which these are engaged, but this endeavour would not be a practical priority if identity interests were sufficiently protected by the suite of ethical concerns that already inform disclosure policies and practices. In this section, I will explain why information subjects' identity

---

[50] This example is not premised on the assumption that chromosomal or other kinds of testing can be used to determine sex, which is not a binary category, but it does assume that some kinds of testing may reveal differences in sex development that might be useful, for example in explaining amenorrhea or infertility.

[51] Walker and Rogers 2017.

interests are neither reducible to nor coextensive with the other interests most commonly invoked when it comes to ethical governance of subjects' access to personal bioinformation.

As highlighted in Chapters 2 and 5, the interests and concerns most commonly invoked include protection of information subjects' health, avoidance of psychological distress, promotion of autonomy, and respect for privacy and private life, with the idea of personal utility attracting increasing attention. It will not be possible to provide comprehensive mappings of all the ways each of these differs from our interest in narrative self-constitution. However, I will provide a sketch of the broad contours of divergence and intersection to demonstrate that our informational identity interests would not be met by attention to these other interests alone and that identity, therefore, requires attention in its own right and on its own terms.

Psychological Distress

As previously noted, the risk of psychological distress is often cited as grounds for *not* providing non-actionable, probabilistic genetic test results. And there is an exception to information subjects' legal entitlements to access their personal health data in UK data protection law if it would cause 'serious harm' to their 'mental health'.[52] As the discussions of the preceding chapters make clear, although threats to the inhabitability of our self-narratives may indeed be experienced as distressing, their personal and ethical significance is not reducible to this distress. Nor is it necessary for narrative harms to manifest in distress or psychological damage for them to have serious ramifications for our well-being and practical capacities. As previously noted, distress is not straightforwardly correlated with identity harms. Valued insights into our biological lives may initially be deeply upsetting to hear, and welcome but ill-founded self-descriptors may end up jeopardising narrative sustainability and intelligibility. Thinking in terms of identity impacts, therefore, requires us to look beyond emotional distress as the sole or paradigmatic harm associated with encounters with personal bioinformation. Conversely, if we are equipped to recognise when identity harms might be at the root of someone's distress or anxiety, we may then be in a stronger position to assess whether offering epistemic, interpretive, or personal tools of

---

[52] Data Protection Act 2018, Schedule 3, Part 2(5).

narrative reconstruction might be an effective means of averting or alleviating this distress.

Clinical Actionability

Many legal provisions and policies governing subjects' access to bioinformation – from instituting of screening programmes, to duties to weigh relatives' interests in knowing about genetic risk, or return of individual research findings – make clinical actionability, including reproductive decision-making, the condition of disclosure.[53] As described in the previous chapter, there are important areas of overlap between personal bioinformation that is clinically actionable or useful for health-related decision-making and that which serves the inhabitability and sustainability of our identity narratives. For example, health protective behaviours may contribute important narrative contents and threads. And restoring health may be prerequisite for having the capacities to engage in self-definition. However, our identity interests extend far beyond preserving or restoring health, for example when it comes to understanding our non-health traits and our relationships to others, or when bioinformation informs the trajectory of our biographies and life projects. And some health insights may be unhelpful or otiose to our self-narratives. The nature and strength of our interests in narrative self-constitution present a credible challenge to assumptions that clinical actionability exhausts or is invariably foremost amongst the ethical grounds for offering findings. Although identity development is not a matter of life or death, it supports capacities that comprise core elements of a rich practical and moral life and, as such, carries comparable ethical weight to many health-related concerns.

Personal Utility and Preparedness

The concepts of 'psychological preparedness' and 'personal utility' are sometimes invoked in attempts to capture information's value beyond its clinical utility. Personal utility is broadly understood as a quality of information that the subject finds useful for reasons other than addressing their health concerns, that they find entertaining, or that piques their curiosity.[54] While it is increasingly common to encounter academic

---

[53] See discussion in Chapter 2.
[54] Bunnik et al. 2014.

proposals that personal utility or preparedness could provide grounds for disclosing some categories of bioinformation, for example individual research findings, it is not clear the extent to which these proposals are reflected in actual healthcare or research practices. Clinical actionability certainly appears to remains the principal consideration.[55] As indicated in Chapter 5, preparedness – understood as adjusting expectations and plans to accommodate future illness – could be one dimension of identity value. Personal utility too may overlap with identity value, but the two are not equivalent. Providing bioinformation solely because it fulfils the recipient's curiosity or assists practical preparedness could be contrary to the recipient's identity interests when the findings are unreliable or when the manner of communication is negligent as to how it impacts valued self-characterisations.[56] Nevertheless, it could be possible to see identity value as a more tightly specified sub-species of personal utility.[57] And the characterisation of narrative identity interests offered here could contribute conceptual focus, cautionary notes, and normative heft to at least some dimensions of the arguments that are already made for the provision of personal bioinformation on grounds of personal utility and preparedness.

Privacy

Privacy interests may not seem immediately relevant here. When it comes to the governance of personal bioinformation, privacy is most commonly invoked in relation to *others'* access to and uses of information about us, rather than our own encounters with it. However, there is one clear sense in which privacy may appear pertinent to disclosures *to* information subjects. Conceptual accounts of what privacy means and the source – if any – of its personal and public value are numerous and vigorously debated.[58] Amongst these are the suggestions that it involves the 'right of the individual to be let alone'[59] and to be 'free from some kinds of intrusions'.[60] These ideas are echoed by Graeme Laurie, who argues that protection of privacy – understood as a metaphorically spatial

---

[55] Ravitsky and Wilfond 2006.
[56] A more refined conception of personal utility that takes the implicit normativity of 'utility' seriously might avert some of these concerns – see Bunnik et al. 2014.
[57] Postan 2016.
[58] Solove 2002.
[59] Brandeis and Warren 1890, p. 193.
[60] Scanlon 1975, p. 315.

'state of (psychological) separateness from others' – provides the rationale for a strong initial, although defeasible, presumption against invading that space by imposing unknown and unsought genetic information on information subjects.[61] Laurie suggests that this kind of spatial privacy is not *intrinsically* valuable but derives value from the instrumental role it can play in protecting other interests. These include 'creating space to develop one's own sense of identity and personality'.[62] The substantial influence of this analysis within bioethics and legal scholarship notwithstanding, spatial privacy does not yet appear to have been used in law to justify upholding the so-called right not to know.[63]

Laurie's conception of spatial privacy and its ethical justification in identity-development terms diverges, however, from the picture of identity development I have presented. Narrative self-constitution does not depend on spatial, social, or epistemic separation. It is an inherently relational undertaking, dependent on interaction, negotiations, and collaboration with others, and is often reliant on their contributions to helping us construct intelligible accounts of ourselves. Furthermore, the arrival of previously unknown and unsought bioinformation may sometimes serve our identity interests. As I shall discuss in the next chapter, it may indeed be difficult to justify unthinkingly imposing personal bioinformation on people on the assumption that they will welcome it. However, such unsought disclosures are contrary to recipients' identity interests when they are detrimental to the inhabitability of their self-narratives, not simply because they violate a necessary state of separateness. The information-related identity interests that I have proposed may be distinguished from interests in spatial privacy because the latter cannot account for the fact that we sometimes have identity interests in receiving unsought bioinformation. A more promising counterpart to identity interests might be found in a different conception of privacy, where privacy is understood in terms of informational control.[64] However, as I shall explain shortly, the exercise of informational control may also fail to track our identity interests.

Autonomy

This brings me to the final comparator: that between identity interests and those in developing and exercising autonomy. This comparison

---

[61] Laurie 2002; Laurie 2014a, p. 41.
[62] Laurie 2014b, p. 58.
[63] Laurie 2014b, p. 58.
[64] Solove 2002.

requires negotiation not only of diverse conceptions of what autonomy means and the conditions for achieving and exercising autonomy, but also of remarkably different claims made about the role of autonomy in relation to information access. These diverse conceptions may be broadly categorised as: those focusing on information subjects' entitlement to choose which information they wish to receive;[65] the value of information as a means for informing discrete autonomous choices and conduct; and the role of information in the development and exercise of the capacities for being an autonomous person. I shall address these three framings in turn, looking first at the choice to know or not to know.

The idea that autonomy is equivalent to the mere exercise of discrete 'consumer' choice is in itself problematic, representing an impoverished view of autonomy and its moral value.[66] Furthermore, while it is easy enough to understand how an 'interest in knowing' can be met through choice, it is notoriously difficult to understand how positions that prioritise 'informational self-determination' would characterise the nature and location of our interests when we do not know that particular information exists at all.[67] Even allowing for its inherent problems, there are clear divergences between this choice model of autonomy and the fulfilment of our identity interests. Chiefly, it is plausible that someone could really want to access personal bioinformation that goes against their underlying identity interest, or reject that which could serve it. And bioinformation that someone is, as yet, unaware of and cannot request could have marked impacts on the inhabitability of their identity. Positing these divergences between presumptively autonomous desires (not) to know and the fulfilment of identity interests is not paradoxical. It is a consequence of adopting a conception of identity interests in which these are not simply equivalent to the fulfilment of preferences but depend on further criteria based in the maintenance of an inhabitable self-narrative. This notwithstanding, recognising that our desires to know and identity interests may diverge does not necessarily mean that protection of identity should prevail in all circumstances – for example, that unwanted information should be forced on subjects on identity grounds.

The version of the relationship between bioinformation and autonomy that is perhaps most familiar in medical law and ethics is that reflected in

---

[65] This framing is exemplified by human rights instruments, such as the 1997 European Convention on Human Rights and Biomedicine, Article 10(2), which enshrine an individual's right to know and to not know biomedical information about themselves.

[66] O'Neill 2002.

[67] Andorno 2004, p. 436; Laurie 2004.

the principle of informed consent, where information about our health and bodies is often seen as important to exercising self-determination in healthcare decisions.[68] Again, equating autonomy with informed consent reflects a disappointingly thin, individualised conception of autonomy. However, it is possible to see, in both bioethics and also in developments in the common law regarding the information provision obligations of healthcare professionals, moves towards a richer construal of the importance of offering information that supports recipients not merely to make choices but to make ones that 'express [their] own character' and contribute to a 'life structured by [their] own values'.[69] Some of our identity interests in accessing bioinformation could coincide with, or be premised upon this objective of making healthcare-related or practical choices that reflect and enact our values. As such, a subset of identity interests might indeed be protected by recognition of the value of personal bioinformation to autonomous agency and informed self-expression in healthcare, and by holding healthcare professionals responsible, under threat of negligence, for providing this information as part of their duty of care.[70] However, this still leaves a substantial tranche of identity interests unrecognised and unprotected. These extend not only to interests in not knowing. It also includes those in accessing information that lacks immediate clinical utility or does not support imminent, discrete, practical decisions, or where withholding it would not lead to clear identifiable material, physical, or psychiatric harm of the kind required to prove negligence.[71] This would leave unprotected less concrete or agency-focused identity harms, such as those associated with being unable to make sense of one's past experiences or to re-evaluate one's personal and moral commitments.

This brings me to the most intricate of the three comparisons, that between self-constitution and our interest in being autonomous, self-determining persons and moral agents. This is intricate because there are such diverse views about what this conception of autonomy involves and what conditions must be fulfilled for someone to be deemed an autonomous person. For example, is it a capacity or result of the exercise of competencies? Does it require substantive independence from outside influences or instead depend on relational contexts? Is it a function of the internal structure of our motives, our reflective processes, or the source

---

[68] O'Neill 2002.

[69] Ronald Dworkin quoted by Lord Steyn in *Chester* v. *Afshar* [2004] UKHL 41 [2004] 4 All ER 587 at para.18. See also Chan et al. 2017.

[70] *Montgomery* v. *Lanarkshire Health Board* [2015] UKSC 11.

[71] *Montgomery* v. *Lanarkshire Health Board* [2015] UKSC 11.

and substantive character of our values?[72] This is not the place to unpack, let alone adjudicate, these debates. However, what is clear is that there is an intimate relationship between the bioinformation-related identity interests, as I have characterised them, and our capabilities to develop and exercise the capacity for autonomy. Here, autonomy is understood in terms of relational practices of critical reflection on one's values and motives, acting in accordance with these within the constraints afforded by embodied and socially embedded lives, and thus 'working out our projects in the world'.[73] Having the capacity for autonomy under this brief definition is, as described in Chapter 3, both a condition for narrative self-constitution and a product of it. However, as also noted in that chapter, autonomy is not the only valuable capacity supported by an inhabitable identity-constituting narrative. Our self-narratives also shape more passive but no less important capacities. They allow us to have a more or less clear sense of who we are and how this is connected to who we have been and who we will be in the future. Our narratives create investment in our own past and future and in our enduring commitments and projects and underpin our loyalties to and relationships with other people, our roles in their lives and theirs in ours, and our membership of groups with shared interests beyond our own agency and control. Our identity interests are entwined with our agency, but they are much more than this. They are also connected to our outlook, interpretations of the world, the nature of our experiences, and our sense of self and self-esteem. Therefore effective recognition of identity interests would protect far more than just our autonomy.

In addition to there being a wide variety of conceptions of personal and moral autonomy there are also differing views about the relationship between information and the development and exercise of autonomy. It will be instructive briefly to compare my account of our information-related identity interests with two contrasting views. At one end of the spectrum sit positions such as that offered by Jurgen Husted, who argues that imposition of unsought personal bioinformation is inherently inimical to autonomy and to autonomous self-development because of its unbidden and uncontrolled impacts.[74] While my account recognises that unsought bioinformation *could* be detrimental to our self-narratives and thus our capacity for autonomy, this is far from necessarily the case. Indeed,

---

[72] For further discussions, see Christman 1989 and Dworkin 1988.
[73] Mackenzie and Stoljar 2000; Young 1982, p. 43.
[74] Husted 2014.

Husted's position is premised on an implausibly individualistic conception of autonomy and sets an unattainably high bar for achieving autonomy or self-development in a world in which we are perpetually assailed by unsought information. As previously noted with respect to spatial privacy, our identity interests lie not in the impossible goal of maintaining an undisturbed self-narrative but in being able to make sense of shifting experiences, minimising and managing risks of deep and enduring disruption, and being supported by others in doing so.

My account also differs from accounts of the relationship between bioinformation and personal autonomy occupying the other end of the spectrum. In contrast to Husted's position, these hold that any epistemically robust bioinformation has the potential to expand options and guide decisions – particularly with respect to our future health and well-being – and so can only enhance autonomy.[75] For example, John Harris and Kirsty Keywood argue, 'where the individual is ignorant of information that bears upon rational life choices she is not in a position to be self-governing. If I lack information, for example about how long my life is likely to continue I cannot make rational plans for the rest of my life.'[76] This perspective resembles the picture I have drawn to the extent that it also makes space for recognising that even unanticipated or unsought bioinformation can enhance our capacities to be authors of our own lives, for example when it provides fresh insights into the risk of future illness. However, Harris and Keywood go further than this. They hold that reliable genetic information about health and future risks is *inherently* and *inevitably* valuable to our capacity for autonomy. This leads them to conclude that an autonomy-based interest in 'not knowing' is a paradox or contradiction in terms. Here, their position diverges from my own. I have drawn a picture of narrativity as a necessarily selective process. What matters is not the comprehensiveness of our self-narratives but their intelligibility and inhabitability. So, while these qualities *can* be jeopardised by gaps in knowledge and understanding, they are equally threatened by attempted factual completism or by incorporating oppressive modes of self-characterisation.

Our information-related identity interests are closely linked to those in having, developing, and exercising the capacity for self-determination but they are not reducible or identical to them. It is not clear to what extent the law or policies governing information disclosure are currently concerned

[75] Harris and Keywood 2001; Vayena 2015.
[76] Harris and Keywood 2001, p. 421.

to protect our interests in developing autonomy understood as the multifaceted capacity of a whole person, or if the focus remains on the thin conception of autonomy as exercise of discrete choices. If laws and policies were to expand into this more ambitious aim, they would need ways of discerning how much and under what circumstances personal bioinformation makes a valuable contribution to being an autonomous person. I want to suggest that the account of identity interests I have offered in this chapter could usefully contribute to judgements of this kind.

Looking at the ways that concerns for autonomy play out in debates about ethical information disclosures and at all the other 'usual suspects' of information disclosure ethics explored above, it is striking the extent to which these focus on the bald question of whether or not to disclose. Many of the discussions of these concerns in the literature are couched in the unhelpful and oppositional language of the 'right to know' and the 'right not to know'. Attending to identity-related interests brings a further important dimension to the ethical landscape by highlighting the central importance of the context and manner in which bioinformation is conveyed. This is a topic to which I will return in the next chapter.

6.7 A Fresh Ethical Dimension

In this chapter, I have brought to a conclusion my case that our encounters with personal bioinformation engage ethically significant interests – interests that cut to the heart of our well-being and the richness of our lives, even though the circumstances and ways in which they are engaged vary between us. These interests are rooted in a multifaceted conception of identity that is not made up of discrete self-descriptors but an interwoven and dynamic whole, the inhabitability of which depends both on the qualities of its contents and also the ways these relate to each other and to our lived experiences. My aims have not only been to highlight the significance of our information-related identity interests but also to demonstrate that these interests introduce a fresh dimension to the ethical landscape. My claim has been that these interests occupy a gap that is neither adequately mapped by existing conceptions of identity value and harm nor sufficiently covered by the suite of other interests and principles that currently dominate ethical frameworks for governance of bioinformation. In the next chapter, I will turn to examine the responsibilities of those who generate and manage our bioinformation to fill this gap by responding to our identity interests, and to consider how they might go about this in practice.

Responsibilities for Disclosure

7.1   Introduction

In this chapter, I will outline what I take to be the broad shape of the ethical responsibilities that fall to those who generate or manage personal bioinformation in respect of its disclosure to information subjects. It will be principally concerned with the nature, source, and extent of various actors' *ethical responsibilities* to meet information subjects' information-related identity interests. As discussed in Chapter 2, the extent of legal and professional responsibilities to provide, or indeed to withhold, personal bioinformation on explicitly identity-focused grounds is currently remarkably limited. These are confined chiefly to meeting conditional entitlements to information about genetic parentage and donor conception. Of course, as also discussed in that chapter, information subjects may well have legal, regulatory, or policy entitlements to, or protections from, information about their health, biology, or bodies, which might coincidentally meet their identity interests on grounds other than those interests themselves – for example, where they have broad subject access rights to their health records, or where concerns about distress from over-diagnosis or lack of clinical actionability means that screening programmes are restricted. However, as I have noted, if these provisions are developed or delivered in ways that are not informed by a clear and robust understanding of the nature and extent of possible impacts on subjects' identities and the ethical significance of these, then there is a predictable and not insubstantial risk that their identity interests will not be met or that they may even be violated.

It has been the aim of this book to fill this conceptual and normative gap and help avert this risk. This chapter represents the final step in fulfilling this purpose – though there will be much further work to be done beyond the scope of the present project, not least in conducting the empirical studies to inform practice in particular circumstances and to develop practicable and effective policy, regulatory, or legal responses to respond appropriately to protect identity interests. Given that identity interests will be affected in different ways by different kinds of personal bioinformation in different contexts and vary between individual information subjects, my intention here is not to make rigid regulatory or policy recommendations, but rather to offer a picture of the responsibilities that should inform these. In the final chapter, I will provide brief examples, in five key disclosure contexts, of what these practical responses would look like if we were to take identity-related responsibilities seriously. In this chapter, I will first outline the shape of what I take to be the four core ethical responsibilities accruing to potential disclosers. I will then examine the ethical foundations for these responsibilities, before returning to look in more detail at what meeting them entails and some of the possible challenges in doing so.[1]

7.2 Responsibilities of Potential Disclosers

The responsibilities to be discussed here relate to disclosures of personal bioinformation to which the potential recipient, the information subject, would not otherwise have direct access. And my focus is, for the most part, limited to responsibilities that accrue to those who hold or have ready access to personal bioinformation about others. As such, it is concerned with responsibilities to disclose bioinformation that already exists, is predictably likely to exist, or is reasonably readily generated, rather than to generate it de novo. Nevertheless, the distinction between conveying existing and generating new information is not a sharp one. This is because whenever information is communicated it will acquire new meanings and connotations, in effect generating new information. And, in order to make it useful, accessible, and comprehensible, almost all of the kinds of bioinformation hitherto mentioned will require analysis and interpretation. I shall argue that the interpretive contributions of disclosers are themselves central to their ethical responsibilities.

The responsibilities that I am proposing correspond to the three information-related interests set out in the previous chapter with some additions and refinements. They may be broadly summarised here as the responsibilities:

To offer, provide, or facilitate, access to personal bioinformation to information subjects where doing so could plausibly contribute to their

---

[1] I will use the phrase 'potential disclosers' to capture those who might be in a position to disclose, not only those who are ready to do so.

developing and maintaining an inhabitable self-narrative in the context of their embodied and socially embedded life;

To do this in a manner that supports the inhabitability of the recipient's self-narrative; and

To protect information subjects from exposure to personal bioinformation that is very likely to threaten the development or maintenance of an inhabitable self-narrative.

In addition to these, and in recognition of the sometimes unpredictable nature of the impacts of personal bioinformation, I want to propose the prior responsibility:

To take reasonable steps to ascertain the likely identity significance of the particular bioinformation to the information subject in the given context, and any likely benefit or detriment to the inhabitability of their self-narrative they could experience from encountering it.

These headline statements of the four responsibilities are given here by way of introduction only. I will explore further below their ethical basis and what is involved in fulfilling them. I will also unpack some possible complexities and challenges in specifying and discharging them. Two key aspects that I will unpack further are, first, that the responsibilities sketched above are pro tanto ones – not absolute but holding in the absence of stronger countervailing reasons to do otherwise. Second, their precise nature and scope will depend on the role of the potential discloser and their relationship to the information subject, and they will carry a greater imperative in some contexts than others. Before exploring these variables, I want first to review the actors to whom these responsibilities accrue and then to explore the ethical grounds for imposing duties on these actors.

Potential Disclosers

Perhaps the most obvious parties to whom the responsibilities listed above apply are healthcare professionals, who care for us, observe our health and well-being, and conduct tests and diagnoses, and investigators leading health-related research studies, who gather and process new data and generate findings about us as research participants. However, as will be clear from the preceding chapters, potentially identity-significant personal bioinformation is generated in a much wider range of contexts than healthcare and primary health research. The list of actors, therefore, who hold others' personal bioinformation or make decisions about when and how it is conveyed to its subject(s) extends, for example, to researchers making secondary use of healthcare data, or data collected for previous studies or held in biobanks. These actors may include not only researchers themselves but also those responsible for managing data resources, research ethics committees, and funders. It includes commercial actors, such as those managing DTC services that offer testing, genomic analysis or body and brain imaging, and those developing, designing, and marketing home test kits, health-tracking devices, or mobile apps which provide users with data about, for example, their diabetes risk, sleep quality, or fitness levels. It includes healthcare providers, professional bodies, and advisory committees, such as NICE, Healthcare Improvement Scotland, or the UK National Screening Committee, who are variously responsible for making decisions about, for example, which screening programmes are offered and to whom and which kinds of predictive, diagnostic, or prognostic tests or health monitoring technologies are available to patients. I also want to suggest that the responsibilities above apply beyond those acting in professional capacities. They extend to private individuals who hold personal bioinformation about another individual – for example about a shared family risk of genetic disease – who does not have direct access to it themselves. This may appear to be an implausibly wide list of parties on whom to impose, perhaps quite demanding and subtle, responsibilities for ascertaining and responding to variable and multifaceted narrative impacts. However, it is intended to provide indications of *potential* bearers of communication responsibilities. They will not all be subject to them or tasked with discharging them in all circumstances.

7.3   Ethical Foundations

The above list of potential disclosers extends far beyond those who we normally consider as having professional or legal duties of care for the health and well-being of information subjects, let alone specific duties to protect the inhabitability of their identities. I am concerned here, however, with the ethical rather than the legal foundations for disclosure responsibilities, even if part of my aim is to provide persuasive grounds for some responsibilities that could or should be enforced in law. The ethical rationale I will set out in this section owes something to both an ethics of care perspective, which emphasises our relationships of mutual dependence and the importance of attention to individual embodied and social needs and vulnerabilities, and a particular conception of beneficence thought of in terms of 'helpfulness', as proposed by Thomas Scanlon.[2]

Anchoring both of these ethical perspectives is the strength of our information-related identity interests. As described in the previous chapters, this strength is grounded in our fundamental interest in developing and maintaining inhabitable identity-constituting narratives and the conditions this establishes for particular valuable experiences and capacities – including understanding who we are and what we value – which play a central role in our fulfilling, practically engaged, embodied, and socially embedded lives. Our information-related identity interests are, therefore, serious and deserve to be recognised and taken seriously by others. As also described in the preceding chapter, bioinformation will not fulfil, or thwart, this basic interest in the same way in every instance and sometimes it will do neither. But when it does have a marked impact, it fulfils a non-fungible substantive, epistemic, or interpretive function in the particularity of our evolving self-narratives. The strength of others' responsibilities to meet our information-related interests will depend, in part, on the degree to which the disclosure in question serves or undermines our more fundamental identity interest.

Vulnerability and Need

We all have myriad interests and needs. Many of them are strong. And other actors are not generally compelled to try to meet all of these. So we need to look further for the full extent of the ethical roots of disclosure responsibilities. In essence – why should anyone else shoulder burdens associated with development of my identity narrative, even if this pursuit matters to me? The answer to this question involves looking to three key considerations: the inherently relational, interpretative, and dialogical nature of self-constitution; the relative lack of control we have over the availability of and our exposure to many kinds of personal bioinformation; and the ways this information may complement, conflict, or compensate for the identity impacts of our lived, embodied experiences.

Because narrative self-constitution is to a great extent an epistemic and interpretive process, one we do not and cannot undertake alone, we are each potentially implicated in the identity projects of those around us. This is especially so where one party holds specific means to make those projects go better or worse – as when others hold, or are in a position to

---

[2] Miller 2013; Scanlon 1998, p. 224.

obtain, bioinformation about us that is not otherwise available to us. In these cases, we are dependent on and vulnerable to their choices about conveying it to us and also to the epistemic asymmetries that their enhanced access to information creates. By this, I mean not only – and perhaps not even chiefly – asymmetries in power that arise from, for example, clinicians, institutions, or family members knowing more about our bodies, minds, or health than we do. As described in Chapter 4, from a narrative perspective particular concerns arise from asymmetries between our own perspectives upon and understandings of the world and the understandings of others – for example mismatches in understandings of our biological biography or our health risks. These mismatches place in jeopardy the correlation between our self-characterisations and how others see us, and thus threaten the externally oriented coherence of our embodied self-narratives and the respectful and supportive recognition of our self-narratives by others. Furthermore, we are often dependent on others for their support in understanding and interpreting new information in constructive ways and, similarly, we are vulnerable to any essentialising, reductive, misleading, stigmatising, or otherwise harmful interpretations that others might apply to it. The nature of this vulnerability warrants closer inspection.

Wendy Rogers, Catriona Makenzie, and Susan Dodds have developed an influential analysis of the concept of vulnerability as it applies to bioethical debates. In accordance with the definition offered by these authors, I understand vulnerability in the present context to mean being 'susceptible to serious harms (physical, psychological, and emotional) with respect to the meeting of one's vital needs – harms that impair one's ability to lead a flourishing life'.[3] Applying the taxonomy developed by Rogers and her co-authors, my claim is that as narrators and occupants of self-constituting narratives we each exist in a state of 'dispositional' 'inherent vulnerability' with respect to the inhabitability of our identities. This is a result of – in their apt description – 'our corporeality, our neediness, our dependence on others, and our affective and social natures' and what this entails for the ways in which we construct our self-narratives, the contexts in which we inhabit them, and the kinds of experiences that threaten their inhabitability.[4] This vulnerability is actualised – becomes 'occurrent' – in particular circumstances, for example when we are awaiting results from a diagnostic test for a serious illness. Some of us will additionally be more

---

[3] Rogers et al. 2012, p. 22.
[4] Rogers et al. 2012, p. 24.

markedly 'situationally' vulnerable if, for example, we live with a mental health disorder that presents particular challenges to our ability to develop a coherent sense of who we are, or if those close to us know something about us that we do not – for example about our genetic parentage – that would sever a key thread in our self-narratives.[5] And even deeper kinds of 'pathogenic vulnerability' may hold in circumstances where our selected modes of self-characterisation, or the intersectional constellations in which we arrange these, are routinely denied recognition or respect by others, when there are no comfortable, socially available master narrative templates that fit these, or when our core threads of self-characterisations are linked to degrading or oppressive stereotypes.[6] I propose that the strength of our basic identity interest and the gravity of our associated vulnerabilities are sufficient to give rise to pro tanto ethical responsibilities in others – individuals and institutions – to support those who are occurrently inherently, situationally, or pathogenically vulnerable. These are responsibilities to minimise threats to the inhabitability of information subjects' self-narratives, where they have the means to do so.

Perhaps the clearest responsibility is to refrain from actively harming information subjects by providing, or imposing, bioinformation in a way that is likely to damage the inhabitability of their identity narrative or their abilities to develop and maintain one. In some cases, the harmful impacts of particular information encounters will be hard to predict, dependent on the disclosure context and existing identity narrative of the recipient. As I shall return to discuss shortly, this indeterminacy is not in itself grounds for relieving potential disclosers of all identity-related responsibilities. Moreover, as discussed in the previous chapter, there are at least two circumstances in which narrative harm is, if not inevitable, then reasonably predictable. The first of these is the provision of information that the discloser knows to be meaningless or misleading, or at least doing so without adequate explanation of these limitations. This might include, for example, the provision of results from a commercial neuroimaging service that purports to deliver diagnoses of serious, complex psychiatric conditions using techniques that lack the necessary capabilities. The second is the provision of information that is predictably likely to be experienced as degrading, stigmatising, or oppressive in the given context – which may well coincide with false or misleading

---

[5] Rogers et al. 2012, p. 24.
[6] Rogers et al. 2012, p. 25.

information – or doing so in a way likely to exacerbate rather than ameliorate the effects of these qualities. This kind of information could include, for example, results of forensic genetic analysis that are derived and presented in such a way as to imply an innate, familial disposition to criminal behaviour.

A Duty to Help

While the responsibility to refrain from actively harmful disclosures is relatively easy to justify, it may seem less obvious why someone would have an ethical responsibility to positively benefit someone else's identity through provision of information. To explain the ethical basis of this further dimension I want to add a complementary lens to that based on need, vulnerability, and interdependence. The second lens is provided by Thomas Scanlon's justification for instating a 'Principle of Helpfulness', which he sets out using the following example:

> Suppose I learn, in the course of conversation with a person, that I have a piece of information that would be of great help to her because it would save her a great deal of time and effort in pursuing her life's project. It would surely be wrong of me to fail (simply out of indifference) to give her this information when there is no compelling reason not to do so. It would be unreasonable to reject a principle requiring us to help others in this way (even when they are not in desperate need), since such a principle would involve no significant sacrifice on our part.[7]

As it happens, Scanlon uses information provision as his example here, but – just as he intends this principle to apply beyond information transactions – I want to hold that it holds not only in instances of offering personal bioinformation, but also those of conveying it in a helpful manner, and withholding bioinformation when doing so would not amount to contemporaneous harm. Scanlon's Principle of Helpfulness takes us beyond moral responsibilities not to harm, which are generally more easily justified, into the realm of responsibilities to those to act for the benefit of others. Moreover, it applies where another's needs are not so urgent as to give rise to a duty to *rescue* but are nevertheless worthy of ethical attention and intervention. The responsibility here is one of supporting others in furthering their significant and legitimate interests. In Scanlon's account this is not intended to include excessively demanding duties. A responsibility to help holds where the ratio of benefit to the

---

[7] Scanlon 1998, p. 224.

information subject to cost to the potential discloser is relatively high. The presence of compelling countervailing reasons and 'significant sacrifices' could be sufficient to override this responsibility to help. I shall indicate what such countervailing considerations could look like in the case of identity-significant bioinformation shortly.[8] As to the nature of the benefit in the context of bioinformation disclosures, this might not be best described in Scanlon's terminology of saving 'time and effort'.[9] However, his characterisation of the benefit in terms of supporting the beneficiary's 'life's project' is strikingly apt where the benefit is one of supporting narrative authorship and narrative inhabitability.[10]

Scanlon's Principle of Helpfulness, with some additional specifications, has been used by Franklin Miller and his co-authors as grounds for researchers' responsibilities to return health-related incidental findings to participants.[11] Here, I seek to apply it beyond return of research findings. Miller and his co-authors suggest that Scanlon's principle would be implausibly broad if, for example, it were read as requiring one to give unsolicited health-related advice to a stranger on a bus. So they seek to further specify it by proposing there must be a professional relationship between the parties and that the potential discloser has legitimate 'privileged access to private information' as a result of this relationship.[12] I, however, do not want to insist that identity-related responsibilities depend on the existence of a formal professional relationship.

I submit that it is reasonable to extend the duty to help more widely because of the importance of our information-related identity interests and because of the range of parties who are in a strong position to serve or frustrate these. However, I would follow Franklin and his co-authors in limiting the duty to those actors whose position, skills, and relationship with the information subject place them in a particular kind of privileged, and indeed powerful, position. This is the position of holding, or being readily able to acquire, bioinformation that the subject would not otherwise have – and which could have significant impacts on their narrative projects – and controlling the subject's access to it. Here, we can call again on the concept of vulnerability introduced above. Information subjects are vulnerable to the inaccessibility of particular bioinformation or to the impacts of exposure to it, and reliant on these actors, and the insights that their expertise or position

---

[8] Scanlon 1998, p. 224.
[9] Scanlon 1998, p. 224.
[10] Scanlon 1998, p. 224.
[11] Miller et al. 2008.
[12] Miller et al. 2008, p. 276.

affords them, to provide, withhold, or help to interpret it. In practice, the ways and extent to which particular actors are able to support others' identity interests, the sacrifice involved in doing so, compelling reasons not to, and the presence of conflicting or coinciding responsibilities will vary with the circumstances. For these reasons, the extent of actors' identity-based responsibilities will vary too. These kinds of countervailing considerations and reasonable limits provide sufficient checks against implausibly unbounded or onerous duties.

Although I am rejecting the existence of a professional relationship as a necessary criterion, the specific roles and skills of potential disclosers *are* relevant to the nature and extent of their responsibilities in several ways. These roles and skills will shape what bioinformation they hold, the nature of their relationship to the information subject, the part they play in generating and controlling the flow of the information, and the power and authority they wield. For example, those conducting medical research generate vast quantities of findings to which participants do not necessarily have access, and many of these findings will not only be health-related but also potentially identity-significant. This is even more likely to be the case where technologies such as neuroimaging or genome sequencing are used and analyses of data from hundreds or thousands of participants are involved. This kind of privileged informational control does not only depend on professional skills. For example, family members will sometimes have knowledge of their own and other family members' susceptibility to hereditary disease through knowledge of their own status and family history.

Vulnerabilities, dependencies, and consequent responsibilities to ascertain and respond to needs are also intimately bound up with the relationship between potential discloser and recipient and to wider pre-existing responsibilities arising from these relationships. For example, healthcare professionals have a particular duty of care for their patients that, while not explicitly extending to identity protection, does encompass wider well-being. And family members, particularly parents, have special responsibilities to nurture the personal development and flourishing of close relatives, particularly their own children, by reason of their relationships with them and the accompanying moral duties to safeguard their well-being. It is not implausible to hold that for parents these duties encompasses, albeit implicitly, that of providing the tools for their children's independent identity-development.[13] I would

---

[13] The presumption of this kind of responsibility might, for example, be evidenced in the emphasis placed on the importance of early-years development and expectations that parents will support their children's learning and increased independence.

further suggest, as illustrated by all three examples discussed in Chapter 5, that we are often in a special position to anticipate the identity-related needs of family members and act as valuable interpretive partners in making personal narrative sense of the implications of newly received personal bioinformation.[14] If, as I am suggesting, ethical responsibilities to support others' information-related identity interest are grounded in the intersection of these interests, information subjects' vulnerability, and the principle of helpfulness, it is not difficult to see how family members' ethical responsibilities can follow from being in this special position.

I want to follow Rogers and her co-authors in suggesting that the causal history of information subjects' identity-related vulnerabilities also have a bearing on others' ethical responsibilities to contribute to rectifying these. These responsibilities are likely to be greater when the potential discloser has played a role in creating these vulnerabilities, for example by providing misleading or poor-quality information that places the future coherence and sustainability of the subject's narrative in jeopardy. This might be the case where, for example, parents have allowed their children to make misplaced assumptions about their genetic parentage. Similarly, some commentators plausibly suggest that, given the central role that state regulators of fertility treatment play in separating donor-conceived individuals from knowledge of their genetic origins, these actors bear a particular moral responsibility for facilitating access to information about donor origins.[15] In these circumstances the source of the duty perhaps goes beyond helpfulness to something closer to justice.

A related line of reasoning – this time with respect to responsibilities to support the interpretation of bioinformation – may be applied to those who invite particular reliance and trust on the part of information subjects by occupying positions of authority, or by presenting bioinformation as providing especially authoritative and objective insights into subjects' embodied lives. As observed in Chapter 5, there appears to be a close connection between subjects' perceptions of bioinformation's epistemic strength and identity significance, and particular narrative harms may follow from misplaced dependence on unreliable or unsuitable findings. For those who occupy positions of presumed epistemic authority, the responsibility to convey bioinformation in a narrative-supporting fashion

---

[14] We might reasonably extend this 'special position' beyond family to long-standing friends.

[15] See Ravitsky 2016.

implies two things – a requirement to support information subjects in making sense of and understanding the limitations of any bioinformation one supplies within one's field of expertise, and a requirement to maintain humility about the legitimacy and limits to one's own abilities to prescribe the narrative role that the information subject ascribes to it.

7.4 Limiting Considerations

As indicated above, those who hold or control the generation and dissemination of potentially identity-significant personal bioinformation are not subject to absolute obligations to meet, or strive to meet, information subjects' identity interests in all circumstances. These are pro tanto responsibilities which hold in the absence of stronger reasons to do otherwise. Identity-related responsibilities will rarely operate in isolation, they comprise part of a wider suite of considerations, including their relationship to the information subject, which potential disclosers must also take into account. Chief amongst the considerations that operate as limiting factors on identity-related responsibilities is the presence of other competing interests.

The first set of limiting factors are information subjects' own potentially competing interests. For example, a responsibility to avert the risk of identity harm from exposure to a distressing diagnosis or risk information will need to be weighed against any potential health benefits of communicating these results. For example, a brother may be relieved of the responsibility to protect his sister from learning of his own susceptibility to treatment-responsive hereditary cancer when the benefits to her of averting serious illness and premature death are substantial, even if he knows this knowledge threatens to disrupt her life, potentially causing her to feel dissociated from her body and her role as a mother.

Responsibilities to disclose or withhold also need to be weighed against the interests of the potential discloser themselves and those of third parties. So, in the present example, the brother may also be relieved of the responsibility to withhold potentially identity-harming risk information from his sister if he knows that it would be of substantial clinical value to her children to know when they reach adulthood or if the effort to conceal his own risk status and subsequent screening and treatment from her would place unsustainable restrictions on his life and their relationship. These examples illustrate the ways in which our identity interests are entangled with and interdependent upon the needs and interests of others. And it is possible that identity interests will be in play on both sides of the disclosure equation. For example, an individual's identity interests in knowing the identity of her genetic mother will need to be weighed against the mother's interests in maintaining the inhabitability of her own narrative and privacy, as well as that of her family.[16]

Relevant countervailing considerations are not limited to responsibilities to particular identifiable others. Public and group interests are also implicated. For example, ethical responsibilities of researchers to communicate individual, identity-significant research findings to participants must be weighed against the possible threat to realising the socially valuable ends of research that might result from the investment of scarce time and research resources in identifying, validating, offering, and communicating these findings.[17] And it is possible that a particular information subject's identity interests could be in tension with those of other members of groups to whom they belong or of the group qua collective. For example, we might imagine circumstances in which some of those living with mental health diagnoses view neurological explanations of their mental illness as alienating and reductive and thus experience the choices of others to seek neurological diagnoses for the same condition as harming the intelligibility and comfort of their own self-narratives by shifting the meaning and connotations of living with the diagnosis in undesirable ways.

The challenge of course remains in examples such as those sketched above of how to weigh identity interests and responsibilities against competing demands or, more specifically, to decide what weight identity should carry in these cases. The picture I have developed in this book does not provide a neat formula for doing so. Much will depend on the nature of the information in question, the characteristics of the potential recipient, the disclosure context, and the relationships between those involved. Weighing of diverse, incommensurable, and sometimes indeterminate competing interests engaged by information (non)disclosure is a notoriously difficult problem – one which is hardly unique to my identity-based argument. Indeed, these dilemmas are familiar from long-standing discussions of ethical decision-making in clinical genetics and the many pages written about the 'right to know' and 'right not to know' genetic information – for example where its clinical value to the one

---

[16] Similar reasoning was used in the majority judgment in *Odièvre* v. *France* – see Chapter 2 for further discussion.
[17] Miller et al. 2008.

subject must be weighed against harm to the privacy of another.[18] Recognising and responding to identity interests does not remove the need to weigh such demands, it adds another important consideration to the mix. However, this does not necessarily mean that this addition further muddies these already obscure waters. On the contrary, thinking in terms of identity will sometimes offer a much-needed means of clarifying and giving substance to several existing, sometimes under-conceptualised, or inchoate ethical concerns that may transpire to be at least in part 'about identity'. For example, if we are equipped to recognise identity interests and the ways in which these can be met, we may be in a stronger position to judge circumstances in which, for example, informational autonomy or spatial privacy do in fact warrant protection, what kinds of personal utility should be taken seriously, or what might lie beneath expressions of distress or anxiety. In these cases, excavating the identity-related roots or aspects of these concerns could offer a way of understanding what is really at stake, the normative heft of privacy or informational control, and how these concerns might best be addressed.

My aim in this book has not been to demonstrate that identity-related interests and responsibilities should always prevail whenever they come up against conflicting demands. Rather I have sought to show that they are a legitimate and ethically significant part of disclosure decision-making practices and policies and warrant being taken seriously alongside other established ethical, legal, and practical considerations. Identity-based disclosure responsibilities may coincide with or run contrary to other obligations, they may function as complementary grounds for disclosure or countervailing reasons not to. They can provide at least as compelling grounds for or against disclosure as privacy, confidentiality, or autonomy concerns do and will indeed often be closely linked to these in the ways described in the previous chapter. While it seems likely that health concerns – especially those with implications for serious illness, death, or profound pain and suffering – will usually carry greater weight, not all health concerns will be this grave. Where health threats are not substantial, identity interests may give considerations of clinical utility a run for their money. This is not solely a matter of competing interests, however. As illustrated in the preceding chapters, people's identity interests often coincide with clinical utility. In these circumstances, the former may provide greater imperatives to provide findings where clinical utility alone is not yet wholly decisive, for example where

---

[18] See, for example, essays in Chadwick et al. 2014.

there is a decision to be made about the relative benefits of instituting health screening programme.

A key part of potential disclosers' responsibilities is, therefore, to conduct a serious and thoughtful weighing exercise that gives identity interests their due alongside, and in counterpoint to, other interests. However, the idea that these responsibilities start and stop at simply weighing conflicting interests ignores further critical ethical dimensions of decision-making and communication practices. As I shall now discuss, these entail responsibilities, first to attend carefully to where potential recipients' identity interests lie, and subsequently to communicate personal bioinformation in a way that seeks to minimise narrative harm and support narrative development. The second of these holds irrespective of whether identity or another consideration prevails in the decision about whether and what to disclose.

7.5   Ascertaining Where Interests Lie

Before potential disclosers can understand what is ethically required of them, they need to know what information subjects' identity interests might look like and how best these may be met. I have suggested above that our identity-related responsibilities include those to attend to the informational needs and vulnerabilities of others and that this entails taking reasonable steps to ascertain where these lie. In contrast to assessing, for example, clinical utility, this is undoubtedly not a straightforward task. It would be potentially detrimental to recipients to make a wrong call about identity value. However, it would also be unjust to impose disclosure responsibilities on others if they had no reasonable practicable way of ascertaining this value.

The most immediate way of meeting this challenge is clearly to ask the potential recipient what they want or do not want to know and to offer them the option of receiving it. Or rather, it is not simply to *ask* but to engage in a reciprocally informing, collaborative exploration of their needs and desired ends to ascertain whether and how the information might meet these, as part of the process of raising the possibility of and offering access to it. This undertaking needs to be 'reciprocal' and 'collaborative' because, as Jackie Leach Scully highlights – in writing about genetic counselling – there are likely to be epistemic, experiential, and interpretive gaps and divergences on both sides which need to be bridged if recipients' interests are to be effectively and appropriately met.[19] Scully emphasises

---

[19] Scully 2009.

the importance of attending to and learning from potential recipients, refraining from assuming that their informational needs will be like the discloser's own, and approaching, as far as possible, an appreciation of their particular needs and perspective. This perspective will be 'shaped by a unique constellation' of variables and may be very different from our own.[20] This chimes with what was said in Chapter 6 – that the identity significance of particular personal bioinformation and its value, or harmfulness, are ultimately shaped by the interpretive perspective supplied by the particularity of the subject's existing identity narrative and circumstances. Scully argues that understanding informational interests requires 'a particular quality of attention towards the real, embodied other'.[21] She cautions, however, that the potential discloser's understanding of the needs and perspective of the potential recipient is unlikely ever to be perfect because of the different experiences, social position, and worldviews of the parties involved. Due to the particularity of each of our interpretive perspectives, Scully further suggests that the ethically appropriate attitude and approach of the potential discloser will be one that respects the 'residual unknowability' and 'ontological "otherness"' of the recipient.[22] This provides not only a strong rationale for the *practical* necessity of carefully attending to the informational needs of potential recipients but also for the *ethical* requirement to do so. This notwithstanding, potential disclosers' abilities to meet this requirement in practice may face challenges.

Obstacles to Ascertaining

The first such challenge is that, in many cases, information subjects will be unaware that there is something to be known at all. And asking them if they would want to know means effectively revealing, or revealing enough of, precisely what could be detrimental to their identity. For example, it is likely to be difficult to enquire whether someone would find it useful to know more about their parentage or about family medical history without thereby indicating that their existing beliefs about these matters are misplaced or incomplete, thus potentially seeding narrative discord and discomfort. In some circumstances, the challenge of enquiring about 'unknown unknowns' may be a stubborn one. However, it is

---

[20] Scully 2009, p. 224.
[21] Scully 2009, p. 226.
[22] Scully 2009, pp. 225, 227.

not unique to navigating identity interests. It is, for example, a notoriously thorny issue in genetic privacy debates.[23] Indeed, recognising the possibility, nature, and ethical significance of identity interests might offer some useful insights to this long-standing puzzle. The dilemma of disclosing unknown unsought bioinformation is commonly raised where genetic findings could have clinical or practical utility for the recipient, but there is a fear that revelation might be accompanied by 'undesirable' personal consequences. The harm implicit in this undesirability is often of vague provenance, scale, or significance. If disclosers are in a position to recognise when these feared harms comprise narrative detriment – as they sometimes will – they will be better placed to assess the risks of disclosure and to put in place the interpretive support that could help avert or ameliorate some of the gravest narrative harms should they arise. I will return to examine what this support could look like shortly.

Sometimes, practicalities or resource constraints will preclude truly individualised, collaborative prior discussion of identity interests – for example, where information-dependent decisions, such as whether to undergo surgery, are time-critical, when it is prohibitively costly and impractical to personalise the feedback practices from a large research study, or where bioinformation is automatically delivered by wearable personal devices. In other cases, meanwhile, individualised consideration of whether to disclose may seem otiose, either because the information has overwhelming clinical value, or because its practical value is negligible and there seems to be a highly likely and serious threat of harm to identity. While remaining mindful of what has been said above about potential disclosers' limited capacities to imagine others' identity needs, in cases such as these, it may be necessary and desirable to institute broad identity-responsive disclosure policies.

These policies need not be wholly blunt instruments. Empirical studies of the kinds explored in Chapter 5 can provide valuable insights. Genetic counselling tools, such as the *BRCA* Self-Concept Scale, offer evidence-based means of identifying how different population subgroups may respond to disclosure.[24] And, even if it is not possible to predict precise narrative harms or benefits, it may be possible to anticipate when identity impacts of some kind could be afoot. As described in the previous chapter, identity-significance is shaped not only by the narrative

---

[23] See Laurie 2002.
[24] Esplen et al. 2009.

perspectives of recipients but also by a cluster of publicly discernible factors. These include the nature and scale of the consequences for information subjects' health and bodies, and the prior meanings and identity relevance ascribed by shared social and cultural practices to the information and the biological states of affairs it reports. Similarly, it is possible to anticipate when particular kinds of information are likely to be inimical to inhabitable self-narratives because they are false, misleading, stigmatising, or otherwise restrictive of self-authorship. It will also often be possible to discern when particular situational or pathogenic vulnerabilities arising from, for example, living with stigmatising conditions or in the shadow of oppressive stereotypes might make particular kinds of bioinformation particularly valuable or identity-threatening. These various anticipatory methods might not deliver infallible insights at an individual level. However, they can help mark out territory in which attention to identity impacts is particularly warranted and where identity-supporting methods of communication are a high priority. Such disclosure policies will of course need to remain flexible and responsive to individual circumstances and emerging evidence.

Navigating Choice

I have suggested that potential disclosers should discuss with information subjects what they might wish to know. But what should be done when subjects' wishes appear to run sharply contrary to others' careful and thoughtful assessment of their identity interests? This dilemma arises because, as I have argued, our identity interests are located in the development and maintenance of an inhabitable self-narrative, not solely in fulfilment of the sheer choice to know or not to know. This does not mean that inhabitability and choice are unconnected. Being able to exercise choice is a key to the agential skills and self-esteem that allow us to be confident authors of our own narratives. And it is of course the case that we will often be the best judges of our own narrative needs. However, we can also be mistaken. The empirical research discussed in Chapter 5 illustrates how, for example, people's actual and longer-term reactions to learning of disease susceptibility can differ markedly from their prior expectations. And it is possible to imagine, for example, someone fervently seeking access to individual findings from their participation in a psychiatric neuroimaging study, believing these will give them the insights they need to make significant personal and professional changes, when these findings are simply not reliable or meaningful at an individual level. Conversely, we might imagine genomic research revealing that a participant is a carrier of a serious, rare genetic disorder when they have elected not to receive individual feedback. For the purposes of these examples, let us suppose that receipt or ignorance of findings in each case respectively poses a substantial threat to the future intelligibility, comfort, and meaning of the participants' self-narratives.[25] Would the research teams be ethically justified in coercing these participants into maintaining an inhabitable and sustainable identity by denying the findings in the first example and imposing them in the second? I want to suggest that the answer here is not as obviously or invariably in the negative as might sometimes be assumed.

Let us look at some positions from which the answer would be 'no'. Pierre Widmer argues that one has the right to 'adopt and maintain a subjective image of oneself, which may objectively be false'.[26] I would submit that talk of rights here is unhelpful. Not only does it demand that we enquire what this right is based upon – Widmer himself suggests it lies in the preservation of a 'desirable picture' of oneself – but it also unhelpfully collapses the matter of where our interests lie with how others should respond to them. I have argued that it is generally not in our interest to occupy a self-narrative that is unsustainable and at odds with embodied experiences and others' understandings of us and the world, even if it is apparently a 'desirable' one in the sense of being currently untroubled and pleasing. However, it is also important that we respect each other's different worldviews and individuality, which suggests a requirement to recognise and support others' narratives and narrative choices. Might there be limits to this recognition – particularly where the coherence, sustainability, and future comfort of someone's narrative are predictably under threat?

In discussing forms of identity harm, Adam Henschke considers the limits to our ethical obligations to recognise and respect others' self-characterisations. He argues that, while we are not obliged to recognise vicious self-characterisations that harm others, merely 'factually unfounded' ones – for example, that one is a vampire – warrant recognition unless they would result in 'fundamental identity

---

[25] As noted in Chapter 6, it is possible that, in some cases, uncertain but strongly welcomed bioinformation could represent an overall identity benefit. For the purposes of these examples, I am assuming that, on balance, the subjects' choices are most likely to be antithetical to an inhabitable self-narrative overall.

[26] Widmer 1994, p. 184.

instability'.[27] Henschke's conclusion regarding vicious other-harming self-descriptors seems sound. We would not be under a moral obligation to enable a white supremacist to 'prove' their solely European ancestry through genomic analysis – if this were indeed possible – and thus contribute to shoring up their racist commitments. The absence of obligation would hold even if in some sense they might be said to have some kind of thin, individualistically conceived interest in these ends. Here the contrary obligation to prevent the kinds of violence, hate speech, and significant social injustice that could arise from enabling race-based stereotypes and racist activities would outweigh any such identity interest. However, the second part of Henschke's claim seems too strong. Not only would vampire self-characterisation, assuming someone is not in fact a vampire, clearly violate the modified embodied-reality constraint I proposed in Chapter 4 – that an individual's self-narrative should be reasonably consistent with and intelligible in light of both others' experiences of the world and their own experience of their embodiment. It is also likely that, as I have sought to demonstrate, non-trivial identity harms may occur which fall short of Henschke's criterion of fundamental instability. As I have argued, self-characterisations are not discrete identifiers but interdependent threads in a multifaceted identity, and their misleading qualities or fragility have wide practical, personal, and relational repercussions. Properly recognising and, where appropriate, supporting someone's identity development through information disclosure practices, therefore, requires not simply recognising discrete self-descriptors piecemeal but also recognising the inhabitability of the whole of who someone is as a complex intersectional constellation.

For these reasons – while stressing that each case must be considered on its own merits – I would suggest that an information subject's choice to know, or not to know, is not an automatic trump. Rather, potential disclosers have a responsibility to interrogate what is chosen as part of a collaborative exploration of needs and to weigh the competing interests – including the subject's interest in exercising choice and any damage to relationships and trust arising from unwanted impositions or denials – giving identity interests the serious weight they are due. This could, I want to suggest, sometimes lead to withholding desired or imposing unwanted findings. From one perspective, this might be seen as troublingly paternalistic, prioritising others' perceptions of

---

[27] Henschke 2017, pp. 211, 213.

information subjects' well-being over their own choices. However, from the ethical perspective set out in this chapter, it can instead be seen as an appropriate response to the vulnerability of subjects' identities – vulnerability to the onslaught of embodied and social experience and to the significant impacts of bioinformation that could explain, radically reframe, or replace these experiences – and to our dependence on each other when it comes to navigating the world and helping us make sense of who we are.

7.6　Identity-Supporting Communication

The challenges of ascertaining information subjects' needs and predicting the identity value and impacts of particular encounters with personal bioinformation, combined with the fact that in many cases disclosure may be required on other grounds or be otherwise unavoidable, lend a particular imperative to the second of the four responsibilities listed at the start of this chapter. This is the responsibility to communicate personal bioinformation in ways that support narrative benefits and mitigate narrative harms. However, it is not only in these unpredictable and unavoidable circumstances that identity-supporting approaches to disclosure matter. Many of the kinds of bioinformation to which subjects do not have direct access will be probabilistic, ambiguous, or technical. The implications of these for the recipient's health and bodily existence may not be readily understood without professional guidance. Moreover, the identity significance, value, or detriment of personal bioinformation are not necessarily fixed prior to disclosure. These qualities are malleable according to factors including the intentions, focus, and tone of the discloser, the medium in which the information is conveyed, and the accompanying interpretive tools, including further contextualizing information and explanations. As demonstrated by the experiences reported in Chapter 5, the meaning of even non-technical information – for example, about the identity of one's genetic parent – may be altered by the ways and context in which is communicated. Furthermore, as noted throughout this discussion, narrative self-constitution is both an inherently interpretive and relational undertaking. It is not something we can do on our own. It springs from and depends upon discussion and negotiation with others, drawing on divergent and shared experiences and common sources of meaning. We are no less vulnerable to the ways that others help us interpret or hinder us from interpreting the role – or superfluity – of new bioinformation to our self-narratives than we are to whether we receive it at all. This vulnerability extends to the identity significance that those doing the communicating invest in the information they convey and the recognition and respect they afford to our chosen self-narratives and the tools we use to construct these. For these reasons, the requirement to communicate personal bioinformation to information subjects in an identity-supporting manner is neither 'a duty too far' nor an unwarranted imposition into recipients' private domain. It is an irreducible part of the ethical responsibilities of those who generate, hold, and manage our personal bioinformation. In the following section, I will set out the broad parameters and some examples of what identity-supporting disclosure practices look like.

What Does Identity-Support Entail?

Echoing the recommendations of others, including Scully and Christoph Rehmann-Sutter, for ethical communication practices in genetic counselling, I want to suggest that identity-supportive disclosure involves a respectful, but not disengaged, discursive approach, involving two interconnected activities.[28] First, it entails enabling recipients to understand the empirical states of affairs conveyed by information, which Scully refers to as our basic 'conceptualization of causality in the world'.[29] And, second, it entails supporting recipients to consider what this might mean for their embodied, relational identities.

The first requirement involves explaining to the recipient what the information conveys about their past, current, or future physical and mental health, their embodied states, experiences, and capacities, and their relationships to others – not only biological relationships but also those of care, trust, and dependency. The kinds of explanation required will depend on how complex, technical, or unfamiliar the information is. It might, for example, involve discussion of the clinical validity of a test – for example, how effective it is in identifying the condition or trait in question and the meaning of complex probabilistic estimates – and its clinical utility – for example, whether it points to a particular prognosis or effective course of treatment. Just as important as explaining what bioinformation *can* tell the recipient is making plain what it *cannot*. The latter might involve, for example, explaining when techniques are not yet sufficiently mature to deliver reliable insights, whether false positive or

---

[28] Rehmann-Sutter 2009; Scully 2009.
[29] Scully 2009, p. 218.

false negative results are likely, or whether confounding factors introduce uncertainties. These provisos are familiar from widespread existing recommendations for responsible communication of health findings – for example, those produced by DTC genomics – where the ethical imperative is viewed chiefly as that of averting health threats from misdiagnosis or false reassurance.[30] The imperative may be no less strong, however, where potential identity impacts are concerned and where the information concerns traits unrelated to health. Given what I have said in earlier chapters about the risks of false or misleading bioinformation – that these might not only fall short of serving useful explanatory roles in our embodied, relational narratives, but also sow incoherence and jeopardise their future resilience and sustainability – it is clear why transparency about epistemic limitations is relevant to averting not only health harms but identity ones too. Preparing recipients to appreciate bioinformation's epistemic capacities and limitations equips them to use it in a clear-eyed way and to their best advantage in the construction of their self-narratives.

The second requirement is to equip, as far as possible, recipients to assess what the information in question might mean for their accounts of who they are and to enable them to accommodate it in, or reject it from, their ongoing narrative endeavours in as smooth a way as possible. There may not always be a sharp line between this kind of assistance and that of providing guidance about information's empirical robustness. For example, a key aspect of identity-supportive disclosure would be diverting recipients from unwarranted reductionist or essentialising readings of bioinformation that, for example, conveys only probabilistic estimates of susceptibility to disease or dispositions to particular behavioural traits. In such cases deterministic readings might both be factually false and also risk impeding the inhabitability of the recipient's narrative by suggesting that unwanted characteristics are unavoidably self-defining and thereby circumscribing the scope for self-authorship. Averting deterministic readings in such cases straddles factual and self-characterising interpretative support.

At a broad level, acting as an interpretive partner may involve offering ways to counter or ameliorate distressing or disempowering impacts on recipients' defining characteristics and the frameworks within which they evaluate these. It will also involve supporting recipients in finding ways to integrate or reject information from their self-narrative in ways that

---

[30] Bunnik et al. 2011.

preserve or restore its coherence, meaning, comfort, and sustainability. Interpretive and explanatory support should, as far as possible, be delivered as part of a process of ascertaining the recipient's particular informational needs, offering them the opportunity to receive it, preparing them to receive it, and managing the effects of disclosure. Some examples of ways in which this might be achieved could include identifying groups of recipients particularly likely to be vulnerable to stigmatising, oppressive, and distressing impacts of encounters with particular kinds of bioinformation and seeking to challenge these by, for example, offering or helping recipients develop what Hilde Lindemann refers to as 'good counterstories'.[31] These counterstories are alternative narrative templates that provide a fresh perspective on oppressive social norms and which support people to 'resist' and 'uproot' existing, limiting, or degrading 'master narratives' and to replace these with more intelligible, enabling, and fulfilling alternatives.[32] Recipients' feelings of uncertainty and insecurity could be addressed by exploring practical steps they might take to ameliorate these – for example, clinical interventions, protective health behaviours, or engagement with patient groups. Timing of disclosure could also make a difference to the nature of consequences for identity – as illustrated by the markedly different reactions of those learning of donor origins early or later in life.

The experiences explored in Chapter 5 suggest that identity impacts could be substantially influenced for the better by ensuring, as far as possible, that the kinds of information provided correspond to the identity-related role it is likely to fulfil. For example, it is not uncommon for donor-conceived individuals to report that distress and disorientation following disclosure of donor conception is exacerbated by lack of further information about their donors.[33] And someone who hopes that a printed image of a brain scan will help align their family's perception of their mental illness with their own might benefit from counselling about how to discuss their diagnosis with those close to them.[34] Information – both the 'core' personal bioinformation itself and supporting contextual information and explanations – should be conveyed in a clear and accessible way. This means, amongst other considerations, not overburdening recipients with unmanageable detail and not treating disclosure as a one-off event or as a defensive maximal information

---

[31] Lindemann 2001, p. 66.
[32] Lindemann 2001, p. 67.
[33] Ilioi and Golombok 2015.
[34] See discussion in Chapter 5.

'dump'. Attention should also be paid to the medium of communication. For example, images and graphical representations of data may aid understanding. However, as they can also invite risks of unwarranted epistemic and personal reliance – as illustrated by common perceptions that neuroimages convey particularly authoritative, objective, or non-negotiable 'truths about the self' – such reliance may itself need to be anticipated and addressed. These are only sketches of preliminary suggestions. Empirical studies exploring differential narrative impacts would make a valuable contribution to developing more detailed, concrete guidance, and to understanding which individuals or groups might have particular or unexpected needs and vulnerabilities.

Recognising Limits

The requirement for wider interpretive support described above may seem to stray far beyond the legitimate professional roles and expertise of healthcare professionals, researchers, managers of biobanks and data repositories, or those designing and marketing DTC services and devices. While family members, genetic counsellors, and other healthcare professionals may be well-placed to provide the kinds of identity-focused interpretive support described here, many actors will be ill-equipped to do so. Indeed, doing so may be a practical impossibility in some circumstances, for example in research studies comprising thousands of participants, or where a health monitoring app has millions of users. However, to reiterate what I have said above, once an actor is in the business of handling and communicating potentially identity-significant bioinformation – whatever that business is – and in the absence of strong countervailing reasons, managing its identity impacts is not an optional extra or an inconvenience but an integral part of their ethical responsibilities. That said, the interpretive responsibilities I am proposing here need not necessarily fall solely upon or be carried out directly by the parties who generate the findings. Implementing robust referral pathways to suitable third-party sources of information and support, and opportunities to reflect upon identity impacts could in some cases be a wholly appropriate part of discharging the responsibilities described above.

It is nevertheless important to recognise reasonable limits to even well-informed and skilled disclosers' insights into the significance of specific bioinformation to a recipient's unique, multistranded identity narrative. Recipients, in deferring to professionals' insights and expertise on empirical states of affairs, may be inclined to defer to them on narrative matters. This is especially so when disclosers occupy a position of power and authority – as they may well do if they are healthcare professionals, research scientists, or older family members. Thus, there remains a need for humility in the face of individual difference and willingness to listen and learn, not solely to advise and instruct. This takes us back to Scully's valuable warnings about showing 'respect for the ontological "otherness" of the other' and disclosers' responsibilities to 'to comprehend as fully as possible the others' worldviews, and recognize their own cognitive and imaginative limits'.[35]

For all of these reasons, identity-supportive communication – just like enquiries as to informational needs – should involve an interpretive partnership. In Scully's terms, it is a 'joint interpretive and ethical enterprise', characterised by discussion and by listening and learning on the part of the discloser and the recipient.[36] This will allow the former to support the particular narrative needs of the latter as best they can. This kind of approach resembles that used in genetic counselling. However, it implies rather more intervention on the part of the discloser than is commonly associated with genetic counselling, where the principle of 'non-directiveness' is widely viewed as a key aspect of best practice. There is some debate about whether non-directiveness is actually achievable or a virtue in genetic counselling.[37] Rehmann-Sutter suggests that it may be neither, given that communication inevitably shapes the meaning of information and that the desired outcome is not non-direction per se but supporting people in realising their agency and leading fulfilling lives.[38] What is clear, though, is that if communication practices are to enable recipients to consider what the information implies for their identities and to realise their capacities to be authors of their self-narratives, this is unlikely to mean abandoning information subjects to their own devices. Identity-supporting practices will be those in which possible narrative framings of bioinformation are offered for discussion, collaborative reflection, and rejection as well as adoption. Useful support will not be abstract or generic, but responsive to the particular circumstances, needs, and vulnerabilities of the recipient.

I do not want to go so far as to suggest that if potential disclosers cannot ensure identity-supportive communication, personal bioinformation should not be disclosed at all. This would be too strong

---

[35] Scully 2009, pp. 226, 227.
[36] Scully 2009, p. 217.
[37] Rehmann-Sutter 2009.
[38] Rehmann-Sutter 2009.

a condition. As with all the identity-related responsibilities described here, obligations to provide interpretive support must be weighed alongside and against other legitimate ethical concerns and, where necessary, legal and reasonable practical constraints. Efforts to do so should be commensurate with the likelihood and depth of identity harms and benefits. This does not mean, however, that attending to the context and manner of disclosure is simply gold-plating or an optional extra. It is integral to taking seriously the central role of self-constitution in an engaged, fulfilling, and flourishing life. And, as noted above, it is a responsibility that holds even, or rather especially, when other priorities such as health protection prevail over identity interests in decisions about *whether* to disclose. In such cases, the imperative is to minimise identity harms when the disclosure of information that could be inimical to inhabitability is unavoidable.

Undoubtedly, each of the requirements described in this chapter carries significant resource implications. I do not seek to minimise these or to ignore disparities amongst the opportunities and resources available to different categories of disclosers to provide interpretive support. However, the practical, ethical, and regulatory measures taken to protect health, privacy, confidentiality, and autonomy in the governance of personal bioinformation also require time, care, and resources. The purpose of this book has been to demonstrate why interests in developing and maintaining an inhabitable identity deserve equally serious and committed attention.

7.7   Shared Social Responsibilities

Before closing this chapter, I want briefly to note that, on the basis of what has been said so far, it is also necessary to consider how identity-related responsibilities extend beyond particular information encounters and transactions. There is clearly a vast landscape of social, cultural, structural, institutional, and practical factors – including the ways in which bioethics and the law are conducted – that can contribute to or ameliorate stigmatising and oppressive insinuations and stereotypes associated with particular forms of embodiment and self-characterisation. These in turn influence the identity roles fulfilled by associated personal bioinformation. Addressing the responsibilities and means to tackle these wider environmental contributions to the meanings and impacts of personal bioinformation lies beyond the scope of this book. However, it must be recognised that the practical and ethical concerns explored over the previous chapters do not take place in a vacuum but within a malleable interpretive environment in which all of us are implicated as contributors.

As noted in Chapter 6, the identity-significance of particular kinds of bioinformation is often, at least in part, socially constructed. Institutional and group practices contribute not only to the potential positive or negative connotations of this bioinformation and what it conveys, but also to the extent to which these connotations gain narrative purchase. For example, several commentators have speculated that laws entitling donor-conceived individuals to know about their gamete donors on explicit identity-related grounds may contribute to a feedback loop that reinforces perceptions that this knowledge is central to identity development and thus to donor-conceived individuals' desires to know.[39] The law is, of course, not the only possible socially constructed source of identity significance. As noted in Chapter 1, research studies exploring the connections between specific biomarkers and human traits, and the ways the media report or policy-makers use the findings from such studies have the power to contribute to popular perceptions that particular kinds of biological or health-related findings convey especially direct and useful insights into what we are like as individual persons. For these reasons, the kinds of research questions that are asked, which studies receive funding, the ways that publics and participant groups are engaged, the methods used in analysing the data collected, and how the findings are reported and taken up all play a role in constructing identity significance and, thus, in associated narrative benefits or harms.

Recalling what was said in Chapter 6, it is not only futile but also a misunderstanding of the unavoidable contributions of shared social tools and practices to narrative self-authorship to seek to counter potential identity harms by trying to eliminate potential 'external' sources of identity-significance. It would not just be potentially cruel but also an ineffective and misdirected effort to deny those who want to know about their genetic origins the means to find out in an effort to counter the narrative value invested in connections to genetic origins. However, the responsibility rests on all of us who produce, disseminate, and use bioinformation – not only at a personal but also at an aggregate or population level – to use the tools at our disposal to minimise the potential for narrative harms and to support imaginative authorship of varied forms of coherent, meaningful, comfortable, and sustainable self-narratives. This means, for example, eschewing biologically essentialist or

---

[39] Freeman 2015.

deterministic readings of findings or classifications of persons that limit our capacities to shape our own stories, or stigmatise those whose experiences deviate from those of the majority. And we should reject simplistic or hyperbolic reporting and marketing of biomedical research and technologies that misrepresent the extent to which particular kinds of bioinformation can provide reliable or meaningful insights into our embodied lives. It also means approaching the practices and methods by which bioinformation is produced in ways that challenge and resist hurtful, degrading, and oppressive stereotypes and instead contribute to the production of inspiring and enabling counterstories and a rich array of tools that serve diverse approaches to narrative self-constitution.

8

Protecting Identity in Practice

8.1 Introduction

Over the preceding chapters, I have sought to demonstrate that information about our health, bodies, and biology, including our biological relationships to others, can make significant contributions to the narratives by which we characterise ourselves, and which constitute our practical identities. I have argued that these contributions are often profoundly valuable. This is not because this information tells us who we are or defines us but because it plays substantive, explanatory, and interpretive roles which contribute to the inhabitability of our identities in the context of our embodied and socially embedded lives. Personal bioinformation can help us develop self-narratives that remain coherent and sustainable when confronted by embodied experience, and that provide robust interpretive frameworks through which to navigate our lives. I have also explored the ways in which personal bioinformation may threaten the sustainability, comfort, and inhabitability of our embodied identities – as occurs when it invites enduring disruption or equips us poorly to cope with and make sense of embodied, social experiences. I have argued that developing and maintaining an inhabitable identity narrative matters a great deal, not only because it means we have a clear sense of who we are but also because it provides the foundations for core experiential, evaluative, and practical capacities. For these reasons, I have argued there is an ethical imperative to attend to the potential identity impacts, both good and bad, of providing or denying information subjects access to their personal bioinformation. Throughout these arguments, I have sought to meet Heather Widdows's challenge quoted in Chapter 2 – to present a 'picture of the self' that is not 'wrong', such that the legal and ethical structures built upon this picture protect the interests that really matter.[1] It is not possible

---

[1] Widdows 2013, p. 6.

to prove that the picture of narrative self-constitution and the roles of personal bioinformation in our narrative projects developed over the preceding chapters is *true*. But I hope to have demonstrated that it at least accords with our intuitions and experiences of what it means, and what it takes, to develop and inhabit our own senses of who we are as embodied beings and to navigate our enabling and limiting health, bodies, and biology. In doing so, I have sought to offer a robust and plausible conception of identity interests, the recognition of which would make a concrete difference to how access to and disclosures of our personal bioinformation are governed.

8.2　What Would Change?

In what ways would the bioinformation governance landscape look different if it were to embrace the picture of narrative identity impacts, interests, and responsibilities described and defended in this book? The headline answer to this question is simply that information subjects' identity-related interests in whether and how they encounter information about their bodies, biology, and health would be firmly installed amongst, and routinely weighed alongside, the other interests that currently dominate the ethical, policy, and regulatory landscape. This means that identity interests would join the roll call of core interests that currently include health protection, mental well-being, informational and personal autonomy, privacy, and confidentiality. Identity interests would enjoy parity of attention with the most prominent of these. This does not mean they should necessarily prevail or take centre stage. But it does mean that they must be recognised, carefully assessed, taken seriously, and afforded weight commensurate with the central role played by the development and maintenance of an inhabitable, embodied, and relational self-narrative in leading a full, flourishing, and practically engaged life.

Attending and responding to information subjects' narrative needs adds a fresh, new dimension to the governance landscape that, I have argued, is both more conceptually and normatively robust, and less unwarrantedly exceptionalist, than the kinds of harms or benefits currently spoken of in terms of 'identity'. It moves these conversations beyond the dominant focus on genetic risk and genetic parentage. It decouples identity interests from biologically essentialist and deterministic views of the self, while addressing fears that any appeal to the identity value of bioinformation risks committing ethical and empirical essentialist fallacies. At the same time, it firmly installs identity as a morally serious concern, rather than a matter of mere aesthetics, preferences, or loose affiliations. Recognising the embodied nature of narrative self-constitution reveals the varied, variable, but nonetheless critical, substantive, structural, and interpretive roles that personal bioinformation plays in our self-narratives. Having said this, responding to embodied narrative identity interests and responsibilities does not entail a wholesale departure from existing bioethical and regulatory flirtations with identity concerns. Rather, it allows us to make space for recognising the value to information subjects of using biological insights as constitutive and interpretive tools in self-understanding, and to appreciate the harms of biological essentialism and fatalism in terms of harm to and constraints upon self-authorship. It reveals the narrative richness that may be derived from familial and biosocial affiliations and the profound risks of subjects building their self-conceptions on unreliable or meaningless findings. It demonstrates why particular biologically informed self-descriptors matter, not necessarily because of any discrete labels lost or gained but because of the effects on the coherence, sustainability, and inhabitability of the inter-interpretive, intersectional whole.

The analysis I have offered demonstrates why identity interests warrant the attention of those who produce, process, and manage our bioinformation in ways that, for example, vaguer appeals that we should recognise 'personal utility', seek to satisfy curiosity, enable 'psychological preparedness', or avert distress might not. But, again, this also does not mean that the ideas and needs referred to in these terms are necessarily without substance. They are often reaching for something interesting and valuable. Being in a position to understand where and how these might overlap with the desire and need to construct an inhabitable self-narrative provides potential disclosers with clarity and legitimate grounds to respond to them if and when they do.

For all these reasons, it might be assumed that attention to identity interests and responsibilities would lead to greater entitlements to personal bioinformation by information subjects and access to wider classes of information on additional grounds. And, in some contexts, this would be true. It would take us beyond the 'usual suspects' that currently provide criteria for disclosure in healthcare and health research – serious health impacts, clinical actionability, or utility in reproductive decision-making. It would also expand upon the relatively isolated recognition afforded to the identity significance of genetic parentage and donor conception. The arguments I have presented provide grounds for the

UK courts and the European Court of Human Rights not only to abandon talk of knowledge of genetic origins 'completing' or providing the 'truth' about applicants' identities but also to recognise and protect 'rights to know' – and, indeed, not to know – under the Article 8 'right to identity' across a much broader range of personal bioinformation. It could point to a richer set of considerations when it comes to introducing susceptibility testing or screening programmes for common complex conditions – such as *APOE* testing for elevated Alzheimer's risk – where the analytic and clinical validity of the genetic test is sound, but the immediate clinical actionability of testing remains somewhat equivocal. In circumstances where there is good evidence of the potential identity value of results and possible identity harms are manageable, this could provide grounds to support screening. I will return below to consider how it might also change feedback policies to participants of individual research findings.

However, recognition of identity interests would not only or inevitably lead to more frequent and widespread disclosures. It would lead to reduced subject access in contexts where there are risks of identity harm that cannot be adequately mitigated by the manner of disclosure. These would not only include disclosures that could cause lasting narrative disruption and distress but also extend to communication of misleading or unreliable bioinformation that would render recipients' narratives vulnerable to future embodied experience. Furthermore, sources of bioinformation that are currently regarded as harmless fun, such as genomic analysis of non-health traits or sleep tracking – where the 'fun' is implicitly connected to something like greater self-knowledge – could prove harder to justify in cases where the epistemic qualities of the information do not support presumptions of narrative value.

In other circumstances, it is less clear whether recognition of identity interest would direct us predominantly towards greater or to less availability of bioinformation. For example, the benefits of widespread adoption of whole genome sequencing in newborn screening programmes could, from one perspective, be viewed as analogous to early disclosure of donor conception – that is, as providing useful tools with which an individual can build a resilient, sustainable self-narrative. However, from another perspective, it may be seen as permitting parents' knowledge of their child's embodied vulnerabilities in ways that preempt the child's own self-authorship. This concern echoes longstanding worries about biomedical practices that foreclose a child's 'open future'.[2]

---

[2] Davis 1997.

Arbitrating between these contrasting perspectives on the identity impacts of genomic screening of new-borns will require looking carefully at evidence of families' experiences. The picture of identity impacts presented in this book cannot answer this question on its own, but it can provide an essential tool with which to assess the evidence.

As I have emphasised throughout, responding to identity interests has wider implications than the question of *whether* to disclose. A bioinformation governance landscape informed by my analysis would be one in which much closer attention is paid to the ways in which potentially identity-significant bioinformation is communicated and to the wider interpretive context in which this takes place. Emphasis on the ways in which health information is disclosed has gained increasing prominence over recent years, for example in debates about governance of DTC genomics and discussions of ethical responsibilities to return individual research findings. The latter is increasingly turning from the question of whether to share findings with participants to questions about how this should be done.[3] Attention to identity interests lends grist to these developments and extends their relevance to other disclosure contexts. Informational transactions beyond clinical genetics would benefit from the kinds of skills and personal support currently largely restricted to genetic counselling. As noted in Chapter 7, the requirement to communicate in an identity-supportive manner should not be restricted to instances in which bioinformation is disclosed expressly to meet narrative needs. Just as important, if not more so, is the provision of identity support where disclosure of potentially identity-significant information is necessitated on non-identity grounds.

A key conclusion of this enquiry is that the identity impacts of encounters with personal bioinformation are not uniform: they may be positive, negative, or neutral; different people have varying experiences of similar bioinformation; and impacts differ between types of bioinformation and disclosure contexts. For these reasons, as well as the sheer variety of settings and ways in which we might encounter information about our own health, bodies, and biology, it is not possible to provide uniform recommendations for reforms to policy, practice, or the law to protect and promote identity interests in all instances. It is, however, possible to offer some broad indications for priorities and reforms in a handful of areas in which subject access is widely debated, including some of the

---

[3] Postan 2021.

illustrative examples that have accompanied and informed my arguments up to this point. I will start here with the issue that initially motivated the questions pursued in this book – donor-conceived individuals' access to information about their conception and their donors.

8.3   Five Disclosure Contexts

Donor Conception

As previously discussed, UK regulation and professional guidance regarding donor-conceived individuals' access to information about their conception and donors are already explicitly informed by the potential value of this knowledge to their identities and the relative benefits of learning of donor origins in early childhood.[4] Parents planning to tell and donor-conceived people hoping to access information are each directed to and encouraged to take up opportunities for advice and counselling. Apart from the sometimes essentialist talk of 'identity completion' underpinning them, these existing measures seem likely to broadly serve donor-conceived individuals' narrative identity interests as I have characterised them. The picture I have presented does, however, suggest some possible adjustments to current regulation and practice.

In view of parents' interests in constructing their own narratives and their invaluable role in supporting those of their children, coercive methods of enforcing early disclosure of donor conception are likely to be disproportionate, insufficiently context-sensitive, and counterproductive. This is particularly so if these methods increased the likelihood of children being confronted by information in uncomfortable, stigmatising, or under-supported ways. However, the importance of being able to make narrative sense of new bioinformation and integrate it early into one's developing identity points to the need, first, for sufficient state funding of counselling and support services and, second, for information availability and provision that appropriately match donor-conceived individuals' needs. Achieving the second of these requires addressing the time lag – which under UK regulations could be more than a decade – between when families are encouraged to introduce the topic of donor conception and when offspring have access to non-identifying and identifying details about the donor. This might be addressed by reducing the minimum age at which non-identifying information is available – it is

---

[4] See Chapters 2 and 5.

currently sixteen – and revisiting the age – currently eighteen – at which one is legally entitled to apply to the regulator, the HFEA, to learn if one is donor-conceived or to receive identifying donor information.[5] Any reforms should be based on empirical evidence of what donor-conceived individuals as a group, and particular segments of this group – for example those conceived using donor eggs or embryos, or those from single parent families – wish to know, and of the relevant risks and benefits to all involved.

As noted in Chapter 5, people conceived using MRT in the UK are not currently entitled to identifying information about donors of the eggs that supplied their healthy mitochondria. In light of my claim that the identity value of knowledge of donor origins lies in its biographical, sense-making, and relational narrative roles, rather than in fulfilling a genetically determinist view of identity, there is little justification for any such disparities in the legal entitlements to donor information. Indeed, through its insistence on linking only nuclear DNA to potential identity interests, the current law risks promulgating a restrictive and deterministic view of identity.[6] Those conceived using mitochondrial donation should have the same information entitlements and opportunities to receive support and counselling as those conceived using one egg.[7] As Jackie Leach Scully argues, there is also a responsibility on all of us to help develop master narratives – for example, through media reporting and the arts – that alleviate rather than contribute experiences of stigma or alienation by those conceived using novel assisted reproductive technologies.[8]

Individual Research Findings

As noted in the preceding chapters, health research ethics continues to wrestle with ethical questions surrounding the return of individual research findings to participants.[9] The arguments I have set out in this

---

[5] Human Fertilisation and Embryology Act 1990 (as amended), s.31ZA.

[6] See Chapter 2 and Department of Health, 'Mitochondrial Donation: Government response to the consultation on draft regulations to permit the use of new treatment techniques to prevent the transmission of a serious mitochondrial disease from mother to child' (2014).

[7] See also Appleby 2018.

[8] Scully 2017.

[9] The practical cogency and ethical relevance of the distinction between intended and incidental findings are increasingly questioned – particularly in exploratory and data-led research. See Eckstein et al. 2014.

chapter suggest that researchers have conditional ethical responsibilities to offer participants the option of receiving individual findings – irrespective of whether they are intended or 'incidental' – that could plausibly carry significant identity value. They also have responsibilities, when feeding back any findings – individual or aggregate – to do so in an identity-supporting manner. These proposals go beyond the most widely endorsed recommendations to offer individual findings that are clinically actionable, concern serious health risks, or are necessary for reproductive decision-making. However, requiring researchers to offer potentially identity-significant findings is likely to be less demanding than suggestions that they should return all those exhibiting the amorphous quality of 'personal utility'. The responsibilities recommended here – echoing Franklin Miller and his co-authors – are founded upon the Principle of Helpfulness and researchers' privileged access and interpretive capacities in respect of bioinformation that participants could not otherwise obtain.[10] They also arise from researchers' causal role in participants' vulnerability to the epistemic asymmetry in their relationship. In addition, it is apparent from experiences reported in Chapter 5 that the meaning and comfort of participants' self-narratives are often intimately bound up with their decisions to take part in research at all and the nature of their experiences of participating. For example, they may volunteer to participate in order to express solidarity with others susceptible to the same disease and feel positive about the experience of doing so and optimistic about how findings might help their family members . Proper recognition of participants' narrative investment in and vulnerability to the ways in which research is conducted and its outputs suggests grounds for strong pro tanto responsibilities to respect potential identity impacts in the ways that studies are designed and conducted, including the policies for returning findings.[11]

Widening return policies to include potentially identity-significant findings would impose a greater burden on researchers to assess, verify, quality assure, and communicate a wider range of individual findings. However, as with any feedback policy, it will still be appropriate to weigh the identity benefits to participants against possible risks, including uses of resources that detract from the pursuit and social value of the study. My suggestion is not that identity interests should always prevail, but that they warrant being taken seriously. It is worth noting that there is no obvious reason to limit these recommendations to health research

[10] Miller et al. 2008.
[11] For further discussion see, Postan 2021.

alone. They would extend to all studies producing personal bioinformation with potential identity significance.

These recommendations bring us back to the example of Ilana sketched in the opening chapter. Ilana regrets that the feedback policy of the research biobank in which she is a participant means that she will only be informed of potentially serious abnormalities found during data collection and will not be contacted with subsequent research findings. Her desire to learn of familial genetic disease risks extends beyond any immediate health concerns to encompass the significance of these risks to her values, life plans, relationship with her own mother, and the way she thinks about of her own parental role. Would Ilana's identity interests be sufficiently great to require feedback of these findings? My answer is a conditional one. On one hand, even if findings about, for example, Ilana's *APOE* variant carrier status would only give rise to a probabilistic risk estimate of Alzheimer's disease and would not be clinically actionable, the arguments presented in the intervening chapters urge us to take seriously Ilana's view these would still be of substantial identity value to her. And this value is no less, and perhaps decidedly greater, than her friend Sam's desire to know about her distant ancestry given the epistemic limitations of Sam's genealogical information. If those governing the biobank itself had access to Ilana's *APOE* variant status, and the resources required to verify their quality and meaning were not excessive, they could well have an identity-based responsibility to offer these to Ilana and to do so in an identity-supporting way.[12] However, if they only become apparent in subsequent studies, third-party researchers' responsibilities to report back to Ilana would depend on, amongst other considerations, their temporal and relational proximity to her, the practicability of reidentifying individual data subjects, and the quantity of sufficiently reliable findings produced by their study. Any of these factors could mean that attempts to meet Ilana's identity interests would be prohibitively resource-intensive.

Confidentiality and Consent in Healthcare

Two further areas in which I want to suggest that information subjects' identity interests ought to join protection of their health and reproductive decision-making as key considerations are, first, healthcare

---

[12] Cf. UK Biobank's policy on the return of potentially serious incidental findings, Gibson et al. 2017.

professionals' deliberations about when it would be justifiable to break the confidence of a patient for whom the bioinformation is also 'personal' and, second, when deciding the kinds of risk information that patients should be given in seeking their consent to medical procedures. As observed in Chapter 2, in the UK health professionals have a legal obligation to weigh the importance of maintaining patient confidentiality against the opportunity to mitigate significant risk of serious harm to family members, with whom they also have professional relationships, by disclosing their patient's health information.[13] And the legal test for the kinds of 'material risk' that patients should be told about when consenting to medical procedures is now based upon what a reasonable patient would want to know in the circumstances, rather than a professional assessment of what is relevant.[14] Failure to weigh in the first context, or to provide the requisite information in the second, may be grounds for action in negligence.

The arguments I have presented suggest that 'significant harm', 'material risk', and 'reasonably want to know' could plausibly be read as encompassing serious epistemic and interpretive threats to the inhabitability of the recipient's self-narrative, given the harm that narrative incoherence and loss of meaning pose to their well-being and capacity to lead a flourishing life. If identity harms are understood in this way, it is possible to see how, for example, a patient's refusal to share their carrier status for a rare genetic disorder with a close family member for whom it could carry significant identity value could ground *ethical* and *legal* responsibilities on the part of the healthcare professionals involved. For these professionals, their responsibilities include the requirement to weigh this identity value against private and public interests in preserving the patient's confidentiality and if, having done so, they were to find the identity value carried greater weight they would be justified in breaking their patient's confidence. Similarly, a care team considering, for example, what should be discussed with a patient due to undergo neurosurgery to alleviate the symptoms of Parkinson's disease, would be obliged to assess the likely identity significance to the patient of knowing that restored independent living and personality impacts could affect their relationship with their life partner, and not only to focus on disclosing the direct physical risks of the neurosurgical procedure.

---

[13] Dove et al. 2019.

[14] *Montgomery v. Lanarkshire Health Board* [2015] UKSC 11, at [87].

For there to be a legal remedy grounded in negligence for a failure to disclose identity-significant information in either of these cases, the courts would need to judge it fair, just, and reasonable to impose such a duty on non-disclosing parties. Furthermore, identity harms would need to be recognised as a relevant category of damage. Currently, these categories include pain, suffering, or loss of capabilities arising from physical and psychiatric injury, or material loss, for example of earnings.[15] Although the arguments presented in this book suggest that identity harms – at their most acute – should be included amongst these on grounds of parity of severity, it is not clear that a court would see it this way. Nevertheless, Graeme Laurie and his co-authors have speculated whether there might be grounds to anticipate courts' greater willingness to recognise a wider class of damages in UK negligence cases. These grounds include the circumstances under which compensation for 'hurt to feelings' is awarded under Scots law, and intimations in recent years that UK courts are taking a more expansive view of relevant categories of harm in negligence cases to include interference with patients' rights to live and plan their lives in accordance with their wishes and values.[16] Identity impacts could plausibly be captured under these wider categories of harm.

DTC Genomics

Online DTC genomics services present a particularly apt context in which to apply the arguments of this book. These services offer a wide variety of potentially identity-significant personal bioinformation, ranging from the presence of genetic variants associated with serious diseases – such as the *BRCA1/2* mutations – to findings that are unrelated to health – for example, ancestral information or susceptibility to early hair loss. And, as previously noted, these services are marketed as providing straightforward insights into users' identities. In doing so, service providers incur reliance and occupy the kinds of causal roles that, I have suggested, engender particular responsibilities to protect the identity interests of those rendered situationally vulnerable by their activities. However, as ample critical analyses of DTC genomics have observed, while the technical capabilities of these services to correctly identify the genomic markers of interest are

---

[15] Laurie et al. 2019.
[16] Laurie 2009; Laurie et al. 2019, p. 389.

generally not in question, the robustness, certainty, and meaningfulness of the inferences then drawn from these to particular traits, susceptibilities, or ancestral connections are considerably more dubious.[17] Anyone may use these services without prior analysis of family risk or counselling, which would normally precede genetic testing in healthcare settings. And results are reported via online portals accompanied by explanations of their variable detail and quality.[18] Even detailed explanatory materials, however, cannot provide discursive support or interpretations that are responsive to personal circumstances.[19] For these reasons, DTC genomics may be seen as a perfect storm for readily foreseeable identity harms. This risk is heightened by the sheer quantity of results delivered at once. Scott Roberts and his co-authors have suggested that the relatively sanguine and distress-free responses they have observed amongst people learning of susceptibility to single multifactorial disorders – for example, as seen in the REVEAL study – are unlikely to be sustained if findings about multiple conditions were to be simultaneously disclosed.[20] Reports of multiple findings – some serious, some surprising, many meaningless – could stretch users' resilience and capacities to make sense of complex probabilistic, population-risk-relative, and caveated results. This is the situation imagined in the vignette sketched at the start of Chapter 1. Sam's experiences capture the narrative turmoil or insecurity that may arise from unexpected revelations, such as absent genetic relationships within families. They also indicate the disproportionate weight that Sam invests in somewhat speculative 'fun' ancestral or trait information. Meanwhile Sam misunderstands or dismisses her probabilistic disease susceptibility estimates as puzzling or hard-to-interpret, yet these are likely to be of far greater consequence to her embodied and relational experiences.

Much of the current ethical concern about DTC genomics focuses on the risk of serious harm to health from inadequately explained or misunderstood health risk information.[21] Other commentators, however, regard such concerns as excessively paternalistic.[22] And some cite

---

[17] See, Bunnik et al. 2011; Skirton et al. 2012.

[18] Skirton et al. 2012.

[19] One online DTC service, 23andMe, encourages users to speak to a genetic counsellor or healthcare professionals before and after seeking health-related reports and offers basic advice on, for example, continuing to attend the screening and pursue other healthy behaviours, see '23andMe Genetic Health Risk Reports: What you should know' www.23andme.com/en-gb/test-info/genetic-health (accessed 18 July 2021).

[20] Roberts et al. 2011.

[21] See, for example, House of Commons Science and Technology Committee 2021.

[22] Green and Farahany 2014.

'personal utility' as sufficient ethical justification for providing results.[23] The conditions for meeting a test of personal utility might amount to little more than feeding the recipient's curiosity or expanding their practical options. In contrast, the bar set by the preceding analysis for realising identity value and averting narrative harms is considerably higher. And while avoiding paternalism may be desirable, self-efficacy and self-authorship are unlikely to be achieved by abandoning service users to make their own choices and navigate a tangle of perhaps unexpected and overwhelming results with little support. Furthermore, it is evident that the potential for narrative harm extends beyond the threats to identity most commonly raised in relation to DTC genomics – namely encouraging unwarranted geneticised views of the self and naturalising human differences in divisive ways – troubling though these possible consequences are.[24] Chief amongst the wider harms brought to light by a narrative analysis are those of constructing precarious identity narratives upon misunderstood, partially understood, or misleading results in such a way that they invite unnecessary reinterpretation of prior experiences, render the recipients' narrative coherence freshly vulnerable to embodied experiences, or foster a narrative that provides a poor interpretive framework for navigating the world. In a somewhat different vein, user data collected by DTC services is often subsequently sold for commercial and research purposes in ways users do not always fully appreciate.[25] In such cases, user's bodies and narratives may be implicated in projects and purposes that undermine their values and their account of the kind of person they are.[26]

The picture of identity interests and corollary responsibilities developed over this and the preceding chapters suggests that DTC genomics warrants either much stronger regulation or reformed delivery models. At the very least, it points to the need for personal, discursive, identity-supporting feedback of findings, with opportunities for users to ask questions and receive counselling; significant reduction of the numbers and kinds of tests offered to remove those that are incapable of providing reliable or meaningful insights, though these need not be limited only to those that are clinically actionable; greater transparency about the nature and purpose of future analyses and about commercial and third-party uses of the data collected; and straightforward means for users to opt out

---

[23] Vayena 2015.
[24] Cf. Nordgren and Juengst 2009.
[25] Bunnik et al. 2011.
[26] McMillan et al. 2021.

of such uses.[27] It also supports calls for more honest and measured marketing of these services, so as to make the epistemic limitations of the test results absolutely clear and to remove implications that they reveal predetermined 'truths' about the self.

Personal Devices

DTC genomics is not the only context in which potentially ambiguous, identity-significant bioinformation is delivered directly to information subjects without the intercession of expert guidance and advice. Healthcare delivery is increasingly reliant on self-management of chronic conditions and use of eHealth technologies, driven by resource constraints, ageing populations, and necessities imposed by global pandemics.[28] Uses of personal self-monitoring devices to track behaviours and characteristics associated with health and well-being, including activity levels, sleep quality, concentration, mental health, and fertility, are also rapidly expanding.[29] This means that an increasing proportion of the personal bioinformation we encounter is delivered directly to us by mobile, wearable, and implanted technologies. Some of these such as wearable fitness monitors are widely available consumer devices. Others are highly specialised predictive, diagnostic, or assistive technologies – for example, surgically implanted BCIs that monitor brain activity to warn users of epileptic seizures.[30]

Although people will usually be able to choose whether to use such devices, they are often passive in their exposure to the bioinformation these deliver.[31] This immediacy, combined with the limited scope to provide integrated, personalised, interpretative support through a digital interface, creates a particular imperative to ensure the quality, reliability, and transparency of the bioinformation generated. This is not only important because of the serious health consequences of erroneous

---

[27] I have suggested above that information providers may reasonably devolve interpretive support to those best equipped to provide it. However, the generic signposting to national genetic health services offered by many existing DTC services hardly fulfils this responsibility and risks overwhelming healthcare providers.

[28] World Health Organization 2021.

[29] Ajana 2020.

[30] Gilbert et al. 2019.

[31] Even this element of choice may not be present if, for example, public health authorities require users to install infection exposure applications on their mobile phones or if social media platforms deliver unsolicited mental health alerts and advice based on algorithmic analysis of users' browsing behaviour, search terms, and keystrokes – see Jain et al. 2015.

medical advice. Attention to potential identity impacts highlights how the information generated may represent more than just health advice or entertainment. For example, some users of BCIs that predict epileptic seizures report that they now feel 'more capable' and as if they have 'found' themselves, while others feel oppressed by reminders of an illness they would prefer to deny.[32] Meanwhile, users of consumer devices may rely on their outputs to explain experiences such as periods of poor concentration or fatigue, anticipate future events such as pregnancy, or characterise themselves as, for example, 'a poor sleeper' or a 'calm person'.

When this occurs, the information supplied by these devices offers ready narrative contents and tools. These may be viewed as having substantial identity value, for all the constitutive, explanatory, and interpretive reasons described in the preceding chapters. As argued in Chapter 4, there are insufficient grounds to assume that bioinformation from personal devices will wholly usurp users' direct, phenomenological experiences of their own bodies and health in their accounts of who they are, rather than complementing these.[33] Similarly, we should not assume that if this information alters users' sense of who they are that this necessarily represents problematic 'estrangement', rather than an integral aspect of dynamic narrative development.[34] However, the potential for harm to users' identities from misleading, intrusive, or distressing alerts or feedback should not be taken lightly. This points to the need to manage users' expectations of what insights their devices can, and cannot, reliably deliver and to assess critically the balance of potential identity harms, especially where the bioinformation supplied is of questionable quality or practical value.[35] It adds weight to existing calls to ensure the suitability of the algorithms and training data used to ensure that these devices provide accurate outputs and advice.[36] It also suggests a need for conscientious decision-making and risk assessment by developers to avoid potentially stigmatising, essentialising, or divisive mean of classifying users' status or performance and highlights the need to design information interfaces that support user's agency in, comprehension of, and critical engagement with the data produced.[37]

---

[32] Gilbert 2015, p. 5.
[33] Cf. Lupton 2013.
[34] Cf. Gilbert et al. 2019.
[35] Peake et al. 2018.
[36] Fenech et al. 2018.
[37] For further discussion, see Postan 2020.

8.4 Future Challenges

The five contexts discussed above are only a small sample of those in which identity-significant encounters with personal bioinformation occur. It will be possible, to varying degrees, to extrapolate beyond the brief recommendations I have made here to many other settings and scenarios. The arguments I have presented in this book have focused on questions of when, why, and how individual information subjects should have access to information about their health, bodies, and biology on identity grounds. I have intentionally set aside ethical concerns about how other people use these kinds of information to characterise and categorise us, as these matters have hitherto received greater attention in the bioethical and legal literature. I have sought to turn our attention instead to our reflexive uses of our own bioinformation to constitute our embodied identity narratives, as well as to the involuntary impacts that this information may have on our narrative projects. Nevertheless, the preceding discussions have made clear that our projects of self-constitution, the tools we use in these narrative endeavours, and the meanings assigned to these tools are closely entwined with the behaviours, interpretive work, and narrative projects of other people.

It seems that these informational and narrative interdependences will only grow and become more complex over the coming years, as – driven by, amongst other factors, the quest for precision medicine, commercial interests, and public health emergencies including global pandemics – increasing quantities of findings about our traits, susceptibilities, and behaviours are derived not from our own bodies, or even from those of our close relatives, but from analysis of 'big data'.[38] These include not only big *health* data drawn from patient records and health research programmes but also those derived from surveillance in the public sphere and monitoring of our online behaviours, using the powerful analytical capacities of artificial intelligence and machine learning.[39] These developments will not alter the imperative to attend to individual encounters with information derived from our own bodies and those close to us. However, they introduce a new kind of distance between the subjects and sources of personal bioinformation. And they will add weight to the cautions I have voiced – to be alert to the identity impacts of the sheer quantities of personal bioinformation that confront us and to the increasingly remote relationships between those producing and processing our

---

[38] Henschke 2017; Raghupathi and Raghupathi 2014.
[39] Henschke 2017.

bioinformation and us. These factors have profound implications for the abilities of these actors to anticipate our identity needs, to help us interpret bioinformation in identity-supporting ways, and to know that this information is personal to us at all.

These developments also add fresh dimensions to identity concerns, as algorithm-driven analyses categorise us in new ways, introducing new forms of self-description, grouping us with those with whom we have had no previous connection, and fragmenting longstanding affiliations. It remains to be seen how our embodied, socially embedded self-narratives – and their qualities of inhabitability – respond to these changes, particularly if they contribute to a widening epistemic gap between our lived experiences and what bioinformation conveys. The preceding discussions offer some intimations of how our narrative undertakings might adapt and respond and how we might be protected from some of the possible narrative blows. These discussions also suggest that in fast-evolving, data-driven environments identity concerns supply an added ethical imperative not only to attend when and how our personal bioinformation is communicated to us, the imperative I have focused on in this book, but also to ask with greater urgency why and for whose benefit this information is produced at all.

Ajana, Btihaj. (2010) 'Recombinant Identities: Biometrics and Narrative Bioethics'. *Journal of Bioethical Inquiry* 7 (2): 237–58.

(2020) 'Personal Metrics: Users' Experiences and Perceptions of Self-Tracking Practices and Data'. *Social Science Information* 59 (4): 654–78.

Akandji-Kombe, Jean-François. (2007) *Positive Obligations under the European Convention on Human Rights: A Guide to the Implementation of the European Convention on Human Rights. Human Rights Handbooks (No. 7).* Strasbourg: Council of Europe.

Alaimo, Stacy, and Susan J Hekman. (2008) 'Introduction: Emerging Models of Materiality in Feminist Theory'. In *Material Feminisms*, edited by Stacy Alaimo and Susan J Hekman. Bloomington: Indiana University Press: 1–22.

Alpert, Sheri. (2012) 'The Specter of Commercial Neuroimaging'. *AJOB Neuroscience* 3 (4): 56–8.

Anderson, James A, and Judy Illes. (2012) 'Neuroimaging and Mental Health: Drowning in a Sea of Acrimony'. *AJOB Neuroscience* 3 (4): 42–3.

Anderson, James A, Ania Mizgalewicz, and Judy Illes. (2013) 'Triangulating Perspectives on Functional Neuroimaging for Disorders of Mental Health'. *BMC Psychiatry* 13 (1): 1–11.

Andorno, Roberto. (2004) 'The Right Not to Know: An Autonomy Based Approach'. *Journal of Medical Ethics* 30 (5): 435–9.

Annas, George J, and Sherman Elias. (2014) '23andMe and the FDA'. *New England Journal of Medicine* 370 (11): 985–8.

Appleby, John. (2018) 'Should Mitochondrial Donation Be Anonymous?'. *The Journal of Medicine and Philosophy* 43 (2): 261–80.

Appleby, John B, Lucy Blake, and Tabitha Freeman. (2012) 'Is Disclosure in the Best Interests of Children Conceived by Donation?'. In *Reproductive Donation: Practice, Policy and Bioethics*, edited by Martin Richards, Guido Pennings and John B Appleby. Cambridge: Cambridge University Press: 231–49.

Ashida, Sato, Laura M Koehly, J Scott Roberts et al. (2010) 'The Role of Disease Perceptions and Results Sharing in Psychological Adaptation after Genetic

Susceptibility Testing: The REVEAL Study'. *European Journal of Human Genetics* 18 (12): 1296–301.

Atkins, Emily R, and Peter K Panegyres. (2011) 'The Clinical Utility of Gene Testing for Alzheimer's Disease'. *Neurology International* 3 (1): 1–3.

Atkins, Kim. (2008) 'Narrative Identity and Practical Continuity'. In *Practical Identity and Narrative Agency*, edited by Catriona Mackenzie and Kim Atkins. New York: Routledge: 78–98.

Barclay, Linda. (2000) 'Autonomy and the Social Self'. In *Relational Autonomy: Feminist Perspectives on Automony, Agency, and the Social Self*, edited by Catriona Mackenzie and Natalie Stoljar. Oxford: Oxford University Press: 52–71.

Baylis, Françoise. (2012) 'The Self in Situ: A Relational Account of Personal Identity'. In *Being Relational: Reflections on Relational Theory and Health Law*, edited by Jocelyn Downie and Jennifer J Llewellyn. Vancouver: UBC Press: 109–31.

Beeson, Diane R, Patricia K Jennings, and Wendy Kramer. (2011) 'Offspring Searching for Their Sperm Donors: How Family Type Shapes the Process'. *Human Reproduction* 26 (9): 2415–24.

Bemelmans, Sonja, Krista Tromp, Eline Bunnik et al. (2016) 'Psychological, Behavioral and Social Effects of Disclosing Alzheimer's Disease Biomarkers to Research Participants: A Systematic Review'. *Alzheimer's Research & Therapy* 8 (1): 1–17.

Ben-David, Shelly, and David Kealy. (2020) 'Identity in the Context of Early Psychosis: A Review of Recent Research'. *Psychosis* 12 (1): 68–78.

Berkman, Benjamin E, Sara Chandros Hull, and Lisa Eckstein. (2014) 'The Unintended Implications of Blurring the Line between Research and Clinical Care in a Genomic Age'. *Personalized Medicine* 11 (3): 285–95.

Besson, Samantha. (2007) 'Enforcing the Child's Right to Know Her Origins: Contrasting Approaches under the Convention on the Rights of the Child and the European Convention on Human Rights'. *International Journal of Law, Policy and the Family* 21 (2): 137–59.

Blake, Lucy, Vasanti Jadva, and Susan Golombok. (2014) 'Parent Psychological Adjustment, Donor Conception and Disclosure: A Follow-up over 10 Years'. *Human Reproduction* 29 (11): 2487–96.

Blauwhoff, Richard J. (2008) 'Tracing Down the Historical Development of the Legal Concept of the Right to Know One's Origins: Has "to Know or Not to Know" Ever Been the Legal Question?'. *Utrecht Law Review* 4 (2): 99–116.

Blyth, Eric. (2012) 'Genes R Us? Making Sense of Genetic and Non-Genetic Relationships Following Anonymous Donor Insemination'. *Reproductive Biomedicine Online* 24 (7): 719–26.

Blyth, Eric, and Lucy Frith. (2009) 'Donor-Conceived People's Access to Genetic and Biographical History: An Analysis of Provisions in Different

Jurisdictions Permitting Disclosure of Donor Identity'. *International Journal of Law, Policy and the Family* 23 (2): 174–91.

Borgelt, Emily L, Daniel Z Buchman, and Judy Illes. (2011) '"This Is Why You've Been Suffering": Reflections of Providers on Neuroimaging in Mental Health Care'. *Journal of Bioethical Inquiry* 8 (1): 15–25.

(2012) 'Neuroimaging in Mental Health Care: Voices in Translation'. *Frontiers in Human Neuroscience* 6: 293–7.

Borry, Pascal, Paul Schotsmans, and Kris Dierickx. (2004) 'What Is the Role of Empirical Research in Bioethical Reflection and Decision-Making? An Ethical Analysis'. *Medicine, Health Care and Philosophy* 7 (1): 41–53.

Bortolotti, Lisa. (2013) 'The Relative Importance of Undesirable Truths'. *Medicine, Health Care and Philosophy* 16 (4): 683–90.

Brandeis, Louis, and Samuel Warren. (1890) 'The Right to Privacy'. *Harvard Law Review* 4 (5): 193–220.

Brandon, Priscilla. (2016) 'Body and Self: An Entangled Narrative'. *Phenomenology and the Cognitive Sciences* 15 (1): 67–83.

British Medical Association. (2019) Access to Health Records. www.bma.org.uk /media/2821/bma-access-to-health-records-june-20.pdf.

Bryman, Alan. (2016) *Social Research Methods*. Oxford: Oxford University Press.

Buchanan, Allen. (1988) 'Advance Directives and the Personal Identity Problem'. *Philosophy & Public Affairs* 17 (4): 277–302.

Buchman, Daniel Z, Emily L Borgelt, Louise Whiteley, and Judy Illes. (2013) 'Neurobiological Narratives: Experiences of Mood Disorder through the Lens of Neuroimaging'. *Sociology of Health & Illness* 35 (1): 66–81.

Bulgin, Dominique, Paula Tanabe, and Coretta Jenerette. (2018) 'Stigma of Sickle Cell Disease: A Systematic Review'. *Issues in Mental Health Nursing* 39 (8): 675–86.

Bunnik, Eline M, A Cecile JW Janssens, and Maartje HN Schermer. (2014) 'Personal Utility in Genomic Testing: Is There Such a Thing?'. *Journal of Medical Ethics* 41 (4): 322–6.

Bunnik, Eline M, Maartje HN Schermer, and A Cecile JW Janssens. (2011) 'Personal Genome Testing: Test Characteristics to Clarify the Discourse on Ethical, Legal and Societal Issues'. *BMC Medical Ethics* 12 (1): 1–13.

Butow, Phyllis N, Elizabeth A Lobb, Alexandra Barratt, Bettina Meiser, and Katherine M Tucker. (2003) 'Psychological Outcomes and Risk Perception after Genetic Testing and Counselling in Breast Cancer: A Systematic Review'. *Medical Journal of Australia* 178 (2): 77–81.

Calhoun, Cheshire. (2000) 'Losing Oneself'. In *Relational Autonomy*, edited by Catriona Mackenzie and Natalie Stoljar. Oxford: Oxford University Press: 193–211.

Callus, Thérèse. (2004) 'Tempered Hope? A Qualified Right to Know One's Genetic Origin: Odièvre v France'. *The Modern Law Review* 67 (4): 658–69.

Camporesi, Silvia. (2019) 'When Does an Advantage Become Unfair? Empirical and Normative Concerns in Semenya's Case'. *Journal of Medical Ethics* 45 (11): 700–4.

Carel, Havi. (2011) 'Phenomenology and Its Application in Medicine'. *Theoretical Medicine and Bioethics* 32 (1): 33–46.

(2016) *Phenomenology of Illness*. Oxford: Oxford University Press.

Carter, Pam, Graeme T Laurie, and Mary Dixon-Woods. (2015) 'The Social Licence for Research: Why Care.Data Ran into Trouble'. *Journal of Medical Ethics* 41 (5): 404–9.

Cassam, Quassim. (2011) 'The Embodied Self'. In *The Oxford Handbook of the Self*, edited by Shaun Gallagher. Oxford: Oxford University Press: 139–56.

Chadwick, Ruth, Mairi Levitt, and Darren Shickle. (2014) *The Right to Know and the Right Not to Know: Genetic Privacy and Responsibility*. Cambridge: Cambridge University Press.

Chan, Sarah, Sarah Cunningham-Burley, Giulia de Togni et al. (2020) 'Beyond Binaries: Dissolving the Empirical/Normative Divide'. *AJOB Empirical Bioethics* 11 (1): 17–19.

Chan, Sarah W, Ed Tulloch, E Sarah Cooper et al. (2017) 'Montgomery and Informed Consent: Where Are We Now?'. *BMJ* 357–9.

Chilibeck, Gillian, Margaret Lock, and Megha Sehdev. (2011) 'Postgenomics, Uncertain Futures, and the Familiarization of Susceptibility Genes'. *Social Science & Medicine* 72 (11): 1768–75.

Christensen, Kurt D, Jason Karlawish, J Scott Roberts et al. (2020) 'Disclosing Genetic Risk for Alzheimer's Dementia to Individuals with Mild Cognitive Impairment'. *Alzheimer's & Dementia: Translational Research & Clinical Interventions* 6 (1): e12002.

Christensen, Kurt D, J Scott Roberts, Wendy R Uhlmann, and Robert C Green. (2011) 'Changes to Perceptions of the Pros and Cons of Genetic Susceptibility Testing after APOE Genotyping for Alzheimer Disease Risk'. *Genetics in Medicine* 13 (5): 409–14.

Christman, John, ed. (1989) *The Inner Citadel: Essays on Individual Autonomy*. New York: Oxford University Press.

(1991) 'Autonomy and Personal History'. *Canadian Journal of Philosophy* 21 (1): 1–24.

(2004) 'Narrative Unity as a Condition of Personhood'. *Metaphilosophy* 35 (5): 695–713.

(2015) 'Telling Our Own Stories: Narrative Selves and Oppressive Circumstance'. In *The Philosophy of Autobiography*, edited by Christopher Cowley. Chicago: University of Chicago Press: 122–40.

Cohn, Simon. (2010) 'Picturing the Brain Inside, Revealing the Illness Outside: A Comparison of the Different Meanings Attributed to Brain Scans by Scientists and Patients'. In *Technologized Images, Technologized Bodies,* edited by Jeanette Edwards, Penelope Harvey, and Peter Wade. New York: Berghahn Books: 65–84.

Cooper, Deborah, Natalie Limet, Ian McClung, and Stephen M Lawrie. (2013) 'Towards Clinically Useful Neuroimaging in Psychiatric Practice'. *The British Journal of Psychiatry* 203 (4): 242–4.

Corsico, Paolo. (2021) '"It's All About Delivery": Researchers' and Health Professionals' Views on the Moral Challenges of Accessing Neurobiological Information in the Context of Psychosis'. *BMC Medical Ethics* 22 (1): 1–15.

Council for International Organizations of Medical Sciences. (2016) International Ethical Guidelines for Health-Related Research Involving Humans. www.cioms.ch/wp-content/uploads/2017/01/WEB-CIOMS-EthicalGuidelines.pdf

Crawshaw, Marilyn, and Ken Daniels. (2019) 'Revisiting the Use of "Counselling" as a Means of Preparing Prospective Parents to Meet the Emerging Psychosocial Needs of Families That Have Used Gamete Donation'. *Families, Relationships and Societies* 8 (3): 395–409.

d'Agincourt-Canning, Lori. (2006) 'Genetic Testing for Hereditary Breast and Ovarian Cancer: Responsibility and Choice'. *Qualitative Health Research* 16 (1): 97–118.

Daniels, Ken R., Victoria M. Grace, and Wayne R. Gillett. (2011) 'Factors Associated with Parents' Decisions to Tell Their Adult Offspring About the Offspring's Donor Conception'. *Human Reproduction* 26 (10): 2783–90.

Davis, Dena S. (1997) 'Genetic Dilemmas and the Child's Right to an Open Future'. *Hastings Center Report* 27 (2): 7–15.

Davis, Nicola (2020) 'Long-Term Offenders Have Different Brain Structure, Study Says'. *The Guardian.* www.theguardian.com/science/2020/feb/17/long-term-offenders-have-different-brain-structure-study-says#:~:text=Now%20researchers%20say%20they%20have,who%20transgressed%20only%20as%20adolescents

de Melo-Martín, Inmaculada. (2014) 'The Ethics of Anonymous Gamete Donation: Is There a Right to Know One's Genetic Origins?'. *Hastings Center Report* 44 (2): 28–35.

(2016) 'How Best to Protect the Vital Interests of Donor-Conceived Individuals: Prohibiting or Mandating Anonymity in Gamete Donations?' *Reproductive Biomedicine & Society Online* 3: 100–8. https://doi.org/10.1016/j.rbms.2017.01.003.

De Winter, Jan. (2016) *Interests and Epistemic Integrity in Science: A New Framework to Assess Interest Influences in Scientific Research Processes.* Lanham: Rowman & Littlefield.

DeGrazia, David. (2005) *Human Identity and Bioethics.* Cambridge: Cambridge University Press.

Department of Health. (2001) Donor Information Consultation: Providing Information About Gamete and Embryo Donors.

(2014) Mitochondrial Donation: Government Response to the Consultation on Draft Regulations to Permit the Use of New Treatment Techniques to Prevent the Transmission of a Serious Mitochondrial Disease from Mother to Child. www.assets.publishing.service.gov.uk/government/uploads/sys tem/uploads/attachment_data/file/332881/Consultation_response.pdf

Dove, Edward S, Vicky Chico, Michael Fay et al. (2019) 'Familial Genetic Risks: How Can We Better Navigate Patient Confidentiality and Appropriate Risk Disclosure to Relatives?'. *Journal of Medical Ethics* 45 (8): 504–7.

Dubov, Alex, and Steven Shoptawb. (2020) 'The Value and Ethics of Using Technology to Contain the Covid-19 Epidemic'. *The American Journal of Bioethics* 20 (7): W7–W11.

Dumit, Joseph. (2003) 'Is It Me or My Brain? Depression and Neuroscientific Facts'. *Journal of Medical Humanities* 24 (1): 35–47.

(2004) *Picturing Personhood: Brain Scans and Biomedical Identity*. Princeton: Princeton University Press.

Dworkin, Gerald. (1988) *The Theory and Practice of Autonomy*. Cambridge: Cambridge University Press.

Eckert, Susan Larusse, Heather Katzen, J Scott Roberts et al. (2006) 'Recall of Disclosed Apolipoprotein E Genotype and Lifetime Risk Estimate for Alzheimer's Disease: The REVEAL Study'. *Genetics in Medicine* 8 (12): 746–51.

Eckstein, Lisa, Jeremy R Garrett, and Benjamin E Berkman. (2014) 'A Framework for Analyzing the Ethics of Disclosing Genetic Research Findings'. *The Journal of Law, Medicine & Ethics* 42 (2): 190–207.

Edelman, Marian Wright. (2015) 'It's Hard to Be What You Can't See'. Huffington Post, 21 August. www.huffpost.com/entry/its-hard-to-be-what-you-c_b_ 8022776.

Eijkholt, Marleen. (2010) 'Sterilisation and the Birth of a Right: Effective Access to Medical Records'. *Medical Law Review* 18 (1): 96–102.

Esplen, Mary Jane, Noreen Stuckless, Jonathan Hunter et al. (2009) 'The BRCA Self-Concept Scale: A New Instrument to Measure Self-Concept in BRCA1/2 Mutation Carriers'. *Psycho-Oncology* 18 (11): 1216–29.

Etkin, Amit. (2019) 'A Reckoning and Research Agenda for Neuroimaging in Psychiatry'. *American Journal of Psychiatry* 176 (7): 507–11.

Farah, Martha J. (2014) 'Brain Images, Babies, and Bathwater: Critiquing Critiques of Functional Neuroimaging'. *Hastings Center Report* 44 (s2): S19–S30.

Farah, Martha J, and Seth J Gillihan. (2012) 'The Puzzle of Neuroimaging and Psychiatric Diagnosis: Technology and Nosology in an Evolving Discipline'. *AJOB Neuroscience* 3 (4): 31–41.

Farrer, Lindsay A, L Adrienne Cupples, Jonathan L Haines et al. (1997) 'Effects of Age, Sex, and Ethnicity on the Association between Apolipoprotein E Genotype and Alzheimer Disease: A Meta-Analysis'. *JAMA* 278 (16): 1349–56.

Feinberg, Joel. (1984) *Harm to Others: The Moral Limits of the Criminal Law*, vol. 1. Oxford: Oxford University Press.

Fenech, Matthew, Nika Strukelj, and Olly Buston. (2018) *Ethical, Social, and Political Challenges of Artificial Intelligence in Health*. London: Wellcome Trust & Future Advocacy.

Floridi, Luciano. (2019) 'Semantic Conceptions of Information'. In *Stanford Encyclopedia of Philosophy*, edited by Edward N Zalta. www.plato.stanford .edu/archives/win2019/entries/information-semantic/.

Fortin, Jane. (2011) 'Children's Right to Know Their Origins – Too Far, Too Fast?'. *Child and Family Law Quarterly* 21 (3): 336–55.

Foster, Morris W, John J Mulvihill, and Richard R Sharp. (2009) 'Evaluating the Utility of Personal Genomic Information'. *Genetics in Medicine* 11 (8): 570–4.

Freeman, Tabitha. (2014) 'Introduction'. In *Relatedness in Assisted Reproduction*, edited by Tabitha Freeman, Susanna Graham, Fatemeh Ebtehaj and Martin Richards. Cambridge: Cambridge University Press: 1–18.

(2015) 'Gamete Donation, Information Sharing and the Best Interests of the Child: An Overview of the Psychosocial Evidence'. *Monash Bioethics Review* 33 (1): 45–63.

Freeman, Tabitha, Kate Bourne, Jadva Vasanti, and Venessa Smith. (2014) 'Making Connections: Contact between Sperm Donor Relations'. In *Relatedness in Assisted Reproduction*, edited by Tabitha Freeman, Susanna Graham, Fatemeh Ebtehaj, and Martin Richards. Cambridge: Cambridge University Press: 270–95.

Freeman, Tabitha, and Susan Golombok. (2012) 'Donor Insemination: A Follow-up Study of Disclosure Decisions, Family Relationships and Child Adjustment at Adolescence'. *Reproductive Biomedicine Online* 25 (2): 193–203.

Frith, Lucy, Eric Blyth, Marilyn Crawshaw, and Olga van den Akker. (2018a) 'Searching for "Relations" Using a DNA Linking Register by Adults Conceived Following Sperm Donation'. *BioSocieties* 13 (1): 170–89.

(2018b) 'Secrets and Disclosure in Donor Conception'. *Sociology of Health & Illness* 40 (1): 188–203.

Gallagher, Shaun. (2006) *How the Body Shapes the Mind*. Wotton-under-Edge: Clarendon Press.

Gergen, Kenneth J, and Mary M Gergen. (1988) 'Narrative and the Self as Relationship'. *Advances in Experimental Social Psychology* 21 (1): 17–56.

Gibbon, Sahra. (2007) 'Charity, Breast Cancer Activism and the Iconic Figure of the BRCA Carrier'. In *Biosocialities, Genetics and the Social Sciences: Making Biologies and Identities*, edited by Sahra Gibbon and Carlos Novas. Abingdon: Routledge: 19–37.

Gibbon, Sahra, and Carlos Novas. (2007) 'Introduction'. In *Biosocialities, Genetics and the Social Sciences: Making Biologies and Identities*, edited by Sahra Gibbon and Carlos Novas. London: Routledge: 1–18.

Gibson, Lorna M, Thomas J Littlejohns, Ligia Adamska et al. (2017) 'Impact of Detecting Potentially Serious Incidental Findings During Multi-Modal Imaging'. *Wellcome Open Research* 2: 114.

Giddens, Anthony. (1991) *Modernity and Self-Identity: Self and Society in the Late Modern Age*. Cambridge: Polity Press in association with Blackwell.

Gilbert, Frederic. (2015) 'A Threat to Autonomy? The Intrusion of Predictive Brain Implants'. *AJOB Neuroscience* 6 (4): 4–11.

Gilbert, Frederic, Mark Cook, Terrence O'Brien, and Judy Illes. (2019) 'Embodiment and Estrangement: Results from a First-in-Human "Intelligent BCI" Trial'. *Science and Engineering Ethics* 25 (1): 83–96.

Giordano, James. (2012) 'Neuroimaging in Psychiatry: Approaching the Puzzle as a Piece of the Bigger Picture(S)'. *AJOB Neuroscience* 3 (4): 54–6.

Glannon, Walter. (2009) 'Our Brains Are Not Us'. *Bioethics* 23 (6): 321–9.

Glover, Jonathan. (1988) *I: The Philosophy and Psychology of Personal Identity*. London: Penguin.

Golombok, Susan. (2017) 'Disclosure and Donor-Conceived Children'. *Human Reproduction* 32 (7): 1532–6.

Golombok, Susan, Anne Brewaeys, Michele T. Giavazzi et al. (2002) 'The European Study of Assisted Reproduction Families: The Transition to Adolescence'. *Human Reproduction* 17 (3): 830–40.

Gooding, Holly C, Erin L Linnenbringer, Jeffrey Burack et al. (2006) 'Genetic Susceptibility Testing for Alzheimer Disease: Motivation to Obtain Information and Control as Precursors to Coping with Increased Risk'. *Patient Education and Counseling* 64 (1–3): 259–67.

Green, Robert C, and Nita A Farahany. (2014) 'Regulation: The FDA Is Overcautious on Consumer Genomics'. *Nature News* 505 (7483): 286.

Hacking, Ian. (1995) 'The Looping Effect of Human Kinds'. In *Causal Cognition: A Multi-Disciplinary Debate*, edited by Dan Sperber, David Premack and A James Premack. New York: Oxford University Press: 351–83.

(1999) *The Social Construction of What?* Cambridge, MA: Harvard University Press.

(2004) 'Between Michel Foucault and Erving Goffman: Between Discourse in the Abstract and Face-to-Face Interaction'. *Economy and Society* 33 (3): 277–302.

Hallowell, Nina. (1999) 'Doing the Right Thing: Genetic Risk and Responsibility'. *Sociology of Health & Illness* 21 (5): 597–621.

Hallowell, Nina, Sarah Cooke, Gillian Crawford et al. (2010) 'An Investigation of Patients' Motivations for Their Participation in Genetics-Related Research'. *Journal of Medical Ethics* 36 (1): 37–45.

Hallowell, Nina, Claire Foster, Rosalind Eeles, et al. (2004) 'Accommodating Risk: Responses to BRCA1/2 Genetic Testing of Women Who Have Had Cancer'. *Social Science & Medicine* 59 (3): 553–65.

Hallowell, Nina, Claire Foster, Ros Eeles et al. (2003) 'Balancing Autonomy and Responsibility: The Ethics of Generating and Disclosing Genetic Information'. *Journal of Medical Ethics* 29 (2): 74–9.

Haraway, Donna. (2006) 'A Manifesto for Cyborgs: Science, Technology, and Socialist Feminism in the 1980s'. In *International Handbook of Virtual Learning Environments*, vol. 1, edited by Joel Weiss, Jason Nolan, Jeremy Hunsinger and Peter Trifonas. New York: Springer: 117–58.

Hardcastle, Valerie Gray. (2008) *Constructing the Self.* Amsterdam: John Benjamins.

Harper, Joyce C, Debbie Kennett, and Dan Reisel. (2016) 'The End of Donor Anonymity: How Genetic Testing Is Likely to Drive Anonymous Gamete Donation out of Business'. *Human Reproduction* 31 (6): 1135–40.

Harris, John, and Kirsty Keywood. (2001) 'Ignorance, Information and Autonomy'. *Theoretical Medicine and Bioethics* 22 (5): 415–36.

Haslanger, Sally. (2009) 'Family, Ancestry and Self: What Is the Moral Significance of Biological Ties?'. *Adoption & Culture* 2: 91–122.

Hauskeller, Christine. (2004) 'Genes, Genomes and Identity. Projections on Matter'. *New Genetics and Society* 23 (3): 285–99.

(2006) 'Human Genomics as Identity Politics.' Award Paper for Young Scholar Conference, Cornell University, 7–9 April. https://citeseerx.ist.psu.edu/view doc/download?doi=10.1.1.571.6238&rep=rep1&type=pdf.

Hedgecoe, Adam M. (2004) 'Critical Bioethics: Beyond the Social Science Critique of Applied Ethics'. *Bioethics* 18 (2): 120–43.

Henschke, Adam. (2010) 'Did You Just Say What I Think You Said? Talking About Genes, Identity and Information'. *Identity in the Information Society* 3 (3): 435–56.

(2017) *Ethics in an Age of Surveillance: Personal Information and Virtual Identities.* Cambridge: Cambridge University Press.

Heshka, Jodi T, Crystal Palleschi, Heather Howley, Brenda Wilson, and Philip S Wells. (2008) 'A Systematic Review of Perceived Risks, Psychological and Behavioral Impacts of Genetic Testing'. *Genetics in Medicine* 10 (1): 19–32.

Hesse-Biber, Sharlene, and Chen An. (2016) 'Genetic Testing and Post-Testing Decision Making among BRCA-Positive Mutation Women: A Psychosocial Approach'. *Journal of Genetic Counseling* 25 (5): 978–92.

Hewitt, Geraldine. (2002) 'Missing Links: Identity Issues of Donor Conceived People'. *Journal of Fertility Counselling* 9: 14–19.

Hickey, Blake Anthony, Taryn Chalmers, Phillip Newton et al. (2021) 'Smart Devices and Wearable Technologies to Detect and Monitor Mental Health Conditions and Stress: A Systematic Review'. *Sensors* 21 (10): 3461.

House of Commons Science and Technology Committee. (2021) Direct-to-Consumer Genomic Testing. www.publications.parliament.uk/pa/cm5802/cmselect/cmsctech/94/9403.htm

Huckvale, Kit, Svetha Venkatesh, and Helen Christensen. (2019) 'Toward Clinical Digital Phenotyping: A Timely Opportunity to Consider Purpose, Quality, and Safety'. *npj Digital Medicine* 2 (1): 1–11.

Human Fertilisation and Embryology Authority. (2019) HFEA Code of Practice, 9th ed. www.portal.hfea.gov.uk/media/1605/2019-12-03-code-of-practice-december-2019.pdf.

Hurley, Ann C, Rose Harvey, J Scott Roberts et al. (2005) 'Genetic Susceptibility for Alzheimer's Disease: Why Did Adult Offspring Seek Testing?'. *American Journal of Alzheimer's Disease and Other Dementias* 20 (6): 374–81.

Husted, Jørgen. (2014) 'Autonomy and a Right Not to Know'. In *The Right to Know and the Right Not to Know: Genetic Privacy and Responsibility*, edited by Ruth Chadwick, Mairi Levitt, and Darren Shickle. Cambridge: Cambridge University Press: 24–38.

Ienca, Marcello, and Roberto Andorno. (2017) 'Towards New Human Rights in the Age of Neuroscience and Neurotechnology'. *Life Sciences, Society and Policy* 13 (1): 1–27.

Ilioi, Elena, Lucy Blake, Vasanti Jadva, Gabriela Roman, and Susan Golombok. (2017) 'The Role of Age of Disclosure of Biological Origins in the Psychological Wellbeing of Adolescents Conceived by Reproductive Donation: A Longitudinal Study from Age 1 to Age 14'. *Journal of Child Psychology and Psychiatry* 58 (3): 315–24.

Ilioi, Elena Cristiana, and Susan Golombok. (2015) 'Psychological Adjustment in Adolescents Conceived by Assisted Reproduction Techniques: A Systematic Review'. *Human Reproduction Update* 21 (1): 84–96.

Illes, Judy, Sofia Lombera, Jarett Rosenberg, and Bruce Arnow. (2008) 'In the Mind's Eye: Provider and Patient Attitudes on Functional Brain Imaging'. *Journal of Psychiatric Research* 43 (2): 107–14.

Jadva, Vasanti, Tabitha Freeman, Wendy Kramer, and Susan Golombok. (2009) 'The Experiences of Adolescents and Adults Conceived by Sperm Donation: Comparisons by Age of Disclosure and Family Type'. *Human Reproduction* 24 (8): 1909–19.

Jain, Sachin H, Brian W Powers, Jared B Hawkins, and John S Brownstein. (2015) 'The Digital Phenotype'. *Nature Biotechnology* 33 (5): 462–3.

Jenkins, Richard. (2014) *Social Identity*. London: Routledge.

Johnston, Carolyn, and Jane Kaye. (2004) 'Does the UK Biobank Have a Legal Obligation to Feedback Individual Findings to Participants?'. *Medical Law Review* 12 (3): 239–67.

Joyce, Kelly. (2005) 'Appealing Images: Magnetic Resonance Imaging and the Production of Authoritative Knowledge'. *Social Studies of Science* 35 (3): 437–62.

Kamenova, Kalina, Amir Reshef, and Timothy Caulfield. (2014) 'Angelina Jolie's Faulty Gene: Newspaper Coverage of a Celebrity's Preventive Bilateral Mastectomy in Canada, the United States, and the United Kingdom'. *Genetics in Medicine* 16 (7): 522–8.

Kay, Jackie. (2011) *Red Dust Road: An Autobiographical Journey*. London: Atlas.

Kellmeyer, Philipp. (2017) 'Ethical and Legal Implications of the Methodological Crisis in Neuroimaging'. *Cambridge Quarterly of Healthcare Ethics* 26 (4): 530–54.

(2021) 'Big Brain Data: On the Responsible Use of Brain Data from Clinical and Consumer-Directed Neurotechnological Devices'. *Neuroethics* 14 (1): 83–98.

Kenett, Jeanette, and Steve Matthews. (2008) 'Normative Agency'. In *Practical Identity and Narrative Agency*, edited by Catriona Mackenzie and Kim Atkins. New York: Routledge: 212–31.

Kirkman, Maggie. (2003) 'Parents' Contributions to the Narrative Identity of Offspring of Donor-Assisted Conception'. *Social Science & Medicine* 57 (11): 2229–42.

(2004) 'Genetic Connection and Relationships in Narratives of Donor Assisted Conception'. *Australian Journal of Emerging Technologies and Society* 2 (1). www.hdl.handle.net/11343/33590

Klitzman, Robert. (2009) '"Am I My Genes?": Questions of Identity among Individuals Confronting Genetic Disease'. *Genetics in Medicine* 11 (12): 880–9.

Konrad, Monica. (2005) *Narrating the New Predictive Genetics: Ethics, Ethnography, and Science*. Cambridge: Cambridge University Press.

Korsgaard, Christine. (1996) *The Sources of Normativity*. Cambridge: Cambridge University Press.

(2009) *Self-Constitution: Agency, Identity, and Integrity*. Oxford: Oxford University Press.

Kreitmair, Karola, and Mildred Cho. (2017) 'The Neuroethical Future of Wearable and Mobile Health Technology'. In *Neuroethics: Anticipating the Future*, edited by Judy Illes. Oxford: Oxford University Press: 80–107.

Kreitmair, Karola V. (2019) 'Dimensions of Ethical Direct-to-Consumer Neurotechnologies'. *AJOB Neuroscience* 10 (4): 152–66.

Kuhn, Thomas S. (2012) *The Structure of Scientific Revolutions*, 50th Anniversary ed. Chicago: University of Chicago Press.

Latour, Bruno, and Steve Woolgar. (1979) *Laboratory Life: The Social Construction of Scientific Facts*. Princeton: Princeton University Press.

Laurie, Graeme. (2002) *Genetic Privacy: A Challenge to Medico-Legal Norms*. Cambridge: Cambridge University Press.

(2004) 'The Right Not to Know: An Autonomy Based Approach – A Response to Andorno'. *Journal of Medical Ethics* 30 (5): 439–40.

(2009) 'Personality, Privacy and Autonomy in Medical Law'. In *Rights of Personality in Scots Law: A Comparative Perspective*, edited by Niall R Whitty and Reinhard Zimmermann. Dundee: Dundee University Press: 453–83.

(2014a) 'Privacy and the Right Not to Know: A Plea for Conceptual Clarity'. In *The Right to Know and the Right Not to Know: Genetic Privacy and Responsibility*, edited by Ruth Chadwick, Mairi Levitt and Darren Shickle. Cambridge: Cambridge University Press: 38–51.

(2014b) 'Recognizing the Right Not to Know: Conceptual, Professional, and Legal Implications'. *The Journal of Law, Medicine & Ethics* 42 (1): 53–63.

Laurie, Graeme, Shaun Harmon, and Edward Dove. (2019) *Mason and Mccall Smith's Law and Medical Ethics*, 11th ed. Oxford: Oxford University Press.

Lawrie, Stephen M, Sue Fletcher-Watson, Heather C Whalley, and Andrew M McIntosh. (2019) 'Predicting Major Mental Illness: Ethical and Practical Considerations'. *BJPsych Open* 5 (2): 1–5.

Lawton, Georgina. (2021) *Raceless: In Search of Family, Identity, and the Truth About Where I Belong*. London: Sphere.

Lebowitz, Matthew S. (2014) 'Biological Conceptualizations of Mental Disorders among Affected Individuals: A Review of Correlates and Consequences'. *Clinical Psychology: Science and Practice* 21 (1): 67–83.

Lennon, Kathleen. (2019) 'Feminist Perspectives on the Body'. In *Stanford Encyclopedia of Philosophy*, Fall ed., edited by Edward N Zalta. www.plato.stanford.edu/archives/fall2019/entries/feminist-body/

Lennon, Kathleen, Stella Gonzalez-Arnal, and Gill Jagger. (2012) 'Introduction' In *Embodied Selves*, edited by Stella Gonzalez-Arnal, Gill Jagger, and Kathleen Lennon. Palgrave Macmillan: 1–11.

Levy-Lahad, Ephrat, Raphael Catane, Shlomit Eisenberg et al. (1997) 'Founder BRCA1 and BRCA2 Mutations in Ashkenazi Jews in Israel: Frequency and Differential Penetrance in Ovarian Cancer and in Breast-Ovarian Cancer Families'. *American Journal of Human Genetics* 60 (5): 1059.

Lillehammer, Hallvard. (2014) 'Who Cares Where You Came From? Cultivating Virtues of Indifference'. In *Relatedness in Assisted Reproduction*, edited by Tabitha Freeman, Susanna Graham, Fatemeh Ebtehaj, and Martin Richards. Cambridge: Cambridge University Press: 97–112.

Lim, Jacqueline, Mariette Macluran, Melanie Price, Barbara Bennett, and Phyllis Butow. (2004) 'Short-and Long-Term Impact of Receiving Genetic Mutation Results in Women at Increased Risk for Hereditary Breast Cancer'. *Journal of Genetic Counseling* 13 (2): 115–33.

Lindemann, Hilde. (2016) *Holding and Letting Go: The Social Practice of Personal Identities*. Oxford: Oxford University Press.

(2001) *Damaged Identities, Narrative Repair*. Ithaca: Cornell University Press.

Lineweaver, Tara T, Mark W Bondi, Douglas Galasko, and David P Salmon. (2014) 'Effect of Knowledge of APOE Genotype on Subjective and Objective Memory Performance in Healthy Older Adults'. *American Journal of Psychiatry* 171 (2): 201–8.

Littlejohns, Thomas J, Jo Holliday, Lorna M Gibson et al. (2020) 'The UK Biobank Imaging Enhancement of 100,000 Participants: Rationale, Data Collection, Management and Future Directions'. *Nature Communications* 11 (1): 1–12.

Lloyd, Genevieve. (2003) *Being in Time: Selves and Narrators in Philosophy and Literature*. London: Routledge.

Lock, Margaret. (2008) 'Biosociality and Susceptibility Genes: A Cautionary Tale'. In *Biosocialities, Genetics and the Social Sciences: Making Biologies and Identities*, edited by Sahra Gibbon and Carlos Novas. London: Routledge: 56–78.

Lock, Margaret, Sarah Cunningham-Burley, Sarah Franklin et al. (2005) 'Eclipse of the Gene and the Return of Divination 1'. *Current Anthropology* 46 (S5): S47–S70.

Lock, Margaret, Julia Freeman, Gillian Chilibeck et al. (2007) 'Susceptibility Genes and the Question of Embodied Identity'. *Medical Anthropology Quarterly* 21 (3): 256–76.

Lock, Margaret, Julia Freeman, Rosemary Sharples, and Stephanie Lloyd. (2006) 'When It Runs in the Family: Putting Susceptibility Genes in Perspective'. *Public Understanding of Science* 15 (3): 277–300.

Loughlin, Michael, George Lewith, and Torkel Falkenberg. (2013) 'Science, Practice and Mythology: A Definition and Examination of the Implications of Scientism in Medicine'. *Health Care Analysis* 21 (2): 1–16.

Lupton, Deborah. (2013) 'Quantifying the Body: Monitoring and Measuring Health in the Age of Mhealth Technologies'. *Critical Public Health* 23 (4): 393–403.

Lynch, Henry T, Carrie Snyder, Jane F Lynch et al. (2006) 'Patient Responses to the Disclosure of BRCA Mutation Tests in Hereditary Breast-Ovarian Cancer Families'. *Cancer Genetics and Cytogenetics* 165 (2): 91–7.

Machado, Helena, and Rafaela Granja. (2020) 'Emerging DNA Technologies and Stigmatization'. In *Forensic Genetics in the Governance of Crime*, edited by Helena Machado and Rafaela Granja. Singapore: Palgrave Pivot: 85–104.

MacIntyre, Alasdair C. (1985) *After Virtue: A Study in Moral Theory*, 2nd ed. London: Duckworth.

Mackenzie, Catriona. (2000) 'Imagining Oneself Otherwise'. In *Relational Autonomy*, edited by Catriona Mackenzie and Natalie Stoljar. Oxford: Oxford University Press: 124–51.

(2007) 'Bare Personhood? Velleman on Selfhood'. *Philosophical Explorations* 10 (3): 263–81.

(2008a) 'Introduction: Practical Identity and Narrative Agency'. In *Practical Identity and Narrative Agency*, edited by Catriona Mackenzie and Kim Atkins. London: Routledge: 1–28.

(2008b) 'Imagination, Identity, and Self-Transformation'. In *Practical Identity and Narrative Agency*, edited by Kim Atkins and Catriona Mackenzie. London: Routledge: 121–45.

(2009) 'Personal Identity, Narrative Integration, and Embodiment'. In *Embodiment and Agency*, edited by Sue Campbell, Letitia Maynell, and Susan Sherwin. Pennsylvania: Pennsylvania State University Press: 100–25.

Mackenzie, Catriona, and Jacqui Poltera. (2010) 'Narrative Integration, Fragmented Selves, and Autonomy'. *Hypatia* 25 (1): 31–54.

(2011) 'Narrative Identity and Autonomy: Reply to Commentaries'. *MIT Symposia on Gender, Race and Philosophy* 7 (1): 1–9.

Mackenzie, Catriona, and Jackie Leach Scully. (2007) 'Moral Imagination, Disability and Embodiment'. *Journal of Applied Philosophy* 24 (4): 335–51.

Mackenzie, Catriona, and Natalie Stoljar. (2000) 'Introduction: Autonomy Reconfigured'. In *Relational Autonomy: Feminist Perspectives on Automony, Agency, and the Social Self*, edited by Catriona Mackenzie and Natalie Stoljar. Oxford: Oxford University Press: 3–31.

Mackenzie, Catriona, and Mary Walker. (2015) 'Neurotechnologies, Personal Identity and the Ethics of Authenticity'. In *Handbook of Neuroethics*, edited by Jens Clausen and Neil Levy. Dordrecht: Springer: 373–92.

Mahlstedt, Patricia P, Kathleen LaBounty, and William Thomas Kennedy. (2010) 'The Views of Adult Offspring of Sperm Donation: Essential Feedback for the Development of Ethical Guidelines within the Practice of Assisted Reproductive Technology in the United States'. *Fertility and Sterility* 93 (7): 2236–46.

Marshall, Jill. (2014) *Human Rights Law and Personal Identity*. London: Routledge.

Martin, Emily. (2010) 'Self-Making and the Brain'. *Subjectivity* 3 (4): 366–81.

McConkie-Rosell, Allyn, and Brenda M DeVellis. (2000) 'Threat to Parental Role: A Possible Mechanism of Altered Self-Concept Related to Carrier Knowledge'. *Journal of Genetic Counseling* 9 (4): 285–302.

McGuinness, Sheelagh, Bert-Jaap Koops, and Eva Asscher. (2010) 'Genetics, Information and Identity'. *Identity in the Information Society* 3 (3): 415–21.

McMillan, Catriona, Edward Dove, Graeme Laurie et al. (2021) 'Beyond Categorisation: Refining the Relationship between Subjects and Objects in Health Research Regulation'. *Law, Innovation and Technology* 13 (1): 194–222.

Mella, Sara, Barbara Muzzatti, Riccardo Dolcetti et al.(2017) 'Emotional Impact on the Results of BRCA1 and BRCA2 Genetic Test: An Observational Retrospective Study'. *Hereditary Cancer in Clinical Practice* 15 (1): 1–7.

Merleau-Ponty, Maurice. (1962) *Phenomenology of Perception*, translated by Colin Smith. London: Routledge.

Meyers, Diana T. (2000) 'Intersectional Identity and the Authentic Self? Opposites Attract'. In *Relational Autonomy: Feminist Perspectives on Automony, Agency, and the Social Self*, edited by Catriona Mackenzie and Natalie Stoljar. Oxford: Oxford University Press: 151–80.

Miller, Franklin G, Michelle M Mello, and Steven Joffe. (2008) 'Incidental Findings in Human Subjects Research: What Do Investigators Owe Research Participants?'. *The Journal of Law, Medicine & Ethics* 36 (2): 271–9.

Miller, Sarah Clark. (2013) *The Ethics of Need: Agency, Dignity, and Obligation.* London: Routledge.

Molewijk, Bert, Anne M Stiggelbout, Wilma Otten et al. (2004) 'Scientific Contribution. Empirical Data and Moral Theory. A Plea for Integrated Empirical Ethics'. *Medicine, Health Care and Philosophy* 7 (1): 55–69.

Mozersky, Jessica, and Galen Joseph. (2010) 'Case Studies in the Co-Production of Populations and Genetics: The Making of "at Risk Populations" in BRCA Genetics'. *BioSocieties* 5 (4): 415–39.

Murdoch, Iris. (2013) *The Sovereignty of Good.* London: Routledge.

National Institute for Health and Care Excellence. (2013, updated 2019) Guidelines: Familial Breast Cancer: Classification and Care of People at Risk of Familial Breast Cancer and Management of Breast Cancer and Related Risks in People with a Family History of Breast Cancer (Cg164). www.nice.org.uk/guidance/cg164

Nazroo, James Y, Kamaldeep S Bhui, and James Rhodes. (2020) 'Where Next for Understanding Race/Ethnic Inequalities in Severe Mental Illness? Structural, Interpersonal and Institutional Racism'. *Sociology of Health & Illness* 42 (2): 262–76.

Nelson, Alondra. (2008) 'Bio Science: Genetic Genealogy Testing and the Pursuit of African Ancestry'. *Social Studies of Science* 38 (5): 759–83.

   (2016) *The Social Life of DNA: Race, Reparations, and Reconciliation after the Genome.* Boston: Beacon Press.

Nelson, Jamie Lindemann. (1992) 'Genetic Narratives: Biology, Stories, and the Definition of the Family'. *Health Matrix* 2: 71.

Niedenthal, Paula M. (2007) 'Embodying Emotion'. *Science* 316 (5827): 1002–5.

Nordgren, Anders, and Eric T. Juengst. (2009) 'Can Genomics Tell Me Who I Am? Essentialistic Rhetoric in Direct-to-Consumer DNA Testing'. *New Genetics and Society* 28 (2): 157–72.

Novas, Carlos, and Nikolas Rose. (2001) 'Genetic Risk and the Birth of the Somatic Individual'. *Economy and Society* 29 (4): 485–513.

Nuffield Council on Bioethics. (2013) Donor Conception: Ethical Aspects of Information Sharing. www.nuffieldbioethics.org/publications/donor-conception

Nussbaum, Martha Craven. (2006) *Frontiers of Justice: Disability, Nationality, Species Membership*. Cambridge, MA: Belknap Press.

O'Connor, Cliodhna, and Helene Joffe. (2013) 'How Has Neuroscience Affected Lay Understandings of Personhood? A Review of the Evidence'. *Public Understanding of Science* 22 (3): 254–68.

O'Connor, Cliodhna, Geraint Rees, and Helene Joffe. (2012) 'Neuroscience in the Public Sphere'. *Neuron* 74 (2): 220–6.

O'Neill, Onora. (2002) *Autonomy and Trust in Bioethics: Gifford Lectures*. Cambridge: Cambridge University Press.

Parens, Erik, and Paul S Appelbaum. (2019) 'On What We Have Learned and Still Need to Learn About the Psychosocial Impacts of Genetic Testing'. *Hastings Center Report* 49 (S1): S2–S9. https://doi.org/10.1002/hast.1011.

Parfit, Derek. (1984) *Reasons and Persons*. Oxford: Oxford University Press.

Parker, Michael, and Anneke M Lucassen. (2004) 'Genetic Information: A Joint Account?'. *BMJ* 329 (7458): 165–7.

Parry, Bronwyn. (2013) 'Knowing Mycellf™: Personalized Medicine and the Economization of Prospective Knowledge About Bodily Fate'. In *Knowledge and the Economy*, edited by Peter Meusburger, Johannes Glückler, and Martina el Meskioui. Knowledge and Space (Klaus Tschira Symposia). Dordrecht: Springer: 157–71.

Peake, Jonathan M, Graham Kerr, and John P Sullivan. (2018) 'A Critical Review of Consumer Wearables, Mobile Applications, and Equipment for Providing Biofeedback, Monitoring Stress, and Sleep in Physically Active Populations'. *Frontiers in Physiology* 9: 743.

Pennings, Guido. (2017) 'Disclosure of Donor Conception, Age of Disclosure and the Well-Being of Donor Offspring'. *Human Reproduction* 32 (5): 969–73.

Pickersgill, Martyn. (2011) '"Promising" Therapies: Neuroscience, Clinical Practice, and the Treatment of Psychopathy'. *Sociology of Health & Illness* 33 (3): 448–64.

Pickersgill, Martyn, Sarah Cunningham-Burley, and Paul Martin. (2011) 'Constituting Neurologic Subjects: Neuroscience, Subjectivity and the Mundane Significance of the Brain'. *Subjectivity* 4 (3): 346–65.

Pinto-Basto, Jorge, Bárbara Guimarães, Elina Rantanen et al. (2010) 'Scope of Definitions of Genetic Testing: Evidence from a Eurogentest Survey'. *Journal of Community Genetics* 1 (1): 29–35.

Postan, Emily. (2016) 'Defining Ourselves: Personal Bioinformation as a Tool of Narrative Self-Conception'. *Journal of Bioethical Inquiry* 13 (1): 133–51.

   (2021) 'Narrative Devices: Neurotechnologies, Information, and Self-Constitution'. *Neuroethics* 14: 231–251.

   (2021) 'Changing Identities in Disclosure of Research Findings'. In *The Cambridge Handbook of Health Research Regulation*, edited by Graeme Laurie, Edward Dove, Agomoni Ganguli-Mitra et al. Cambridge: Cambridge University Press.

Rabinow, Paul. (2010) 'Artificiality and Enlightenment: From Sociobiology to Biosociality'. *Politix* 90(2): 21–46.

Racine, Eric, Ofek Bar-Ilan, and Judy Illes. (2005) 'fMRI in the Public Eye'. *Nature Review Neuroscience* 6 (2): 159–64.

Racine, Eric, Sarah Waldman, Jarett Rosenberg, and Judy Illes. (2010) 'Contemporary Neuroscience in the Media'. *Social Science & Medicine* 71 (4): 725–33.

Raghupathi, Wullianallur, and Viju Raghupathi. (2014) 'Big Data Analytics in Healthcare: Promise and Potential'. *Health Information Science and Systems* 2 (1): 1–10.

Ramos, Renato T. (2012) 'The Conceptual Limits of Neuroimaging in Psychiatric Diagnosis'. *AJOB Neuroscience* 3 (4): 52–3.

Ravelingien, An, Veerle Provoost, and Guido Pennings. (2013) 'Donor-Conceived Children Looking for Their Sperm Donor: What Do They Want to Know?'. *Facts, Views & Vision in ObGyn* 5 (4): 257–64.

Ravitsky, Vardit. (2010) '"Knowing Where You Come From": The Rights of Donor-Conceived Individuals and the Meaning of Genetic Relatedness'. *Minnesota Journal of Law, Science & Technology* 11 (2): 655–84.

   (2014) 'Autonomous Choice and the Right to Know One's Genetic Origins'. *Hastings Center Report* 44 (2): 36–7.

   (2016) 'Donor Conception and Lack of Access to Genetic Heritage'. *American Journal of Bioethics* 16 (12): 45–6.

Ravitsky, Vardit, and Benjamin S Wilfond. (2006) 'Disclosing Individual Genetic Results to Research Participants'. *American Journal of Bioethics* 6 (6): 8–17.

Read, John. (2007) 'Why Promoting Biological Ideology Increases Prejudice against People Labelled "Schizophrenic"'. *Australian Psychologist* 42 (2): 118–28.

Readings, Jennifer, Lucy Blake, Polly Casey et al. (2011) 'Secrecy, Disclosure and Everything in-Between: Decisions of Parents of Children Conceived by

Donor Insemination, Egg Donation and Surrogacy'. *Reproductive Biomedicine Online* 22 (5): 485–95.

Rehmann-Sutter, Christoph. (2009) 'Allowing Agency: An Ethical Model for Communicating Personal Genetic Information'. In *Disclosure Dilemmas: Ethics of Genetic Prognosis after the 'Right to Know/Not to Know' Debate*, edited by Christoph Rehmann-Sutter and Hansjakob Müller. Farnham: Ashgate: 242–73.

Richards, Martin. (2014) 'A British History of Collaborative Reproduction and the Rise of the Genetic Connection'. In *Relatedness in Assisted Reproduction*, edited by Tabitha Freeman, Susanna Graham, Fatemeh Ebtehaj, and Martin Richards. Cambridge: Cambridge University Press: 21–43.

Ricoeur, Paul. (1992) *Oneself as Another*, translated by Kathleen Blamey. Chicago: University of Chicago Press.

Riessman, Catherine Kohler. (2008) *Narrative Methods for the Human Sciences*. Los Angeles: Sage.

Roberts, J Scott. (2012) 'Genetic Testing for Risk of Alzheimer's Disease: Benefit or Burden?'. *Neurodegenerative Disease Management* 2 (2): 141–4.

Roberts, J Scott, Kurt D Christensen, and Robert C Green. (2011) 'Using Alzheimer's Disease as a Model for Genetic Risk Disclosure: Implications for Personal Genomics'. *Clinical Genetics* 80 (5): 407–14.

Roberts, J Scott, L Adrienne Cupples, Norman R Relkin et al. (2005) 'Genetic Risk Assessment for Adult Children of People with Alzheimer's Disease: The Risk Evaluation and Education for Alzheimer's Disease (Reveal) Study'. *Journal of Geriatric Psychiatry and Neurology* 18 (4): 250–5.

Roberts, J Scott, and Wendy R Uhlmann. (2013) 'Genetic Susceptibility Testing for Neurodegenerative Diseases: Ethical and Practice Issues'. *Progress in Neurobiology* 110: 89–101.

Roberts, Scott J, Susan A LaRusse, Heather Katzen et al. (2003) 'Reasons for Seeking Genetic Susceptibility Testing among First-Degree Relatives of People with Alzheimer Disease'. *Alzheimer Disease & Associated Disorders* 17 (2): 86–93.

Roe, David, and Larry Davidson. (2005) 'Self and Narrative in Schizophrenia: Time to Author a New Story'. *Medical Humanities* 31 (2): 89–94.

Rogers, Wendy, Catriona Mackenzie, and Susan Dodds. (2012) 'Why Bioethics Needs a Concept of Vulnerability'. *International Journal of Feminist Approaches to Bioethics* 5 (2): 11–38.

Rose, Diana, Constantina Papoulias, James MacCabe, and Jennifer Walke. (2015) 'Service Users' and Carers' Views on Research Towards Stratified Medicine in Psychiatry: A Qualitative Study'. *BMC Research Notes* 8 (1): 1–9.

Rose, Nikolas. (2007) *Politics of Life Itself: Biomedicine, Power, and Subjectivity in the Twenty-First Century*. Princeton: Princeton University Press.

Rose, Nikolas S, and Joelle M Abi-Rached. (2013) *Neuro: The New Brain Sciences and the Management of the Mind*. Princeton: Princeton University Press.

Roskies, Adina L. (2008) 'Neuroimaging and Inferential Distance'. *Neuroethics* 1 (1): 19–30.

Rowbottom, Darrell P. (2019) 'Scientific Realism: What It Is, the Contemporary Debate, and New Directions'. *Synthese* 196 (2): 451–84.

Rowley, Jennifer. (2007) 'The Wisdom Hierarchy: Representations of the DIKW Hierarchy'. *Journal of Information Science* 33 (2): 163–80.

Royal, Charmaine D, John Novembre, Stephanie M Fullerton et al. (2010) 'Inferring Genetic Ancestry: Opportunities, Challenges, and Implications'. *The American Journal of Human Genetics* 86 (5): 661–73.

The Royal Marsden NHS Foundation Trust. (2016) Patient Information: A Beginner's Guide to BRCA1 and BRCA2. www.patientinfolibrary.royalmarsden.nhs.uk /brca1brac2

Sabatello, Maya, and Eric Juengst. (2019) 'Genomic Essentialism: Its Provenance and Trajectory as an Anticipatory Ethical Concern'. *Hastings Center Report* 49: S10–S18.

Saini, Angela. (2019) *Superior: The Return of Race Science*. Boston: Beacon Press.

Saks, Elyn R. (2007) *The Centre Cannot Hold*. London: Virago.

Scanlon, Thomas. (1975) 'Thomson on Privacy'. *Philosophy & Public Affairs* 4 (4): 315–22.

   (1998) *What We Owe to Each Other*. Cambridge: Belknap Press of Harvard University Press.

Schechtman, Marya. (1996) *The Constitution of Selves*. Ithaca: Cornell University Press.

   (2007) 'Stories, Lives, and Basic Survival: A Refinement and Defense of the Narrative View'. *Royal Institute of Philosophy Supplements* 60: 155–78.

   (2012) 'Making the Truth: Self-Understanding, Self-Constitution, Neuroscience, and Narrative'. *AJOB Neuroscience* 3 (4): 75–6.

   (2014) *Staying Alive: Personal Identity, Practical Concerns, and the Unity of a Life*. Oxford: Oxford University Press.

Scheib, Joanna E, Maura Riordan, and Susan Rubin. (2003) 'Choosing Identity-Release Sperm Donors: The Parents' Perspective 13–18 Years Later'. *Human Reproduction* 18 (5): 1115–27.

Schrijvers, Anne, Henny Bos, Floor van Rooij et al. (2019) 'Being a Donor-Child: Wishes for Parental Support, Peer Support and Counseling'. *Journal of Psychosomatic Obstetrics & Gynecology* 40 (1): 29–37.

Scott, Susie, Lindsay Prior, Fiona Wood, and Johnathan Gray. (2005) 'Repositioning the Patient: The Implications of Being "at Risk"'. *Social Science & Medicine* 60 (8): 1869–79.

Scully, Jackie Leach. (2008) *Disability Bioethics: Moral Bodies, Moral Difference*. Lanham: Rowman & Littlefield.

(2009) 'Receiving and Interpreting Information: A Joint Enterprise'. In *Disclosure Dilemmas: Ethics of Genetic Prognosis after the 'Right to Know/ Not to Know' Debate*, edited by Christoph Rehmann-Sutter and Hansjakob Müller. Farnham: Ashgate: 216–29.

(2017) 'A Mitochondrial Story: Mitochondrial Replacement, Identity and Narrative'. *Bioethics* 31 (1): 37–45.

Sharon, Tamar. (2017) 'Self-Tracking for Health and the Quantified Self: Re-Articulating Autonomy, Solidarity, and Authenticity in an Age of Personalized Healthcare'. *Philosophy & Technology* 30 (1): 93–121.

Sharon, Tamar, and Federica Lucivero. (2019) 'Introduction to the Special Theme: The Expansion of the Health Data Ecosystem – Rethinking Data Ethics and Governance'. *Big Data and Society* 6 (2): 1–5.

Shaw, Alison. (2006) 'The Contingency of the "Genetic Link" in the Construction of Kinship and Inheritance: An Anthropological Perspective'. In *Freedom and Responsibility in Reproductive Choice*, edited by John R Spencer and Antje Du Bois-Pedain. London: Hart Publishing: 73–90.

Shildrick, Margrit. (2005) 'Introduction: Beyond the Body of Bioethics'. In *Ethics of the Body: Postconventional Challenges*, edited by Margrit Shildrick and Roxanne Mykitiuk. Cambridge, MA: MIT Press: 1–24.

Skinner, David. (2020) 'Forensic Genetics and the Prediction of Race: What Is the Problem?'. *BioSocieties* 15 (3): 329–49.

Skirton, Heather, Lesley Goldsmith, Leigh Jackson, and Anita O'Connor. (2012) 'Direct to Consumer Genetic Testing: A Systematic Review of Position Statements, Policies and Recommendations'. *Clinical Genetics* 82 (3): 210–18.

Solove, Daniel J. (2002) 'Conceptualizing Privacy'. *California Law Review* 90: 1087.

Somers, Margaret R. (1994) 'The Narrative Constitution of Identity: A Relational and Network Approach'. *Theory and Society* 23: 605–49.

Staudt, Michael D, Eric Z Herring, Keming Gao, Jonathan P Miller, and Jennifer A Sweet. (2019) 'Evolution in the Treatment of Psychiatric Disorders: From Psychosurgery to Psychopharmacology to Neuromodulation'. *Frontiers in Neuroscience* 13: 1–10.

Stewart, George. (1992) 'Interpreting the Child's Right to Identity in the UN Convention on the Rights of the Child'. *Family Law Quarterly* 26: 221–4.

Strawson, Galen. (2008) 'Against Narrativity'. In *Real Materialism and Other Essays*, edited by Galen Strawson. Oxford: Clarendon Press: 189–208.

Sunstein, Cass R. (1996) 'On the Expressive Function of Law'. *University of Pennsylvania Law Review* 144 (5): 2021–53.

Tallandini, Maria Anna, Liviana Zanchettin, Giorgio Gronchi et al. (2016) 'Parental Disclosure of Assisted Reproductive Technology (Art)

Conception to Their Children: A Systematic and Meta-Analytic Review'. *Human Reproduction* 31 (6): 1275–87.

Taylor, Charles. (1989) *Sources of the Self: The Making of the Modern Identity.* Cambridge: Cambridge University Press.

(1992) *The Ethics of Authenticity.* Cambridge, MA: Harvard University Press.

Taylor, Mark. (2012) *Genetic Data and the Law: A Critical Perspective on Privacy Protection.* Cambridge: Cambridge University Press.

Thom, Robyn, and Helen M Farrell. (2019) 'Neuroimaging in Psychiatry: Potentials and Pitfalls'. *Current Psychiatry* 18 (12): 27–34.

Topol, Eric. (2018) 'Blood, Sweat and Tears in Biotech: The Theranos Story'. *Nature* 557 (7706): 306–8.

Turkmendag, Ilke. (2012) 'The Donor-Conceived Child's "Right to Personal Identity": The Public Debate on Donor Anonymity in the United Kingdom'. *Journal of Law and Society* 39 (1): 58–75.

Turner, Amanda J, and Adrian Coyle. (2000) 'What Does It Mean to Be a Donor Offspring? The Identity Experiences of Adults Conceived by Donor Insemination and the Implications for Counselling and Therapy'. *Human Reproduction* 15 (9): 2041–51.

UK National Screening Committee. (2015) Criteria for Appraising the Viability, Effectiveness and Appropriateness of a Screening Programme. www.gov.uk/government/publications/evidence-review-criteria-national-screening-programmes/criteria-for-appraising-the-viability-effectiveness-and-appropriateness-of-a-screening-programme.

Underhill, Meghan L, Robin M Lally, Marc T Kiviniemi, Christine Murekeyisoni, and Suzanne S Dickerson. (2012) 'Living My Family's Story: Identifying the Lived Experience in Healthy Women at Risk for Hereditary Breast Cancer'. *Cancer Nursing* 35 (6): 493.

Van Assche, Kristof, Serge Gutwirth, and Sigrid Sterckx. (2013) 'Protecting Dignitary Interests of Biobank Research Participants: Lessons from *Havasupai Tribe v Arizona Board of Regents*'. *Law, Innovation and Technology* 5 (1): 54–84.

Van Fraassen, Bas C. (1980) *The Scientific Image.* Oxford: Oxford University Press.

Vayena, Effy. (2015) 'Direct-to-Consumer Genomics on the Scales of Autonomy'. *Journal of Medical Ethics* 41 (4): 310–14.

Vayena, Effy, Alessandro Blasimme, and I Glenn Cohen. (2018) 'Machine Learning in Medicine: Addressing Ethical Challenges'. *PLOS Medicine* 15 (11): e1002689.

Velleman, J David. (1996) 'Self to Self'. *The Philosophical Review* 105 (1): 39–76.

(2005a) 'Self as Narrator'. In *Autonomy and the Challenges to Liberalism: New Essays*, edited by John Christman and Joel Anderson. Cambridge: Cambridge University Press: 56–76.

(2005b) 'Family History'. *Philosophical Papers* 34 (3): 357–78.

(2006) *Self to Self: Selected Essays*. Cambridge: Cambridge University Press.

(2008) 'The Gift of Life'. *Philosophy & Public Affairs* 36 (3): 245–66.

Vodermaier, Andrea, Mary Jane Esplen, and Christine Maheu. (2010) 'Can Self-Esteem, Mastery and Perceived Stigma Predict Long-Term Adjustment in Women Carrying a BRCA1/2-Mutation? Evidence from a Multi-Center Study'. *Familial Cancer* 9 (3): 305–11.

Wachbroit, Robert. (2002) 'Genetic Determinism, Genetic Reductionism, and Genetic Essentialism' In *Encyclopedia of Ethical, Legal and Policy Issues in Biotechnology*, edited by Thomas H. Murray and Maxwell J. Mehlman. New York: John Wiley: 352–6.

Wade, Christopher H. (2019) 'What Is the Psychosocial Impact of Providing Genetic and Genomic Health Information to Individuals? An Overview of Systematic Reviews'. *Hastings Center Report* 49 (S1): S88–S96. https://doi .org/10.1002/hast.1021

Walker, Mary Jean. (2012) 'Neuroscience, Self-Understanding, and Narrative Truth'. *AJOB Neuroscience* 3 (4): 63–74.

(2019) 'Two Senses of Narrative Unification'. *Philosophical Explorations* 22 (1): 78–93.

Walker, Mary Jean, and Wendy A Rogers. (2017) 'Diagnosis, Narrative Identity, and Asymptomatic Disease'. *Theoretical Medicine and Bioethics* 38 (4): 307–21.

Weiner, Kate, Paul Martin, Martin Richards, and Richard Tutton. (2017) 'Have We Seen the Geneticisation of Society? Expectations and Evidence'. *Sociology of Health & Illness* 39 (7): 989–1004.

Widdows, Heather. (2013) *The Connected Self: The Ethics and Governance of the Genetic Individual*. Cambridge: Cambridge University Press.

Widmer, Pierre. (1994) *Human Rights Issues in Research on Medical Genetics*. Strasbourg: Council of Europe.

Wilson, Margaret. (2002) 'Six Views of Embodied Cognition'. *Psychonomic Bulletin & Review* 9 (4): 625–36.

Wilson, Sarah. (1997) 'Identity, Genealogy and the Social Family: The Case of Donor Insemination'. *International Journal of Law, Policy and the Family* 11 (2): 270–97.

Wisdom, Jennifer P., Kevin Bruce, Goal Auzeen Saedi, Teresa Weis, and Carla A Green. (2008) '"Stealing Me from Myself": Identity and Recovery in Personal Accounts of Mental Illness'. *Australian and New Zealand Journal of Psychiatry* 42 (6): 489–95.

Witz, Anne. (2000) 'Whose Body Matters? Feminist Sociology and the Corporeal Turn in Sociology and Feminism'. *Body & Society* 6 (2): 1–24.

Wolf, Susan M, Frances P Lawrenz, Charles A Nelson et al. (2008) 'Managing Incidental Findings in Human Subjects Research: Analysis and Recommendations'. *The Journal of Law, Medicine & Ethics* 36 (2): 219–48.

World Health Organization. (2021) Global Strategy on Digital Health 2020–2025. www.who.int/docs/default-source/documents/gs4dhdaa2a9f352b0445 bafbc79ca799dce4d.pdf

Xafis, Vicki, G Owen Schaefer, Markus K Labude et al. (2019) 'An Ethics Framework for Big Data in Health and Research'. *Asian Bioethics Review* 11 (3): 227–54.

Young, Iris Marion. (2005) 'Throwing Like a Girl: A Phenomenology of Feminine Body Comportment Motility and Spatiality'. In *On Female Body Experience: 'Throwing Like a Girl' and Other Essays.* Oxford: Oxford University Press: 27–45.

Young, Robert. (1982) 'The Value of Autonomy'. *The Philosophical Quarterly* 32 (126): 35–44.

Zadeh, Sophie, Elena Ilioi, Vasanti Jadva, and Susan Golombok. (2018) 'The Perspectives of Adolescents Conceived Using Surrogacy, Egg or Sperm Donation'. *Human Reproduction* 33 (6): 1099–106.

Zeiler, Kristin. (2009) 'Symposium on Genetics, Identity and Ethics'. *New Genetics and Society* 28 (2): 153–6.

Abi-Rached, Joelle, 10, 54
access to personal bioinformation.
    see under personal
    bioinformation
ADHD (attention-deficit hyperactivity
    disorder), 205
advisory committees, potential
    bioinformation disclosers
    and, 221
affiliative self-fashioning, 54
African Americans, ancestry tracing by,
    54, 178
African ancestry tracing, 196, 206
African heritage, identity harms
    and, 204
Alaimo, Stacy, 92
Alzheimer's disease, 188
    desire to contribute to research
        concerning, 147, 177
    preventive/therapeutic interventions
        for, 145
    testing for, 44, 141–4, 156, 174, 250
ancestry tracing
    African Americans ancestry tracing
        and, 54, 178
    African ancestry tracing and,
        196, 206
    Black British ancestry tracing and,
        54, 178
anxiety, 209
APOE (Apolipoprotein E) gene, 141
APOE testing for risk of Alzheimer's
    disease, 44, 141–4, 174
    counselling and education about, 148
    motivations for undergoing, 146, 177
    reactions to receiving results from,
        150–3
    recommendations regarding access/
        disclosure, 250

Article 8 of the European Convention
    on Human Rights (ECHR),
    33–7, 250
    access to health records and, 41, 45
articulation constraint
    role of personal bioinformation in
        meeting, 103
    Schechtman on, 72
Ashkenazi Jewish populations, *BRCA*-
    related cancers and, 155
Asperger's syndrome, 101
asymptomatic disease, 85, 115
Atkins, Kim, 62, 96, 97
attention-deficit hyperactivity disorder
    (ADHD), 205
autonomy, 77–8, 212–17

Baylis, Françoise, 69, 95
BCIs (brain-computer interfaces), 260
biobanks (vignette concerning
        participation in), 1, 221, 255
biological essentialism, 48–51, 110–13
    beyond biological essentialism
        and, 51
    reactions against, 50
bioethics, 3
biography, 101, 106, 198
    donor conception and, 132, 137, 140
    genetic parentage and, 58, 107
    genetic risk and, 149
bioinformation governance, 5, 247–63
bioinformation, personal. *see* personal
        bioinformation
biosocial identity-making, 54
biosociality, 54
bipolar disorder, 158
Black British, ancestry tracing by,
        54, 178
Blyth, Eric, 137

bodily doubt, 92
Bortolotti, Lisa, 108
the brain, 10, 15, 20, 49
brain scans, 1, 9, 162 *see also*
    neuroimaging
brain-computer interfaces (BCIs), 260
Brandon, Priscilla, 97
BRCA genes
    breast/ovarian cancer risk and, 141
    the governance landscape and, 257
BRCA-related cancers, Ashkenazi
    Jewish populations and, 155
BRCA Self-Concept Scale, 234
BRCA testing, 44, 141–4, 191
    age at which it is sought, 146
    BRCA activism and, 155, 178
    desire to contribute to research
        concerning, 147
    motivations for participating in,
        145, 146
    reactions to receiving results from,
        150–3
breast cancer, 141
Buchman, Daniel, 163, 167

cancer, breast/ovarian, 141
Carel, Havi, 92, 117
Caribbean heritage, identity harms
    and, 204
case studies, list of, xiv
Cassam, Quassim, 94
characterisation, identity as, 24, 25
the 'characterization question', 23
Chilibeck, Gillian, 148
choice (not) to know, 7, 27, 213
    autonomy and, 213
    navigating choice and, 237
Christman, John, 70, 79, 83
CIOMS (Council for International
    Organizations of Medical
    Sciences) Guidelines, disclosure
    of health research findings
    and, 43
clinical actionability, 7, 8, 142, 210
clinical utility, 142, 169, 231
coherence. *see* narrative coherence
Cohn, Simon, 163, 165, 166
colorectal cancer, 112

comfortable narratives, 185
communication, identity-supporting,
    238–44
competing interests, disclosure and,
    229–32
conceptual and normative foundations,
    filling gaps in, 46–60, 197–205
confidentiality, family information and,
    42, 255
consent, 214, 255
constraints on self-constituting
    narratives, 72
constructed identity significance,
    191, 196
Corsico, Paolo, 168, 170
Council for International
    Organizations of Medical
    Sciences (CIOMS) Guidelines,
    disclosure of health research
    findings and, 43
counterstories, 197

d'Agincourt-Canning, Lori, 146, 147,
    155, 157
damaging narrative contents,
    202–5, 224
Data Protection Act 2018 (DPA), 41,
    45, 209
data, as distinguished from
    information, 13
Davidson, Larry, 169
DeGrazia, David, 62, 78
de Melo-Martín, Inmaculada, 52
depression, 114, 158, 162
determinism, 48
diabetes, Type-1, 207
direct-to-consumer (DTC) genomic
    testing services. *see* DTC
    (direct-to-consumer) genomic
    testing services
disability paradox, 191
disclosure of bioinformation, 5–7, 12,
    14, 16 *see also under* personal
    bioinformation
    debates about, 18
    identity interests in, 18
    recommendations regarding, 247–63
discrimination, 55, 204

distress
   narrative disruption and, 105, 138, 250
   relationship to and distinction from
      identity interests, 209
donor conception, 15, 19, 174, 188
   donor anonymity and, 38
   encounters with, 19
   the governance landscape and, 252
   illustrative example concerning, 19,
      124–41
      information subjects' experiences
         of, 127–35
      narrative impacts and, 135–41
      types of information involved, 124
   information about
      discovery of, 126
      donor-conceived individuals' legal
         entitlements to, 37–40, 126
      mitochondrial replacement
         therapy and, 40, 197, 253
      parental disclosure of, 38, 125–6
      recommendations regarding,
         252–3
   preference for/importance of
      knowing and, 135
   Ravitsky on, 47
   responsibilities for disclosure
      and, 241
   social context and, 192
   UK regulations and, 37–40, 124
Donor Sibling Registry, 132
DPA (Data Protection Act 2018), 41, 45
DSD (differences in sex development),
      damaging narrative contents
      and, 203
DTC (direct-to-consumer) genomic
      testing services, 7, 9, 18, 44, 126,
      192, 257–9
   ancestry tracing and, 54, 196, 206
   bioinformation governance issues
      and, 251
   genetic-essentialist assumptions
      and, 49
   misleading information and, 201
   potential bioinformation disclosers
      and, 221
   recommendations regarding access/
      disclosure, 257–9

responsible communication of
      health information and, 240
   vignette concerning, 1, 2
Dumit, Joseph, 163, 165, 180
duty to help, 225–9

Edelman, Marian Wright, 197
Embodied Narratives
   case studies, list of, xiv
   guide to the chapters in this book,
      28–30
   terminology used in this book, 12–28
embodiment, 90–4
   identity significance of, 190
   narrative identity and, 94–8
empirical bioethics, 121
entitlements to personal
      bioinformation in law, 31–42
epilepsy, 103, 261
epistemic qualities of bioinformation,
      113–18, 200
ethical responsibilities for disclosure of
      bioinformation, 218–48
   ethical foundations of, 221–9
   limiting considerations and, 229–32
   shared social responsibilities
      and, 244
European (Oviedo) Convention on
      Human Rights and
      Biomedicine, 32, 33
European Convention on Human
      Rights (ECHR), Article, 8 of
   access to health records and, 41, 45
   right to identity and, 33–8, 250
European Court of Human Rights
      (ECtHR), 34, 250
European General Data Protection
      Regulation (GDPR), 41
European Study of Assisted
      Reproduction Families, 126
exclusion, 55, 79, 82
experiences, identity narratives and, 175
external coherence, 103, 104

FDA (Food and Drug Administration),
      direct-to-consumer genomic
      testing services and, 44
feminist theories of self, 91

first-personal narration, 69

fMRI (functional magnetic resonance imaging), 158

Food and Drug Administration (FDA), direct-to-consumer genomic testing services and, 44

forensic genetic analysis, 204, 225

Fraassen, Bas van, 114

Freeman, Tabitha, 39, 138, 192

Frith, Lucy, 132, 138

functional magnetic resonance imaging (fMRI), 158

future challenges for access to personal bioinformation, 262

GDI (General Definition of Information), 13

GDPR (European General Data Protection Regulation), 41

General Definition of Information (GDI), 13

genetic ancestry tracing, 8, 9, 54, 206
  African American ancestry tracing and, 54, 178
  African ancestry tracing and, 196
  Black British ancestry tracing and, 178
  unreliability of, 206

genetic essentialism, 50, 140

genetic identity, 47

genetic information, 3, 8
  issues of wider entitlement and, 40
  'right to know' or 'not to know' and, 6

genetic parentage, 35, 46, 47, 107, 124
  knowledge of, 10
  Lillehammer on, 111
  Velleman on, 58

genetic risk, 19
  illustrative example concerning, 141–58
    information subjects' experiences of encounters with, 144–53
    narrative impacts of, 153–8
    type of bioinformation involved, 141–4
    recommendations regarding access/ disclosure and, 221

the 'genetic self', 48

genetic testing, 141–58, 192, 195 see also DTC (direct-to-consumer) genomic testing services

Gibbon, Sahra, 53, 54, 155, 178

Glover, Jonathan, 70, 80

Gooding, Holly, 145

governance, 5, 247–63

group identity, 26

Hacking, Ian, 53, 96

Hallowell, Nina, 146

Haraway, Donna, 191

Harris, John, 216

Haslanger, Sally, 52

Hauskeller, Christine, 46
  intra-species classifications and, 53, 55
  on reifying social distinctions, 9

the Havasupai people, 26

health research
  bioinformation generated by, 4, 43
  feedback of findings from, 6, 18, 43, 230, 253–5
  identity harms and, 204
  potential bioinformation disclosers and, 17, 220

health status, identity significance and, 190, 193

Healthcare Improvement Scotland, potential bioinformation disclosers and, 221

healthcare information
  clinical actionability and, 210
  right to access records of, 41, 45
  secondary research uses of, 4, 43, 221

healthcare professionals, as potential bioinformation disclosers, 220

Hekman, Susan, 92

helpfulness, 225–9, 254

Henschke, Adam, 21

hermeneutic role of bioinformation, 113–18

HFEA (Human Fertilisation and Embryology Authority), 38, 39
  applying to for donor information, 126
  the governance landscape and, 253

home test kit companies, potential
bioinformation disclosers
and, 221
HRA (Human Rights Act 1998), 33,
38
Human Fertilisation and Embryology
Act 1990 (HFE Act), 38
Human Fertilisation and Embryology
Authority (HFEA), 38, 39
applying to for donor
information, 126
the governance landscape and, 253
Human Rights Act 1998 (HRA), 33, 38

identity, 1–30
bioinformation impacts and, 8
constituting vs. revealing, 108
definitions of, 20–8
as a multi-stranded whole, 180
narrative theories of, 61–86
question of 'who we are' and, 3, 5
right to, under European
Convention on Human Rights
(ECHR), 33–7, 250
role of bioinformation in, 98–109
identity harms, 86, 199–205, 223
identity interests, 10, 181–219
ascertaining where they lie, 232–8
distinguishing from other interests,
208–17
fundamental identity interest and,
183–6
governance issues and, 247–63
information-related, 186–90
legal entitlements and, 31–40, 218
protection of, 2, 11, 12, 33–8, 45–6
relationships between structure and
contents, 205–8
responsibilities for meeting, 219–46
identity narratives, 57–86, 172–80, 198
the body and, 94–8
contents of, 65, 86, 87, 99, 202–8, 224
fundamental identity interest and,
183–6
inhabitability of, 186
knowledge of genetic parentage and,
135–41
negative impacts and, 178

personal bioinformation as a tool of,
98–109
vulnerability and, 223
identity significance of bioinformation,
190–7
contexts of, 190–4
social construction of, 196
identity-supporting disclosure
practices, 238–44
identity value, 43, 210
Illes, Judy, 166
illustrative examples of encounters with
bioinformation, 19, 120–72
image (public persona), 21
imaging services, potential
bioinformation disclosers
and, 221
implanted devices, 103, 260
individual research findings, feedback
of, 6, 18, 43, 230, 253–5
infertility, 103
information, as distinguished from
data, 13
information-related identity interests,
186–90
information subjects, 3, 16
entitlements to access personal
bioinformation and, 8, 31–42
information interests of, 5–8
informed consent, 214, 255
inhabitable narratives, 186
intelligibility, 64, 73, 75, 77, 83
harm to caused by misleading
information, 201
internal, 103
internal coherence, 103, 104
International Declaration on Human
Genetic Data, 32
International Human Rights Law, 32
interpretation, 13
interpretive frameworks, 14, 96, 105

Jolie, Angelina, 53
Juengst, Eric, 44, 49, 201

Kennett, Jeanette, 77
Keywood, Kirsty, 216
KH and Others v. *Slovakia*, 37

Kirkman, Maggie, 59, 132
    on family stories and narrative
        identity, 140
    on ignorance of donor origins, 139
    on parents as key collaborators in
        helping donor-conceived
        individuals, 134
Klitzman, Robert, 57, 153
Korsgaard, Christine, 24, 87

Laurie, Graeme, 211, 257
legal entitlements to personal
        bioinformation, 31–42, 45–6
Lillehammer, Hallvard, 110, 113
the lived body, 91
Lloyd, Genevieve, 67
Lock, Margaret, 51, 148, 156
Loughlin, Michael, 116
Lupton, Deborah, 52, 116
Lynch syndrome, 100

MacIntyre, Alasdair, 62, 68, 94
Mackenzie, Catriona, 23, 24, 62
    on achievability, 84
    on biological realities, 106
    the body and, 95, 96, 98
    on capacities and capabilities, 79
    on characteristics, 116
    on coherence, 82
    on identity harms, 203
    on identity narratives, 63, 74
    on internal goods, 78
    on interpretive frameworks, 96
    on making sense of who we are, 76
    on narrative contents, 65
    on the relative integration of identity
        narratives, 82
    on Saks, 80, 169
    on the self over time, 64
    on Strawson, 80
magnetic resonance imaging
        (MRI), 158
major depressive disorder (MDD),
        158, 162
MAOA gene, identity harms and, 204
Maori populations, 204
Marshall, Jill, 35, 37, 46, 51
master narratives, 68, 87, 196

the material body, 91
Matthews, Steve, 77
MDD (major depressive disorder),
        158, 162
meaningfulness, 14, 64, 87, 184
memories and experiences, identity
        narratives and, 175
mental health status, 158
    responsibilities for disclosure
        and, 241
    vulnerability and, 224
Merleau-Ponty, Maurice, 91
Meyers, Diana, 81
    on achievability, 83
    emergent intelligibility and, 77
    on figurations, 196
    on intersectional identities, 81
    on self-descriptors, 194
Mikulic v. *Croatia*, genetic parentage
        and, 35
Miller, Franklin, 226, 254
misleading information, 200–2,
        224
mitochondrial replacement therapy
        (MRT), 18, 40, 197
mobile apps
    potential bioinformation disclosers
        and, 221
    tracking pandemics and, 6, 260
MRI (magnetic resonance
        imaging), 158
MRT (mitochondrial replacement
        therapy), 18, 40, 197
Murdoch, Iris, 78

narrative coherence, 74
    achievability of, 82
    external, 103, 104
    harm to caused by misleading
        information, 201
    internal, 103, 104
    objections to, 79–86
    recapped, 183
    the value of, 79–81, 104, 205–8
narrative contents, 65, 99
    as damaging, 202–5, 224
    as meaningful, 87
    as relate to structure, 86, 205–8

narrative context, of identity
  significance, 193
narrative identity, theories of, 61–88
  the body in, 94–8
narrative self-constitution, 61–88, 94
narratives. *see* identity narratives
narrativity, 58, 82, 86, 172–80
  importance of according to
    Atkins, 97
  interpretation and, 66, 100
  relational, 67
  requirements of, 71, 80
National Institute for Health and Care
  Excellence (NICE)
  BRCA screening guidelines and, 142
  potential bioinformation disclosers
    and, 221
need, vulnerability and, 222–5
Nelson, Alondra, 54, 178, 196
Nelson, Hilde Lindemann, 62, 68, 196
  on counterstories, 83, 241
  on the early chapters of our lives, 137
  on first-personal narration, 70
  on identity narratives, 74
  on oppressive master narratives, 87
Nelson, Jamie, 58
  on how our lives connect with those
    of others, 137
  on the opening pages of our
    biographies, 107
neural activity, 9
neurobiological self, 54
neuroessentialism, 49
neuroimaging, 10, 49, 175, 195
  communication context and, 193
  data from, algorithmic analyses
    of, 159
  motivations for, 162
  psychiatric neuroimaging and, 20,
    158–72
neuroscience, reportings of in non-
  specialist media, 9
neurotechnologies, 49
NICE (National Institute for Health
  and Care Excellence)
  BRCA screening guidelines and, 142
  potential bioinformation disclosers
    and, 221

Nordgren, Anders, 44, 49, 201
normative and conceptual foundations,
  filling gaps in, 46–60, 197–205
normative roles, 102–8
normativity, 60, 63, 78, 88
Novas, Carlos
  biographical narration and, 57
  risk identity and, 54, 56, 156
Nuffield Council on Bioethics, 47,
  135, 140
numerical identity, 21
Nussbaum, Martha, 85, 87

Odièvre v. *France*, 36
oppressive conditions, 80, 83
oppressive master narratives, 87
origins cases, in European Court of
  Human Rights (ECtHR), 33–7
ovarian cancer, 141
overactive thyroid, 103

pandemics
  bioinformation collection and, 4
  tracking exposure/immunity via
    mobile apps, 6, 260
Parry, Bronwyn, 51
personal bioinformation, 5, 16
  access to
    by information subjects, 8, 17
    future challenges for, 262
    information subjects' entitlements
      in law and, 31–42
    knowledge of genetic parentage
      and, 10
  concerns about identity relevance
    and, 110–18
  contexts in which encountered, 3,
    16–20, 120–80
  contribution to embodied narratives
    and, 119
  defined, 13–16
  epistemic qualities of, 113–18, 200
  examples of encounters with, 4,
    16–20, 120–72
  identity significance of, 190–7
  interpretive context and, 100
  as a narrative tool, 98–109
  normative roles and, 102–8

personal identity, 22
personal utility, 43, 210, 254
PET (positron emission
        tomography), 158
phenomenology, embodiment and,
        52, 91
Pickersgill, Martyn, 167
policy research, potential
        bioinformation disclosers
        and, 221
Poltera, Jacqui, 62
    on identity narratives, 74
    on narrative coherence, 82, 84
    on narrative scepticism, 80
    on Saks, 80, 169
positron emission tomography
        (PET), 158
potential bioinformation disclosers,
        responsibilities of, 219–46
practical identity, 23
practical self-characterisation, 25
preparedness, 145, 210
principle of helpfulness, 225–9, 254
privacy, 6, 7, 45, 211
psychiatric neuroimaging
    encounters with, 20
    illustrative example concerning,
        158–72
        information subjects' experiences
            and, 161–7
        narrative impacts of, 167–72
        type of bioinformation involved,
            158–61
psychological distress
    narrative disruption and, 105, 138, 250
    relationship to and distinction from
        identity interests, 209
psychological preparedness, 145, 210
psychosis, 158, 204
public persona (image), 21

racial/ethnic profiling for forensic
        purposes, 204
Racine, Eric, 49
racism
    misuses of genetic science and, 55
    oppressive master narratives and, 87
Ravitsky, Vardit, 9, 47

reality constraint, 73
reductionism, 48
Rehmann-Sutter, Christoph, 239, 243
relational narrativity, 67–9, 240
relational roles, 28, 65, 68, 185, 189
relational self-constitution, 137
REVEAL Study, 143, 144–51
    importance of interpretive context
        and, 188
    participant counselling and, 148
rheumatoid arthritis, 101, 105
Ricoeur, Paul, 86, 97
right to identity
    under European Convention on
        Human Rights (ECHR),
        33–7, 250
    Human Rights Act (HRA) and,
        33, 38
    under United Nations Convention
        on the Rights of the Child
        (UNCRC), 33
'right to know' or 'not to know', 2,
        6, 217
right to respect for private and family
        life, European Convention on
        Human Rights (ECHR) and,
        33–7, 41, 45, 250
rights, 182
risk identity, 54, 56, 156
Roberts, Scott, 258
Roe, David, 169
Rogers, Wendy, 60, 115, 117
    on coherence, concerning
        asymptomatic disease, 85
    on narrative identity and
        asymptomatic disease, 208
    on vulnerability, 223, 228
Rose v. *Secretary of State for Health*, 38
Rose, Nikolas
    narratives and, 57
    risk identity and, 54, 56, 156
    on self-characterisation, 10

Saks, Elyn, 80, 169
Scanlon, Thomas, 222, 225
Schechtman, Marya, 76, 77, 86
    articulation constraint and, 103
    the body and, 94, 99

on capacities, 85
on coherence, 84
on constraints on self-constituting
    narratives, 69, 72
on identity as characterisation, 25
on intelligibility, 81
on narrative identity, 61, 63, 65, 66,
    71, 193
on practical identity, 23
on prenarrative truth about the
    self, 109
reality constraint and, 73, 104
on relational narrativity, 68
schizophrenia, 80, 158, 169
    damaging narrative contents
        and, 203
    psychiatric neuroimaging and, 163
screening programmes, 17, 18, 41,
    221, 250
Scully, Jackie Leach, 239
    on ascertaining where others'
        interests lie, 232, 243
    on mitochondrial replacement
        therapy, 60, 197
self-characterisation, 25, 35, 48, 63
self-constituting narratives, 61–88, 94
    coherence and, 74
    constraints on, 72–5
    contents of, 65
    objections to, 70–2
    practical and evaluative capacities
        of, 75–9
selfhood, 63
self-narratives. *see* identity narratives
shared social responsibilities, 244
Shildrick, Margrit, 91, 92
sickle cell disease, 204
single-photon emission computed
    tomography (SPECT), 158
sleep-monitoring apps, 116
smart technologies, 4, 18, 44
    potential bioinformation disclosers
        and, 221
    tracking pandemics and, 6, 260
social construction, of identity
    significance, 191
social identity, 24
social responsibilities, shared, 244

somatic identity, 54
species identity, 21
SPECT (single-photon emission
    computed tomography), 158
Stewart, George, 33
Strawson, Galen, 70, 79
structure of identity, as relates to
    contents, 205–8
subject access rights under the Data
    Protection Act (DPA), 41, 45
sustainability, 184, 201

Taylor, Charles, 62, 67, 77
    the body and, 94
    on identity, 78, 86
    on relational narrativity, 68
    on self-constitution, 68
Taylor, Mark, 14, 15
terminology used in this book, 12–28
thyroid disease, 103
tracking devices, 44
    governance and, 260
    pandemics and, 6, 260
    potential bioinformation disclosers
        and, 221
transphobia, oppressive master
    narratives and, 87
Type-1 diabetes, 207

UK Donor Conceived Register, 126
UK Longitudinal Study of Assisted
    Reproduction Families,
    126, 131
UK National Screening Committee,
    41, 221
UNCRC (United Nations Convention
    on the Rights of the Child), 33
unification, 75
Universal Declaration of Human
    Rights, 32

Velleman, David, 62
    on acquaintance with genetic
        parents, 58, 107, 137
    on observing family resemblances,
        117, 137
    on self-narratives, 75
vulnerability, 222–5, 226, 238

Walker, Mary, 60, 62
  on achievability, 83
  on brain data, 10
  on characteristics, 70
  on coherence, concerning
     asymptomatic disease, 85, 208
  distortion of self-conceptions and,
     115, 117
  on dramatic personal changes,
     76, 111

on identity narratives, 74
on making sense of who we are,
   76
on 'revealing identity', 108
Widdows, Heather, 27, 60, 247
Wilson, Sarah, 58, 107, 136
worthwhile narratives, 58, 87,
   184

Young, Iris Marion, 93, 191

Books in the Series

Marcus Radetzki, Marian Radetzki and Niklas Juth
Genes and Insurance: Ethical, Legal and Economic Issues

Ruth Macklin
Double Standards in Medical Research in Developing Countries

Donna Dickenson
Property in the Body: Feminist Perspectives

Matti Häyry, Ruth Chadwick, Vilhjálmur Árnason and Gardar Árnason
The Ethics and Governance of Human Genetic Databases: European Perspectives

J. K. Mason
The Troubled Pregnancy: Legal Wrongs and Rights in Reproduction

Daniel Sperling
Posthumous Interests: Legal and Ethical Perspectives

Keith Syrett
Law, Legitimacy and the Rationing of Health Care: A Contextual and Comparative Perspective

Alasdair Maclean
Autonomy, Informed Consent and Medical Law: A Relational Change

Heather Widdows and Caroline Mullen
The Governance of Genetic Information: Who Decides?

David Price
Human Tissue in Transplantation and Research: A Model Legal and Ethical Donation Framework

Matti Häyry
Rationality and the Genetic Challenge: Making People Better?

Mary Donnelly
Healthcare Decision-Making and the Law: Autonomy, Capacity and the Limits of Liberalism

Anne-Maree Farrell, David Price and Muireann Quigley
Organ Shortage: Ethics, Law and Pragmatism

Sara Fovargue
Xenotransplantation and Risk: Regulating a Developing Biotechnology

John Coggon
What Makes Health Public?: A Critical Evaluation of Moral, Legal, and Political Claims in Public Health

Mark Taylor
Genetic Data and the Law: A Critical Perspective on Privacy Protection

Anne-Maree Farrell
The Politics of Blood: Ethics, Innovation and the Regulation of Risk

Stephen W. Smith
End-of-Life Decisions in Medical Care: Principles and Policies for Regulating the Dying Process

Michael Parker
Ethical Problems and Genetics Practice

William W. Lowrance
Privacy, Confidentiality, and Health Research

Kerry Lynn Macintosh
Human Cloning: Four Fallacies and Their Legal Consequence

Heather Widdows
The Connected Self: The Ethics and Governance of the Genetic Individual

Amel Alghrani, Rebecca Bennett and Suzanne Ost
Bioethics, Medicine and the Criminal Law Volume I: The Criminal Law and Bioethical Conflict: Walking the Tightrope

Danielle Griffiths and Andrew Sanders
Bioethics, Medicine and the Criminal Law Volume II: Medicine, Crime and Society

Margaret Brazier and Suzanne Ost
Bioethics, Medicine and the Criminal Law Volume III: Medicine and Bioethics in the Theatre of the Criminal Process

Sigrid Sterckx, Kasper Raus and Freddy Mortier
Continuous Sedation at the End of Life: Ethical, Clinical and Legal Perspectives

A. M. Viens, John Coggon and Anthony S. Kessel
Criminal Law, Philosophy and Public Health Practice

Ruth Chadwick, Mairi Levitt and Darren Shickle
The Right to Know and the Right Not to Know: Genetic Privacy and Responsibility

Eleanor D. Kinney
The Affordable Care Act and Medicare in Comparative Context

Katri Lõhmus
Caring Autonomy: European Human Rights Law and the Challenge of Individualism

Catherine Stanton and Hannah Quirk
Criminalising Contagion: Legal and Ethical Challenges of Disease Transmission and the Criminal Law

Sharona Hoffman
Electronic Health Records and Medical Big Data: Law and Policy

Barbara Prainsack and Alena Buyx
Solidarity in Biomedicine and Beyond

Camillia Kong
Mental Capacity in Relationship: Decision-Making, Dialogue, and Autonomy

Oliver Quick
Regulating Patient Safety: The End of Professional Dominance?

Thana Cristina de Campos
The Global Health Crisis: Ethical Responsibilities

Jonathan Ives, Michael Dunn and Alan Cribb
Empirical Bioethics: Theoretical and Practical Perspectives

Alan Merry and Warren Brookbanks
Merry and McCall Smith's Errors, Medicine and the Law (second edition)

Donna Dickenson
Property in the Body: Feminist Perspectives (second edition)

Rosie Harding
Duties to Care: Dementia, Relationality and Law

Ruud ter Meulen
Solidarity and Justice in Health and Social Care

David Albert Jones, Chris Gastmans and Calum MacKellar
Euthanasia and Assisted Suicide: Lessons from Belgium

Muireann Quigley
Self-Ownership, Property Rights, and the Human Body: A Legal Perspective

Françoise Baylis and Alice Dreger
Bioethics in Action

John Keown
Euthanasia, Ethics and Public Policy: An Argument against Legislation (second edition)

Amel Alghrani
Regulating Assisted Reproductive Technologies: New Horizons

Britta van Beers, Sigrid Sterckx and Donna Dickenson
Personalised Medicine, Individual Choice and the Common Good

David G. Kirchhoffer and Bernadette J. Richards
Beyond Autonomy: Limits and Alternatives to Informed Consent in Research Ethics and Law

Markus Wolfensberger and Anthony Wrigley
Trust in Medicine: Its Nature, Justification, Significance, and Decline

Catriona A. W. McMillan
The Human Embryo in vitro: Breaking the Legal Stalemate

Benjamin Peter White and Lindy Willmott (editors)
International Perspectives on End-of-Life Law Reform: Politics, Persuasion and Persistence

Carolyn Adams, Judy Allen and Felicity Flack
Sharing Linked Data for Health Research: Toward Better Decision Making

Milton Keynes UK
Ingram Content Group UK Ltd.
UKHW021952191123
432891UK00015B/113